CAPITALISM WITH A COMRADE'S FACE

CAPITALISM WITH A COMRADE'S FACE

Studies in the Postcommunist Transition

Roman Frydman
Kenneth Murphy
Andrzej Rapaczynski

Central European University Press
Budapest

Central European University Press
Október 6. utca 12.
H-1051 Budapest
Hungary

ISBN 963 9116 06 8 Cloth
ISBN 963 9116 11 4 Paperback

Printed in Hungary

Contents

List of Figures

List of Tables

Preface

Enthusiasm is not fashionable nowadays. The fall of communism was not accompanied by the exuberance with which the Old World once greeted the American Revolution or the sense of triumph across Europe that accompanied the end of Nazi Germany. Yet it is no exaggeration to say that the process that began in 1989 has ushered in, at least so far, the greatest extension of freedom the world has ever known.

That is not to say that this phenomenal—and, frankly, entirely unexpected—disintegration of the specter that had haunted Europe, and the globe, for most of this century made the postcommunist world definitively "safe for democracy." Communism is dead, no doubt, and with it, for the foreseeable future, the ghost of totalitarianism in Europe (though not without nostalgic longings in places such as Belarus). In this sense, no matter what comes after communism in many parts of the former Soviet empire, it is hard to believe that the future will not bring a comparative increase in political decency, greater freedom for individuals, and, in most places, greater economic prosperity.

These freedoms are nothing to scoff at, but it is no great feat to best communism on any of these scores. What the people who rejoiced at the fall of the Berlin Wall hoped for was something much more than that: not just a decrease in thuggery, want, and oppression, but the establishment of genuine democracies from the Elbe to Kamchatka and of functioning market economies from the Baltics to Bishkek. These hopes and ideals are not yet dead; indeed, the chances that they may be realized seem no worse today than six or seven years ago in the headiest days of "postcommunist transition." The transition from communism, however, is in many ways longer and more arduous than many people (innocently) first expected, and backsliding in many places is also a realistic possibility. What is perhaps most difficult to contemplate, especially for those who greeted the fall of communism with the greatest surge of enthusiasm, is the daily ordeal of the transition itself.

The word "transition" holds as its primary definition the movement or passage from one state or set of circumstances to another. But history is more than a bad habit, and a clean, revolutionary break with the past is almost never possible. What most onlookers and participants alike in the revolutions of 1989 and 1991 failed to recognize was that the new postcommunist societies must, at least for a time, retain a good deal of the old. This residue of the obsolete should not be considered the result of obtuseness and ignorance alone (even if their motley armies are never to be underestimated). There are active and pervasive influences that bind the transition societies to the past and on occasion cause even the best-intentioned reformers to seek to recover the moribund. Those who would engineer escape from these influences must be aware of the captivity the socialist past imposed and continues to nurture.

Indeed, the idea that a clean break with the past, the political equivalent of a scorched earth policy, is still more doubtful as a course of conduct for reform-minded statesmen than for men of war. Quite apart from the natural tendency of politicians to cling to the past (no matter how tried and untrue), and quite independently of the constraints on change imposed by the imperatives of democratic, or even semidemocratic, legitimacy, the postcommunist transition is not from a state of backwardness to modernity, but from one highly developed (although thoroughly *mis*-developed) society to another. This means not only that the forces of the past are that much stronger, but also that its edifices embody an enormous social effort, one that was paid for with a body count, the sweat and blood of generations. Most of the industrial and institutional white elephants produced at such a price are a grim instance of what economists dismiss with the phrase "sunk cost"—an expenditure that must be given up for lost without as much as a backward glance. In reality, however, it is not always clear what is and what is not a white elephant, and the most vexing problem for political leaders—their advisors and outside critics, too—is to determine what aspects from the past can be salvaged and what cannot, and must not, be saved.

Nor is it always clear to what state of affairs the transition is supposed to lead the countries of Eastern Europe and the newly independent states (NIS). "Democracy" and "market economy" are always listed by politicians and commentators alike in the postcommunist region as among their ultimate aims. But the meaning of these terms is much less clear in practice than on the page or speaker's rostrum. If democracy is defined as a system in which the most important leaders are freely elected and the basic rights of individuals are respected, most countries in the postcommunist region already are, to greater and lesser degrees, democratic. If price liberalization, moderate levels of state ownership, and the absence of central planning are the hallmarks of a market economy, most transition countries are either already there or well on the way to this goal. It is in the interstices of the two, however, in a political and economic system with the capacity to generate sustained growth and stable political institutions, that the benefits of both democracy and a market economy are secured. On this score, alas, there is still a lot of doubt about the future of many postcommunist countries.

Indeed, the very institutional shape that democracy and the market economy are likely to take in the region if the transition is successful is a matter of constant, insistent debate. Is a form of presidentialism, of Westminster-style parliamentarism, or of federalism the most appropriate system for any given transition country? Can a majoritarian or a proportional system of representation best insure political stability? Will the tripartite model of labor relations found in today's Germany or the more adversarial type of trade unionism found in the Anglo-Saxon countries better contribute to labor peace, high employment, and economic prosperity? Will institutional ownership of corporate property and so-called internal capital markets be more likely to provide effective corporate governance for business enterprises in transition, or is a more individualistic model involving highly capitalized stock markets and markets for corporate control more likely to do this vital job? Will the state remain the main provider of retirement funds and social services, or will more market-oriented solutions prevail?

These are not technical questions, but rather fundamental milestones defining the concrete forms of democratic and market regimes to which the postcommunist countries are in transition. There are many types of democratic regimes and many variations on the idea of a market economy, some of which work well in some places yet, when transplanted, not at all in others. Institutions, after all, are not hothouse plants. Presidentialism works well in the United States, but led to dictatorships in most South American countries that tried it (and some elsewhere, such as France in 1848). Close relations between the state, employers, and labor unions may have been instrumental in the process of rebuilding Germany from the ruins of Hitler's War, but they nearly wrecked Great Britain during the same postwar decades. Decisions—some overt, some incremental, some by default—are now being made in Warsaw, Moscow, Ljubljana, and the other postcommunist capitals that very well may determine how successful their democratic and economic systems will one day turn out to be.

In addition to its primary meaning, the word "transition" can also carry with it a connotation of brevity. Broad public enthusiasm for dramatic social changes and sacrifices can be maintained for only brief moments—the famous "windows of opportunity" that journalists and historians like to talk about. Even if it were known what to save and what to sacrifice from the entire order of the old regime, even if there were no doubts as to where today's changes are leading, and if a tropism toward inertia were not at issue, politics would exact its price on policy. Traditions within any society sometimes cannot withstand scrutiny; not everyone—perhaps only a daring few—are willing to see the implicit examined explicitly. At times of great social stress and dislocation, a simple consideration of alternative policies can seem a corrosive enterprise, a process of exposure that may cost the best-intentioned reformer his or her chance to lead. Add to this general fear of change and uncertainty the truth that there are many who stand to lose from the transition; in fact, the more radical the change, the more numerous the losers, from managers and workers whose jobs are suddenly insecure, to intellectuals who are no longer venerated models, to the well-connected for whom relations with the old elites guaranteed privileged access to scarce consumer goods. Together, the "losers" form a ready-made coalition capable of stalling the transition or even bringing it to an outright halt.

Fundamentally, the most important reason why transition from one political/economic regime to another is slow is that reform is not a science. What bridges the gap between democratic faith and reality is not detailed knowledge of every way station on the road on which society is heading and how to reach each one, but a set of institutions that accumulate from many distinct and seemingly unconnected decisions—some right, some wrong—and embody the collective experience of what works for a society and what does not. Institutions are mostly a product of history, not design, and they are needed precisely because human beings have only very imperfect knowledge of

how societies work. Like the market whose invisible hand some-
how mysteriously coordinates what central planners could never
bring together, so institutions—which are to the market what
wheels and spokes are to a machine—are mileposts toward
which human beings habitually orient their behavior in order to
reduce the uncertainty implicit in any complex, temporally extended endeavor.

The essays collected in this book are attempts to describe
this new institutional order *in statu nascendi*. Their genesis says
something important about them: they were written originally
for newspapers on both sides of the old Iron Curtain. Except for
two essays on Slovakia and Croatia, which expose abuses in the
economic reform processes in those troubled countries, each
essay takes on a particular institutional aspect of the transition,
be it privatization, banking, social security, labor relations, or
international trade, and attempts to give a snapshot of its development that is both instructive and understandable to a wide
general audience of people living with the day-to-day consequences of the transition.

As in all collections of occasional pieces written over a prolonged period of time, some things are said more than once, and
some parts are considerably different in texture than others.
Moreover, because events in the region change so fast, it would
be futile to try and keep every essay up-to-date in all respects.
This is the curse of all collections, but these defects also have
advantages, if not virtues, for the essay format allows us to cover
a range of topics that might be awkward to encompass within
the confines of a unified text. More importantly, the absence of
the need to develop a single, straight line of thought throughout
the entire book permits us to look at our central subject from a
variety of angles and vantage points—historical at times, critical
at others—that we hope add up to something more than even
the most rigorous exposition of a single point of view.

This catholic perspective extends from content to method.
The institutions we are describing here are mostly within the
province of economics. In the opinion of the great majority of
professional writers on economics, however, that discipline is not
properly political or historical. By this they mean, first of all, that
economics should steer clear of questions that require for their
answers an explicit statement of political or moral values; and
secondly, that economic writing should confine itself to those
problems of allocation and efficiency for which its established

techniques are so well adapted. In the circumstances of the post-communist transition, however, this purist, "scientific" attitude is largely inappropriate. The postcommunist transition is not a technical problem for which economics can be treated as a tool box to be used for the examination, repair, or outright replacement of this or that broken part. This is no moment that, in a minor modification of the scriptural parable, the bland should lead the bland. Instead, economic discussion in the region nowadays must harken back to the early days of the discipline, when the writings of Smith, Ricardo, and Mill demonstrated the extraordinary capacity of economic thought to elucidate the problems of epochal social, political, and historical change.

By divorcing itself from the need to struggle with the elements of the political and social world, however recalcitrant they may be, conventional modern economics has ensured its technical virtuosity and its internal consistency, but often at the cost of social relevance. Proclamations and aphorisms are not considered economics unless they follow and elucidate some equation or other. These essays, with their insistent emphasis on the connectedness of economic and noneconomic processes, are an early effort to mark out some of the boundaries within which the lasting institutional outcomes of the transition from communism are to be sought. Whether the partial sacrifice of scientific precision is warranted by this task is for the reader to judge.

Acknowledgments

The essays included in this volume have been aided in a variety of ways by many individuals. First and foremost, we are grateful to Rebecca Schumann, Simon Nellis, Pavel Sinev, Melissa Fleer, and Josh LaPorte for their help and dedication to our common research efforts. The research on which these essays are based could not have been undertaken without the aid of Lindita Xhillari in Albania, Igo Pelipas in Belarus, Spartak Keremidchiev and Todor Gradev in Bulgaria, Eva Klvacova and Jan Mladek in the Czech Republic, Ailu Kukumagi in Estonia, Attila Havas and Andras Koroseny in Hungary, Katarina Khmenchuk and Viacheslav Kozlov in Kazakhstan, Asel Djusebekova and Marat Temirkanov in Kyrgyzstan, Velga Vilne, Daira Baranova, and Tatjana Muravska in Latvia, Romas Lazutka in Lithuania, Trajko Slaveski in Macedonia, Sergui Botezatu in Moldova, Joanna Dzialo and Agnieszka Rybinska in Poland, Liviu Gaita in Romania, Maxim Kvasha and Sergei Vinokur in Russia, Eugen Jurzyca and Andrej Juris in Slovakia, Franci Krizanic in Slovenia, Miroslva Didukh, Valentin Lavrinenko, Natalia Tchourikova, and Viktor Stepenenko in Ukraine, and Alisher Djumanov in Uzbekistan.

As with all of the work undertaken by the Privatization Project, this book would not have been possible without the generous and unfailing support of George Soros. We are also grateful to the Eurasia Foundation and the Pew Charitable Trusts for their assistance over the years.

1
Privatization
The Permanent Revolution

Since privatization (the transfer of economic assets from the public to the private sector) began in the postcommunist world, it is easy to misunderstand and mischaracterize its impact. Some appearances deceive, others are revealing. Some all-too-common jibes (for example, that privatization breeds corruption) are partly accurate, others are instantly dated by the region's often exploding rates of economic growth. For any assessment of the results of privatization, look hard, and evidence for opposite conclusions can be found. The privatization process is one of external success and internal contradictions.

Even though it is obviously easier to nationalize than to denationalize, what is happening in countries attempting the transition from a complete state economy to something in the direction of its opposite is, at least in theory, the greatest exchange ever of property between private citizens and their governments in modern history. According to the European Bank for Reconstruction and Development (EBRD), the private sector has emerged from nowhere to dominate the economies of Estonia, Poland, the Czech Republic, Russia, Slovenia, Slovakia, Moldova, and Kyrgyzstan (see table 1.1 and figure 1.1). Once unthinkable notions about private ownership and private economic power (which create diffuse sources of political power) are now the norm: private television stations flourish in, to cite just two surprising examples, Romania and Ukraine; Latvia's national airline (following the bankruptcy of the state-run line) is in the hands of private shareholders; private pension schemes provide a growing share of social security protection to citizens in the

Table 1.1

Public Sector Share of GDP and Employment Accounted for by Private Sector (Including Cooperatives) in Eastern Europe and the Former Soviet Union

Country	Share GDP (%)*	Share Employment (%)†
Belarus	15	40.2
Kazakhstan	25	9
Moldova	30	47
Uzbekistan	30	59.7
Ukraine	35	24.5
FYR Macedonia	40	na
Kyrgyzstan	40	0
Romania	40	51.4
Bulgaria	45	34.7
Croatia	45	46.6
Slovenia	45	na
Lithuania	55	61.5
Russia	55	51
Albania	60	na
Hungary	60	59.4
Latvia	60	58
Poland	60	59.8
Slovak Republic	60	31.9
Estonia	65	na
Czech Republic	70	na

* Share GDP is a rough estimate as of mid-1995 by the EBRD.
† Share Employment is calculated as of 1994 except for Hungary and Moldova, where data for 1993 are used.

Source: EBRD Transition Report, 1995.

Czech Republic. Almost everywhere in the region, the private sector is fast becoming the best hope for an improvement in living standards.

Now that the privatization process—in tandem with the freeing of prices and the fight against inflation—has helped to construct the broad outlines of a market economy, it is time to examine in some detail the impact of privatization (and the variety of privatization strategies that governments have pursued) on economic development. Three issues almost instantly emerge on center stage. The first is the resistance to reform of many businesses despite the change in ownership from state to private

Figure 1.1

Public Sector Share of GDP and Employment Accounted for by Private Sector (Including Cooperatives) in Eastern Europe and the Former Soviet Union

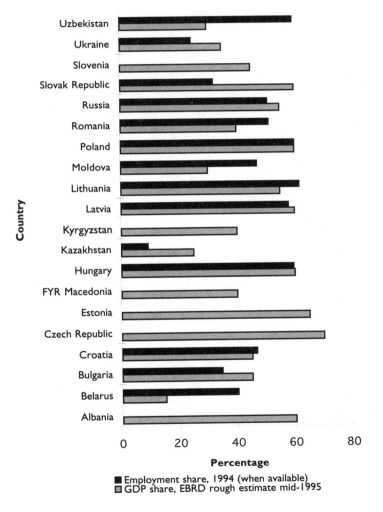

■ Employment share, 1994 (when available)
□ GDP share, EBRD rough estimate mid-1995

Note: The term "private sector" is a broad concept that includes, in some countries, collective farms and companies with only minority nonstate ownership. Employment share figure is for 1993.
Source: EBRD Transition Report, 1995.

hands. In many cases, indeed, privatization has not produced the hard decisions about restructuring that its advocates wanted and expected. Murky ownership of many industries, exacerbated by the large ownership stakes that the state retains almost everywhere in the region, contributes to this wounded result. Even in the Czech Republic, upheld as a paragon of privatized virtues by so many commentators (and by the proud Czechs most of all), many privatized firms have managed so far to avoid the root-and-branch reform that the architects of the country's mass privatization program envisioned, in part because the premier Vaclav Klaus, though sounding like Margaret Thatcher, is as keen on protecting jobs as any nostalgic Swedish socialist.

Second is the belief that in most transition countries it is hard, if not impossible, to persuade a majority of ordinary people that privatization is beneficial to them, a stricture much in evidence over the past half-decade. In the run-up to the Russian presidential elections of June/July 1996, for example, Boris Yeltsin sacked his most successful minister, one-time privatization czar Anatoli Chubais, merely to appease widespread dismay at the results of privatization. Once President Yeltsin was re-elected, however, Chubais' managerial talents, honed in the vast privatization effort that he commanded between 1991 and 1994, carried him back to the center of Russian power, and he became first deputy prime minister in the Kremlin. In Romania, Ion Iliescu based his penultimate campaign for the presidency on the populist-statist slogan, "We are not selling out the country."

Ex-communist, post-communist, once-and-future communist: no matter the hyphenation and its masking or mocking intent, resentment at the effects of privatization was one of the factors that ushered communism's political heirs back into political power in Poland, Hungary, and Lithuania within only a few years of communism's short demise. Only in the Czech Republic, Moldova, and Estonia have privatization's advocates built effective electoral machines on the basis of successful strategies. Indeed, one of the striking features of the Russian presidential campaign of 1996 was President Yeltsin's early failure to recognize that there was a constituency that supported his reforms. Only when Anatoli Chubais assumed a central role in the campaign organization did Yeltsin's forces begin to make direct appeals to this pro-privatization audience.

The third issue concerns privatization's impact on the state. Many people within and without the region hoped that divesting government of business decision making would not only encourage economic efficiency in a growing private sector, but would also make the state itself more efficient and effective in carrying out its reduced role. Indeed, the lack of reform of the state is pivotal to understanding the privatization process as a whole.

This last issue hints at a plausible explanation for the dilatory approach to privatization taken by governments that is often evident in the transition countries. Despite the huge prestige opponents to the regime gained after the collapse of communism, only the Czech, Estonian, Kyrgyz, Moldovan, Slovak, and Russian reform governments steeled themselves to take decisive actions on privatization early in the transition. Noncommunist leaders in Hungary, Slovenia, and Croatia—countries that, it was wrongly supposed, had advantages due to the somewhat decentralized nature of their socialist economies—probably believed that little fast action in privatization was necessary. Others—Latvia, Bulgaria, Romania, and Uzbekistan—fretted over what privatization plan to pursue. Saddest of all, under the erratic leadership of Aleksander Lukashenka, the government of Belarus opted to stick its head in the sand, condemning privatization as well as all other reforms while retreating into the tried-and-failed Leninism that collapsed in 1991.

No matter the speed at which it was undertaken, when posed as an economic cure-all privatization was bound to disappoint. Some ministers saw it as a way to close yawning budget deficits through pricey sales, others as a means to inject a source of income into, say, harried pension systems. (Macedonia, to cite just one example, earmarks 15% of all privatization revenues or an equal percent of the shares in privatized firms to the national pension fund.) Workers wanted firms to be privatized into their own hands. Pensioners and state employees wanted compensation. Ex-owners claimed that only restitution of property would bring justice. Average people everywhere in the region merely wanted their (supposedly) fair share of the spoils.

Given such often grandiose expectations, a widespread letdown was perhaps inevitable. Moreover, a more fundamental division was also at work. Most economists saw privatization as a means to develop genuine owners who would employ assets in a far more efficient way than the state. But politicians instinctively recognized that privatization was as much about power as efficiency and sought to skew the process to either their own direct benefit or to the benefit of their supporters, cronies, or clans. So extravagance and cynicism contributed to what followed: both not only shaped and misshaped the privatization process, but also affected evaluations of the impact of shifting the economy into private hands.

1.1 The Magic Bullet

As the postcommunist transition began, there was something almost touching about the enthusiasm manifested in the way some reformers and their advisors responded to the notion of privatization. Early thinking on privatization—theoretical and programmatic—was dominated by a somewhat naive belief in the magic powers of capitalism. Under communism, enterprises were hopelessly inefficient because the state stuck its nose in the business of business unceasingly. So the credo of privatization at its inception in the postcommunist world was: get the state out of business; release the forces of private enterprise; let specialists do what they do best, rather than knuckle under to dictates from party apparatchiks—then industry will start moving.

What most transition country leaders did *not* reckon with at all was that years of communist misallocation of resources and mismanagement of industry had become embedded deeply in the capital stock of the economy: firms were often located in the middle of nowhere, far from raw materials and sources of skilled labor; many enterprises were too big or too small and too vertically integrated (meaning that they tried to produce every component themselves in order not to rely on suppliers as inefficiently managed as they); there was too much heavy industry and an overemphasis on the military, too much focus on producing quantity and too little on assuring quality. It was as if the communists themselves, because of a kind of misguided ideological pride, conspired to make and keep their industry out-of-date.

It was thus misleading to blame the problems of transition economies on state ownership alone—something that brings to mind the somewhat sluggish performance of Western utilities or state airlines, or even those patronage-ridden wastrels, Italy's state-owned conglomerates. Many transition country leaders (as well as their Western advisors) averted their eyes from the fact that most of existing industry, with its voracious appetite for subsidies, was worse than useless. No matter how rapid, no move from the autarky of the socialist camp, with its rigged markets, five-year plans, and shoddy goods, to the exposed fields of international competition could ever transform these dinosaurs into viable industries.

In dealing with the communist legacy, expectations that capitalism would magically make former state enterprises work were thus always a childish fantasy. Indeed, the primary genius of capitalism is not its miraculous powers to make things work better; it is what the Austrian economist Joseph Schumpeter called "creative destruction," that is, the ability to *drive out* from the marketplace firms that cannot compete effectively in terms of either price or of quality. So what capitalism was bound to bring to the transition countries was a housecleaning of monumental, indeed chilling, proportions: the sweeping away of any number of substandard firms accumulated over fifty or more years during which things were uncreatively added, but never creatively destroyed.

Every postcommunist economy, to be sure, is burdened by its share of industrial dinosaurs, but not each to the same degree, and the pain of transition is directly proportional to the amount of creative destruction that market forces are apt to inflict on the former state sector. The greater the proportion of firms without any reason for their existence under the new conditions, the less privatization can do to soften the hard landing in a competitive environment. Under any regime, the nonreformable, value-subtracting firms must be closed if they are not to drain resources needed in other, more dynamic sectors of the economy. Whether or not to privatize such white elephants is, therefore, not a decision concerning their potential efficiency (the odds are that they have little or none at all), but rather one concerning the *political costs* of their closure under the systems of private or public ownership.

Privatization—if it is meant seriously as withdrawal of both the state's interference *and* its subsidies—is bound to make many firms go broke, often very quickly. Here is the fundamental political contradiction of privatization: what in the long run is in the interest of everyone—a leaner, more efficient economy—is certain to produce a lot of pain for many, usually ordinary people, in the short run. That many of the workers involved had little or no say in the incompetent decisions of the socialist era that sealed their industry's fate makes the process of restructuring all the harder for them to accept passively. No surprise then that attitude of most governments to privatization is best described by the words of the peasant girl in Mozart's opera *Don Giovanni:* "I would like to, and I am afraid."

1.2 Unrecognized Privatizations

So far, whatever creative destruction has taken place in most postcommunist countries is due not to privatization, at least not to the official programs people are talking about, but to macroeconomic reform. In order to stabilize currencies and put the state budget in order, governments had to cut subsidies lavished by the communists on their inefficient creations (see figure 1.2). Russian industrial subsidies have crashed since 1992, falling from 32% of GDP to 6% in 1994. Poland cut enterprise subsidies from 16% of GDP in 1986 to 3.3% in 1992. In country after country, the figures are similarly dramatic.

Slashed subsidies do force managers to wield the knife: the 150 to 200 largest firms in Hungary and the Czech Republic reduced their workforces by 57% and 32% respectively between 1989 and 1993. Looked at from this point of view, the much-deplored falls in industrial output in most postcommunist countries were for the most part actually the pruning of inefficient production and the necessary shrinkage of the bloated state sector. The figures are as follows: in Albania, 44% in 1992; in Belarus, 11% in 1993; in Estonia, 25.8% in 1992 alone; Bulgaria, 27.8% (1991); Croatia, 28.5% (1991); Czech Republic, 22.3% (1991); Macedonia, 17.3% (1992); Hungary, 18.2% (1991); Kazakhstan, 28% (1994); Kyrgyzstan, 25% (1992); Latvia, 48.7% (1992); Lithuania, 50.9% (1992); Moldova, 25% (1992); Poland, 26.1% (1990); Romania, 21.9% (1992); Russia, 18.8% (1992); Slovakia, 17.6% (1991); Slovenia, 13.2% (1992); Ukraine, 28% (1994); and in Uzbekistan, 12.3% in 1992.

As a side effect of this process, much unheralded privatization has been taking place. When the crunch of the Polish shock therapy of 1991–92 really came to be felt by state firms, many enterprises responded by selling assets they had hoarded because of the previous regime's chronic shortages. Thousands of trucks sold by desperate state companies, for example, formed the basis of Poland's thriving private-sector trucking and wholesaling industries. Without the real estate leased from cash-starved state firms, the growth of the private sector, particularly in service industries, in such countries as Hungary and Russia,

Figure 1.2

Government Spending Patterns

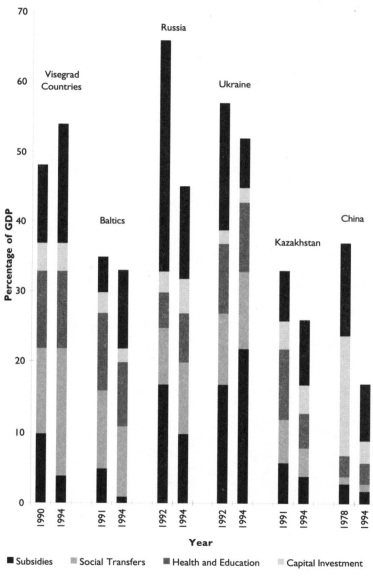

Source: EBRD Transition Report, 1995.

would have been impossible. In most countries, probably more assets have so far migrated in this way from the state to the private sector than in official privatization programs.

1.3 Constructing the Capitalist Order

Unlike Lenin's revolutionaries of 1917, the makers of the privatization revolution were not about to leap blindly or blithely into the unknown. There was no need to conjure out of thin air, as Lenin and his Bolsheviks had once done, a vision of the society that they wanted to create. A market economy in the manner of those already in existence in the developed world was their goal from the outset. But so fretful were these reformers of the terrors of the unknown—and so noxious was the Bolshevik precedent of government by imagination—that they would not envision a road·ahead that had not been traveled before. So cautious a vision is perhaps understandable among leaders who had lived all their lives with the dismal consequences of Lenin's improvisations and experiments. But these self-imposed limits, in turn, led to a fundamental misunderstanding and misinterpretation of the unprecedented nature of what privatization really entailed during the postcommunist transition.

In looking for tested mechanisms of privatization, it was clear that Britain's Margaret Thatcher was the first to make privatization a politically fashionable and workable policy. In 1979, she succeeded in convincing a plurality of the British people that she could put much of British state-owned industry, share by share, on the market. By selling a number of large state firms, such as British Telecom, British Airlines, and British Steel, below what the secondary market would bring, she raised revenues for the budget (thus allowing her government to be more generous than her fiscal conservatism would otherwise permit) and created millions of new shareholders who—to the shock of the Labour Party—abandoned Britain's traditional class-based politics to become firm backers of her Conservative Party.

Politicians are fast learners, and many countries—from Brazil to Mexico to the Philippines—and political leaders of all ideological stripes—including socialists in Spain, France, and Portugal—soon followed Britain's lead. When East Germany reunited with West Germany, a big push was made to sell eastern industries through a specially created agency, the Treuhandanstalt. Given the almost unbroken successes of sales in the West (both in terms of yielding revenue for governments and, quite often, in restoring doddering state companies to health—witness the robust vitality nowadays of British Airlines, British Telecom, and British Steel), it was almost natural for the new East European and NIS (newly independent states) governments—encouraged by their Western advisors, for whom Thatcher's sales were the only thing they knew—to see this as the right path for their countries as well.

Nothing could have been more wrong. Where market institutions exist, as in Thatcher's Britain, privatization is merely the sale of a few state-owned enterprises. State companies in Great Britain, even if somewhat less efficient, were basically a product of the surrounding capitalist culture. The sale of state enterprises, although a big job, was also a rather standard operation, not that different from taking public a closely held corporation by issuing shares to investors at large. A number of investment banks stood ready to underwrite the issue and to sell it to the public.

In the transition countries, by contrast, privatization must be a *systemic change:* its task is to introduce capital markets, to make genuine firm valuation possible, to create the environment in which, day in and day out, normal market transactions can take place. Above all, the very scale of the problem transcends anything known in the annals of economic history. While Margaret Thatcher's sales of a few large firms during her first ten years in office was considered a great success, Russia alone had over 200,000 state enterprises to privatize, Poland had some 8,000, Uzbekistan 3,000, Latvia and Slovenia 1,500 each, Moldova 1,300, and even tiny Estonia and Macedonia had close to a 1,000 state enterprises to privatize. By any reckoning, following the British model would have taken forever, monopolizing political energy (and talent) to the detriment of other vital reforms.

What the transition countries needed was an innovative solution corresponding to the scale and uniqueness of the task at hand. But in politics new ideas are usually either hard to come by or risky business, and the temptation to fight the next war with weapons inherited from the last war is a sin of which not only generals can be guilty.

1.4 The Insiders' Party

In this world, however, what gets done is usually not a matter of ideas, either good or bad, but of naked political power. Indeed, while a key idea behind privatization was to depoliticize the economy, there was no way to evict politics from the privatization process itself.

The hardscrabble task of effective privatization was bound to be painful, as overmanned and often insolvent firms shed labor, new owners fired old incompetent managers, and production of unsaleable goods shrank. Privatization, however, was not only going to make some people miserable; it was also certain to make a small group of others very rich, almost instantly. In a social transfer of wealth of such unprecedented magnitude, various political groups were bound to be activated and energized.

A head start in politics is eighty percent of victory, and the best organized groups are usually the winners. In transition countries, the first to mobilize were the insiders: the workers and management of state enterprises facing privatization. They were not only the most immediately affected, but also felt entitled to take over. Privatization was evidently supposed to throw out the bath water but leave the children with free run of the nursery.

Reasons for this can be found in the history of communist-era reforms. It is indeed a strange irony of privatization that countries that had tried to decentralize managerial control under communism—Yugoslavia under Tito, Hungary under Kadar, the Soviet Union under Gorbachev—saw later efforts at privatizing hurt, not helped, by the results of these attempted reforms. Decentralization conferred more power on enterprise managers and workers and allowed them to develop a network of connections to managers and workers in other firms. Over time, these interests fused into something of a potent and cohesive lobby to promote insider interests.

Only when Hungary, for example, gave its managers a virtual veto power over how a firm was to be privatized did the first postcommunist government's privatization program get off the ground. Poland, where workers had also effectively organized under Solidarity and other unions, ended up with its privatization stalled by an alliance of worker-manager opposition. Because Romania's government during the presidency of Ion Iliescu (1990–1996) bungled its privatization, the only privatized firms that appeared in these years came from (usually corrupt) management-employee buyouts (MEBOs). The price of rapid privatization in Russia was the nearly complete insider control of all privatized firms, a topic discussed in further detail below.

Even before communism disintegrated, insiders—the very people who ran state industries, and usually ran them into the ground—jumped on the bandwagon of private property. In the limbo that most enterprises had fallen into during the last days of the old regime, factory managers were quick to spin off valuable assets into special firms under their control, leaving the state with hollow shells and massive debts.

A common ruse went something like this: You are the boss of a state firm that makes, say, bricks. You set up a firm in your son or daughter's name to which you sell 10,000 tons of bricks at or below cost price. You have the state firm you run lend money to the new private company you own and control to make the purchase. The new company then sells the bricks at market prices, pays back the loan, and reaps a big profit. Repeat this for a year or two, and suddenly you are a rich man. In the meantime, however, the state firm has slid downhill. So you make a rock-bottom bid for it. The government says yes, pleased to get another loser off its books.

Anyone who says that transition country managers are incapable of innovation ought to look at the myriad corruptions they have employed to strip valuable assets or gain ownership of the firms outright. Two examples: Managers of Tutun, a tobacco maker in Macedonia, pillaged their firm by financial manipulation. In 1990, Tutun's manager, Vasko Kuzmanovski, paid for his firm a sum equal to its supposed book value. Here's the catch: he borrowed the money (at close to no interest) from Tutun itself. The same device, rubber-stamped by the plant's employees, was used by Lithuanian ex-premier Lubys in a managerial buyout of Jonava Nitric, a fertilizer plant and one of the largest factories in the Baltics.

Everywhere, the politically connected were usually the biggest winners. The case of a former head of KISZ, the Hungarian communist youth organization, Imre Nagy (not to be confused with Hungary's premier during the 1956 revolution), is typical. In 1990, Nagy's one-man company, Vallalkozas Szervezes Kft., purchased from the old communist party its four newspapers (including Hungary's biggest daily, *Nepszabadsag*) for a mere 1.5 million forints. In less than a year, *Nepszabadsag* alone fetched over 100 million forints.

Although some countries, such as Hungary, moved (often under public pressure) to curb the worst abuses of spontaneous privatization once the new regime was in power, insider scams become chronic when privatization was stalled. Bulgaria is a textbook case. So commonplace are insider deals in Bulgaria that there is a name for them: *Positano,* from the street where the reformed communists, now socialists, have their party headquarters. By the late 1980s and early 1990s, abuse of the leasing system was the favored ploy. The case of Briljant, a factory in the old Roman town of Plovdiv, is typical. Briljant's bosses secured a DM 300,000 loan from the First Private Bank of Sofia, supposedly to buy new equipment. New machinery was secured all right, but at double the market price through First Leasing House of Sofia, a subsidiary of the bank. Bank insiders and Briljant's managers pocketed the difference.

By 1996 in Bulgaria, a more insidious ploy became, sad to say, even more popular. Privatizations were routinely corrupted under the rule of law. If insiders lost out in their bids for a company, they merely went to court and had a friendly judge annul the auction. Slanchev Den, once a luxury spa for high-ranking communist apparatchiks on the Black Sea, was clawed back by its managers through such dubious court proceedings.

Insiders are, of course, not bad *per se.* Many Western management theorists reckon that when managers own a piece of their firm, their incentives to push for increased efficiency and greater profits grow. But managers, and even more so the employees, have a multitude of conflicting interests in the firm—above all their employment. The problem insiders pose in the transition countries is derived from the fact that they usually "own" more than a small sliver of their firms and are not subject to external oversight. Add to this that employees of overmanned firms and incompetent communist managers have the most to lose in genuine restructuring, which means layoffs and dismissals, and you have a recipe for failure. Restructuring will fail unless real power in the firm is vested in people committed to *defend the interests of capital.* These are unlikely to be insiders whose conflicting interests distort their behavior.

1.5 Sold Out

Against the predations of insiders, prosecution has proven itself to be a puny weapon. Faced simultaneously by the overriding need to restructure economies and the political firestorms ignited by spontaneous privatization, governments needed to get a handle on what was, in the early postcommunist years, fast becoming an out-of-control process. National privatization policies were needed. In devising them, governments soon hit a fork in the road: the choice was between trying to sell a large part of state industries and the untried and populist-sounding route of giveaways. The road of privatization through sales was well traveled by others such as Margaret Thatcher, and politicians, being politicians, usually act in a spirit of "better the devil we know." Most, at least at first, opted for the tried-and-(with luck) true.

As noted previously, what is true and effective in one set of circumstances may be woefully inadequate elsewhere. So it is with privatization through sales. Certainly sales offered a number of alluring prospects, a supposed bonanza for depleted treasuries being the greatest, of course. Many governments bent backward trying to service the monumental debt payments with which the promiscuous borrowings of the old communist regimes had saddled them. Others (Poland most importantly) defaulted, but still needed large sums to keep ladling out social services (no politician likes to incur the opposition of the old, widows, and orphans).

The idea that privatization can help to balance a national government's budget is dangerous nonsense when applied to the transition economies. Even if they were to succeed in replenishing state coffers, such sales would simply drain scarce capital from the very private sector that privatization is meant to create. After all, privatization was intended to transfer assets to the private sector, not the other way around.

A moment's reflection is enough to show that the hope for large revenues from privatization of most state enterprises was a pipe dream from the start. The only potential buyers for state companies with enough cash are foreigners, but they are often more imaginary than actual. Except for natural monopolies and a few lucrative plums, such as telecoms, transport, and even television, foreigners, contrary to the region's naive belief, were not keen on buying postcommunist dinosaurs. Of all the transition countries, only Hungary attracted enough direct foreign investments to make a bit of difference in its privatization program, and even there, most foreign investments went into utilities and greenfield (new) projects, rather than the more typical postcommunist enterprises. In other countries, especially the NIS, foreign investment is still pitifully small and likely to stay that way until confidence in reform grows, and a private economy is created by genuine privatization protected by law.

Selling to foreigners is also a political hot potato. The assets offered are usually worth little, if anything. And yet, if the price is low enough to reflect this abject state of affairs, the bureaucrats making the sale are bound to be accused of selling off the family silver to strangers and of being corrupt to boot. (In fact, because such sales are indeed politically suicidal, the suspicion of corruption is often well founded.)

That the very idea of selling thousands of companies to domestic buyers is preposterous becomes clear when one looks at the stock of domestic savings in most countries in transition. Private assets, always rather meager under a regime implacably opposed, by definition, to private capital, were made even more pitiful by postcommunist inflation. In Poland, for example, if people in 1990 were to spend half of their accumulated savings on shares of privatized firms (a completely unrealistic assumption that would mean a collapse of the new private sector), they would have enough money to pay for a mere 5–8% of the book value of Polish state firms!

What this shows is that if a sales program is to result in privatization of a significant portion of the postcommunist state sector, prices would have to be so low that the term "sale" does not really apply. Much to the distaste of those who said that only sales result in "real owners," "giveaway" better describes what actually happens in the course of this form of privatization— except it is not a giveaway to all citizens, but to a select group which happens to be allowed to "buy" state assets for a song. That this is an invitation to political patronage of all kinds (and the mischief that implies), on the one hand, and outright corruption, on the other, should be self-evident.

1.6 Sold Slow

Sales in all their variations—tenders, auctions, MEBOs, initial public offerings (IPOs)—have another serious drawback: they are also terribly slow. Take the case of IPOs. The carefully prepared public stock offerings that took place in Poland in the early years of reform, after a lot of time and effort, resulted in little more than two dozen privatizations. Despite making IPOs a focus of official privatization efforts in 1994–95, Romania managed to privatize only one company, Apullum Alba Iulia, in this way. The records of IPOs in Hungary, Lithuania, and Slovenia are equally dismal, says the World Bank. Other methods produce somewhat better results, but still the numbers are not impressive.

Of course, theoretically speaking, one *could* simply auction off thousands of companies without any minimum prices or conditions imposed. But in fact this never happens; politicians would be skinned alive for the prices that resulted, and by renouncing conditions that last beyond the auction or sale they would emasculate themselves as ministers and could no longer exercise their *power*. It is only through giving out contracts for consulting firms that do valuations, getting points for "saving jobs" through requiring that the new owners keep the firm's bloated employment, and conditioning sales on specific postprivatization investments (as if bureaucrats who had fifty years to run their countries suddenly knew better than future private owners what investments will make sense) that privatization bureaucrats can stay in business. Because of the need to establish such conditions, the sale of a candy factory to Jacobs Suchard of Switzerland, for example, took more than four hundred days to run Bucharest's bureaucratic gauntlet in 1994.

So sales go slowly. Putting a "fair" price on state firms is difficult (particularly given the idiocies of socialist accounting methods), time-consuming, and one more invitation to dishonesty and political piracy. Indeed, underestimating value is the easiest get-rich-quick scheme around. When it came time to sell off Slovenia's state oil company, to cite just one example, auditors put such a cheap price on it that the sale had to be stopped (in the nick of time) when it came out that the company's managers stood to make a windfall profit of $30 million.

Negotiations between governments and potential buyers are also interminable, and this problem is complicated even more by the choice of salesmen. At the heart of the privatization programs throughout the region are government privatization agencies specially constructed to handle the transition. Not surprisingly, these bodies suffer from much the same incompetence and political interference—habits inherited from the socialist era—as any other part of transition country government. In the huge lobby of Croatia's National Property Fund, indeed, there is a telling example of the new and the old: a smiling receptionist at a flickering computer screen and a clock with no hands.

One of the problems with governments running businesses (selling companies is certainly a business, and a difficult one at that) is that political objectives nearly always trump the economic objectives. In Lithuania, the Central Property Commission is merely an ad hoc group with members drawn on a temporary basis from other ministries. Members are torn in their loyalty between the CPC and their regular departments. Added confusion arises because, when enterprises are corporatized, there is no established procedure to decide which ministry nominates members to the firm's new board of directors, so board membership becomes a form of partisan political payoff. (Curiously, the perk of board membership began its life as a payoff in the region in quite the reverse way: in Hungary in the late 1980s, board seats were bestowed as a favor from newly corporatized company managers to their political patrons.)

Presidents Franjo Tudjman of Croatia and Ion Iliescu of Romania have also made this type of payoff a central means for maintaining the loyalty of their far-from-unified political machines, with well-paying board seats dangled before party members to keep them in line. In Kyrgyzstan, a sham privatization converted the State Property Fund from a regulatory body into three supposedly commercial organizations. All three became insolvent, due largely to the interest-free loans made not to newly privatized firms, but to friends in the state sector. Never one for subtleties, Slovakia's premier Vladimir Meciar, during the second of the three prime ministries he has held since the breakup of Czechoslovakia, simply appointed himself head of the presidium of the National Property Fund.

Politics also often dictates that firms in which privatization would result in large-scale layoffs not be privatized. Kyrgyzstan, Latvia, Macedonia, and Uzbekistan, therefore, use their privatization agencies as something akin to industrial hospitals. Needless to say, despite many life support measures (usually costing taxpayers a pretty penny), most patients never recover. (Latvia, alone it seems, has been willing to shut down at least some of these sick giants, perhaps because most of their employees were nonvoting ethnic Russians.) Romania's method was to hamstring its sales process even more by creating a gamut of oversight boards—a Court of Audit, State Financial Control Board, Prime

Minister's Control Corps, and Financial Guard—that sales must run through before any privatization deal can be consummated. Small wonder then that after four years a mere 8% of the share capital in Romanian state firms has actually been privatized.

Another popular delaying trick is to announce that some companies are too valuable or "strategic" to risk having them fall into private hands. In Romania under Iliescu, tobacco processing, urban transport, and even scholarly publications were deemed "sensitive" industries not subject to privatization. Slovakia's government designated wide sectors of the economy—telecoms, post, gas, oil, electricity, arms, civil engineering, pharmaceuticals, forestry, water, even a stud farm—as too strategic to be left entirely to the private sector. *In toto* property worth SK 150 billion (nearly 40% of the total valuation given to state companies before privatization) was placed under this special protection in 1995. So long as the Slovak premier Vladimir Meciar remains in power, many of the firms included are unlikely to be privatized; in others the Slovak government will maintain control through its so-called golden share, minority stakes that give it an effective veto over how ostensibly private firms are run.

Given these limits, it is no surprise then that only Hungary (with its large foreign investment) and Estonia (with neighboring Finland looking for a toehold in the Baltic markets) privatized a significant part of their economies by sales. And what gets privatized is usually given for a song to managers and political cronies. In theory, Albania's privatizations were to be conducted through open auctions. Instead, exemptions have been the rule rather than the exception. In a recent study the Tirana-based economists A. Mancellaria and N. Koci say that only eight firms out of 239 in the auction under examination were actually sold in this way. For one reason or another, the other 231 were exempted, and the less transparent methods used to privatize the firms predictably benefit the political friends of President Berisha, who wants to build a constituency for his anticommunist policies.

1.7 Big Graft and Small Gains

Such corruption is as nothing compared to what can be found in Slovakia. Here the governments of Vladimir Meciar junked the open and equitable system inherited from the mass privatization initiated by Czechoslovakia in 1990–91 in favor of a policy of selected giveaways, in which members of the government, the ruling parties, and their families and friends reap the richest rewards. A realistic fear is that this new class will carry on in the same failed ways as during the socialist era, insisting on subsidies, monopoly power, tax holidays, and friendly regulation. Moreover, the political class gets more than a say over how business is conducted; it can insist that the spoils from industries controlled by their cronies enrich their political coffers, giving their parties a powerful leg up in running electoral campaigns—an advantage Meciar used for all it was worth in recapturing the government in the autumn of 1994.

Rarely, however, can privatizations have been more private than in the case of Russia's energy and mineral resources sector. Once it was decided to shut foreign firms out of the bidding for shares in privatized oil and gas firms, the government (and not reluctantly) was obliged to sell off the crown jewels of Russian industry in rather murky ways to powerful insiders and the few domestic figures willing and able to ante up.

Among the oddest and (so it turned out to be) most politically damaging devices the Russian government hit upon to cash in on its equity holdings in the energy and resources sectors was to invite would-be bidders to make loans to the government, secured by parcels of government-held shares in big natural resource producers. If the government does not pay back the loans by September 1996, the lenders—mostly Russia's powerful private banks—take control of the state's shares of many valuable companies the government used for security. The deals show every sign of having been rigged for the convenience of insiders, who snapped up blocks of energy sector shares at fire-sale prices. With no money set in the Russian budget to pay back the loans, lenders looked assured of reaping rich rewards.

Sales may be slow, but when governments say that they want to speed up the process, look out. Parliamentary debates over a so-called Law to Accelerate Privatization stalled Romania's mass privatization scheme throughout 1995 and well into 1996, all the better for the country's nomenklatura to continue the grab for riches which sales gave to them. When a new mass privatization law at last emerged from this limbo, a caveat ratified ownerships acquired in all previous privatizations (96–97% were MEBOs), no matter how dubious.

In selling state assets, perhaps governments should think small. Privatization of shops, restaurants, and other service companies—what is known as "small privatization"—which was most often accomplished through sales has usually been an unqualified success. Why? Although insiders were nearly always favored (the Czechs were the solitary exception here), separation of ownership and management in such small businesses is not desirable, and secondary markets developed rather quickly, allowing insiders to sell their new acquisitions for an immediate windfall to someone truly interested in investing in the business. (Where small privatization did not work, as in Russia, the state put a lot of restrictions on resale, employee dismissals, and change in the line of business—for example, if the shop was a barber shop, so it must remain.)

Rapid privatization of retail operations delivered immediate and tangible benefits in the countries where it was tried. In 1990, less than a year after communism's collapse, for example, there were over 300,000 private stores operating in Poland. Dreary state stores with empty shelves gave way to brightly painted private outlets meeting the long-suppressed needs of consumers. In even the most laggard country, shops and kiosks broadened dramatically the variety of goods on offer. Such individual and family-run businesses soon became nimble in reallocating resources and introducing more modern business methods, most importantly in demanding and getting from other small private businessmen an improved distribution system. Politically, these small business owners and their employees delivered significant support for reform politicians.

1.8 The Giveaway Way

If sales could not deliver sweeping privatization, at least not quickly, what strategy would succeed in doing so? A few private firms in a sea of state companies was not the decisive break with the state-owned economies of the past that the postcommunist countries needed. So how could a "critical mass" of private firms be created?

The sheer size and complexity of privatization seemed to counsel against simple remedies. Yet the most daring privatization adventure is, at its heart, a simple scheme. Riddled with the sorts of caveats and exceptions to be found in most sales privatization programs, the blueprint for mass privatization undertaken by the Czechs would have been unworkable. Instead they wielded a broad brush and can fairly claim (despite a serious balance of trade crisis in the spring of 1997, a result of the government's timid postprivatization strategies) unique economic as well as political successes, a tricky balance.

A giveaway to the wide public was the privatization method pioneered by the leaders of what was then still Czechoslovakia. Slovaks inherited the scheme after the "velvet divorce," but a series of governments headed by Vladimir Meciar since Slovak independence have done everything they could to gut the program and undo its effects. Under the Czech scheme, each adult citizen would buy privatization vouchers for a nominal sum. These vouchers could then be converted into shares of privatized companies at a gigantic multistage central auction during which hundreds of companies were offered simultaneously. (Two "waves" of such sales resulted in the privatization of most state firms.) An individual could take part in the auction or exchange vouchers for shares in an investment fund which then used this "voucher capital" to bid for much larger stakes in many auctioned companies.

The amazing—and unique in transition countries—thing about the Czech program was that insiders received no special treatment whatsoever. Nor, also uniquely, were the most valuable state enterprises excluded from the program; firms had no choice but to privatize, though they were given some breathing room in how to go about it. This made the vouchers, which carried no puffed-up monetary face value, truly attractive. The reason why nearly all adult Czechs chose to participate was that, given the high value of the assets on offer, many privatization funds could promise a more than tenfold return in one year.

In their fears about potential and real abuses of the process, most leaders of transition countries ended up throwing out the baby with the bathwater by devising overregulated privatization programs (see table 1.2 and figure 1.3 to 1.7). Czech premier Vaclav Klaus' policies, however, were shaped not by fears but by an utter commitment to let the market decide. It can be argued, however, that Klaus has given the Czechs too much of a good thing: lack of government regulatory oversight has contributed mightily to the woeful state of the Prague Stock Exchange. The hands of investment fund officers were not tied, and they could decide on any promotion and investment strategy they liked.

Table 1.2

Methods of Privatization for Medium- and Large-Sized Enterprises in Six Transition Economies (Percentages of Total)

Country	Sale to outside owners	MEBO*	Equal-access voucher privatization†	Restitution	Other ‡	Still in state hands
Czech Republic						
By number §	32	0	22(e)	9	28	10
By value #	5	0	50	2	3	40
Estonia **						
By number	64	30	0	0	2	4
By value	60	12	3	10	0	15
Hungary						
By number	38	7	0	0	33	22
By value	40	2	0	4	12	42
Lithuania						
By number	<1	3-5	65–70	0	0	25–30
By value	<1	3-5	50–60	0	0	35–45
Poland						
By number	2	30	6	0	8	54
Russia ‖						
By number	0	55	11	0	0	34

* MEBO stands for Management-Employee Buy Out.

† Equal-access voucher privatization refers to privatization through voucher schemes that didn't include preferences for special groups, such as managers or employees. For this reason, although most Russian companies were privatized through a voucher program, the end result was MEBO because of preferences given to insiders in the program.

‡ Includes transfers to municipalities or social insurance organizations, debt-equity swaps, and sales through insolvency proceedings.

§ Number of privatized firms as a share of all formerly state-owned firms. Includes parts of firms restructured prior to privatization. It should be noted that sorting by number highlights majority ownership after privatization. Take the example of the Czech Republic: the state is a majority owner in only 10% of medium- to large-sized enterprises.

‖ Includes assets sold for cash as part of the voucher privatization program through June 1994.

Value of firms privatized as a share of the value of all formerly state-owned firms. Data for Poland and Russia are unavailable. It should be noted that sorting by value highlights portfolio holdings after privatization. Again, take the example of the Czech Republic: the state owns holdings equal to 40% of the share capital of medium- to large-sized companies, while it has majority ownership in only 10% of companies.

** Does not include some infrastructure firms. All management buyouts were part of competitive, open tenders. In thirteen cases citizens could exchange vouchers for minority shares in firms sold to a core investor.

Note: Data are as of end 1995.

Source: Gray, 1996; World Bank.

Figure 1.3

Method of Privatization for Medium- and Large-sized Enterprises in the Czech Republic (Percentage of Total by Value)

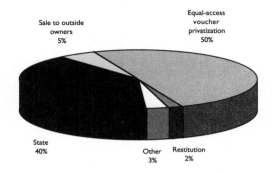

Note: Although the Czech state still has a large portfolio of shares in privatized companies (40% of share capital privatized), it should be noted that it is a majority shareholder in only 10% of all former state-owned companies.
Source: World Bank.

Figure 1.4

Method of Privatization for Medium- and Large-sized Enterprises in Hungary (Percentage of Total by Value)

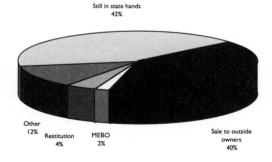

Note: Although the Hungarian state still has a large portfolio of shares in privatized companies (42% of share capital privatized), it should be noted that it is a majority shareholder in only 22% of all former state-owned companies.
Source: World Bank.

Figure 1.5

**Method of Privatization of Medium- and Large-sized
Enterprises in Poland (Percentage of Total by Number)**

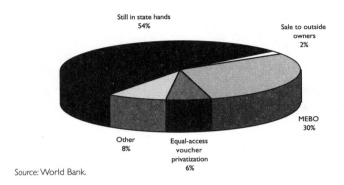

Still in state hands
54%

Sale to outside
owners
2%

MEBO
30%

Other
8%

Equal-access
voucher
privatization
6%

Source: World Bank.

Figure 1.6

**Method of Privatization for Medium- and Large-sized
Enterprises in Russia (Percentage of Total by Number)**

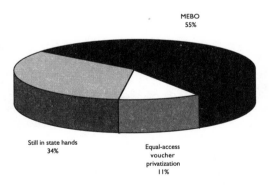

MEBO
55%

Still in state hands
34%

Equal-access
voucher
privatization
11%

Note: Equal-access privatization refers to privatization through voucher schemes that didn't
include special preferences for certain groups, such as managers or employees. For this reason,
although most Russian companies were privatized through a voucher program, the end result was
MEBO because of preferences given to insiders in the program.
Source: World Bank.

Figure 1.7

Method of Privatization for Medium- and Large-sized Enterprises in Estonia (Percentage of Total by Value)

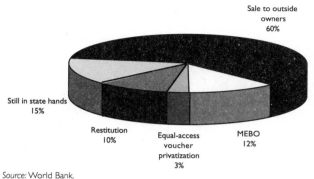

Sale to outside owners
60%

Still in state hands
15%

Restitution
10%

Equal-access
voucher
privatization
3%

MEBO
12%

Source: World Bank.

The thinking behind this mass privatization was based on a few simple but important assumptions:

- The state should not try to make money on privatization: this slows down the process and, except when monopolies such as telecoms are sold, usually fails as well. (That the Czechs were not saddled with heavy government debts, as were Poland and Hungary, made it easier for them to avoid this blunder.)

- Privatizing individual companies is a difficult business; no easier, in fact, than running them. Hence, a state that failed at running firms for fifty years would not be allowed to wreck privatization by trying to engineer the postprivatization structure of firms either. The important thing was to get the state out of business decision making as quickly as possible and leave in place a system open enough to evolve on its own.

- Privatize privatization: the investment funds at the heart of mass privatization were never conceived as the last word in the new system. They were, however, expected to do what state bureaucrats would not: decide which companies to sell and to whom, find qualified "core" investors, lead the restructuring effort—in short, begin the work of creating real businesses.

1.9 Pale Imitations

The apparent success of the Czechs on the political as much as the economic front and a growing realization that sales were unlikely to produce meaningful results made the Czech model popular with subsequent reformers elsewhere—or so it seemed as country after country jumped on the voucher bandwagon.

Russia pursued a mass privatization program consciously modeled on that of the Czechs. So too Kyrgyzstan and Moldova. Poland endlessly discussed and inched toward its own mass privatization plan. Romania bests everyone by having not one but two. Lithuania, Ukraine, and Bulgaria have made various half-hearted moves to implement their imitations of a voucher scheme.

Even wayward Belarus stopped its long march backward long enough to announce in the spring of 1996 its own spin on mass privatization. After only a few weeks, and despite all the pain inflicted by the government's lack of reform, the program attracted more than 5.6 million Belarusians to apply for vouchers, 70% of the eligible population. (To be sure, their actions may be little more than wishful thinking, given the snail's pace of Belarus' privatization up to now: at most, says the EBRD, 15% of GDP is in private hands. Indeed, today the few private companies that run afoul of President Lukashenka, such as Agroprombank, are renationalized by the sort of Leninist legality abandoned almost everywhere else in the ex-communist world.)

But as in art, copies pale against the original. Russia is the most interesting case. "Fast and loose" is probably the best way to sum up its privatization policy. No one doubts that it has been extraordinarily swift. Between January 1993 and June 1994, an estimated 14,000 to 15,000 companies were privatized through various giveaways, including voucher auctions. Over 60% of Russian industry is now in nominally private hands. Most critically, the power and control of the central and branch ministries—the heart of communism's economic darkness—was shattered, hopefully forever.

The problem is that the private hands that gained control of privatized firms are usually the same ones that ran Russia's economy into a ditch under socialism. The program's architects, under the leadership of Anatoli Chubais, apparently believed (probably correctly) that the weak Russian government would never get privatization off the ground without the support of an important constituency, and that if insiders did not benefit directly, first, and in a big way, they would form an insurmountable roadblock to privatization.

To buy insider support, managers and employees received all sorts of preferences. Of these, the most important was the right to buy majority stakes in their firms at outdated book value. "Buy" is in fact a misnomer. Inflation had eaten into these book values to such an extent that a Volga car on the books of a Moscow taxi company by August 1992 was worth a mere Rb 2,000 to Rb 3,000, that is, $10 to $15. By buying a voucher on the secondary market at a 50% discount to its nominal value and using it to pay the state for shares, these prices could be cut by half again. Here is a sale as a giveaway if there ever was one.

So skewed was the process that voucher privatization resulted in near-absolute insider domination of Russian industry, with managers and workers in control of about two-thirds of the shares in privatized firms. Up to 30% of shares were sold at voucher auctions open to the public (with insiders trying, by fair means and foul, to buy up these shares as well; cases of intimidation and unannounced auctions were not unknown). Remaining shares have remained in the hands of the state, which is the largest single shareholder in most firms, though to meet budget shortfalls, beginning in late 1996, the Kremlin has started selling some key oil and infrastructure holdings.

Was this deal with insiders akin to Faust's pact with the devil? It is too early to say. Pernicious side effects are already visible; whether or not they are chronic is still to be determined. After shares are consolidated in the hands of insiders, trading virtually stops. Outsiders sometimes try to put a foot in the door by attempting to buy shares directly from workers, but these attempts fail because management threatens to dismiss workers who sell their shares—unless it is to the managers themselves, of course. Managers also balk at opening the shareholders' registry and refuse to record transactions of which they disapprove. (Moldova was one of the first to crack down on this abuse by creating its State Registry Coordination Unit.)

Privatizing Russia, a study by Maxim Boyko, Andrei Shleifer, and Robert Vishny (all once advisors to Chubais) argues that these side effects were a necessary price to pay if privatization was to be secured in any form. The fundamental cause of economic inefficiency in the communist system was the Leviathan-like influence of politics over economic affairs. Privatization's purpose was to see that industry was removed from state control. This depoliticization was far more important, say the study's authors, than the particular corporate structures that emerged from it.

But are Russian firms doing better under the new system? The jury is still out, to be sure, and some observers see signs of change. Others do not, and the improvement, if any, is certainly not dramatic. Although the backs of the old branch ministries and trusts have certainly been broken, a worrying concentration of ownership has emerged among a few big Moscow-based banks.

The long-term hope of Russian privatization must be that insider ownership is inherently unstable. Eventually, the well of revenues tapped by diverting enterprise assets to other private companies, or from pocketing employee shares on the cheap, will run dry. If the government is prepared to close the spigot of state subsidies even more, managers might be forced to turn to sources of finance that will bring outside influence to bear. But for now, the main effect of the Russian giveaways has been to entrench existing insiders, including the largely incompetent nomenklatura management. Perhaps most ominously, as we shall see presently, the political payoff of the great insider give-away is sometimes questionable in terms of their influence on policymaking. Boris Yeltsin's reelection as president, however, would not have been likely without the financial support of the new elite created by privatization.

1.10 Polish Hesitations

Poland after Solidarity's victory of 1989 was the cradle of many ideas that led to the new giveaways. Although the first postcommunist government got bogged down in ill-starred IPOs and other sales, discussions of giveaway schemes were ripe in early 1990. Janusz Lewandowski, future minister of privatization, had even proposed a voucher program as far back as the 1980s.

While the Poles dithered and quarreled until the political opportunity of the reform governments evaporated, Lewandowski and his successors (with the help of the London investment house of Warburg) continued to dream up ever more complicated giveaway schemes. In conscious contrast to the Czechs, who relied on market spontaneity, the Polish plan was to spoon-feed small investors with shares of state-sponsored, indeed, state-organized, investment funds. Each fund would marry a foreign management firm with a local institution and a politically packed board of directors. Shares of each privatized company were divided into identical packets, with a "lead" fund holding one large bloc and the rest distributed evenly among everyone else.

When, after three years of political fumbling, Poland's mass privatization program got off the ground in the autumn of 1996, the number and size of the companies to be privatized (participation was voluntary) shrank so much that the term "mass" privatization became a joke. Fifteen National Investment Funds (NIFs) were made overseers of 512 mostly small companies of dubious worth. Fund managers were given ten-year contracts and large state-subsidized fees to improve company performance.

No sooner were the funds created than feuding broke out between state-appointed board members and the foreign managers. Two funds tried to kick foreigners off their management teams, Fund 11 evicted American bankers Wasserstein Perela, and Fund 13 Japan's Yamaichi International and a Hong Kong group, Regent Pacific. Only when the government stepped in, fearing the ignominious collapse of its long-delayed and loudly trumpeted program, and removed board members hostile to foreign participation was this abuse stopped.

Chauvinism and cultural clashes fan the resentments of local board members. But more serious sources of dispute are opposing attitudes toward the restructuring of firms. Many NIF board members see their job as doctoring sick companies and the funds as little more than industrial hospital wards. NIF advisors usually prefer to practice triage: sacrifice terminally ill companies in order to save scarce resources for firms with the best potential for long-term health and profits. With the government throwing its weight behind NIF industrial quacks, the mass privatization program to which it paid lip service soon became bogged down in a morass of politically inspired restructuring, meaning that in most cases (the closure of the Gdansk shipyard, birthplace of Solidarity, being a rare exception), no real restructuring has taken place at all.

More generally, experiences with privatization funds throughout the region are mixed. Most funds are not reliable corporate governance watchdogs. A number of fly-by-night operations in Russia collapsed in disgrace. Romanian Private Ownership Funds (POFs) are self-promoting rent-seekers, with no concern for their shareholders. Lithuania's funds also either ignore their shareholders or buy their silence. Invalda, a fund with 26,000 shareholders owning parts of sixty companies and another twenty outright, paid its shareholders dividends of 10% since its founding, though only half its firms make money.

1.11 Czech It Out?

So giveaways turn out to be no panacea either, at least not everywhere. Are they really doing as well as is billed in booming Prague?

The main problem with Czech privatization is the ownership structure of the funds; more precisely, of the management companies that usually exercise total control of them. In some ways, what happened is easy to understand. Mass privatization was a logistical nightmare, with its need to distribute vouchers, convince individual citizens to participate, and assure that privatized companies did not end up owned by thousands or even millions of small shareholders. This last point was the most worrying, for fragmented ownership is almost equivalent to no ownership at all. Such a pattern of nonownership would leave firms at the mercy of their insiders, and we have seen what that means. This is why investment funds that concentrate ownership control on behalf of dispersed owners are a necessary element of mass giveaway.

To ensure that investment funds with some degree of public confidence were created, the Czechs allowed existing state banks to form and manage privatization funds. The gambit paid off, in the sense that the process was smooth and 70% of voucher holders opted to deposit their vouchers with funds. But it is undeniable that a price was paid. Eager to insulate themselves from outsider control and to gain control of as many Czech firms as possible in one fell swoop, the bank funds promptly used a good portion of their vouchers to buy bank shares.

Czech funds and the banking system soon became embedded in a dense web of cross-ownerships. Take the case of Prvni Investicni, the biggest investment company and a subsidiary of Investicni Banka. It administers fourteen funds, two of which (Bankovni Investicni and Rentierky Investicni) have over 50% of their holdings in the banking sector. Indeed, of the six largest Czech banks and financial groups—Komercni, Ceska Sporitelna, Ceskoslovenska Obchodni, Investicnia a Postovni, Zivnobanka, and Ceska Pojistovna (Czech Insurance)—only Zivnobanka does not have a piece of Komercni, Ceska Sporitelna, and Ceska Polistovna. Cross-ownership ranges anywhere from 50% for Ceska Pojistovna to something near zero for Ceskoslovenska Obchodni. With the networks illustrated above "you do not negotiate a transaction," says one fund manager, "you negotiate as part of a relationship."

Some academic observers are not bothered by the power of the Czech banks, pointing to the fact that the country had traditionally followed the German model of universal banking in which financial institutions both lend money to companies and serve as corporate monitors. But although this model served Germany well for decades (it is now being rethought in its homeland), is it the right one for the new Czech circumstances? In theory, such ownership is supposed to work well because information about firms gleaned through close lending relations between a firm and bank, further consummated through seats on company boards, allows banks to monitor company managers and permits shareholders to reduce their risks.

So goes the theory. In practice, these close links make many economists in the region go weak at the knees. First, there is suspicion that Czech investment funds prefer to use their power to pressure companies whose shares they control into buying financial services from the fund's banking master rather than to restructure their operations. (Lithuania tries to curb this risk through banning bank shareholdings in investment funds.)

Second, the system breeds insider dealing and inhibits transparency, which consequently retards the development of capital markets. Prices on the Prague Stock Exchange (or the rival RM-System) are often a mystery, and most deals (estimates go as high as 90%) are struck in private. Funds get a sneak preview of company books and investment decisions through the seats they control and manipulate on company boards and can often influence the market to the detriment of small (often their own) shareholders.

Third, with bureaucratic cultures derived from their mother institutions, bank funds are reputed to be lazy. They care less about monitoring managers and restructuring than about lucrative seats on the boards of the companies in their portfolios. Consequently, managers still claim to trade off shareholder interests against those of employees and other shareholders.

But perhaps the greatest danger of the Czech experiment is continued high levels of state ownership of banks themselves. The Fund of National Property (FNP) is often the biggest shareholder in the banks, with 48% in Komercni (the country's biggest) and 40% in Ceska Sporitelna. Cescoslovenska Obchodni has even more government strings attached: 20% is owned by the FNP, 20% by the Ministry of Finance, 27% by the Czech National Bank, and 24% by the Slovak National Bank.

As long as the government is in the hands of parties (and individuals) committed to nonintervention, its stake in the banks may not be a big problem. But if the government were to change hands, a new regime could lean on banks to, in turn, lean on funds that control most of the Czech economy. By the standards of depoliticization, does this amount to successful privatization?

Despite these question marks, prospects for the Czech experiment are better than most. Spurred by more aggressive nonbank investment funds, much restructuring is undoubtedly going on. Managers do get fired, payrolls are cut down to size, and pressure by outside owners on managers is greater than in any other transition country.

Perhaps the most important change of all is a tidal wave of ownership reconfiguration taking place. In this "privatized privatization," known as the "third wave" (the first two being the official auctions that took place during mass privatization), investment funds are putting together controlling packages of many firms and selling them to interested foreign and domestic investors.

By 1995, powerful outsider players began to enter the fray. The Bahamas-based corporate raider Michael Dingman, in cooperation with Harvard Funds, purchased controlling interest in some of the most important Czech companies. These shares were managed by Dingman's famously no-nonsense Stratton Holdings. Other deals were smaller, but an estimated five hundred companies quietly changed hands that year. Nothing comparable—even in absolute terms, not just relative to the small size of the Czech Republic—has yet taken place anywhere else.

The largest investment funds are also feeling the heat. Plzenska Banka, after being taken over by the upstart private financial group Motoinvest, began a buying frenzy of investment privatization fund shares. Frightened by this challenge, the banks managing the most powerful funds—Komercni Banka, Zivnostenska Banka, and Ceskoslovenska Obchodni Banka—bought back at a high price shares acquired by Plzenska. Unwilling to pay such greenmail, Creditanstalt and a number of others were forced to sell their funds to the Motoinvest group.

Even the transparency of the so far rather shady deals might be increasing. New laws to protect minority shareholders and increase disclosure requirements were passed on the initiative of Tomas Jezek (the first Czech privatization minister and, later, the Prague Stock Exchange's reform-minded chairman). However, only when the Czech balance-of-trade crisis in the spring of 1997 threatened to spread to the capital markets did Premier Klaus assent to putting real teeth into the bourse's watchdogs.

1.12 The Politics of Privatization

In democracies, the worst that can befall a government that badly miscalculates a policy is time spent as an opposition party. In many transition countries, however, reform governments carried with them not the fear of a spell in the political wilderness, but the nightmare of elimination altogether: the return to power of a communist apparatus that would snuff out not only privatization, but democracy as well.

Add to this the fact that no government in any country likes a planned increase in unemployment, nor do they like taking on entrenched lobbies or facing vengeful strikes; they do so, if they do so, in the belief that the consequent unpopularity will be limited or short-lived and eventually outweighed by a wider recognition that their actions were necessary. Privatization, therefore, was more than a bet on the future of the economy, it was a desperate political gamble as well.

Indeed, politicians understood from the start of the process of transformation that privatization was as much about power as about economic efficiency. All, in the end, sought to skew the privatization process to their electoral benefit. Their political choices, however, will have long-term consequences for the health of their countries's economies and politics beyond the next election. The bet governments made in their choice of privatization programs was between appeasing existing lobbies, such as insiders, and creating entirely new constituencies. In essence, it was a choice between the past and the future. The worry for those who gambled on the future was this: would there be enough time for new constituencies to take shape (and organize as voting blocs) before the gamblers would have to face their voters again?

Prague's Vaclav Klaus, as we have seen, was the sole leader to roll the dice in this high stakes game. His macroeconomic and stabilization policies, despite doses of Thatcherite rhetoric, may have trimmed and fudged far more than those undertaken in Poland, Estonia, or Latvia. And they did, indeed, succeed in muting the political shock of transition by dampening down the pain of unemployment. But where Klaus and his government excelled was in pushing through in record time the most extensive privatization scheme ever undertaken. Almost single-handedly, this action not only put zest into Klaus' government, but also created a new cadre of reform enthusiasts.

To be sure, the Czech privatization route posed obvious political risks, not least that rapid change may produce the unsettling impression of things being out of control. But by shunning insiders (for the most part), the moral basis of the old socialist politics was fatally weakened—a situation helped in no small measure by formal legal curbs on the communists. Because envy and resentment are not the ingredients of political stability, mass privatization needed to spawn a broad spectrum of people who considered themselves "winners" in the grand gamble of privatization. Here Klaus succeeded, probably beyond expectations, in creating from scratch a powerful electoral constituency, one unconnected to the old ways of doing things: tens of thousands of shopkeepers who had purchased their stores at genuinely open auction; thousands who had property that had been confiscated by the communists restored to them, and were thus likely to be unwavering in their support; and many new shareholders in privatized large firms. Here, indeed, the lessons of Prime Minister Thatcher's privatizations were correctly applied as large swathes of the population became interested shareholders in Klaus' success. A survey in 1996 of 1,450 Czechs by the Institute of Sociology of the Czech Academy of Sciences shows the depth of this support. Some 79% of the respondents who participated in both waves of voucher privatization declared themselves satisfied with the process of reform; only 37% of those who participated in one wave, or sat out the reforms altogether, voiced similar support. Entrepreneurs and those who had property restituted to them support reform even more robustly, with 76% of the former and 66% of the latter endorsing the country's emerging economy. Moreover, by giving birth to powerful private financial institutions dependent on the continuation of reform, Klaus also created a financial support system for his efforts.

Did appeasement of insiders elsewhere deliver political benefits to the appeasers? If so, they are hard to find. Reform governments that assumed that they could overcome or cover up envy and resentment at insider privileges soon learned that they could do neither. Leading reform politicians in Estonia, Lithuania, Hungary, Poland, and Russia were often rudely turfed onto the street at the first opportunity by voters who deeply resented the special benefits afforded insiders.

This inability of reform politicians to forge a political base among insiders—indeed, the scale of insider ingratitude—is stunning. For example, as compared with those working in new or even state firms, employees in privatized Russian companies are the least likely to vote for reform politicians and among the most nostalgic for communists, reports a 1996 survey by J. Earle and R. Rose ("Causes and Consequences of Privatization: An Empirical Study of Economic Behavior and Political Attitudes in

Table 1.3

Voting Behavior of Russian Employees

Column Percent	Budgetary organization	State enterprise	Privatized firm	New private	Other	Sample
Approval of Yeltsin (n=980)						
	13.5	13.5	8.6	21.0	8.7	12.8
Candidate for President (n=480)						
Leftist	8.4	5.1	12.0	1.1	7.5	7.4
Nationalist	20.9	32.8	32.8	25.1	46.5	29.2
Reformer	51.9	43.6	32.3	49.0	45.5	43.3
Centrist	18.7	18.5	23.0	24.9	0.5	20.1
Party (n=423)						
Leftist	22.4	16.9	24.7	1.9	14.4	19.3
Nationalist	18.0	26.7	30.8	34.8	43.3	26.8
Reformer	36.6	30.2	23.2	55.5	41.8	32.4
Centrist	23.0	26.2	21.2	7.8	0.6	21.5
Ownership composition						
	24.8	31.9	28.8	12.5	2.0	100

Source: Earl and Rose (1996).

Russia"). Moreover, these employees are equally stodgy in their economics; they are the most negative about their firms and are openly unwilling to work to improve things (see table 1.3).

Because the attitudes of Russian managers were not surveyed, it is impossible to say where their political loyalties now lie, though studies of where Russia's political parties go to get financial backing hint that such managers provided the lifeblood of finance for the communist Gennadi Zyuganov's presidential campaign in 1996. But a glimpse at Hungarian insider managers gives a clue. When asked about their view of the political and economic changes since 1990, Hungarian managers were harshly pessimistic, longing for state aid, and supportive of a redistributive system (see table 1.4). Indeed, the greater insider control a manager has of his firm, the more he seems to yearn for the old ways of socialism.

This is a far cry from the strong support for reform found within Czech managing circles, a clear reason why Vaclav Klaus broke form with other reform politicians in not getting the electoral boot, but instead holding on to power in the May 1996 Czech elections—granted, by the skin of his teeth, as Klaus was forced to form a minority government, his coalition claiming

Table 1.4

Managerial Attitudes in the Czech Republic and Hungary

Opinion	Agree/Disagree (%)	
	Czech Rep.	Hungary
Changes in the economic system are positive	83/1	21/42
Changes in the economic system are generally positive	81/1	35/16
Political and economic future of the country is promising	92/0	45/27
Prevailing political climate is favorable for business	60/23	28/69
State does not provide enough assistance to existing businesses	50/33	79/18
State pays insufficient attention to social justice	13/70	53/42
State overtaxes companies in my business	43/42	74/25
Sample size	151	234

Source: Data based on Privatization Project/World Bank spring 1995 survey.

only 99 of the 200 seats in parliament—Klaus was reelected not just for his radicalism, but also for his results. Mass privatization was the first step in proving that market economies can deliver the goods to more than a few.

1.13 Where to From Here?

Against the odds, privatization in a number of transition countries shows that the broad superstructure of a capitalist economy can be put in place (historically speaking) much faster than many expected. Indeed, by the increasing pressure it puts on state enterprises as well as its continuous strengthening of the private sector, privatization is a big contributor to the robust growth some transition countries are now seeing. And it has demonstrated its centrality if the role of the state in the economy is to be redefined.

At the start of the privatization process, democracy was a help, not a hindrance. This is unusual because in long-standing democracies, consistent, lasting public support for tough economic medicine has often proved to be elusive. Certainly, Estonia, the Czech Republic, Russia, Albania, and Moldova had the luxury of initiating the toughest parts of their privatization programs with broad democratic backing, both within their parliaments and among the people at large. In each, it now seems clear, privatization spawned a number of independent institutions—stock markets, banks, shareholders, and other private property owners—that will, as time passes and economies begin to grow, continue to strengthen free-market democracy.

If pursued energetically, as in the Czech Republic, privatization actually energizes rather than devours the impulse to reform. A number of countries, indeed, are now moving beyond the industrial and small business privatization that dominated the first years of the process of transition. Following Hungary's lead—where it was an effort born of budgetary desperation—Estonia, though running a budget surplus, is well down the road in plans to privatize its basic infrastructure: railways, ports, telecoms, and the national power grid. Latvia and Kyrgyzstan are making sounds about moving in this direction, too.

But other transition countries continue to face instability in pressing their privatization programs forward in the wake of public uncertainty and insider opposition. The longer they wait and fritter away the special "window of opportunity" provided by the

Figure 1.8

Extent of Privatization

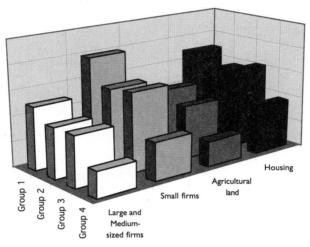

Note: Privatization by type of asset and country group. Data are for 1995 and are simple averages of estimates for the countries in each group.

Country groups are as follows:

Group 1: Poland, Slovenia, Hungary, Croatia, FYR Macedonia, Czech Republic, Slovakia
Group 2: Estonia, Lithuania, Bulgaria, Latvia, Albania, Romania, Mongolia
Group 3: Kyrgyzstan, Russia, Moldova, Armenia, Georgia, Kazakhstan
Group 4: Uzbekistan, Ukraine, Belarus, Azerbaijan, Tajikistan, Turkmenistan

Source: EBRD Transition Report, 1995; World Bank staff estimates.

fall of communism, the more "normal" democratic politics becomes, with special interests clamoring ever more effectively for exceptions and privileges, and the tougher it will be to take decisive action (see figure 1.8).

Many places—and this is clearly a reason for long-term hope—seem to have developed the political maturity necessary for constancy of purpose in privatization and, hence, success. The determination with which governments stick to reform efforts (though, no doubt, at times in a stop-and-go fashion) and are rewarded for it by voters (such as in the Czech Republic, Slovenia, and the less-developed Moldova) suggests to optimists that public recognition of the general benefits of privatization is beginning to take hold.

There are laggards, of course: Ukraine pays a high price for its faint-hearted reforms (though the irony is that most Ukrainians blame reform, not the absence of it, for their woes). Macedonia, Uzbekistan, and Belarus still fail to acknowledge that state-dominated industries do not work and are a ceaseless drain on the treasury, though in late 1996, Uzbekistan's president Islam Karimov seemed poised to bite the bullet and embrace mass privatization, and Romania's flawed privatization program seems destined, despite government interventions, to undermine ongoing state control of supposedly privatized industry. Nonetheless, signs of a new maturity should not be taken for granted: populism and short-termism may merely be in remission, preparing to rear their heads if prosperity does not reach the general population soon.

Austere governments such as those in Prague, Chisinau, Tallinn, and Riga may be voted winners so long as memories of communism are still fresh in people's minds. Once they fade, the lure of subsidies and renationalization may come back. In some cases, notably Russia, despite Boris Yeltsin's reelection in July 1996, the big fear is that privatization may still fall victim to political instability, even if the process itself has gone too far to be reversed easily.

The reason why privatization remains an issue in dispute is often a matter of institutions. Privatization's results and prospects reflect the fact that countries are making do with immature political and economic arrangements. The most extreme examples are Ukraine, Bulgaria, and most of all, Belarus, where heavily centralized governments have not found a sensible way to redefine their roles and where the legal framework for (and public support of) private property is ephemeral. The politics of privatization in many other countries is dogged either by explicit restrictions and maintenance of large swathes of state control, or by outright corruption. It is hard to think of any transition country in which the new instituional setup is complete.

From its birth in the region, privatization was an awesome and awe-inspiring task. Succeed, and the link between state and economy would be broken, hopefully forever; fail, and the transition from communism itself would be placed at risk. The lesson that most governments—some vehemently, others by paying lip service—say that they learned during the first few years of privatization and restructuring is that a muscular private sector is vital to the future well-being of their countries and that privatization is an essential tool in reaching this goal. The lesson that none of them has fully been able to decipher is how to make all their new privatized "owners" begin to behave like real owners. That code is yet to be broken.

2
Capitalism with a Comrade's Face

To the myriad reformers who assumed power in the socialist world after communism's collapse, privatization was always a necessary step in the postcommunist transition to free markets and democracy, a move away from absolute domination of the economy by the state and from the economic evils traceable to a lack of "real owners" capable of monitoring the behavior of enterprise managers. For much of the population, the goals of the privatization process were never entirely clear or comprehensible; what was clear was that privatization would inevitably make some people rich. And the public feared, indeed expected, that the people who would be made rich by privatization would be the very same people who had been oppressing them for decades: the communist nomenklatura.

That reformers were right in principle in their move toward privatization is not seriously questioned; after all, there is no known example of a successful modern economy without a market based on private property. Whether what is going on under the name of privatization in most countries of Eastern Europe and the former Soviet Union can be described as a transition to such a successful property-based market economy is a question on which the jury is still out. Where the verdict is in, however, is that in most countries the people did not err in their rush to judgment: the old nomenklatura has, indeed, mutated into the new capitalist class.

According to a former leading politician in Romania, 80% of new Romanian millionaires were part of the Ceausescu-era nomenklatura; many had been in the arms industry and have since built their fortunes on arms trading (skirting the arms embargo on Croatia and Serbia was a particular boon). A survey of

Russia's top one hundred businessmen compiled by Moscow's Applied Politics Institute found that 61 % of the country's new rich were members of the ex-nomenklatura. A Polish economist who traced the careers of several hundred top nomenklatura from 1988 to 1993 found that over half of them turned up as top private sector executives. The numbers in Hungary are reported to be even higher than in Poland.

Hence, the million-dollar question on which much of the future of Eastern Europe may depend: Does the fact that privatization was hijacked by the very people of the old regime it was intended to tame mean that the region's march toward greater justice and economic efficiency will be stymied as well?

2.1 The Nomenklatura Unbound

In many countries of the former socialist camp, political personnel changes in the wake of communism's demise were much less than one might have expected. The faces atop and within the state apparatus of Romania, Belarus, or Ukraine are, after all, not that different from those who had ruled in the 1980s (though their style of governing has been significantly transformed). But even in those countries in which the collapse of the old regime was accompanied by the old political elites' eviction from power, such as in Poland, Russia, and Hungary, the big surprise was that party members were soon gliding with relative ease from politburos into boardrooms of many companies. "Whenever I meet with a big Hungarian company," said an American diplomat-turned-investment banker, "I invariably am seated across the table from someone I once negotiated with when Hungary was communist."

To be sure, the profile varies in different countries. In the Czech Republic, nomenklatura managers have not been particularly successful in retaining their control of the levers of economic power on the enterprise level. (They were more successful in retaining some power in the banking industry, though not in gaining ownership.) In Poland, managers used (and abused) their entrenched positions to block privatization of the biggest enterprises, thus preserving much of their control, but could not convert this control into full property rights. (They were much more successful in gaining such title to property in smaller firms.) In Russia, the power of the nomenklatura managers was unbroken by privatization, but even there workers had to be given a share, and some of the most valuable natural resources are still owned in an unclear (and thus insecure) way. Titles are also clouded in Hungary, where managerial control comes together with a web of immensely complicated corporate cross-holdings that make the very concept of ownership problematic.

But with the possible exception of the Czech Republic, the nomenklatura has been extremely successful at converting its political domination into economic might. The countries where the communists lost (at least temporarily) their hold on political power may indeed provide the most ironic twist of the postcommunist transformation: liberating the economy from a state run by the nomenklatura has liberated the nomenklatura as well.

Under the old regime, the nomenklatura's privileges were paid for by submission to the tyrannical will of the communist party and its political leaders. (This was, in many ways, a comfortable servitude. Even nowadays, some managers look with wonder, and perhaps even indignation, on those who advocated escape.) It was only the always precarious position of these managers in the bureaucratic pyramid that enabled the members of the communist elite to appropriate for themselves much of the return from the nation's economic assets. Under the new system, emancipated from control by the political center, the nomenklatura gained title to these assets, and the new order gave them legal protection for their privileged status as property holders. By making them into owners of capital, privatization thus allowed the former nomenklatura managers to preserve their stranglehold on economic resources, while also giving them the freedom that the old regime denied them. Indeed, privatization has even given a degree of legitimacy to the nomenklatura's spoils that the old regime miserably failed to provide as it tried to justify them through an ideology rather than the ancient and venerable institution of private property.

Here is the true paradox of privatization: it allowed (or at least went a long way toward allowing) members of the nomenklatura to achieve something they could not have hoped for even under communism. Only in countries such as Ukraine, where the economy remains dominated by value-subtracting industrial white elephants, has the nomenklatura maintained an almost united front against large-scale privatization. Ukrainian industrial bosses appear to know that their huge factories have value only as political chips (with privatization inevitably leading to their closure) and so prefer to stay closely linked to the state with its handouts and rigged markets. In the more "advanced" postcommunist countries, in which there were more valuable assets to be appropriated by those who had enough power to lay their hands on them, the new owners also like to get their share of political largesse. But they are no longer satisfied with being dependent on the state; like all survivalists they want to turn *their* environment to their individual advantage; they now want the state to serve their needs. The return of the communists to power in a number of the countries in transition must be viewed in light of this role reversal.

2.2 The Resistible Rise of the Kleptoklatura

How did this transformation of the nomenklatura happen? The story actually begins a few years before the final collapse of the communist system. In countries such as Hungary, Poland, and Russia, personal enrichment of party ranks became a semi-official part of the desperate, last-gasp "reform" policies pursued by reform-minded communist regimes such as Mikhail Gorbachev's in Russia. As the policies of *perestroika* and its regional clones increasingly stressed the importance of markets and provided a limited space for private property, the comrades themselves were, of course, the best equipped and best placed to take advantage of the new opportunities. Indeed, the policy turned out to be so popular among the middle (enterprise level) nomenklatura that the top brass rather quickly lost control of the process.

The resulting scramble for riches came to be known as "spontaneous privatization." Its most notorious examples were in Hungary in 1988 and 1989, during the last months of the communist regime, when the authorities introduced new laws allowing conversion of state enterprises into corporate legal forms, such as joint-stock and limited-liability companies. Factory managers and their cronies manipulated these laws to insulate themselves from any external control, spinning valuable assets into separate subsidiaries of which they became part owners and leaving the state with empty shells and liabilities.

Spontaneous privatization was soon spreading throughout the region. After Nicolae Ceausescu's bloody fall, a former Securitate secret policeman, Gheorgehe Urzica, quickly came to own a string of luxury shops in Bucharest, places which had never been officially privatized. What started with a few stores and small companies often ended up with theft on a grand scale, especially where, as in Romania, the old elites maintained their hold on the state beyond the collapse of the regime that had brought them to power. Victor Stanculescu, one-time head of the quartering corps for Ceausescu's army and later a member of the provisional tribunal that sentenced the dictator to death, became the owner of Romania's leading arms exporting firms, companies which had never been publicly put up for sale. A Polish banker in Lodz complained in 1995 that most of his bank's bad loans were made by the old guard to their cronies (who were by then in the newly favored private sector) during the few months in which the Mazowiecki government ruled in coalition with the communists.

But no country can compare with that of Russia, whose enormous wealth and natural resources fell prey to a few modern-day robber barons with a party pedigree. In what reportedly began as a conscious Soviet policy of placing various party officials into key economic posts, men like Sergei Yegorov, former chairman of the State Bank of the Soviet Union and head of the financial department of the Communist Party Central Committee, became among the richest men in Russia and, in Yegorov's case, the chairman of the Commercial Banks' Association. Gorbachev's prime minister, Nikolai Ryzhkov, also made a switch "from plan to clan" and is now chairman of the Tveruniversal Bank.

Connections to the often corrupt new authorities can also yield pretty good results. For example, in November 1995, Russia's huge Uneximbank, a firm with close ties to President Yeltsin's former security chief and drinking buddy Alexander Karzhakov, was victorious in an auction to control 38% of Norilsk Nickel, the world's largest producer of that commodity (as well as of platinum and cobalt). Uneximbank, which is partly owned by Norilsk Nickel (making the whole transaction a family affair), had been charged with managing the auction, and its winning bid was only half that offered by a competitor. Indeed, the $170 million Uneximbank offered was a mere $100,000 above the minimum bid level set by—wait for it—Uneximbank, who had been named by the government as the auctioneers.

The theft of the century, perhaps indeed of all time, was that of the Russian energy sector, which accounts for at least 17% of Russia's GDP. The assets of the oil giant Gazprom alone are valued in hundreds of billions of dollars. (According to most estimates it dwarfs General Motors, long believed to be the largest industrial company in the world.) Although such companies as Gazprom were excluded from the official privatization program, 60% of stakes in them have ended up, in ways that no one clearly understands, in the hands of a few company insiders, favored politicians, and banks run by the ex-nomenklatura. Among the major shareholders of Gazprom is rumored to be its former boss, now prime minister, Victor Chernomyrdin. Chernomyrdin denies any involvement in the company's affairs nowadays, but few believe his protestations, particularly as his son is building a lavish mansion within a wooded Gazprom estate. (Russia seems to be the only democracy in the world in which the net worth of the prime minister is estimated with a potential error of a few hundred million dollars.)

Nor are comrades from the secret police lagging behind their ex-party cronies. Oleg Kalugin, Russian's one-time dissident KGB general, has become one of his country's richest men, trading around the world in "scrap" steel from decrepit state factories. Radu Tinu, who used to be a regional deputy head of the Securitate, is now one of the richest businessmen in Timisoara, where the Romanian revolution started.

Such business dealings are enough to evoke the worst nightmare of postcommunist transformation: that former secret police networks have been converted into national and international business structures which, often allied with organized crime, are setting up commercial empires throughout the Eurasian continent. The vision of a small, secretive elite, tied to the old regime, recombining, reinventing, and reconstituting itself on a large scale within the new order may not be the most realistic of dangers, even if it cannot be fully discounted. But in the somewhat conspiratorial mindset of a significant segment of the East European and ex-Soviet public, it may go a long way to delegitimize the new democratic regime.

2.3 The Faustian Bargain

Ironically, some of the greatest gains by the nomenklatura were made neither through backroom deals in the waning days of the old regime nor through outright theft and bribery in the postcommunist period. They were made perfectly legally through the various privatization programs designed and executed by the new reform-minded governments of Eastern Europe and the newly independent states of the Soviet Union.

Russia is, again, a prime example. In order to be able to push through their ambitious program of quick privatization, Russian reformers, led by Anatoly Chubais, had to ensure that they had the support of some sufficiently powerful political and economic forces within the old system. Otherwise, their reforms would go nowhere in the apparatchik-dominated Duma. The program had to have some losers and some winners, and the winners could not all be in the future.

Chubais chose as the main losers in the Russian privatization program the most inefficient and deadening structures of the old regime: the old centralized industrial bureaucracies such as branch ministries, industrial associations, trusts, and other lobbies for socialist stagnation and the status quo. The main winners, the forces with which the reformers allied themselves in the great push for quick privatization, were to be the managers and the workers of individual state enterprises, provided they broke away from the old structures.

Company managers, for Chubais and his allies, were the lesser evil. Concessions in the privatization program, giving them partial ownership and outright control over their enterprises, were designed to assure their support. The gamble paid off beyond the wildest expectations of the small band of reformers who gathered about Yegor Gaidar and Chubais in dachas on the outskirts of Moscow in the winter of 1991–92 to devise the privatization of the socialist state. The old centralized industrial structures were successfully, and rather swiftly, dispatched to the dustbin of history. Some 14,000 companies, an absolutely unprecedented number, were privatized between January 1992 and the end of June 1994 through a combination of insider buy-outs (or, given the ridiculously low prices, giveaways) and voucher auctions.

The price for this? Enterprise insiders—managers and workers—emerged as majority owners of nearly 70% of Russian enterprises. Although top management directly acquired "only" 9% of the shares through the mechanism Chubais established, and workers ended up with 56%, shortly afterwards managers resorted to a series of measures designed to increase their stakes. They started buying up workers' shares, while at the same time preventing workers from selling to outsiders. Those who resisted were threatened with dismissal. Managers held tight to company registers and simply refused to record share transactions of which they disapproved. They bought up still more shares at public voucher auctions (which could be made less public if the managers had the sympathy of local Property Fund officials in charge of running the auctions). And many formed separate private companies that they or their families would control and siphoned to them money and the most valuable assets of their enterprises. One way or another, they ended up owning the lion's share of the new capitalist property.

Here, in a savage irony, reformers charged with the task of undoing Marx's dismal handiwork seemed, instead, only to prove socialism's founder correct in at least one of his prophecies. Production is dominated, he said in *Capital,* by "magnates . . . who usurp and monopolize all advantages in this process of transformation." In the early stages of privatization, indeed, the authority of the nomenklatura managers appeared as total as that exercised by the great capitalists of the Victorian Age as portrayed by Marx. Privatization itself seemed to be set in their interest alone. By all visible evidence, decision-making power in many privatized firms is theirs.

In no other country was the nomenklatura grab for new property as successful as in Russia. But on a smaller scale, a similar pattern of political alliance between the governing reformers and the enterprise-level nomenklatura was often the only successful mix in the drive to privatize. Whenever the Polish or Hungarian authorities attempted to privatize over the heads of the entrenched pre-1989 managers, they encountered interminable obstacles, delays, and difficulties. All the while, many firms, as long as they remained owned by the state, were hemorrhaging money and value by the day. Only when the state decided to give them in one way or another to their managers—through a form of "leasing" (in Poland), subsidized credits (Hungary), or fully leveraged buyouts (Romania)—did privatization have a chance.

2.4 Like a Phoenix from the Ashes

The penultimate chapter of the *nomenklatura rediviva* is the return to political power of the by-now-former communists—this time no longer as the "vanguard of the proletariat," but rather as the tail wagged by the nomenklatura-capitalist dog. This chapter is still largely unwritten, despite the experiences of such countries as Hungary, Poland, and Bulgaria.

The electoral victory of the ex-communists comes in part from the public's disgust with the corruption and disenchantment with seemingly slow economic improvement. In a strange irony, both may have much to do with the nomenklatura's behavior. Will their victory now usher in a new spiral of abuse?

Although Hungarian privatization policy has become still somewhat friendlier to management since the return to power of the so-called ex-communists, the victorious socialists under Prime Minister Gyula Horn did not introduce any radical changes to the reform strategies already underway. Until late 1995, Polish communists also had their hands tied by the need to govern in a coalition and by the aggressive presidency of Lech Walesa. They could not, therefore, attempt any radical moves, but they were ruthless in placing their henchmen on the boards of state companies, staffing local governments with their supporters and distributing patronage positions among their allies. They stalled as long as they could the moribund mass privatization program and attempted to emasculate its antinomenklatura elements by insisting that privatization fund managers have personal experience in running state enterprises. Until being routed in parliamentary elections in the spring of 1997, Bulgaria's government of ex-communists, too, attempted to make sure that nomenklatura managers gained control of the investment funds that dominated the companies included in that country's oft-postponed, and easily manipulated when in force, mass privatization program.

Political manipulation of privatization can set a country back. Slovakia was one of the early success stories of reform. Mass privatization as practiced by its early postcommunist governments laid the foundation for vibrant economic growth and low inflation. But the third government of Vladimir Meciar, which assumed power in late 1994, twisted the privatization process into a political patronage machine. State property—from the choicest morsels such as the giant energy firm Slovnaft to small town hall recreation centers—was sold to handpicked insiders in a naked bid by Meciar to establish a client business class loyal to his regime. That process negated some of the industrial restructuring initiated by the mass privatization investment funds that Meciar sterilized and helped undermine Slovakia's bid for early entry into NATO. In November 1995, indeed, the European Union delivered a strongly worded *demarche* to Meciar that warned against continuation of his thuggery and corporatist strategies, and when the first list of five postcommunist countries to begin membership negotiations with the European Commission was announced, Slovakia was not among them.

2.5 Survival of the Unfittest

"Meet the new boss, same as the old boss" is a line English rockers the Who used to sing. Nowadays few can blame Polish, Hungarian, Russian, Romanian, and other reformers from turning that old rock anthem into a new political lament. The nomenklatura, in transforming itself into a ruling kleptoklatura, seems determined to make the old socialist Pierre Proudhon's dictum ring true: "All property is theft."

But apart from undermining somewhat the legitimacy of the new regime—perhaps of a private property regime itself—is there something economically wrong with the nomenklatura's success? If economists are not alarmed at management buyouts in the West—indeed, they tend to think that owner-managed companies often have distinct advantages over firms with widely dispersed ownership—why should we be concerned about the future of the postcommunist recovery just because *their* managers also want to have a share of their enterprises? Isn't this just the normal blues following every exhilarating revolutionary change, when romantic freedom fighters must make room for pedestrian and not always pure businessmen?

There is a grain of truth in this. No society, after all, can be reshaped overnight. Elites everywhere always contain a large number of talented people (even though under such regimes as communism and fascism, the elites are immoral and unscrupulous). Some of these people, indeed, would be successful within any political system. Their communist pedigree should not matter, especially when experienced entrepreneurial talent is in short supply.

But what matters is not just the unsavory past of the *nouveaux riches* of this new model nomenklaturadom. It is the fact that many among the nomenklatura would not make it under most democratic and free market systems. At best, they rose to the top for their political loyalty rather than business or professional qualifications. At worst, their advancement was based on the principle of a truly negative selection, with the more talented and honest people quickly bested in the Byzantine machinations of the party bureaucracy by sycophants and thugs. Moreover, there is little evidence that the kleptoklatura thinks all that differently from its socialist-era forebears. Belief in monopoly, autarky, and capital investment appear to remain nomenklatura dogma, though the near bankruptcy of most states has forced a realization among them that new subsidized capital investment for their firms may not be in the cards for years to come. These three articles of faith reinforce each other and threaten long-term economic health.

The postcommunist transition thus requires, for economic as much as for political reasons, that many of the old guard make room for the next generation of business leaders. It is this process that gets stymied by the managerial entrenchment resulting from nomenklatura privatization.

Another reason why this nomenklatura capitalism matters is that it prevents an evolution of corporate governance that is necessary if Eastern Europe is to join the world economy. Owner-managed companies of moderate size can have very beneficial economic effects, as Germany, with its *Mittelstand,* has shown for many decades. But unless a few people or families are to own most of a country's wealth, large industrial enterprises require a separation of ownership and managerial control. And when managers do not own more than a small share of their companies (when they are mostly "agents" rather than "principals"), their performance must be monitored so that they work for the owners rather than slacken and enrich themselves at the owners' expense.

The danger of such "agency problems," as economists call them, particularly serious in the transition countries of Eastern Europe and the ex-Soviet Union, where managerial pilfering of social (and thus nobody's) property has a long tradition. The only way to combat this is to make sure that all productive assets have a clear outside owner, a genuine capitalist in the boardroom, who can protect the interests of the company (and, indirectly, society) against the rapaciousness of unscrupulous insiders.

In this context, the moral unacceptability of nomenklatura capitalism also has economic significance. The new regimes, albeit imperfect, have a certain (and growing) degree of democratic transparency which today makes naked theft far more difficult. Nomenklatura acquisitions, therefore, must be partly hidden and partly clothed in some kind of legitimizing garment. These embellishments and subterfuges are not just a proverbial fig leaf; indeed, they may be quite costly in terms of future inefficiency. To hide nomenklatura ownership, inefficient structures (such as the impenetrable maze of Hungarian corporate cross-holdings) may need to be created, and because they distort the legal environment, they are likely to make *all* ownership weaker. Or to legitimize managerial grabbing, workers must be given the lion's share of a company, which makes any future restructuring (often requiring layoffs and changing old and inefficient ways) that much more difficult.

2.6 A House Divided?

Visitors to the postcommunist countries often hear complaints that little has really changed, that the nomenklatura is as strong as ever, and that privatization has merely tinkered at the rigging on the side of the party regime. This is patently not true. An entirely new class of entrepreneurs owning their own businesses is playing an ever-increasing role. Much of privatization, especially of smaller firms, is also producing the kind of restructuring necessary to move many countries on the way to solid growth. (And privatization has also brought political benefits. The Czech Republic's Vaclav Klaus is the only reformer in the region to win reelection in an environment in which he faced no real neocommunist threat. In Russia, Boris Yeltsin succeeded in winning a second term as president and quickly brought Anatoly Chubais, the central figure in the country's privatization program, back into the center of power in the Kremlin. Even in Moldova, privatization minister Ceslav Ciobanu partly attributes reconciliation between the government in Chisinau and the secessionist Transdniester region to the economic stability privatization has helped bring about.) But privatization is certainly not moving along the course expected by most reformers. The forces of the past have simply shown themselves to be much stronger and more resilient than anyone expected.

To damn privatization because it has been hijacked in part by the old nomenklatura would be foolish. There is no way East Europeans could have maintained their overgrown public sector or shrunk it without some unexpected side effects. But neither should the massive coup by the ex-communists be ignored, for as long as the nomenklatura remain powerful players on the region's business scene, their presence will have potentially serious consequences. Given a competent business organization, capital is now available throughout the postcommunist world, but the mere possession of capital is no guarantee that the requisite talent can be obtained and organized so that a firm will prosper. Privatized firms must rely, on the main, on external sources for this talent. Unlike capital, it is not something a firm can supply to itself.

The hopeful sign here is that, according to many observers, the ties that bind the nomenklatura are dissolving. The peak of its influence was the remarkable social contract made with the briefly dominant reformers in the heady early days of reform; if the nomenklatura permitted democratic and market reforms to proceed, the reformers would permit the nomenklatura to become rich. There are hints, however, that this Faustian bargain may be costly for the devil as well. Shortly after its consummation, privatization began to place uncontainable pressures on the nomenklatura as, first, the unity of the kleptoklatura and the old central bosses began to crumble and, then, the interests of those who managed to snap up genuinely viable businesses began to diverge from those who needed continuous state support. This shift has been disguised because, as was true under socialism, the position of the nomenklatura was thought to be immutable. That decision-making power should move outside the charmed circle of the nomenklatura seems unnatural to its members, and those within such firms who argue for such a dispersal seem to be in search of frivolous novelty. Yet for successful nomenklatura capitalists, the economic liberalization at the heart of privatization contains within it elements of great appeal. Here is where and when the logic of nomenklatura control begins to unravel. After all, why steal Gazprom if you cannot make billions from it!

Habits of the past will certainly continue, with many nomenklatura managers forming alliances of convenience with their former political soulmates. But the long-term hope for privatization, for growth, and for democracy must be this: a nomenklatura divided against itself cannot stand.

3
Privatization and Two of Its Enemies
Slovakia and Croatia

3.1 Marching Backwards: Slovakia's Counterrevolution

"Why can't they," wailed Professor Henry Higgins about women in the George Bernard Shaw play *Pygmalion,* "be more like us?" With far more tact but equal impatience, businessmen attempting to make their way in Slovakia tend to reel back, asking: "Why can't the Slovaks be more like the Czechs?"

Slovak authorities bridle at that comparison. "At the time of the divorce," says Pavel Ochotnicky, chief economist at state-owned savings bank Slovenska Sporitelna, "Czechs had all the essentials of a state—army, police, the very idea of ruling a country. In 1991 we began from scratch."

Under communism, indeed, ministers in Bratislava were little more than marionettes manipulated by party leaders in Prague. (Sometimes these communist bosses were ethnic Slovaks, such as Alexander Dubcek and Gustav Husak, but Slovak powerlessness persisted all the same.) Even after five years of independence, central government remains small. But key offices of state are now established and preside over a stabilization program bringing low inflation (under 10% annually since 1995) and the second fastest GDP growth in the ex-socialist world. In 1994–95, for example, hard currency reserves doubled and the trade deficit halved, with exports to OECD countries in 1994 alone skyrocketing almost 50%, to $2.6 billion.

Despite all this progress, businessmen were still anxious in August 1995 in Bratislava, sweating as much from psychological stress as from summer heat. Why, then, didn't the Slovak government stick to a privatization scheme that worked? Why did bureaucrats at every level appear so aggressive? Has Slovakia become a reformer's nightmare, a place where East Europeans are frittering away their initial success?

3.1.1 Meciar's Counterrevolution

The main reason for this bleak assessment is the third government of Vladimir Meciar, formed in November 1994. Two things characterize Meciar's style of politics. On one level, his government signified the return of a clique descending, in part, from the old communist nomenklatura, which brings with it many discredited communist habits. "People are starting to govern as in the old days," says Brigita Schmgnerov, an opposition deputy and former minister. "The first rule is to escape responsibility for any decision. The second is that every decision must benefit the rulers."

Patronage indeed lubricates Meciar's political machine. Purges carried out during his ministries removed over 4,000 business, government, and media leaders in favor of Meciar cronies. State jobs such as teacher, postman, industrial manager, or TV director come only with a recommendation by the cadre of Meciar's Movement for a Democratic Slovakia (HZDS) and its coalition partners, the Slovak National Party (SNP) and the Workers Party (ZRS). The antimonopoly office, to cite one of many examples, was no longer headed by young technocrats who jibbed the first independent Slovak governments into dismantling state monopolies. Under Meciar it has been bossed by an ex-carpenter commonly referred to as "Woodenhead" who does not dare to question the wisdom of the powers above him.

More ominously, in a bid for total control, Meciar tried in May 1995 to impeach his nemesis, President Michal Kovac, falling twenty votes short of the necessary two-thirds majority. (The silver lining in this was that Meciar could not even deliver all of his coalition's votes, a sign that his rule is not the irresistible steamroller he claims it to be.) In a cloak-and-dagger fashion, Kovac's son was kidnapped near Bratislava and later discovered half-conscious in an abandoned car outside Vienna. It was believed that Meciar's police wanted to facilitate in this way his extradition to Germany, where the younger Kovac was wanted for questioning on a tax matter. (Unlike Austria, Slovakia lacks an extradition treaty with Germany.)

On another level, Meciar's regime harks back to an even older tradition of Mitteleuropean politics: the virulent strain of corporatist authoritarianism of the 1930s and 1940s. The pattern, sadly, is all too familiar: divisions within a democratic government incite calls for strong medicine—on the one hand, to stop seeming political rot and, on the other, to invest the state with not only material power but also the imponderable force of majesty. Throughout the region, that terrible majesty assumed the form of race-based, demagogic states such as the rump Slovak Republic ruled, under Hitler's tutelage, by Monsignor Tiso.

Given Meciar's deeds and that precedent, few can blame Slovaks for experiencing a disconcerting sense of deja vu. Example: Meciar himself proclaimed the government's intent to restrict births among Slovakia's Gypsies. (Luckily, the assault has been merely verbal, with no formal legislative follow-up so far.) More covertly, state industries, following the classic corporatist design, are frequently hived off in secret deals to Meciar's political and personal cronies. From Slovnaft, the monopoly state oil company, to the armaments firms being collected into a holding company controlled by Julius Toth (a former HZDS finance minister), Meciar is bludgeoning Slovak industry into a political money and patronage machine.

Slovak reform is quickly becoming a part of this spoils system. "Abusing the privatization program is not merely politics," says Gabriela Kaliska, a former opposition member of parliament. "It is the main part of the counterrevolution." What Meciar's regime is attempting to undo is Slovakia's bid for a free market and a democratic society.

3.1.2 The Early Successes

Central Europe has nearly six years of experience with what works in privatization and what does not. Three fundamental questions face any would-be privatizer: Should property be given away or should it be sold? Should preferences be given to insiders (that is, the old managers and workers), or should restructuring be entrusted to new outside owners? What institutions should replace the state in monitoring and supervising the managers of privatized enterprises?

A giveaway to the general population was the privatization strategy followed by the then Czechoslovakia and continued in Slovakia during its first year of independence. Every adult citizen was entitled to buy for a nominal sum the same number of privatization vouchers, which could be invested, either directly at auction or through investment funds, in a long list of firms being privatized. No privileges were given to insiders, and enterprises were compelled to privatize, though they were given some latitude in how to go about it. Few restrictions hindered new investment funds that offered their shares in exchange for vouchers held by the population. The funds then invested their new "voucher capital" to acquire large blocks of shares in privatized enterprises.

The result was quite impressive. Some 503 big Slovak companies were privatized in the first round of the voucher privatization scheme agreed to by the old Czechoslovak federation. Combined with the 10,000 small businesses sold during the small privatization program, these firms produce nearly 60% of Slovak GDP. Employment in this new private sector is growing on average 2% per year, whereas employment in the state sector continues to fall. Ownership was dispersed, kick-starting the development of capital markets. At the same time, a number of large funds held significant enough stakes to exert pressure on the management of privatized enterprises. The hold of the old central nomenklatura was being broken, fueling an economic and political renewal.

What the architects of this "mass privatization" understood (even if it went against the advice of most Western experts) was that sales under East European conditions would be both excruciatingly slow and bring little or no revenue to the state. Few foreigners were willing to buy (and if done on a sufficiently large scale, such foreign acquisitions would be nothing short of political dynamite). Prospective domestic buyers lacked the capital necessary to purchase large industrial enterprises, and except in the case of a few good firms, sales at realistic prices thus would lead to little or no privatization. Countries such as Poland and Hungary, for example, expected big windfalls from direct sales but were disappointed, and most big enterprises remained in state hands.

To make sales brisk, assets must be sold far below their value. This is what makes them so attractive to people like Meciar, for such sales are also, in truth, giveaways. But unlike the open and equitable distributions through a voucher scheme used in the Czech Republic and Slovakia in the early days of independence, Meciar's direct sales are selective giveaways in which those who control the government, and their friends, reap rich rewards.

3.1.3 Steals and Deals

Instead of building on Slovakia's earlier success, Meciar attempted to undermine this progress. Throughout each of his three ministries, Meciar vigorously attacked the mass privatization program and ultimately cancelled its second wave even though 3.5 million people had already purchased vouchers. Meciar claimed that direct sales were superior to mass privatization because sales could inject money into the treasury even as they built up a class of native owners. Because these sales were conducted in secret and their terms were unknown, however, it was impossible to verify whether or not they contributed much, if anything, to the government's purse. Still, the fact that 39% of Slovnaft shares were sold directly to a Meciar supporter for less than half of their quoted price on the Bratislava Stock Exchange indicates that maximizing revenues was far from a government priority.

Since returning to power for the third time in November 1994, Meciar's government has held a "fire sale" of state firms. In six months property valued at SK 20 billion was sold, with the National Property Fund (NPF) getting back barely SK 3 billion. Compare this with the SK 35 billion the NPF obtained through direct sales between 1991 and 1994 (about one-third of which were conducted by Meciar's previous governments). By converting his nomenklatura cronies and nationalist allies into outright owners of Slovakia's enterprises, Meciar inhibits a prime goal of privatization: depoliticization of the economy. The political vetting of sales that Meciar's regime undertakes and the inevitable quid pro quo that such deals entail mean that powerful new links are forged between those who control industry and those who rule the political machine. The new business class can insist on subsidies, tariff protection, monopoly power, tax concessions, and friendly regulation. And the new political class can insist that the spoils of crony businesses enrich the coffers of political parties and the pockets of politicians.

With direct sales, windfalls abound (for the blessed few). Take the case of the energy company Slovnaft. First, the government fused it with Benzinoil, giving Slovnaft up to 90% of oil and gas distribution in Slovakia, extending its sway into next door Moravia. In August 1995 it sold a 39% stake in Slovnaft (reportedly for half the price Slovnaft shares were fetching on the open market, and for no down payment) to Slovintegra a.s., a private company controlled by Slovnaft's general director, Slavomir Hatina. Although some outside shareholders exist (the EBRD is one), Hatina gained near-majority control of the company through this sale combined with the SK 1.2 billion worth of Slovnaft equity he secured in earlier direct sales. A supporter of HZDS since its founding and, it is said, a key financial backer of the party through his control of Slovnaft's purse, Hatina sits atop the most valuable property in Slovakia.

Or, consider the case of Julius Toth, the finance minister of Meciar's previous government. From his Kosice redoubt, Toth controls the country's sole private bank, a big daily newspaper, and the VSZ steelworks and has been put in charge of the holding company that will receive a majority of Slovakia's armaments manufacturers. VSZ alone is responsible for 16% of industrial production and 26% of exports. Together with Slovnaft, with its 7% share of industrial production, the two companies had revenues equal to 8% of Slovakia's GDP in 1993. So these deals are not peanuts.

Two factors matter in direct sales: political links and division of the spoils among the coalition partners. ZOS Vrutky, a profitable monopoly rail construction firm, for example, was to be acquired by the wife of SNP deputy Vitazoslav Moric. When reports of the proposed sale caused a scandal, ZOS Vrutky was sold to a legal entity, the beneficial owner of which is reported to be no other than Mrs. Moric. Tire-maker Matador Puchov was turned into a joint-stock company in which workers got 20% of the shares, and managers, led by Stefan Rosina, a close associate of Finance Minister Jan Ducky, received 80%. But when outsiders try to acquire assets, even when they are likely to pay a more realistic price, they are shown the door. A lawyer for an Austrian company shut out in its bid for a piece of Slovnaft says: "It isn't because we are foreign that they don't want us to invest. They don't want to sell shares in the company because they want to keep all the profits for themselves."

Mimicking their bosses in Bratislava, local politicians create their own spoils system. In Zilina, the town council empowered the mayor to sell directly—and without review—any property with a value of SK 800,000 or less. Soon after, the mayor sold to an HZDS supporter for SK 125,000 a villa valued at SK 5 million, which rented annually for SK 750,000. Later he sold a SK 10 million villa to the chairman of Matica Slovenska (a supposedly non-profit pro-Meciar group devoted to nationalist causes) for SK 1.0. "I am resolved to promote and assist Matica for as long as I live," says Mayor Slota. And he does. Matica also received, for a similar SK 1.0, the profitable printing presses of the state firm Neografia Martin.

Vague and malleable laws invite lawlessness. Although only two new privatization acts have been passed since 1992, amendments have occurred, on average, every fifty-one days. Even when Slovakia's high court speaks, the government feels no compulsion to act. One noisy affair is that of Novaky Chemical a.s. On November 3, 1994, the NPF agreed to sell 51% of Novaky to the Czech firm Inekon, which deposited $2.5 million as a down payment. That day, Meciar's third ministry took office and immediately nullified the deal. Six months later, the Constitutional Court declared unconstitutional the act which authorized this and many other nullifications. Even so, Inekon was not given its shares, despite quiet intervention by Czech diplomats and a contract provision that imposes a SK 50,000 fine for each day of further delay.

Laws also provide camouflage. An example is the 1994 change to the statutes governing the NPF. Before 1994, privatizations were vetted by the cabinet and officials of the Ministry of Privatization, a process that subjected sales to some public and parliamentary scrutiny. Saying that he wanted to depoliticize sales, Meciar shifted all oversight to the NPF's presidium, equally packed with the men of his coalition. Now decisions can be made much more swiftly and without disclosure to or scrutiny by the opposition.

3.1.4 Strategic Retreats
What he cannot spin off to his cronies, Meciar wanted, in the good old corporatist tradition, to keep under direct state control. Indeed, Meciar's law on so-called strategic industries was carefully designed to bolster the interests of the political classes by providing them a long-term source of patronage, while at the same time holding potential competitors (especially foreigners) at bay. Certain companies in areas such as telecoms, postal services, gas, oil, electricity, arms, civil engineering, pharmaceuticals, forestry, water, and even a stud farm, were deemed too impor-

tant to be left entirely to private owners and the market. Property worth SK 150 billion (nearly 40% of the total valuation given to the entire list of Slovak state companies before privatization) was designated as strategic. One-third of these would, says Meciar, never be privatized in any way. Others would be privatized through direct sales but only after the NPF transferred to the relevant ministry the firms' "golden shares" (that is, shares with special voting rights), which, though minority stakes, will command the power to shape business decisions. Here is a return to ministerial management on the sly. And Meciar's track record does not augur well: managers at Slovak Telecom, Slovak Power, and Slovak Energy Factories were dismissed in the past year for "political insufficiencies."

Having to grope their way through the maze of ministerial, NPF, and private shares established by the strategic industries act is certain to deter foreign investors, for it is impossible to say which firms are covered by what provisions of the act, or how the state will acquire its "golden shares" in previously privatized firms. "This is nationalization by default," says Vladimir Miskovsky, a former privatization official. "If it persists, this program will doom industries in desperate need of foreign investment, like telecoms, to continuing decay."

3.1.5 Bouncing Bonds

Perhaps the most brazen attack on previous Slovak reform efforts was the outright cancellation of a program well on the way to realization. Upon resuming the premiership in November 1994, Meciar immediately suspended the second wave of voucher mass privatization; even he could not ignore the fact that 3.5 million Slovaks had paid the equivalent of a week's average wage to subscribe to the second wave of vouchers. Meciar also needed to placate the IMF, which insisted that Slovakia systematically privatize if a standby loan agreement was to be maintained. (Because the old Czechoslovak clearing system for international trade was scheduled to shut down October 1, 1995, the government became keen to maintain this option.) After months of waffling, Meciar cancelled the voucher system in July, and a new wrinkle, bond privatization, was announced. Because its real purpose was political, the scheme (a veto of the bill by President Kovac was overridden when parliament reconvened in September 1995) promised to be more mess than mass.

The scheme was transparently simple—and simply transparent. Everyone with a voucher was to receive in its place a bond, guaranteed by the National Property Fund (NPF), worth SK 10,000 and carrying an annual 11 % interest rate. There were two major ways in which bonds were to be used: to help to purchase a home or a flat or to pay off installment debts incurred in the direct purchase of a company from the NPF. As distinct from the voucher system, what the bond scheme lacked was an automatic conversion of the bonds into shares of a large number of privatized enterprises through the system of auctions open to all on equal terms. Allowing bonds to be used to pay NPF debts exposed the scheme's hidden intent. Only firms that the NPF chose were sold. Insiders who bought their shares through direct sales from the NPF (putting down little of the usually low asking price) could then buy the bonds at a discount from ordinary Slovaks and use the face value to pare down even further their privatization debts. The scheme mainly served Meciar's political purposes: insider's route to ownership is greased, while outside control and oversight are effectively excluded.

Economists at the Slovak National Bank also feared that the bonds, acting as direct injections into the money supply, would incite inflation. Because they were guaranteed by the NPF, which was unlikely to secure enough reserves to pay them off when they came due in 2001 because direct sales of NPF's assets were not likely to generate enough revenue. Thus, either a massive default or the government being forced to print money to pay off the bonds was the anticipated consequence.

3.1.6 Outsiders Out

In line with its commitment to nomenklatura control, Meciar's government aimed its lowest blows at the investment funds created in the first wave of voucher privatization. Despite their limitations, investment funds, representing millions of small shareholders, were the main outside investors with the power to take on the often thankless task of challenging managers and pushing for enterprise restructuring. By gaining control of two-thirds of the vouchers, the funds acquired a strong voice in newly privatized businesses—but this was precisely what earned them Meciar's hostility. For the coalition's ex-communist and nationalist firebrands, the funds were wicked speculators who robbed Slovaks of their heritage and, in the words of Stefan Gavornik, head of the NPF's presidium, needed to be "punished." How far was he willing to go? "Law," said the ever-loyal Gavornik, "is not an issue in privatization."

The bond privatization act damned Slovakia's investment funds as superfluous. Their role was to be taken over by the state, at least until Meciar's cronies become outright owners. Until the installment debt of a direct sale is paid off, an amendment to the NPF's charter, passed in July 1995, granted the NPF oversight of business decisions such as investment, management changes, layoffs, and company bylaws in all companies on their way to privatization.

Meciar's ire exacts its costs. The 160 new investment funds set up for the second wave were offered a scant SK 500,000 (about $100) per fund by the government, to be divvied up as compensation. A second line of attack against the investment funds restricted their holding to no more than 10% of a company's shares. Because the first wave allowed for bigger holdings, many funds took stakes of 20% and 25% in some companies. Under pressure from Meciar, many were forced to sell these "excess" share on the cheap to insiders.

Attacks on the funds were made on many fronts. PSIP fund, Slovakia's second largest, had its license revoked on technical grounds. Stewardship of PSIP, which collected 25% of second-wave vouchers, was given to Harvard Capital and Consulting, Slovakia, whose most powerful board member, Vladimir Lexa, happened to be the father of Ivan Lexa, Meciar's secret-police chief. Trading in shares of VUB Kupon Fund were suspended by the Ministry of Finance after VUB sold a one-third stake in the fund to Nomura Securities. To get along, some funds went along. For example, Cassoviainvest took a minority stake in Agrizempa a.s., which was sold by direct sale to Meciar supporters. Other fund managers dithered nervously in the office of Rudolf Lachkovic, president of the Association of Investment Managers and Investment Funds, fearing fresh assaults even as they looked to the Kosice-based Constitutional Court to restore their rights.

3.1.7 Meciar Bound?

Despite all Meciar's machinations, recreating a politically controlled economy will not be simple. The market genie may not be so easy to reimprision in its bottle. Moreover, if Meciar's erstwhile cronies, like Slavomir Hatina, are to reap maximum profits from their new holdings, they will need the foreign shareholders and capital markets that Meciar's government suppresses. Will the beneficiaries of Meciar's efforts remain Meciar loyalists in the future, or will self-interest shatter the corporatist connections he is seeking to forge?

Hints that Meciar's political privatizations breed dodgy allies are visible. P. Maisky, once an HZDS industrial backer, is an opposition supporter now that he controls most of the companies he set out to acquire in 1991. Some observers also interpret Julius Toth's absence from Meciar's third government as a sign that the powerful former finance minister's loyalty may be wavering. And, it is said in Bratislava, Hatina threw his weight against the government's strategic industries proposal when it was being debated in parliament in early 1996, perhaps a sign that he was beginning to doubt the need to tie his interests to Meciar's fate. The big unknown is how long it will take men like Toth and other handpicked insider owners to respond to real business incentives.

Equally important, Slovakia's infant constitutional system influences the political struggle. Though lacking history's sanction, powerful bodies are arrayed (but not yet allied) against Meciar. Despite being a former Meciar supporter, President Kovac repeatedly flexed his independence by vetoing key HZDS legislation and (as during a summer visit to Washington in 1995) by convincing foreign leaders to rebuke Meciar's authoritarian ways. The Slovak National Bank has rebuffed efforts to trim its anti-inflation program. Slovakia's Catholic bishops (backtracking from some grim early political gaffes, such as being present when a monument to Monsignor Tiso was unveiled) have preached derisively against Meciar's cloaking his regime in Catholic garb. The Constitutional Court, though packed with old-line communist prosecutors, gutted Meciar's economic program by declaring key HZDS laws unconstitutional.

Today these institutions may have shallow roots. Yet their legitimacy is no less than Meciar's own, and in preserving their independence against Meciar's encroachments, they provide centers of countervailing power in politics that privatization should provide in business. The odds that Slovakia's independent institutions will grow, not fade, will be enhanced if international institutions, foreign governments, and outside public opinion actively support this trend. (Here the silence of Czech premier Vaclav Klaus has been deafening, though, truth be told, Czech president Vaclav Havel did call Meciar a "paranoid" in the spring of 1997.) But only a combination of political and economic forces is likely to curtail Meciar's ambitions. That prospect is Slovakia's hope, and its continuing crisis.

3.2 Privatization Paranoid Style: Croatia

A mere five years after breaking away from Yugoslavia and gaining their national independence, Croats nowadays discuss the future not with the brashness you would expect but use, instead, an odd grammatical tense. Call it the "concealed assumptive": a future conditional embroidered with such murmured phrases as "if it is not already too late" or "security permitting" or the ever-popular "if appropriately dealt with." After the Bosnia peace accords were signed late in 1995, despite unwritten and unstated caveats, far-reaching reforms were nonetheless anticipated in Croatia. President Franjo Tudjman's signature on the twenty-one conditions insisted upon by the Council of Europe in Croatia's membership application, moreover, seemed to point in the direction of democracy, free markets, and the European Union.

In the months that followed, however, optimism faded. By crafting a myriad of electoral coalitions in a series of spring and summer elections in 1995, opposition parties swept to victory in most cities, including Zagreb, as the share of Tudjman's ruling Croatian Democratic Union (HDZ) fell, denying him the two-thirds parliamentary majority needed to rewrite the constitution. Unaccustomed to defeat, indeed, embittered at these rebuffs, Tudjman's regime soon began wheeling out the familiar tools of oppression: elections rigged or discarded, corrupted privatization, state monopolies reinvigorated, legalized suppression of free speech. In a novel example of authoritarian inventiveness, the independent paper *Panorama* was shut down for environmental law violations. (Such authoritarian inventiveness is somewhat characteristic of Tudjman's rule. The two hundred sanctions-busting artillery pieces and rocket launchers used to devastating effect in the Krajina offensive of 1995 were listed on import documents as "giraffes.")

None of this surprises even the most casual observer of the Croat political scene. Ever since Yugoslavia disintegrated, Croatia's importance in Western peace plans allowed Tudjman's regime literally to get away with murder. Sanctions applied with vigor on Serbia were routinely ignored by Croatia—witness the scandal over the Clinton administration's winking at Iranian arms shipments (with Croatia acting as the conduit) to the Bosnian government.

This international tacit acquiescence extends to Croat domestic affairs as well. Two years after Croatia's victory over the rebellious enclave of Serb-held Krajina, followed by the flight of 500,000 Serb refugees, Tudjman's government has done nothing to reassure the country's few remaining ethnic Serb citizens, a silence matched by the West. In April 1996 in the village of Kricka, a deliberate withdrawal of police protection left Serb homes (most occupied by old people too infirm to flee) to be mined without protest. Lower-level harassment of Serbs is tolerated by Tudjman's government, too. Only when the Helsinki Watch committee's Zagreb office, not Western diplomats, kicked up a fuss were Serbs in that village connected to the electricity supply Croat residents had used for months. Such silence leads Ivan Cicak, the Helsinki Watch committee's Zagreb president, to suspect that "the West endorses Tudjman's long-term goal of an ethnically pure state."

In diplomacy as elsewhere, willful blindness is both habit-forming and debilitating, like any addiction. To continuously look the other way from Tudjman's abuses—as the United States does deliberately and Germany does by default, having washed its hands in disappointment (recognizing Croatia's independence was, after all, reunified Germany's first big "go-it-alone" foreign policy initiative)—is dangerously shortsighted. Apparently, fearing that democracy acts as a medium through which long-suppressed nationalist fever can explode, Western political leaders believe that a little democracy is a dangerous thing in postcommunist Yugoslavia.

This is one of the biggest fallacies about the political dynamics of Eastern Europe during the postcommunist transition. Far from unleashing pent-up nationalist feeling, democratic politics in the region, as in most other places, tends to diffuse upswells of nationalist fervor. It is enough to look at such postcommunist countries as Poland and Hungary, or Croatia's northern neighbor, Slovenia, all of which allow democracy full rein, to see that the radical, nationalist right is usually a weak or spent force in a pluralist political environment. Even in Russia, despite catastrophic economic decline and the humiliating loss of empire, Zhirinovsky's ersatz "Black Hundreds" are a ranting, but declining, minority, with the June/July 1996 presidential election revealing them as possessing far less support than, say, Jean Marie Le Pen's National Front routinely receives in much more stable and prosperous France. By the same token, where authoritarianism has taken hold—from Serbia to Uzbekistan—fevered nationalism has been raising its ugly head.

By its tolerance of Tudjman's ethnic and political abuses, the West may incite what it most fears in Croatia: abuses by the regime which will provoke such unrest that Tudjman is pressured to play the nationalist card even more heavy-handedly in order to cling to power. This in turn may both lead to a more aggressive international posture by Croatia, threatening the Bosnian accords, and also usher in a nastier ethnic climate at home, with Serbs increasingly and publicly branded as enemies within. Here is an old dialectic of power in the region: recall that the nationalistic specter of external enemies was a fundamental bedrock of Soviet-style repression. It is all too easy for Western diplomats to assume that without Tudjman an even bloodier Croatia would be both imminent and unavoidable. Such thinking exonerates them from the search for options and peaceful reforms and passes to others the burden of action. But what if they are wrong?

3.2.1 Tribal Glue

Tudjman's oppressions may sometimes be silky smooth, but often they show an iron fist hidden within the general's white dress gloves. In October 1995, for example, Ivo Skrabalo (vice president of the liberal Croatian Social Liberal Party, HSLS) was declared the winner of a parliament seat for Zagreb. Within hours the result was overturned by Tudjman's handpicked electoral commission when absentee ballots cast by seamen (Zagreb is far from the coast) and prison inmates miraculously appeared. No surprise that most of these votes went the HDZ way. Throughout the latter half of 1995 and through all 1996, Tudjman stalemated Zagreb municipal elections, using his presidential powers to block a series of opposition figures, chosen by a victorious seven-party coalition, from assuming the mayor's office. Respecting election results was one of the twenty-one conditions Tudjman accepted when he applied to the Council of Europe for Croatia's membership. In such robust chutzpah, Croatian politics proves (once more) that it is not for beginners, outsiders—or optimists.

No elected government in Eastern Europe, indeed, has the monopoly on power Tudjman has enjoyed since 1990. Twice, the HDZ movement he controls has received absolute majorities in parliament. Its haughtiness was fanned by the West's embrace; one favorite ploy such support delivers Tudjman is his ability to isolate his opponents by branding them enemies of America as well as of himself. But Tudjman's ability to disempower other political parties does not eliminate contention from Croatian political life. It simply moves it within HDZ itself. What this means, however, is that political power in Croatia pulses within the straitjacket of HDZ nationalism.

HDZ is no simple monolith, however. Internal upheavals are, if not frequent, incontrovertible nonetheless. In 1994, for example, the left wing of HDZ indulged in an unprecedented act of group indiscipline. Thirty-odd members led by former premier Josip Manolic broke with Tudjman. The issue was Bosnia, but at stake was the total control of political life the president exercises. Tudjman is not a man known for reticence or tact under pressure. Opponents were accused of treating policy as a "circus" and in tight-lipped confrontations told to shut up or get out.

Infighting within HDZ invariably provokes Croatia's small and ever-threatened free press and radio into frenzies of anticipation. Will infighting catalyze (at last) the millennial realignment of Croatian politics: HDZ pragmatists and Croatia's four large democratic opposition parties against HDZ's apostles of "Greater Croatia" and a Balkan apartheid? When Manolic and Stjepan Mestic broke with Tudjman, opposition leaders stood on tiptoe ready to kiss the heretics. However, political realignment was not to be. HDZ has a dread of splits. Despite the loss of some powerful figures, few of the rank-and-file followed Manolic and Mestic into the wilderness. The tribal cohesion of HDZ stood intact for all to see.

Why is this so? One of Croatia's most articulate analysts, Professor Nenad Zakosek of the University of Zagreb, argues that Tudjman's HDZ regime is not an eschatology; it is a survival doctrine. From the moment in 1990 they wrested Croatia from the splintering mass of Yugoslavia, the military men, ex-emigres (defense minister Gojko Susak is a former pizza maker from Toronto), ex-communist apparatchiks and Croat nationalists surrounding President Tudjman lacked a clear vision of a truly better future: they sought instead to hold on to something marginally better (for ethnic Croats) than the past.

Like all revolutionary parties, indeed, HDZ despises any and all opposition. Yet the story of its politics is a story of the various strands of nationalism fighting for dominance of the movement.

One powerful faction is rooted outside the country, among the ethnic Croats of Hercegovina who have the right to vote in Croatia's elections. Another smaller but equally revanchist group looks nostalgically to Croatia's Nazi-era Ustasha government for inspiration. A third grouping contains the cluster of nationally minded communist apparatchiks that Tito and his successors favored in the communist era so as to draw the sting of Croat nationalism from Yugoslav politics.

Because HDZ has the amorphous qualities of a mass movement, not the constancy of a political party, Tudjman must be ideologically pragmatic. This can be as confusing for HDZ members as for outsiders. Even those used to the bland utterances of Western politicians find it hard to pin down what course Tudjman and his colleagues believe they are pursuing. One minute he pledges to HDZ leaders from Hercegovina that no Croats will be sent to stand trial before the Bosnia war crimes tribunal: the next, a Croat general from Hercegovina is on a flight bound for the International Court of Justice in The Hague. Such dealings make it hard to avoid Professor Zakosek's terse conclusion that Croatia's rulers do not have an ideological blueprint to guide or determine policy, only opportunism.

Holding on to power is the one constant goal of HDZ; everything else can be improvised. Croatia is a society in which Western democratic freedoms—say, local government or opposition—are less constitutional rights than displays of intermittent government self-confidence. Its dominant ethos is one of clannish secrecy, embracing not just the cabinet, HDZ party structures (they mimic communist ones, with HDZ party members often "shadowing" official state officers) and the military, but the civil service, the judiciary, mass media, finance, and the education system (a purge of non-HDZ high school principals was undertaken in 1996). Each power base has been recaptured through ruthless loyalty and a supple capacity to suppress or simply ignore policy differences that inevitably arise within a regime lacking proper political opposition.

That combination of loyalty and secrecy robs the leadership in Zagreb of real security and robs party acolytes of certainty. No one ever really knows what the government is collectively thinking. But then it is a mistake to judge Croatian politics by Western or even transition country standards. They are tribal politics and are about survival, pride, masculinity, and muddling through. As

Ivica Racan, leader of the opposition reform-communist group-ing, the Social Democratic Party, and thus someone who should know, remarks: "We like our politicians to be wolves."

3.2.2 One-Man Show

Tudjman affects more than the crisp white military tunics and holidays on the Adriatic isle of Brioni favored by Marshal Tito. In seeking to bring the governmental machine under his thumb, Tudjman crafted a constitution that confers near-absolute execu-tive power on himself. The tame courts can do little to protect constitutional rights against legislative power, and the parliament is in turn a tool of the executive. This is a system that can legally shut down Zagreb's French-language lycee and German-language gymnasium, remove elected county presidents from office and appoint unelected HDZ cronies, and propose a press law that is the most repressive media measure on offer in Eastern Europe.

Postcommunist Croatia is also producing the irony of a bureaucracy even more bloated than that under communism. A reason for this was given by Milan Kovac, HDZ's man atop the state privatization fund, who says that for the foreseeable future Croatia must be able to "shift back and forth along a sliding scale between a war and peace economy." Bureaucrats like Kovac know that this mission depends on the maintenance of state control of the economy in tacit liaison with HDZ elements that rig reforms such as privatization for partisan interests. Thus, Tudjman used delegated executive powers to sack perhaps 40 % of all managers of socially owned business and replace them with HDZ loyalists. This economic purge is complemented by a HDZ bandwagon rolling through almost every institution of Croatian life.

Obstacles to presidential dictate are met in two ways: administrative upheaval and legal quick fixes. Departments, min-istries, and local and regional governments can be merged, moved, or removed at presidential whim. A tier of presidential assistants oversees the work of state ministries. President Tudjman also set to work on university rectors (all four universi-ties are now headed by HDZ party loyalists) and other semi-inde-pendent groups. And for every election, there is a new election law tailored to meet HDZ needs. (Professor Smiljko Sokol, Tudjman's electoral law magician, is one day likely to be reward-ed with the rectorship of the University of Zagreb.) These elec-toral fixes are needed because HDZ's electoral share keeps falling. Even after the Krajina victories of 1995, HDZ's vote fell (a positive sign that nationalism was never as popular among Croatians as Tudjman pretends and the West fears). Indeed, HDZ's vote remained at the same low level in June 1997, yet it remained the top party largely because of opposition disunity. HDZ can now rely on about only 33% of the vote.

3.2.3 Privatization of the State

In Zagreb, people rarely talk about corruption. They talk instead about *dpr* (pronounced "duper"). When something shady or stupid happens, people shake their heads: *Dpr*. Nothing gets done properly because of *dpr*. The word is used to describe a social fabric in which the threads of authority, personality, and profit are pressed together so tightly that they are inseparable. *Dpr* is not exactly corruption. *Dpr* is a kind of greedy collusion among people whose ideas about conflict of interest are structurally underdeveloped. Asked to explain her family's sudden wealth, for example, President Tudjman's wife blithely pointed to royalties gained on the seven editions of her husband's autobiography as the source. "We have our Croatia" is HDZ's slogan, a credo that party officials appear to take literally.

Eager to increase the spoils available to HDZ's supporters, Tudjman early in his rule moved to bring decentralized Croatian enterprises firmly under state (and HDZ) control. The amorphous system of "social ownership" established under Tito gave local managers and employees nearly total control over their firms without giving them actual ownership, which naturally led to serious inefficiencies. The cover for Tudjman's grab for economic power was the plausible claim that the system of social ownership needed reform and that only the government could prevent managers from looting enterprises. What resulted, however, was a form of nationalized theft.

Many of the old managers were dismissed and replaced by HDZ loyalists. Once at the helm, the new men would siphon company funds, often obtained though loans from HDZ-dominated banks, and stash them away in foreign bank accounts. Then, ostensibly as a prelude to privatization, "social ownership" was abolished, and most enterprises were brought under direct state control. This gave HDZ further scope for patronage as thousands of directors were named to newly created company boards, including many HDZ parliamentarians. Given the paltry salaries of members of parliament, directorship income is not peanuts: it often exceeds by two or three times the amount parliamentarians receive from the state for their work. The more loyal his or her vote, the more likely a deputy is to be handed additional directorships by Tudjman and his cronies.

But these were only the first stages in Tudjman's strategy. Controlled privatization was the easiest way to further increase HDZ patronage and balance party factions. Goodies were distributed to the loyal and denied to renegades. HDZ loyalists put in charge of companies could run down their value in order to fix a low price for their eventual sale, which would invariably go to the management itself or to another HDZ backer. In this way, privatization became a patronage tool that allowed a politically well-heeled ex-truck driver with no management skills to become the monopoly owner of the country's dairy distribution system, and a former tavern-musician-turned-general to become one of the biggest landowners of northern Croatia.

Insider dealing did not stop there. Even the cheap prices charged HDZ loyalists were often too much for them. So a new ingredient, manager's credits, was added to the brew. State-controlled banks, primarily the giant Privredna Banka and Zagrebacka Banka, issued unsecured credits to company managers (or firms set up by them) to buy up the company, often using still further discounts granted to employees (who face dismissal if they don't cooperate). Zagreb's Esplanade Hotel, long the city's most luxurious, was practically given away in this way to its managers, who also managed to gather a DM 20 million credit alongside their ownership stake.

More generally, virtually all major bank credits, as with most privatizations, have been really a form of political transfer designed to keep the rival wings of HDZ happy. In the process, new empires are created to fund the HDZ political machine. Two shadowy figures, Miroslav Kutle and Ivica Todoric, oversee this system of patronage. The growing octopus of Todoric's investments (with its financial base in Zagrebacka Banka) serves what is known as the technical wing of HDZ, meaning its ex-communist members. Kutle's empire, with interests in construction, Dalmatian tourist hotels, mining, and breweries, is said to service the interests of Croat nationalists (both of the home-grown variety and the few returned emigres in Tudjman's inner circle).

There are also big plans for the future as the prospect of postwar reconstruction looms large. The capture of public sector industries—"privatized state ownership" in the words of the

Social Democrat Ivica Racan—delivered to HDZ control the most powerful sectors of the economy: energy, finance, and infrastructure. That control is sure to become a new source of patronage as reconstruction begins. Already the workings of this system are clear. In Istria, the government commissioned highway construction from a French company, which then promptly subcontracted the work to local HDZ-affiliated firms, which work very slowly. Not surprisingly, all big Croatian construction firms are now under HDZ's thumb, meaning that the party will be the biggest beneficiary of reconstruction, whether or not what is to be built is actually needed, or actually built.

Drazen Budisa, once the opposition's nominee for the mayoralty of Zagreb, and perhaps its leading figure, argues that such cynical exploitation of contracting practices not only endangers the reconstruction process, but also makes the struggle against corruption so much the harder: transfers to the ruined regions like Krajina and the blighted lands around Osijek in the east will be made in order to provide contracts for industries in HDZ hands. "We are all against corruption. But who can realistically attack reconstruction investments?"

3.2.4 Divide and Misrule

There was a time when Tudjman would have pushed ahead with such deals without worry. But opposition victories are a sign of changing times: elected opposition mayors are far less compliant about corrupted privatizations than HDZ place holders; local prosecutors show signs of being more purposeful in their duties; muckraking papers like *Nacional* and *Feral Tribune* revel in exposing HDZ scams. Fear of exposure on a massive scale, indeed, may be the motivating factor behind Tudjman's obstructing an opposition takeover of Zagreb. He may or may not believe that "democracy cannot mean opposition control of the capital" (his oft-stated rationale for refusing to confirm the freely elected mayor of Zagreb in office), but he assuredly realizes that, should his opponents control Zagreb, disclosure of how the spoils of city property were disposed—Zagreb contained one-third of Croatia's prewar industrial base—will inevitably follow, feeding a growing disdain for HDZ corruption.

Still, it is hard to say who faces the bigger crisis: HDZ or the opposition. As political scientist Ivan Grdesic says, "The opposition parties are torn between making deals with each other or with HDZ for a share in power." Put another way: the opposition's coalition-forming bargains, profitable in the dozens of recent electoral victories, are under threat due to the parties' mutual suspicions. Even more worrying is the fact that these fears are often justified: Tudjman is an expert at seducing local opposition figures into switching sides once they win elections.

Trade unions, too, are subject to divide-and-misrule ploys. Union leaders have been slow to realize what is happening to them, being concerned chiefly with assuring that they keep union property acquired during the communist days. (The Social Democrats—meaning the former communists—are also kept passive by Tudjman's threats to confiscate their property.) New unions, sprouting overnight in response to local circumstances— such as particularly corrupt privatization, as in the case of the spring 1995 strikes at Croatia Bus—can grow so quickly as to catch not just management but the government off-balance. Whether or not they can substitute for political activity only time will tell.

If unions do become politically active, Tudjman is ready with a new law on associations that allows private associations to be stripped of property if a compliant court (and most of them are) says they crossed the line into politics. The union movement is also vulnerable to the factionalism HDZ exploits elsewhere. Deep and often bitter rifts have already emerged between unions committed to limited industrial objectives and those that see trade unionism as the essential condition for effective opposition politics. No sooner do union activities spill over into organized politics than the leadership is decapitated, sometimes in mysterious ways, as when the head of the electrician's union was murdered in 1995.

3.2.5 Tudjman's End Game

Still, domestic pressures are growing month by month, and as a result President Tudjman's international diplomacy is likely to become one more suited to his tough-minded temperament than the pacific posturings on regular display since the Dayton accords of 1995. Thus Croatia will probably (if steathily) reject good-neighbor polices toward Bosnia and will do little to stabilize the insecure Bosnia-Croat federation. (Indeed, the reverse is a far more likely outcome.) Moreover, as HDZ electoral prospects continue to dim (at least in terms of the majoritarian control HDZ exercised over the first five years of Croatian independence), to survive Tudjman seems certain to continue narrowing, not widening, the country's democracy.

Nowadays, what matters most in Croatia is power over the army and patronage. Tudjman's Croatia, indeed, seethes with talk of power. There is growing evidence that the logic of HDZ control will require a new concentration of it. Under such a phase, today's pseudoparliament, semifree press, and considerable freedoms of speech may all be treated as expendable relics. The so-called threat of the return of 500,000 Serbian refugees (polls conducted in late 1996 suggested that 50% of Croats strongly object to their return) can be used to fan public fear and so keep HDZ voters in line. And if Croats no longer rally to the "moral crusade" of, say, incorporating Mostar within the homeland, as opposition deputy Bozo Kovacevic puts it, then at least HDZ supporters can be told their ill-gotten property will be seized or that they will be jailed if the party loses control. Such stratagems may be hard to understand for those who see Croatia as an ally. But President Tudjman is not and never has been comprehensible as a postwar European leader. He is a tribal boss, bred on the culture of one-party rule.

Although there are hints that the moral glue of HDZ is dissolving, scant evidence exists that the jittery dynamics of Tudjman's politics are unsustainable. A divided opposition is far from creating the kind of coherent coalition required for a potential bid for power or even the active obstruction that would force Tudjman to deal on terms other than his own. Theories of democratic evolution in Croatia require of their adherents in Western foreign ministries a leap of blind faith. For all its recent traumas and defeats, HDZ has dozens of stratagems unplayed and lines of defense intact—one being the periodic assertion that Croatia itself is doomed.

Croatia's problems are not merely internal. They affect Europe and America as well. Daily, President Tudjman calls the West's bluff, both in Bosnia and at home. In flaunting his refusal to honor the twenty-one conditions agreed to for Council of Europe membership, he has drawn the day nearer when his international critics must choose between putting some teeth into their democratic commitments or snatching at whatever crumbs of reform may drop from the table of a growing authoritarianism. The choice is only made harder in that genuine commitment requires not the pointless gesture of a diplomatic demarche, or a mere delay in accepting a Croatia under Tudjman's thumb into European institutions such as the Council of Europe. The Council of Europe, indeed, granted Croatia membership on October 16, 1996, after a six-month delay during which Tudjman did nothing at all to meet the conditions initially set for membership; sadly, Croatia fell deeper into its slough of authoritarianism during this supposed rebuke, a break with Tudjman that risks a threat to the fragile peace in Bosnia.

The evidence of the past six years is that Europe and the United States are only too glad to evade hard choices, comfortable in the belief that history or the actuarial tables may get them off the hook. History shows no sign of providing such assistance; despite being riddled with cancer, Tudjman was reelected to a second term as president in June 1997. One way or another, the West is going to have to get its hands dirty in Croatia.

4

Solidarity No More

Reinventing Trade Unions

Trade unions are the lost tribes of the postcommunist world. It is difficult to think of any other group or groups of people in the transition countries who think of themselves as literally leftover, or left out, in the way that trade unionists—whether of the state-dominated variety or from the fiercely independent associations, such as Solidarity, that emerged in the turbulence and economic decay of the 1980s—see themselves as being left behind by the breakdown of communism and the beginning of market economics in the postcommunist nations. Governments throughout the region mostly ignore trade unions in their policymaking, an indifference that extends to the vast majority of rank-and-file union members. Many trade unionists, it seems, have lost everything as gargantuan state industries lose their subsidies, become shut down, or (the rarest option) are privatized. The men and women who in the socialist past worked in the coal pits of Siberia and eastern Ukraine, the shipyards of Poland's Baltic Sea, the steel mills of Slovakia—depending on one another to survive—often had no choice but to learn community. Today, such ties often seem to be all these workers have as huge one-factory or one-pit towns become ghost towns, where it is only the people themselves who refuse to die.

Times of wrenching economic change are rarely positive moments for the trade union movement in any society. Recession and uncertainty almost always tip the balance of power between employers and trade unions in the direction of bosses and owners. This is a fact of life both in advanced free-market economies and in the newly liberated economies of Eastern Europe and the former Soviet Union. Today from the Baltic States to the Black Sea, the shop floor is more often worried about holding onto jobs than fattening pay packets. Even correcting for scarce and unreliable statistics, the trend in Poland, Croatia, Latvia, Estonia, the Czech Republic, Slovakia, Slovenia, and elsewhere is for workers voluntarily to leave the unionized state sector to find better-paying jobs in the region's growing and largely nonunion private sector. So unions are being forced to retreat, often chaotically, on many fronts.

Tactics, practices, and work rules that hardened over the long decades of socialist mismanagement are nowadays being scrutinized harshly by governments, bosses, and at times even by trade union leaders. Rank-and-file members often signify their personal lack of faith in the effectiveness and utility of their unions by opting out of trade unions altogether or, at the very least, balking at making any contribution whatsoever to union war chests. The best International Labor Organization (ILO) estimates are that trade union membership has fallen by, on average, at least one-third everywhere in the transition countries. Thus trade unions for the most part cannot effectively:

- increase or even protect the real incomes or the job security of their members;
- strengthen or protect their organizations' complete independence from either government, their employers, or both;
- influence government policy in ways that benefit trade unionists and the wider economy.

Decline in the prestige of unions comes only a short time after they won some of the most notable battles in the breakdown of communism. From Poland's Solidarity to Bulgaria's Podkrepa, to the impromptu strike committees among the coal miners of Russia, Belarus, and Ukraine in 1991, trade unions were at the frontline of change. A leading role in dismantling the socialist state and crafting new societies was taken for granted by union leaders. Everywhere in the region, however, such hopes have been dashed. Disillusion is, perhaps, at its most severe in Poland, where Solidarity's trade union members view the reforms initiated in the early 1990s by a government composed primarily of Solidarity members as a personal betrayal. Split into warring factions, two distinct union federations now claim the mantle of the old Solidarity. Both groupings are open enemies of Solidarity's former political leaders. Indeed, Solidarity's fractious trade unionists, in a strange and ironic twist, nowadays often find themselves, especially at the local and shop-floor level, increasingly allied with their old persecutors in the former state unions. And, as an added paradox, things for which the courageous independent trade unionists of the 1980s fought—the right to bargain, the right to hold free union elections—have contributed mightily to the decline of these independent unions.

Nonetheless, it would be premature to write off trade unions in the transition countries entirely. However far trade unions have fallen in public esteem and membership prestige, the diminishment they have undergone during the transition is not likely to end the matter. After all, numerous organizations regularly live on despite losing the impulses that originally brought them into being. Official trade unionism's very extensiveness under socialism, and the network of services and benefits these hollow unions provided members, assure that no matter how often today's trade unions are dismissed or ignored by governments, unions cannot be done away with easily. But the old socialist functions have so distorted the notion of what a trade union is that many reformers fail to understand their true role in a modern economy. As the historic voice of the worker in the class struggle, unions had to continue to exist in some form even in the erstwhile workers' states of the Soviet empire. Unions, however, could not be accorded any role that was inconsistent with the goals of the state and party.

Under communism, indeed, unions did little or nothing to channel worker sentiment to employers in state industries. Communist-era unions had a greater resemblance to human resource departments of companies than true worker collectives and, as such, were controlled by management, meaning the communist party apparat. Links between unions and social protection schemes (under socialism unions were often the vehicle for delivering pensions and medical benefits) strain prospects for restructuring both state industries and unions as labor leaders fumble their efforts to define their new role. The spring of 1994, for example, saw some of the first effective nationwide protests by labor unions in the Baltic states and the Czech Republic. The issue? It was not wages and work conditions that incited these sudden signs of industrial unrest, but demands for maintaining the extensive retirement pensions established by the old socialist regimes that brought trade unionists massively into the streets.

Faced with membership indifference and the loss of their traditional (if sometimes sham) role in the economy, unions thus have to reevaluate their position in society. Labor's role in transition country politics remains a lingering question. Should unions and union bosses be kept out of political action, only using their power to bargain directly with employers? Will wages, hours, and working conditions be determined through collective negotiations or legislative imposition? These questions carry further implications: whether the goal of economic liberalization and transformation can be carried out without a thoroughgoing reexamination of the purposes of trade unionism as both an institution and an economic actor.

Trade unions affect the rate of employment and investment and the distribution of economic resources. Concentrated union power tends to promote the political and social rule of either a shop floor oligarchy or of tame unions paralyzed by state concerns. Both outcomes distort the market for labor by restricting its supply or by artificially determining its price. Modern industrial economies, in both politics and economics, depend (even in places as strongly pro-union as Austria and Scandinavia) upon a diffusion of union power that enables most industries to act with some degree of independence in reconciling the cost of labor with other costs of production.

Such economic interpretations of trade unions, however, do not fully explain the inner urges and deep-seated emotional patterns that are at the heart of trade unionism everywhere. Every union, even those on a state leash, can acquire in the eyes of the union's rank-and-file members the status of deliverer of benefits and security that otherwise would not exist. In revolutionary times unions may come to seem a bulwark against want and humiliation. So the first impulse of some unionized workers, if confronted by the prospect of forcible change in their union's status or structure, will usually be to resist. This may go some way to explaining the pronounced revival of the state unions in Poland and Bulgaria that had seemed so utterly discredited a short six years ago, with the rank-and-file apparently rallying to these old structures so that they might act as counterweights to governments, supported by the independent unions, that seemed increasingly hostile to labor's supposed interests.

So old debates about the nature of trade unions—their power and their places in industry, many of which have long been settled in the West—are joined anew. The most prominent is the question of the proper relations between trade unions and government. It is generally believed that former president of Romania Ion Iliescu constantly attempted to use trade unions to intimidate his political opponents. Indeed, in the early years of his rule, Iliescu summoned coal miners to come to Bucharest to break up demonstrations against his regime by students at the University of Bucharest. Such manipulation is not confined to the unscrupulous. The Czech Republic's premier, Vaclav Klaus, has embraced trade unions in a new collaboration with government, within which trade unionist opposition to privatization and infla-tion-fighting will be, for the most part, smothered. In both cases trade unions are seen as valuable institutions that can be used to mediate or retard economic transformation.

4.1 Toward a Social Contract

This struggle is symptomatic of a wider problem in the postcom-munist world. Institutions of power and influence that are fully detached from the state are not well developed—indeed, often are nonexistent—in the region. Relations and interaction bet-ween infant institutions (such as independent unions) and the state are often unwanted, unpredictable, or disorganized—some-times all three at once. Yet unions have long played a useful role in the West as channels through which information and pressure can pass, both between the rank-and-file and the managers, and between workers and the government. Trade unions are both interest groups and instruments of communication. As such, how they develop and what functions they assume (or will be permitted to take on in Eastern Europe) will be critical to the process of economic reform in the transition countries.

In establishing the right of workers collectively to offer or withdraw their labor, unions might help to establish the kind of enforceable social contracts long missing in the countries of to-day's postcommunist world. A contract is an agreement reached voluntarily, quid pro quo, and likely therefore to be observed, or in any event, rightfully enforced. Being voluntary, it has the con-sent of the parties involved. The presumption is not only that one party has agreed to what the other party has freely pro-posed, but also that, in the original meaning of the word, all par-ties have consented—that they have thought, felt, and judged the matter both independently and together. Being a contract, the agreement will, presumably, be specific enough to minimize the inevitable quarrels of misunderstanding or ambitious demands that will arise in the course of a contract. It defines what each one of the parties expects of the other. It will say what are the respective rights and duties of workers and managers. The very process of collective bargaining should make industrial relations both regular and regulated, and through such dealing agreed criteria will exist for adjudicating future disputes.

These are some of the essential characteristics of the constitutional free-market system that is only in its infancy in the region. Free markets can prevail only when every person is bound by lawful contracts. Only when people act as they have promised can they truly cooperate, in business or in any other undertaking. Others outside of the agreement can also depend upon this predictable behavior, and the original parties to the agreement can in turn benefit from others depending on the certainty of these agreements. Reaching consensual agreement is a way to inspire what economists call "reputation effects," making bargains explicit so that deviations are subject to detection and redress. These effects are of fundamental significance for groups such as unions and businesses that engage in numerous transactions with other groups and people, for others are assured that they will engage in a predictable way.

Without enforceable agreements of the type just described, there can be no free markets in labor or anything else, at least not for very long. For the antithesis of this bounded freedom is to be at the mercy of those who act arbitrarily. It is not to know what may be done to you. It is to have no right to an accounting and to have scant means of objecting. Despotism and anarchy prevail in those markets where contracts do not exist or are not upheld. Both, fundamentally, are lawless and arbitrary. Indeed, despotism may be defined as the anarchy of lawless rulers, and anarchy as the despotism of lawless crowds.

From their often violent beginnings in the industrial revolution, unions in the West have all but abandoned their role as bulwarks against oppression and have become sophisticated partners in negotiating contracts concerning a wide variety of issues, both at the company level and at the national political level. In the early days of industrialization, for example, the work force could be treated, for the most part, as a homogenous mass. Few classifications were needed. Workforces in a modern economy, however, are highly differentiated. Rules that regulate seniority, pay, promotions, and pensions for these myriad classes of union employees are voluminous. Unilateral application of these rules, no matter how meticulously undertaken, would most likely seem arbitrary or unjust, at least by some. By helping to frame the rules and by participating in their administration through the grievance machinery that trade agreements usually establish, unions serve to mitigate the feeling that such systems are arbitrary or unjust. It is a measure of the importance of this function that, where unions do not exist, good management practice often calls for the development of some substitute device to handle this task.

In helping to prevent discontent and to dampen feelings of alienation, trade unions also remove barriers to the identification of working-class needs and desires—barriers that once contributed to trade union power. Related to this function, indeed, is the role free and independent unions play in a functioning democracy: they channel to the political arena the desires of labor and engage the workers in a constructive dialogue with the owners in a civil and predictable manner. An institutional framework, whether imposed by law or produced by a system of informal dialogues, balances the power of unions and employers and ultimately leads to stability and an environment for economic growth.

Certainly the existence of unions in Eastern Europe and the NIS may make privatization and economic policymaking more difficult to manage. More identities asserted, more obligations demanded, more organizations in the field: all this points to a more tumultuous politics. If the new trade unions are to be viable actors in reinventing their nation's economic order, they will have to begin by renouncing that project.

4.2 Divorce? What Divorce?

When you have a good thing, said the devil in a French proverb, you organize it. All governments, overtly or covertly, directly or at arm's length, influence the shape, scope, and activities of trade unions. On one side stand those who, starting from the presumption that oversight is power, believe that unions, as one of the commanding forces of the economy, must be under the control or at least the direction of the state. On the other side stand those who start from the presumption that power corrupts and so believe that the unrestrainable, infinitely corruptible state should never control any important aspect of the economy. In between these two poles there exists the vast, muddled majority of countries in the industrial democracies and in Eastern Europe and the NIS who appear to believe in something called the mixed economy, but are not at all sure about what sort of ingredient trade unions are or how they can be successfully measured and mixed into the economic whole. In the transition countries, the spectrum of trade unionism does not move easily from political left to right; there is only modest state control of unions in lagging Lithuania, for example, while the flag-waving free marketeers of the Czech Republic have courted a new state oversight of most union activities.

Links between trade unions and transition country governments now fall into two broad camps. Continental Europe's myriad structures, with their goal of reaching social and industrial harmony, provide the first model. Although there is a superstructure of laws that govern trade unionism, detailed oversight of union activity is lacking. Emphasis is placed on links between unions, government, and employers, by which the interests of all are reconciled in a grand compromise. Industry gives to government and labor a role in economic decision making in exchange for cooperation in solving economic problems. Government is seen as a force for reducing the risks to both junior partners by monitoring investment and employment decisions. Close, long-term relations are forged among all three actors as unions are centralized to deal with their partners on a national scale. Each party is apprised of their partners' plans in the course of these relations, which are sometimes facilitated through formal structures for talks, but are more often conveyed through casual points of contact.

The second type of unionism is modelled on the Anglo-American system that channels unions away from politics and toward local shop-floor matters. This is promoted by a legal framework that defines how unions can behave and organize and the manner in which employers may treat them. Norms by which employers recognize unions and engage in negotiation, mediation, and arbitration are set not by direct bargaining between the two parties—as is the case in the tripartite system—but through law, and employer support for "yellow dog" (meaning tame, employer-run) unions are banned outright. Legal penalties for violations underpin this system, usually enforced by the courts. This narrow focus on immediate material gains, indeed, gave rise to George Bernard Shaw's famous quip that "trade unionism is the capitalism of the proletariat."

Why are labor leaders attracted to either system? The attractions of the second model are easy to see. It provides visible checks on the actions of employers and government. In surrendering some freedoms, unions gain a framework by which their existence and activities are recognized and protected. A willingness by trade unionists to restore links to the state is, on the surface, less easy to understand in countries that have just escaped from the claws of the totalitarian state. Bosses, for example, like this form of unionism because it usually establishes industrywide bargaining that insures that rates of pay are more or less the same for the same kinds of work everywhere in the country. Such dealings bring wage matters within the purview of the state, which is usually the guarantor of the bargain. If the bargain can be influenced to meet political concerns or the economic program of the government, then the level of wages is subject ultimately to state control. One answer to the question of why trade unions in the postcommunist world have often favored the corporatist model may reside in the fact that union leaders in Eastern Europe and the NIS fear chaos and unrest no less than government ministers and employers do. They want hands-on involvement in setting national wage and economic policies in order to protect their members' security.

In Estonia, it has not gone unnoticed by the rank-and-file that the former president of the hardline inflation-fighting central bank, Siim Kallas, was in the heady early days of Estonian national independence the head of the Central Association of Estonian Trade Unions. Trade unionists share the anxiety that the transition to a free market, if left to others, will produce only unemployment, misery, and a deepening of revolutionary conditions. When asked some years ago at a conference of central bankers in Chicago why he, a union leader, pursued monetary policies that meant, in effect, the end of industrial subsidies and thus resulted in large numbers of union workers being thrown out of their jobs, Kallas was blunt: "The only real and lasting jobs are those to be found in a real market economy. Work must reflect demand. Our policies protect real jobs that exist, and create the conditions for new jobs to appear." So a working alliance of state, business, and trade union should look like a body of practical men who have something of value to offer each other in confronting revolutionary chaos.

In many countries, these different models exist side-by-side or are fusing together. The characteristics of each model, however, reveal clear indications as to future economic developments in each country.

4.3 In Germany's Shadow

On the surface, trade unions in the Czech Republic—as in other aspects of that country's transformation—appear to be models for the rest of Eastern Europe and the NIS. A big bang of union elections, undertaken within a year of the Velvet Revolution of November 1989, propelled new faces to the top of large unions. The seventeen old communist-era federations were broken into fifty industry-wide unions, and 80% of leaders were dismissed. Free of heavy-handed state control, some Czech unions have become nimble in dealing with corporate bosses. The extent of modernization among Czech unions is remarkable. But they are far from being the sort of truly independent actors that a modernized Czech economy needs.

The problem is structural: the emerging tripartite system—nationwide employer-employee bargaining brokered by the national government—restores the right of Prague bureaucrats to review wage deals and thus influence how labor is allocated. This may stop the cutting of cozy bargains between old state bosses and their union cronies, but it begs to stifle the independence and initiative that privatization is meant to encourage. Wages and work practices are, in theory, negotiated on a national level and frozen. Thus tripartite dealings hold out the possibility that wages will never find their true equilibrium level in an expanding and free-ish labor market.

That the Czech reformers led by Premier Vaclav Klaus saw a need to lure unions into making national bargains is puzzling. Czech trade unions have no recent history of militancy. Unlike in Poland or Bulgaria, where trade unions manned the barricades in the anticommunist demonstrations of 1989, Czech unions (save for some rude public meetings with communist officials during the final days of the old regime) stood on the sidelines. Since 1989, labor peace has prevailed. Falls in GDP and industrial production have scarcely caused unemployment to rise—a neat trick that seems to defy the laws of Keynesian and neoclassical economic gravity. Continued overmanning in state firms, voluntary withdrawal of some workers from the labor market, and fast growth in the labor-intensive private service economy have all contributed to shortening Czech dole queues. Real monthly wages, indeed, have fallen at less than half the level elsewhere in the region (though how far is a subject of fierce dispute among economists).

A soft landing following the implementation in 1990–92 of the Czech privatization and stabilization programs granted the cabinet of Premier Vaclav Klaus freedom to attack labor market rigidities gradually. Fighting inflation was the priority, and to contain the growth of wages as a component in price increases, the government established a corporatist structure that enticed labor peace by (in theory) granting labor a voice in fixing national economic and investment strategy. Underlying this program was a belief that wage restraints can best be delivered by large, centralized unions that do not bid up labor prices as they compete with each other for members. Jeffrey Sachs and Michael Bruno, in their study "The Economics of Worldwide Stagflation," put forth an empirical case for this idea, arguing that "real wage moderation" is only secured by corporatist union structures which are the "key to achieving low inflation and low unemployment."

Tripartite deals inject the state deeply into business decisions: how many people to employ and at what wage. The first Czech tripartite council, in 1990, was formed "to avoid social tension and to create social consensus." Some of its original tasks—reconciling trade unions to privatization, for example—are now obsolete. Other tasks, such as the tripartite's role in achieving long-term wage restraint, remain ill-defined years later. All the while, the tripartite's role is not purely advisory: it has powers to see that its advice is followed. To some of the council's critics, those powers seem punitive. Others believe that they are used misguidedly. Yet some of the council's twenty-one members—seven from unions, seven representing employer groups, and seven from ministries—fret at the institution's impotence.

Disagreements are over purpose. Produced as a compromise in the jittery early days of reform, the tripartite's functions were never made explicit in law. Originally seen as a talking shop, it now resembles a ministry without a portfolio—frequently assured of its importance, in practice unsure of its tasks. The council has three ill-defined functions (ensnaring unions in the web of privatization, enforcing wage restraint, and casting off industrial subsidies), parts of which have been shed by other ministries, parts of which are still uncomfortably shared. In departmental terms, it is an arbitrator, official statistician, and policeman. Each role invites fresh state intrusions in the market.

Judged by publicity, the first Czech tripartite agreement established national consensus. Appearances, however, deceive. The numerical wage goals it announced were not merely aspirations; they were targets that the government intended to meet. Among them:

- minimum wage of KC 2,000 per month;
- the beginnings of an indexation system, with any 1% rise in inflation over a base rise of 5% causing an automatic 1% salary boost;
- an appropriation (never met) of 25% of the budget to public-work projects, small business support, and labor retraining; and
- severance pay fixed at 65% of salary for the first six months, 60% of net salary for the six months following.

These impositions on business and government may have seemed quite bland at the time, but they hint at a system that is nothing of the sort. Complacency about the state of the labor market in the Czech Republic was shattered with the ending of price controls in January 1991. Inflation roared to 58%, so the minimum wage should have risen by 53% in turn. The government balked, holding the minimum at the tripartite's original level of KC 2,000. Similarly, the government reduced the term of severance pay from twelve months to ten months. The benefit was lowered to 60% of salary for the first six months and to 50% of salary for the remaining months. Ostensibly, this was prudent, at least as politics. Union power to inflate salaries and to preserve overmanning seemed routed.

History shows that there are four approaches to try to prevent unions from overwhelming an economy by wage demands: (1) to bribe them by changing policy on other issues to suit their wishes; (2) to push up unemployment and thus to scare unions into submission (this is an absurdly wasteful strategy, and often fails to hurt the most powerful unions, whose jobs are not at risk); (3) to legislate to limit strikes (this can be useful, but can work only if governments are willing to pay the price of curbing unrest); and (4) to resist union demands directly by sacking strikers or, more often, by sitting out or defying the threat of strikes.

Superficially, Klaus resisted. By breaking its word, his cabinet rebuffed wage-driven inflationary pressures. One need only look at the results of Ukraine's tripartite system in the early 1990s to see why such a break was needed. In April 1993, then Prime Minister Leonid Kuchma and twelve trade union leaders agreed to a system that indexed salaries to a level either 1%, 2%, or 3% above inflation. Direct harm was done to the Ukrainian economy in several ways:

- Wage rises were not linked to productivity. This was an incendiary weakness at a time when Ukraine's economy needed a jolt to its competitiveness.

- The automatic nature of the adjustments made union members less conscious of the effects of inflation, as nobody seemed to lose.

Bias toward better protection for the lowest-paid union members means that wage differentials are abridged and incentives weakened. The corollary is that those workers less favored by indexing (mostly the higher-paid ones) are tempted to greater militancy to make sure that the escalator does not sweep others along faster than themselves. With automatic indexation overwhelming any negotiated adjustment, union leaders lose their bargaining role and are therefore pushed toward even more irresponsible demands in the areas of negotiation still open to them. Labor markets are, in effect, annulled because weak sectors and enterprises face the same level of wage increases irrespective of their productivity or ability to pay. Ultimately, governments pass on the burden for all this in the form of ever-mounting inflation.

Such escapes from economic reality are, in essence, escapes from responsibility, so the Klaus government's refusal to adhere to its imprudent agreements seems wise. But retrenchment of the original tripartite's inflationary indexing in the Czech Republic did not bring less rigidity to the labor market; it shifted rigidity elsewhere in the economy. Wages remain controlled in the most regressive way. Officials are tempted to enforce the tripartite in ways that tell whole sets of industries not to increase their wage payments by more than a certain amount, no matter the impact on any individual business or industry.

In a healthy market economy, the amount wages may rise depends on an industry's profitability and productivity, since only then will salary increases not result in inflationary pressures. In inflationary times, however, profitability figures are not reliable, and the government, bent on controlling price increases, pays scant attention to profits. Across-the-board control of wages is what matters. This is not only a blunt instrument: what can be pushed down for political reasons can also be pushed up. Here is the fundamental flaw of corporatist labor relations: wages are transformed from a microeconomic question into one with nationwide political significance on which cabinets can rise and fall.

To shroud this prospect, 1992's tripartite agreement in the Czech Republic omitted specific promises. Vague pledges to be "active" in promoting employment, providing social protection for the young and invalid, and minimizing GDP decline were what replaced them. Yet one commitment was set in concrete. Tripartite wage rulings, like legislative enactments, were made mandatory.

The 1993 tripartite agreement differed little from the previous year. New pledges to implement requalification programs and to find solutions to the growing problem of unemployment in a few hard-hit regions were adopted. The minimum wage, as agreed to in 1992, was adjusted for inflation. A week after the signing of the 1993 agreement, the powerful Prague metro workers rebelled to wrest a 33% wage hike from the government. Premier Klaus denounced the wage increases. What the government gave to the metro workers was taken from other, weaker unions. Wages became a zero-sum game.

4.4 The Limits of Tripartite Deals

Many countries in the region have decided that the best way to minimize union-driven wage inflation is to establish commissions similar to the Czech tripartite council. Latvia and Lithuania, to cite two examples, have both centered their three-handed industrial bargaining around an indexation that pegs wages to a level fixed somewhat below the rate of inflation. Slovakia has made tripartite indexation statutory. In Russia, unions are demanding that the national tripartite council establish quarterly indexing, and it appears that they may get parliamentary backing. In Poland, the tripartite's central wage bargaining has always been something of a sham, but indexation is being talked up by elements of the left-leaning government. The "one federation, one vote" structure of Romania's early attempts at establishing a tripartite council granted disproportionate power to small federations that remained poodles of the Iliescu government. The institution was short-lived as the larger trade unions refused to sit on the commission, but elements of the Iliescu government periodically try to revive the so-called Tripartite Commission on Social Dialogue.

Hungary is the only country where state-enforced wage indexation is on the way out, instead of on the way farther in. The Interest Reconciliation Council (ET), Hungary's version of the tripartite council, was established in August 1990 after the first democratic elections brought the conservative Democratic Forum into power. Unlike in the Czech Republic, Latvia, and Lithuania, the Hungarian government has been scrupulous in not describing its tripartite talks as effectuating an income policy. It prefers to set cash limits on the total sum to be spent on wages and other fixed costs within big industrial firms and to leave the various company boards to take sole responsibility for the pay-round aspects of the tripartite talks.

Nevertheless Hungary has imported the German system of national wage bargaining whole, something supported by Hungarian employers and unionists alike. German-style centralized bargaining in which strong industry-wide unions negotiate with their respective employer associations to set industry agreements on wages and benefits, coupled with influential worker councils, has seemed to work well for decades (though since the early 1990s it appears that it is beginning to break down, even as German-style national wage bargaining is being exported to its eastern neighbors). Social stability and moderate wage hikes were the strengths of the system. Inflationary leapfrog, where workers in one plant leverage their raises relative to others, is avoided through national deals, and union leaders are forced to reckon the impact of salary increases on job prospects. The economist Fritz Scharpf has argued that the corporatist orientation of German unions allows union leaders to focus on the macroeconomic aspects of their wage demands, for their responsibility is to a nationwide membership, not merely to one factory or enterprise.

The commonplace strategy of wage and price stabilization is to hold wage increases within the amounts that can be paid for by gains in productivity. The amount of productivity gain—

the increase in output per worker—becomes known only over time and differs among firms. Industry-wide union bargaining does not settle for what the individual firm can afford, which could mean different wage rates for different firms. Throughout most of the postwar years, this coercive consensus brought Germany lower unemployment than most of its neighbors. This combination of inflationary firewall and employment elixir was the source of its appeal, particularly when "labor" became recognized as a national interest group, a sort of estate of the realm. Here, on issues national in scope, labor is seen as an essential symbolic group and is asked to define its attitudes on all types of policies.

But there may be an irony in the fact that the German system is being adopted in Eastern Europe and the NIS exactly at the moment when it is coming under intense scrutiny in Germany itself. National wage bargaining may have been uniquely suited to a rapidly growing economy: until recently, Germany, reconstructed de novo from the ruins of World War II, did not know the concept of economic retrenchment. Under conditions of more or less uninterrupted growth, the national wage system can assure stability because, even as the national bargaining moderates wage growth (and hence inflation), the system can deliver continuous wage increases based on the growth of the economy. But when sustained economic prosperity ends, the national wage system begins to show some cracks as well since its rigidities no longer allow for a link between wage increases and increased productivity. In times of retrenchment, such as is necessary in Eastern Europe and the NIS, with entire industries to be closed or restructured, the rigid German system does not seem very appropriate.

Indeed, for these and other reasons, the tradition of setting one basic wage agreement for each industry, rather than allowing each company to negotiate its own deal, looks naive in today's Germany as well. So does the practice of authorizing a single union to organize all the professions in a company. For although Germany remains highly industrialized, services, which employ more nonunionized, part-time or white-collar workers, are claiming a bigger share of GDP. As in all countries, unions in Germany find white-collar workers especially hard to organize. Such workers are apt to change jobs more often, which reduces their loyalty to employers and unions alike; require more flexibility in their working hours to deal with customer demands; and often possess bargaining power with employers due to their skill level. High-tech companies also give unions trouble. At Siemens, for example, less than 20% of the high-tech workforce has joined IG Metall, Germany's biggest union. Contrast this with the 70% of workers unionized at steelmaker Krupp. Krupp is in a shrinking part of the German economy, Siemens in a fast-growing one.

The breakdown of the system of national bargaining in the lands of the former East Germany lays the limits of such dealings bare. At first, German reunification looked like a boon for IG Metall and other big unions. It promised four million new members primed with the creed of worker's rights and labor practices in the east. Rising unemployment quickly spread the message within eastern German union branches that wage contracts guaranteeing equality with westerners regardless of productivity only destroy jobs. Wages in eastern German engineering, for example, already two-thirds of western German levels, quickly reached parity with their western counterparts—that is, if they retained or secured a job. Yet eastern German workers, most of them toiling in outmoded factories, produce far less. Companies are screaming for relief. Manufacturers have demanded that IG Metall delay annual pay boosts. The union is obliged to talk about such requests, but not to bend. So rogue wage agreements are spreading.

Some firms have reached agreements with impromptu worker committees that will cut workers' pay to below the level established in the contracts. And this practice is spreading into the heart of German industry. Employees at Germany's main airline, Lufthansa, shocked unions by forgoing pay raises in 1992. As the German economy continues to weaken, other firms will demand the same flexibility. Neither employers nor workers want to dismantle the system of cooperation that has given Germany decades of relative labor peace. Slackening of this model in the wake of both recession and decayed industries of East Germany should be a warning to those who would transfer the German system in total to the countries of Eastern Europe and the NIS.

Corporatism, which from its infancy in Franco's Spain and Leon Blum's France always held grand (and most often grandiose) ambitions for government to shape national investment and employment strategies without the need to assume the real responsibilities of industrial ownership, has insinuated itself into all aspects of Hungarian trade unionism. Not only are minimum wage rates, working hours, and social benefits made mandatory on employers with the consent of the ET through a Ministry of Labor decree, but labor's voice in investment strategy is also codified, though, so far, no teeth have been put in these decisions. ET rulings are not vetted by parliament; they move directly from commission to ministry, where officials can veto the rulings only if they negate the entire tripartite deal for a given year.

Of the ET's ten committees, unions are strongest on the Wage and Labor Committee and on the Labor Market Committee. Both, through the ET statute, grant unions veto over legislation concerning wages and labor, so wage regulations, the wage scale, holidays, and enterprise working conditions are all subject to strict union review. Other ET agreements—on industrial subsidies or special classes for employee share ownership, to cite two examples—are presented to parliament, or the relevant parliamentary standing committee, by the ET board's director. Union leaders have the right to participate in these hearings and to offer their views on the impact of the ET to the economics and budget committees in the legislature. As of mid-1997, trade unions have availed themselves of this opportunity rarely.

It may be that Hungary's trade union bosses do not want to be seen as abusing a good thing. In many ways they have been able to transform the ET into an extraparliamentary chamber. Here is the danger inherent in tripartite structures. By inducing unions into close collaboration with government, labor militancy may be muted, but an expansion of their influence is inevitable. The decision to grant unions a decisive voice in managing the country's social protection funds is an instance of this trend. When the Act on Self-Government of the Social Security Funds was passed in 1992 by the conservative Democratic Forum government, it was never envisioned that a dyed-in-the-pink trade union boss, Sandor Nagy, would become the ET's controlling voice. The tripartite of the previous year, however, had set nationwide union elections as the instruments for choosing the managers for these social security funds. What the government did not reckon on was the speedy revival that Nagy and his discredited trade union comrades would make in public esteem. So rapid was their return from the political dead that, by the time the act passed parliament, the liberal impulse behind it was already out of date.

Understandably, the politically savvy Nagy has used the position to bolster the old-style industrial unionism. Control of the investment purse strings has given him not only a weapon with which to beat back the challenge of new independent unions (as we will see), but powerful influence over investment strategy in most industries.

Unions may now speak to bosses, public and private, not only as employees but as a block of investors. With assets perhaps ten times larger than the country's biggest private investment fund, the First Hungary Fund, Nagy has the potential to push industries in ways that unions want them to be run. Because the enabling act did not mandate a fiduciary duty on the fund's managers to assure an investment strategy based on profitable returns, the fund may wind up muscling enterprise bosses into protecting production and not long-term growth. Worse still, managerial initiative may be stifled by politically motivated meddling.

Throughout 1995, Nagy was careful not to incite fears that the social security funds would become a backdoor to a renewed socialism. Plans for expanding union influence, however, abound. One oft-speculated scheme involves a requirement that privatized industries hand over, in the form of shares, up to 20% of their profits. These would be held by the fund's managers. It appears that Nagy hopes that in time the social insurance fund will become a majority shareholder in (and virtual owner of) many of these companies. Nagy's colleagues are wary, perhaps recognizing the damage a similar scheme did to Sweden's socialists in the 1970s. Mandatory share transfers alarmed the public and contributed mightily to Sweden's socialist party going down in electoral defeat for the first time since World War II.

Other options being bruited about within and without the parliament include:

- a levy on payrolls as well as on profits that would go directly to the social pension fund; the fund then would be empowered to make loans to companies as well as to acquire additional equity holdings.

- encouragement by tax concessions of voluntary purchases by employees of individual shareholdings, with these shares to be vested in the social pension fund.

- a "citizen's fund" to be raised by taxing all but the lowest incomes. Under this plan, each person could switch his or her contributions among several competitive funds managed by the national social pension fund. This sounds like a good scheme for inculcating individual responsibility for preparing a retiree's future, but with Nagy and his cohorts retaining oversight for investment, it may only cede more power to union interests.

Common to all these alternatives is trade union recognition of Hungary's need for capital. Independent unions fear, rightly, that compulsory social security levies will make it impossible for sound enterprises to attract investment and that what is most likely is that lame ducks—the home of Nagy's core union support—will go on being fattened.

What the social insurance debate symbolizes is a common problem created by the nature of tripartite agreements. Union militancy is tamed at the price of granting labor a near-veto over the structure of industrial relations and investments. Consensus becomes conformity to national goals. In the Czech Republic, Hungary, and Latvia, a few trade union leaders have openly questioned this drift toward a comprehensive "social contract" type of pay-tax-prices settlement. With a high percentage of employment remaining in the state sector, it is clear that, no matter how effectively labor peace is achieved through tripartite arrangements, the form of industrial relations being established through such a comprehensive system assures that it will rarely be a game for two private players only.

4.5 Shaped by Law

Countries where unions helped to rewrite the rules of the political game after the revolutions of 1989 (and in the nations of the former USSR after the failed coup against Mikhail Gorbachev in August 1991) have not established powerful tripartite commissions in the manner of the Czech Republic and Hungary. A legal structure for trade union activism that would guarantee union autonomy from the state was a priority that independent trade unionists fought for in their battle against socialist hegemony, and unions in those countries found the Anglo-American model of the legal protection of union independence more attractive. But beware of having desires fulfilled too completely. The paradox of the success of unions like Poland's Solidarity and

Bulgaria's Podkrepa is that in reforming the legal standing of unions, they may have contributed to an unintended revival of the fortunes of the old state trade union organs.

Before the 1930s, American trade unions survived precariously. Only for a few specialty skills, such as the typography trades within newspapers, did genuine trade unionism prevail. In the coal mines, for example, union leaders literally had to fight for their lives against the rage of state police in places such as West Virginia while nascent unions in the lumber and copper industries were stymied by paid vigilantes. Industry resisted unionism not only by boss thuggery, but primarily through the actions of government—often through the action of state militias sent in to factories to protect strikebreakers. Even more effectively, industry was able to use the law and the courts as a means to thwart the labor movement. Under the common law, labor union activity was punishable as a criminal conspiracy. A later and more sophisticated variant of this method allowed union activity to be enjoined as a combination in restraint of trade prohibited by the Sherman Anti-Trust Act.

Franklin Delano Roosevelt's New Deal radically changed the legal framework of labor-management relations, inciting a revolution in trade union activities. For perhaps the first time ever, a national government threw its weight emphatically behind labor's demand to organize. This support was more than verbal. FDR's National Labor Relations Board aggressively enforced the Wagner Act, which guaranteed workers the right to organize and bargain collectively and imposed a duty on employers to bargain with worker's representatives so as to give labor a voice on issues well beyond wages alone. In effect, what the NLRB did was to force, within the framework of law, the sharing of industrial power that union leaders had long been demanding. By defining and extending the range of compulsory bargaining issues, the NLRB brought into union purview not only wages and hours, but holiday and vacation pay, discharge from employment, bonuses, profit sharing, work loads and conditions, subcontracting shop rules, work schedules and rest periods, merit increases, and finally the vital areas of welfare benefits and pensions.

At the base of these governmental actions was a revolution in law. In giving unions these powers, the law was recognizing a set of group rights over and above those held by individuals. These *group* rights took two explicit forms: first, the legal obligation of an employer to bargain collectively with unions; and second, the granting of exclusive representation rights to a single union within a defined bargaining unit. This, plus the growth of various union devices (maintenance-of-membership clauses in contracts, union shops, etc.), gave American unions a legal protection few unions anywhere in the world had known.

Law, as William Forbath argued in his book "Law and the Shaping of the American Labor Movement," provides powerful incentives for narrowing union programs and enticing pragmatism from trade unionists. Unlike the tripartite model of trade unionism, which sets few legal requirements on union structures, the Anglo-American model relies heavily on a detailed legal framework of union activity. Indeed, by fixing how unions may organize (for example, by imposing internal election regulations), behave (for example, by banning coercive practices), and finance themselves, law becomes the fundamental factor in determining trade union legitimacy. Even monopoly unions can be effectively constrained. Laws such as the U.S. National Labor Relations Act established for unions a formal legal status that requires that they be recognized and dealt with by employers. Such laws also limit the application of union power by, for example, checking the ability of unions to collaborate with each other in widening industrial disputes. From Poland's first postcommunist minister of labor, Jacek Kuron, to a series of labor ministers in Bulgaria, to Estonia's union leader-turned central-banker-turned foreign minister Siim Kallas, the thesis has taken hold that labor responsibility is not achieved through a collective bargaining mechanism that relies on trade unions becoming a partner of employers and the state, but stems from a precise legal code that both outlines the limits of union behavior and sets boundaries on union relations with their membership.

By comparison with the tripartite model of trade unionism, the law-oriented Anglo-American model of trade unionism limits day-to-day government involvement in union affairs by establishing a rather meticulous framework of trade union laws and regulations. The truth of the matter is that although American (and now British) trade unions may moan about the limits and obligations that this legal framework imposes upon them, they recognize that these limitations are a trade-off for something most union leaders consider of extreme value. That "something" is the monopoly power that unions acquire—and then preserve—through government sanction.

The reasons for this grant of monopoly power are fairly simple. The primary purpose of market trade unionism is to eliminate wages as a factor in competition. Where an industry is only partly unionized and wages can therefore be utilized as a competitive lever, a union must either impose a monopoly or go under. The pattern of monopoly, however, changes in different markets. In oligopolistic markets—that is, in industries dominated by a few giant firms—unions eliminate wages as a competitive factor by what is called "pattern bargaining," imposing wage agreements that adhere (somewhat akin to tripartite deals) within all firms in the industry. Although in theory, bargaining is still done between one union and one firm, in practice the agreement is industry wide. In highly competitive or small firms, unions step in and provide a structure to the market, often limiting entry by new startup firms.

Here, by recognizing in law monopoly power, an irony intrudes. Democracy is usually thought of as a system that prevents the establishment and exercise of monopoly power. Elections are competitions that, in theory, check the ability of any political party, or politician, to entrench itself in power by offering electors the chance periodically to kick their elected leaders out of office. Union elections often result in the opposite happening, the causes of which we will examine later on. What is clear in American and British labor history is that, when government sets the terms under which unions organize within enterprises, it inevitably places on the union that wins this organizing effort sole authority to act in collective bargaining for the workers in that firm. Afterward, it is almost impossible for workers to change their union affiliations. Competition among big union federations or even individual unions, one of the key elements in most tripartite systems, is nearly nonexistent under this sort of labor regime.

In many ways, particularly in the United States, but also in the Britain of today, where legal reforms initiated by Margaret Thatcher have weakened large national federations in favor of localized union monopolies, the legal system has worked admirably in enticing unions to concentrate on the specific economic concerns of their members. Legal structures imposed by government prevent unions from making destabilizing incursions into politics. Partisan activity has not been banned as unions remain at the heart of the U.S. Democratic Party and Britain's Labour Party. What has been almost totally eliminated (though only recently in Britain and only because of Thatcherite reforms) are the sorts of political strikes and work stoppages that are, despite the embrace of the state, far from uncommon under the tripartite system.

The complex legal patterns governing labor that have prevailed in America ever since the presidency of Franklin Roosevelt were probably not intended explicitly to grant unions the monopoly power previously discussed. Roosevelt's underlying purposes in restructuring American labor relations laws were threefold:

1. to slash the influence of the communist party in the hierarchy of American unions;

2. to cement labor as a viable institution in the nation's economic life, one acting as a political counterweight to large industries;

3. to draw labor into mutually useful long-term relationships with industry and prevent the economic disruption caused by strikes.

Alluring parallel reforms were also offered to industrial bosses in order to entice them into more peaceful dealing with labor. Employers, in theory, would be inclined to establish more trusting relations with unions and not seek to switch their negotiating partners because of short-term objectives.

Insufficiently accountable union leaders are one negative side effect of the monopoly unions that emerge with government blessing; still, if such leaders are not always negotiating wisely, they are usually delivering sufficient goodies to their membership for their failings not to be noted too bitterly. A recent study by Andrei Shleifer and Robert Vishny, entitled "Corruption," warns of the danger such a monopoly system may pose for Eastern Europe. Shleifer and Vishny believe that monopoly power creates an organized and disciplined system of corruption, one perhaps less damaging than a mad scramble where everyone with the slightest bit of influence grabs all he can. They believe that dominant and disciplined monopolists are likely to deliver on any promises they make in exchange for their bribes. Does this mean that monopoly corruption might be anodyne or even helpful? Probably not, say the authors. Corrupt monopolists will most likely encourage economic activities that allow for bribes to be exacted without detection—at the expense of economically more efficient, or possibly more profitable, activities. This has consistently been the charge made against America's penchant for monopoly unions. Untroubled by any prospect of competition from other trade unions, unions such as America's Teamsters (predominantly a truckers' union) have consistently evidenced a pattern of corruption.

Nowadays, the Shleifer and Vishny thesis is put to the test in Eastern Europe. The outlaw status of independent unions during the communist era against the power of the old state unions inspired a focus on the legal aspects of trade union life by both Solidarity and Podkrepa. Ironically, the reforms that they backed raise the specter of replacing the gargantuan communist union monopoly with American-style local union monopolies. After decades of cossetting, it was believed, most of the state union structures had grown fat and lazy. Legal reforms and restrictions would make them vulnerable to penetration, and perhaps replacement, by independent unions. With chilly new drafts of competition wafting through shop floors, some Solidarity and Podkrepa leaders nowadays wonder wistfully about the cozy ties with the state that they have forsaken. Many of these leaders are stunned at the resilience the state structures have shown in the face of legal reforms. Indeed, the most likely candidates for monopoly status under this legal umbrella are the old state unions, who have found the environment created by legal reform highly congenial.

4.6 Unions and the Law

Two objectives animate those countries that have concentrated on legal reforms: (1) to improve the internal workings of the unions, and (2) to protect individuals from being bullied. Industrial relations were to be based on a code of positive rights, guaranteed both to individuals and to collective bodies. In Estonia, it is planned that these rights will be administered through distinct labor courts. Bulgaria is working toward the establishment of statutory tribunals to deal with industrial disputes by compulsory conciliation and arbitration. (This device is usually viewed as a classic anti-union ploy, but in Bulgaria it nevertheless was pushed by Podkrepa in 1994–95 as a way to validate the position of independent unions in the face of continuing state union vitality.)

There is a logic to recasting union immunity in law in line with that accorded to individuals. One of the surprising legacies of socialism was a facade of labor laws that granted unions a startling amount of independence from the law. To be sure, the right to strike was nonexistent, but as bodies, unions were invested with a sham autonomy that theoretically left them outside the bounds of legal appeal for their actions. Under the Anglo-American legal model now being adopted, no longer would unions that order unlawful action be immune from the legal consequences of their decisions.

Contempt for law was one of the prime symptoms of the so-called "British disease," pre-Margaret Thatcher. Indeed, one of the reasons she came into power, in 1979, was a widespread belief that the 1970s had been a decade when unions could abandon contracts and workers could picket without regard to whether or not the picketers had a direct stake in the dispute. British unions then had a unique position, one that many post-communist governments now feared, so Premier Vaclav Klaus suggested to an audience at the Hoover Institution in 1994. As far back as 1875, Britain's trade unions won immunity from prosecution for criminal conspiracy when their acts were "in furtherance of a trade dispute." From 1906 onward, they were protected against liability for civil damages when inducing breaches of employment or interfering with trade. British unions could thus repudiate agreements made by their leaders with impunity. The advantage of making union funds liable to be penalized (a key requirement in making unions as a body responsible for their acts), as shown by the American experience, is not so much that fewer working days are lost, but that strikes become concentrated around the time of renegotiation of an annual wage contract. Because unions and employers both have a greater incentive to reach a settlement at this time, such strikes have a tendency to cause much less economic damage and are also prone to an emphasis on such practical matters as wages and job security.

In 1991, the Polish minister of labor, Jacek Kuron, was tempted by the notion of making immunity for industrial action dependent on secret ballots being held before a strike, if a proportion of the membership called for it. The law he was developing was to hold that unions that had received the balloted sanction of their members for a strike would not have their funds put at risk for any breaches of the law that might arise during the conduct of such a strike. Strikes held without membership voting in support of industrial action, however, would put union funds at risk should a court one day award damages to employers or third parties. When Kuron left the government, his colleagues walked away from this proposal. Still, the labor code that he backed did make unions financially liable for breaches in collective agreements. Given the perilous state of Polish trade unionism's finances, this is potentially a rule with teeth, although at this point it is not enforced.

Moreover, legal codes limit a union's ability to coerce its members. Individuals are protected against being forced into closed shops (a workplace in which all employees must be members of a union) if they genuinely object on grounds of conscience or personal conviction, though an outright ban on closed shops, such as exists in Germany, has not been included in Bulgaria's trade union code. In Poland, 80% of workers in a firm have to agree to any new closed shop; most workplaces, indeed, have competing unions within them. In Estonia and Bulgaria, contracts requiring suppliers or subcontractors to use only union labor have been voided. An attempt to curtail and depoliticize industrial disruption was made by tightening the definition of a trade dispute to which legal immunities apply.

Turning the socialist-inspired system into one of positive rights, so as to bring union behavior into line with most of the Western industrial economies, is necessary in order to push the power of decision making over strikes away from national federations and down to the shop floor, where the consequences of any decision would be most keenly felt as the costs to the membership (and the employer) of industrial action would be direct and immediately known. In theory, more responsible decision making would arise. Legal mandates on union elections form a second path to establishing such responsible action. Results in this, however, are mixed so far. Union governing bodies choose electoral rules suited to secure their own re-election. Scope for abuse is greatest in unions such as the teachers' and civil service branches of Poland's reformed communist-era union Ogolnopolskie Porozumienie Zwiazkow Zawodowych (National Association of Trade Unions, OPZZ), that use the block-vote system. Under the block-vote system, entire votes of a branch union are thrown behind one particular candidate on a straight show-of-hands majority of those who attend a branch meeting. Political activists usually pack such meetings, perhaps intimidating moderates not to attend them, thus swinging the vote behind their often unrepresentative choices.

Extending the practice of secret ballots to unions was one of the means Prime Minister Thatcher used as a supposed cure for this aspect of the British disease, and the use of such ballots has indeed led to some changes in Polish branch union leadership. The theory behind this rule is simple: most union leaders are elected by only a tiny fraction of their members. This would not matter much if these voters were a random sample of the membership, but they seldom are. Instead, voters in union elections tend to be the most politicized members. This often leads to a union leadership unrepresentative of its members. For example, estimates of the political loyalties of Czech trade unionists suggest that 4.6% are clearly leftist; 15.7% are moderately of the left; 46.4% claim to be centrists; 25.5% are moderately of the right; and 7.9% are hard-right in orientation. Although 80% of union leaders are new men, they still do not reflect the diversity of their members. Most are men of the left. To make union leaders accept the obligation of representing their membership fairly, reform of the election system is required. This will probably require the end of shop-floor votes and the establishment of secret ballots.

Despite being the biggest promoter of the reform of trade union laws, Bulgaria's Podkrepa (the independent trade union federation) has been disadvantaged by these reforms in two ways:

1. By law, for a union to gain the right to represent workers in collective bargaining, it must be able to claim a majority of workers in an enterprise as members. With the old membership lists of the communist era, when union registration was mandatory for every worker, safely in the hands of the Konfederatsija na Nezavisimitev Bolgaria (Confederation of Independent Trade Unions in Bulgaria, KNSB), the successor federation to the old state union, Podkrepa usually finds itself outmanned by paper rank-and-file. Though these "dead soul" members can be a drain on KNSB resources, for workers who fail to pay dues are maintained on the lists and are thus entitled to use of the union's social programs, the KNSB keeps them registered as a trump against Podkrepa's ambitions.

2. It is forced into de facto alliances with the KNSB to keep out "yellow dog" unions that some managers seek to build up as the requisite "social partners" that the law on collective bargaining demands.

Deals such as this, however, have gone some way toward fudging the differences between the old unions and the new, for among trade unionists almost everywhere, "yellow dog" unions are the most despised of institutions. Their banning, even in the face of the vast unemployment unleashed by the Great Depression of the 1930s, was one of the first demands put forward by U.S. labor interests as unions sought to participate in the establishment of Franklin Roosevelt's New Deal.

The requirement that a majority of workers must declare their support for the representation of a particular union in their workplace, one of the key provisions pushed by the Polish Solidarity and the Bulgarian Podkrepa, has promoted the revival of the old trade union federations rather than increase independent power. Such majority rules provide added cover to the old state unions' demands for the lion's share of seats at the collective bargaining table. As has been shown, most workers, even if members in the new independent unions, have at least on paper maintained their membership in the old structures, granting these a distinct advantage when membership rolls are tallied in order to decide which union has gained the right to represent a given workplace.

4.7 Legal Limbo

Nobody is quite sure which group, if any, Ukraine's trade union laws of 1995 were intended to favor. Since the fall of the USSR, no new laws on labor or trade unions have been passed. In theory, unions remain governed by the same socialist codes as before, and no trade union group save the Ukrainian Council of Trade Unions—which ceased to exist in 1991—is recognized in the law itself. This holds even for the semiofficial Federation of Trade Unions of Ukraine (FTUU), which inherited the old structures. Despite this inertia, however, many of the dynamics of the legal model of trade union organization are at play. In Bulgaria and Poland, the legal model unintentionally reinvigorated the state union structures; in Ukraine law has been used to openly favor the old, and irredeemably unreformed, union organs.

Although the law has not altogether stopped new unions from forming, legal fictions have real consequences: Ukraine's labor code vests the shell of the old official unions with distributing many social welfare benefits, bonuses, and housing. Pension and medical benefits, too, remain tied to the old union structures. Lures such as these are the lone comparative advantage enjoyed by the government-sponsored federation set up in early 1992 as the successor to the old state union federation. In a society undergoing a wrenching transition, these attractions are enough to prevent independent unions from making headway. Moreover, the law (unlike in other countries of Eastern Europe, as we will see) does not establish any procedures for undertaking collective agreements when more than one union exists in a firm. Where Podkrepa might welcome such silence from the state, Ukraine's free trade unions have seen this loophole used to blacklist them from participating in many talks. State managers and ministers fix deals as they have always done.

Article 252 of the Labor Code seemingly protects trade union officers from employer pressure, but little in Ukrainian labor relations is ever what it seems on the surface to be. Sacking a trade union leader from his job, no matter the cause cited by the employer, can in theory only be achieved with the (unlikely) approval of the local branch of the FTUU. Such protection, however, is afforded only to "official" shop stewards. Other union activists have no standing in law. Therefore, independent trade unionists, and independent union organizers, act with the gun of unemployment pointed constantly at their heads.

With the economy's seemingly ceaseless downturn, cracks in this legal facade are emerging. Some union-state-industry relations, sealed by legal inertia, look less potent than they once did. FTUU leaders in key industries, such as coal mining, are having to compete for member loyalty, particularly as the Independent Trade Union of Miners, headed by Oleksander Myrl, has established its own legitimacy through a series of wildcat strikes it has called periodically since 1991. That legitimacy also comes by ballot. (It is somewhat ironic that the legal mode of reform is being followed in Ukraine in a voluntary manner by a union that exists, for all intents and purposes, outside the law.) Myrl has been scrupulous in establishing a system that can outlast him. Under his guidance union elections are regular and must be contested. Voting is made easy so that at least 50% of paid-up members vote, and candidates for union office must present clear programs detailing their political and economic views. A written manifesto must be posted in union halls by all candidates. Voting, moreover, is secret, and each vote has equal weight, making fraud difficult.

In the eighteen months since Myrl instituted his internal reforms, voting turnout has roughly doubled to 60%, and is even higher in some local contests. It has not altered the political complexion of the union because Myrl's influence is dominant.

Candidates do submit election addresses, but they are normally mere platitudes. Shop steward advice still carries great weight with the rank-and-file. It is significant that the democrats in the union are strongly in favor of secret ballots, and the old communists who have come over to the independent miners are strongly opposed to them.

Details and consequences of government-mandated election practices and a meticulous legal framework for trade union balloting can be varied. Poland's trade union laws have allowed unions to stick to traditional or individual variants, such as mass meetings of the membership or nominations controlled by the current leadership, in choosing their leaders. But the overarching legal framework has secured a final divorce of union and state. The paradox is that in supporting the construction of this legal edifice, Solidarity's trade union elements also helped to revitalize their bitter rivals, the old state union structures. Combat between these two labor camps now swings back and forth, but increasingly Solidarity's former trade union elements find themselves ever more often on the defensive. It is bitterly ironic, but only a few short years after its political triumph, Solidarity's trade unions have not only bolted the political wing of the movement that they once led, but also find their commitment to trade union independence sorely tested as the temptation of alliance with the old-line OPZZ union grows.

4.8 Self-Inflicted Democracy

Here a greater and sharper irony intrudes. In the years of its underground struggle in the 1980s, Solidarity's focus was primarily political; its interest in day-to-day labor concerns waned for the simple reason that outlaw status inhibited its ability to intervene with managers. Usually prone, borrowing Abba Eban's damning description of the Palestine Liberation Organization (PLO), "to take every opportunity to miss an opportunity," Poland's communist leaders on this occasion acted with rare foresight. The trade union law they introduced after the declaration of martial law in 1981 was astonishingly liberal so far as the official union structures were concerned. Many of the union freedoms Solidarity had pushed for in the hectic months of 1980–81 were now accorded the state union structure. Its national leadership of old-time apparatchiks remained despised, but on the local level these state union organs flourished, gaining a kind of grassroots legitimacy.

A splintering between Solidarity and its trade union supporters could be glimpsed even before communism's fall. Solidarity's leaders spent the 1980s fighting daily battles for survival, not contemplating the hard economic choices that would be needed once the fight was over. Its leaders knew that their demands would one day require that the government take steps to reform the economy that would, in turn, hit trade unions hard. That day came with the formation of the first Solidarity government headed by Premier Tadeusz Mazowiecki. Advent of the so-called shock therapy program, designed by Leszek Balcerowicz, the first postcommunist finance minister, brought Solidarity's latent fault-lines to the surface. Even before the Balcerowicz plan bit hard on state subsidies, a radical wing of Solidarity's trade unions seceded. Seeking to usurp the heroic mantle of the Gdansk summer of 1980, one group of rebel unionists boldly proclaimed itself "Solidarity 80," a signal that Solidarity was in rebellion against itself.

In order to insure fair play for Solidarity's trade unions, the Mazowiecki cabinet had erected a strict code for trade union behavior. By dismantling the formal points of contact between the state and the old union structure, the Mazowiecki government was, in theory, leveling the playing field. Neither Solidarity's former trade unions nor the old state organs much liked the sound of this. Both complained that the government had declared war on trade unions and their role in the economy when neither the constitution nor the economic exigencies demanded a decree of divorce. However, the government's position was clear. The law required that all unions operate on the same basis, that is, according to democratic principles, market forces, and obedience to the labor code.

This meant that unions should no longer be run for social and political rather than economic ends. Therein lies the rub: The two union federations that were hived off from Solidarity—NSZZ Solidarity and Solidarity 80—had earned their spurs as political movements. Such political concerns distort union hierarchies, which forsake their commitment to shop-floor interests in search of a higher game. Chronic over-centralization almost inevitably occurs in politically minded unions. A vicious circle is set in motion: more centralization produces increased focus on politics, an increased interest in politics incites a greater amount of centralization.

The implications of these tendencies for NSZZ Solidarity (by far the larger of the two ex-Solidarity groupings) are at the heart of its failure. On the shop floor, workers saw the old communist union structures as more inclined to concentrate on their personal economic concerns. This belief was a direct result of the communist-era legal reforms that allowed for the rise of the OPZZ in the first place. The law that established the OPZZ, so as not to create a nationwide organ with the potential for independent action, expressly placed power in the state union structure at the local level. From day one, OPZZ stewards had restricted horizons. Their focus was, in theory, their local shop floor membership, nothing more, and any political ambitions among its leaders were quashed, at least temporarily, by the communist debacle of 1989 (although they have since revived in the left-of-center Polish government that ruled between 1993 and 1997).

The OPZZ, the successor federation to the old state trade union structures, was well placed to take advantage of NSZZ Solidarity's evident flaws. With Solidarity forced underground throughout the 1980s, the OPZZ had free rein to establish itself and its legitimacy among workers confronting the harsh and declining Polish economy of the time. Industrial connections and loyalties it forged allowed the OPZZ to marginalize NSZZ Solidarity's national importance as it used the labor code's emphasis on democratic legitimacy to turn its independent rival into a minority representative. As in Bulgaria, the Polish labor code demands that a union achieve the loyalty of a majority of workers in an industry or craft in order to represent them. Results have been similar to those in Bulgaria: laws intended to neutralize the old trade unions have been used, instead, to undermine the laws' intended beneficiaries. Because it was severely restricted in its ability to bargain with employers over wages, for wage discipline was being forced nationwide through the "popiwek" tax—a levy on wage boosts above a fixed norm—NSZZ Solidarity found itself competing on the OPZZ's home ground of delivering social services, where its promises of action seemed less credible than those of the old unions.

Between 1993 and 1997, the OPZZ controlled the most powerful interest group and voting bloc in the Polish government, one which a government dominated by ex-communists could ignore only at its peril. In the face of this, however, Solidarity tried to burnish its credentials as a labor movement. How far the group must still go to reclaim its former mantle was amply demonstrated by a forty-day strike at the Huta Warszawa steel mill in 1996. A poll published by Zycue Warszawy revealed that, despite the loss of 1,600 out of 4,900 jobs at the plant, only half the membership supported the strike.

4.9 Divided We Stand

Solidarity's trade union leaders may see their position as jinxed at home—and idealized by free trade unionists throughout the old Soviet empire. At the invitation of an impromptu strike committee, leaders from NSZZ Solidarity's Gdansk region arrived on April 23, 1991, in the capital of Belarus in order to advise that struggling committee on the formation of a free, alternative trade union. The next day, a press bulletin of the Minsk Strike Committee dated April 25, 1991, tells us, two of those leaders—Jerzy Salmonowitcz and Jan Khalas—were expelled from the USSR for "breaking the passport regime."

Minsk's trade union "August of discontent" in 1991 was briefly modernized by an infusion of Solidarity's hard-won political skills. With the help of Bogdan Borusewicz, chairman of the Gdansk Solidarity local, the Minsk Strike Committee came to acquire the only secret printing house in the capital of Belarus by the time of the August putsch against Mikhail Gorbachev of that year. It was this printing house that issued leaflets urging workers to ignore the orders of the coupmakers.

In a modern industrial economy there is usually a coordinated chain of labor institutions through which workers and managers adjust their conflicts. That process may at times seem inefficient and erratic when academically analyzed, and it may well be so complicated that those who make it work do not fully understand why the mechanisms work as they do. People are as often as not unaware of how they do the things they do successfully. But such devices do work, and through them questions are decided—or forgotten, which is also a form of deciding. When another and conflicting chain of institutions provides another and conflicting set of decisions, dual sovereignty exists. Almost everywhere in Eastern Europe, two sets of union federations exist, demanding allegiance. In all these countries the official federation finds opposed to it not merely hostile impromptu strike committees (as in Ukraine and Belarus), but a rival federation, more chaotically organized, perhaps, but more enthusiastic and more able to command obedience from its members. In many cases this rival organization exists in a kind of legal limbo and is without resources, and not all of its leaders, let alone its members, define their aim as supplanting the established structures. Very often, as in Ukraine, they see themselves as merely supplementing it, perhaps also as preserving it in its social purposes (meaning, delivering pensions and medical benefits). Yet a rival sovereignty they are, and the struggle that arises comes down to a struggle between two rival machines.

That the old unions inherit prestige and material benefits goes with their being entrenched, but with that inherited status also goes most of the liabilities of all the old social institutions. Try as they may to alter these legacies, the old unions find them impossible to blot out. The established union is unpopular for the very reason that it is an obvious and responsible continuation of the old regime and, therefore, bears blame for its huge failings. The independent unions face none of these difficulties. Their early growth, usually underground, was due to the prestige they garnered as voices of opposition. They had, as trade unions go, fewer responsibilities. They did not have to use, even temporarily, the worn-out machinery of state labor management. Indeed, they had the great but fleeting advantage of deriving energy from their roots underground.

Predicting the results of this struggle is a tricky business. The very indefiniteness of labor's role causes a sort of derangement in both their structure and their power. Official unions are restricted by their links to the state, while the independent unions find it difficult to offer any constructive role in a socioeconomic system ill-suited to decentralized initiative. This in turns incites enfeeblement verging on paralysis of both independent unions and the old structure.

Independent unions are small, which is paradoxically both the source of their legitimacy and a cause of their problems. The natural tendency of unions is to expand. The theory, as Mancur Olson has explained in his classic study "The Logic of Collective Action," is that "market forces work against any organization that operates in a part of a market." Unions thus have an interest in organizing to make other firms conform to a wage scale. When only a part of an industry is organized, employers retain, in effect, a reserve army of strikebreakers. Moreover, wide federations inevitably seek to control the door to employment in their industry.

Throughout Eastern Europe and the NIS, relations among independent unions are a patchwork affair. Politics, law, organizational incentives, and history all play a part. In Belarus, unions must register with the state and in the locales where they are formed. Republic-wide organs must register in the Ministry of Justice. Such a process gives officials a powerful say over a union's statutes and its ability to affiliate with other unions because registration can be refused or stalled, thus granting favored unions an advantage in establishing majority support in an enterprise. This process has played a crucial role in the reassertion by Belarus' state-controlled union, the FedTUB, of its dominance in union membership.

4.10 Divide and Misrule

Romania's warring trade unions are a classic example of divide and misrule. The violent revolt in 1989 against the Ceausescu regime led to the virtual collapse of the old communist trade union, the Univnea Generala a Syndicatelor din Romania (General Union of Trade Unions in Romania, UGSR), and to a general shakeup of the old structures active in enterprises. A survey conducted by the Romanian Institute for the Quality of Life shows that about half of all enterprise general managers were thrown out of their jobs between December 1989 and February 1990. Little coups like these opened the door for worker activists to engage in all sorts of trade union formation. Unable to put the trade union genie back in the bottle, the government decided to let a thousand unions—and rivalries—bloom.

In Romania, only fifteen people are required to set up a local enterprise union; only two of these locals are needed to begin a federation; and only two federations are necessary to initiate a national confederation that gains the right to sit with the government during meetings that set the National Collective Contract. Such a confederation can be as small as sixty people, a number easily satisfied, and manipulated, during the Iliescu era. (Poland, too, has laws that allow small groups to form independent unions, but these are abused in a different way. The founders of such unions gain immunity from dismissal, so clever workers have used the law as a dodge to secure their jobs in these uncertain times.) Since the violent events of Bucharest in 1989, no less than four major trade union confederations, each boasting over a million members, and countless smaller confederations have been established, unionizing over 60% of the labor force. Each of these unions fights for members and for influence with the government.

As in Poland, Hungary, and Belarus, fights between new unions and successors, by fragmenting union structures into warring political blocs, inhibit the ability of either to show their muscle, with ambiguous economic effects. Managers are forced to deal with a confusing and sometimes conflicting profusion of union bosses. The fight for influence, members, and power often leads to extremism. In Russia, however, competition among federations has set Mancur Olson's thesis on its ear: by subdividing federations, local union branches have invented ways to make the market work for and not against them.

Alliances between unreconstructed industrial managers and the bosses of Russia's old union federations mask a myriad of more pragmatic dealings between local shop stewards and factory bosses, for Russia today is a mosaic of an economy whose component parts fit uneasily together. Trade unions mirror this. National leadership is often stuck in a rut, but fear for the future has made local leaders open to all sorts of change. When Moscow's Moven Ventilator factory, a fish processing plant, found that financing for privatization was stalled by an overvalued asking price set by the state, employees themselves became a source for the capital desperately needed by the management. In September 1990, the plant's shop-floor leaders agreed with managers to transform the enterprise into a joint-stock company, wholly owned by the bosses and workers. The company offered 6,500 shares at 1,000 rubles apiece. Workers could purchase shares with a down payment of only 200 rubles, borrowing the remainder from the company through a generous ten-year loan. Over 360 of the firm's 490 employees became shareholders. They elected a shareholders' (not a workers'!) council to consult with the directors over big decisions.

This local focus has important consequences, given Russian trade unionism's extensive participation in industrial decision making, for Russia's system of codetermination gives workers the right to sit on the supervisory boards of most companies. In many cases local works councils have the right to nominate 50% of the members of a supervisory board, under a chairman nominated by the shareholders. In companies with under 2,000 workers, the works councils are, in theory, entitled to only a third of the seats on the supervisory board. Firtu (Federation of Russian Trade Unions) has been pushing, without much hope of success, for a say in making these nominations, but its power over local stewards has so decayed that Firtu has been able to assert little authority. Important business changes are negotiated with local stewards, not Firtu. Yet if local union leaders reject such plans, managers can still go ahead—so the prevailing system seems simply to be one of asking the unions twice and keeping them informed about decisions.

Privatization, however, is not so attractive to either the Russian bureaucracy or the gargantuan 60-million-member Firtu. Both (rightly) see it as a threat to their existence. Both have done their best to obstruct local buyouts and innovations. Many shop stewards, in response, saw more promise for their members in breaking away from big federations than in trying to convert these leviathans to reform.

Innovation by desperation on the part of shop stewards is leaving Firtu behind. Russia's code on collective bargaining (Part III, Article 6) allows for deals to be struck by any representative body of workers, so ad hoc committees have sought to cut specific deals in their factories. Such activism is protected by law, for not only can workers not be penalized for labor organizing, elected stewards must be permitted free time to carry out their duties. The Labor Code of 1992, like that of Poland's, prohibits elected union leaders from being dismissed from their jobs at any time within two years of their tenure. Moreover, with elections mandatory and closed shops unlawful, Firtu is unable to discipline wayward branches. Firtu seeks to exert pressure the old-fashioned way, by denying social benefits, but with many of these perks in the control of breakaway organs of Firtu, this threat rings hollow.

Unilateral deals are catching on in Russia and elsewhere. Although many are reached only with the gun of plant closure pointed at the heads of managers and local shop stewards, it is likely that more shots would have been fired were Firtu the sole interlocutor for workers. Indeed, in an informal survey of privatized firms conducted by Germany's Cologne-based trade union institute, 80% of privatized firms have collective agreements that do not extend beyond the factory gate. The implications for this rupture are clear: local unions are taking on for themselves the role of establishing viable relations with local managers. To this end, they can reflect in their collective bargains the sorts of specific changes in work rules that Firtu could never bring itself to countenance and can bring innovative methods of introducing employee capital into play. The advent of such deals has led the supervisory councils that Russia's Labor Code mandates in firms undergoing privatization to abandon the obstructionist role that Firtu envisioned for them when it lobbied for their creation. A majority of workers can transfer this supervisory role to a committee of union leaders. Moreover, even in state industries (defined as those in which the government retains 50% of ownership), collective bargaining agreements are increasingly local in their content. Almost 60% of these deals repudiate the power of unions to sack local managers.

Responsible local trade union leadership is a product of a breakdown of national wage and industrial deals. Having declared their independence, local stewards do not take kindly to national union leaders attempting to return and walk away with their power. This will certainly mean that local unions are likely to become more and more competitive as individual firms fight for survival and markets. That may play into the hands of bosses who will pit union against union, but it also promises the benefit of allowing for manager and worker flexibility. Such cooperation may be due more to a survival instinct than to any real conversion to market-oriented unionism. Yet the fact that deals tied to specific local considerations are struck every day (it seems) without backlash is evidence that the breakdown of national negotiations is a powerful recipe for restructuring. In terms of immediate flexibility, local Russian unions look better placed to innovate than almost anywhere else in the region. The generous benefits to insiders offered in the Russian voucher privatization program has led to substantial worker ownership of the newly privatized firms.

But the benefits derived from feuding federations, if experience in Western Europe is anything to go by, can be short-lived. The nearly hundred years' civil war among France's big trade union federations, the communist-run Confederation Generale du Travail (CGT), the socialist Confederation Francaise Democratique (CFDT), and the largely white-collar Force Ouvriere (FO), has hardened negotiating tactics as federations seek desperately to hold on to their members. Disputes among the big federations have dampened worker enthusiasm for trade unionism as a whole. Only 20% of French workers belong to unions, compared to 44% in Britain, with its unitary Trades Union Congress (TUC). (A paltry 12% of workers belong to unions in the United States.) Only one car worker in five at Renault's Paris plant belongs to a union, although Paris is the most unionized region in the country. Moreover, to enhance their allure to members, the three French federations, like rival shopkeepers in cutthroat competition, frequently cut their dues and other charges. Paltry funds, in turn, prevent French unions from both financing long strikes and establishing effective benefit schemes.

Not only are French unions in every industry divided among the rival confederations, but each confederation is constantly plagued by internal ideological splits. The CGT was for decades in the grip of Stalinists, but now it is controlled by a more social-democratic element. While the unions quarrel, French employers are united in one organization, the Patronat. On average, French unions on strike are successful a mere 9% of the time; 38% of strikes end in compromise; and 52% of strikes fall apart or peter out in total defeat.

When ideology dominates, politics rules. The communist CGT was always scared that major strikes would lose votes for the French Communist party. The CFDT, during the term of French president Francois Mitterrand, had similar inhibitions. Battles between the two unions are conducted in excessively ideological language. The CFDT says that the CGT wants bureaucratic centralism unrelated to the needs of average workers, while the CGT accuses the CFDT of propping up capitalism. The Force Ouvriere regards the communists as worse enemies than the employers and so refuses ever to cooperate with the CGT.

Flaws in the French model of trade union organization are clear: political motivation replaces economic interest as the dominant concern. Moreover, national leaders feel compelled to consult with shop stewards, lest the local leaders become turncoats, taking their membership to a rival federation. Such a focus, however, is a source not of moderation but of extremism in negotiations as radical shop stewards gain the whiphand in setting union demands. The checks and balances that promote union responsibility are absent. Local leaders are in direct competition with other shop stewards for influence, and the loudest usually triumphs. Federations, fearful of losing membership to rivals, can risk growing weaker by disciplining shop stewards or caving in to shop-floor demands in search of power.

Throughout Eastern Europe and the NIS, the fast-growing splits in union movements in Poland, Bulgaria, Hungary, and Ukraine, and embittered rivalries elsewhere work to governments' advantage. Private-sector workers want to break the links that keep public-sector wages up through state subsidies. In Poland and Estonia, they are attacking such public-sector privileges as codetermination and indexed pensions, the cost of which are often seen as financed by their personal taxes.

As the rivalries among French federations have locked unions into marriages with political parties, so too battles among rival union groupings are causing trade union leaders actively to seek political alliances. An ILO poll of trade unionists in the region showed that a majority of shop stewards think that union influence on governments is more a matter of politics than economics. As the first priority of many governments now is to counter inflation, the desire of union leaders to keep employment high is apt to cause a falling out even in the most closely allied parties and unions. By early 1996, the honeymoon between Poland's government of ex-communists and the OPZZ was fraying.

With rival federations becoming the rule, it is unlikely that union leaders in the transition countries will continue to believe that their influence depends on ties with a party in power. For the moment, with a government composed of reformed communists in power, leaders in the old state unions find themselves at the heart of policymaking in Hungary. In Poland, Solidarity's leaders were on the other end of the seesaw for years. Estranged from their former political mates, Solidarity's trade union bosses found themselves excluded from all serious governmental discussions of economic policy. Because of the existence of rival federations such as in Poland, the spirit of heavily politicized unions is likely to live on.

4.11 Critical Masses

This essay has highlighted the trade union structures likely to emerge in Eastern Europe and the NIS under the two dominant union regimes present in modern economies. The consequences of adopting either model are significant, not only for trade unionism, but also for shaping the general economic climate. In choosing the corporatist model, nations invariably create a web of connections that draws the state tightly into all sorts of business decisions. In choosing the legal model of trade unionism, governments relinquish some the influence that the corporatist model gives them to moderate and control wage demands, but the ability of unions themselves to fix wages on a national scale is also curtailed.

Both models of unionism, however, through a variety of devices, do limit the impact of market forces on labor prices, though not necessarily in an inefficient manner. The Czech tripartite has so far prevented that country's unions from becoming as influential as, say, Bulgaria's, yet the structure promises over time to grant Czech unions a level of influence found in heavily unionized Germany. As the German corporatist consensus is shattering under the pressure of the very sort of vast restructuring now underway throughout the postcommunist world, there is a danger that Czech tripartite dealings will begin to hinder reform, not enhance it. Poland's once powerful independent union, Solidarity, has diminished itself through legal barriers partly of its own making. Though competition for labor is being introduced everywhere in Eastern Europe because of the creation of private firms and a less-constrained labor market, it will likely take decades for the links among unions, employers, and the state—hardened over the many decades of socialism—to unwind in ways that allow either model to function as intended.

By the crudest measure of trade union strength—membership—it is clear that, no matter the model of trade unionism being adopted, the labor movement is losing ground everywhere in the region. Neither centralized wage bargaining, the core of the corporatist model, nor local shop-floor negotiations, the usual result of the legal model, has aided unions in meeting their main task: raising real wages. In country after country, wage rises are often falling behind the rate of inflation. This is true under the tripartite regime of the Czech Republic as well as in the Polish legal system.

In terms of immediately establishing a vital union structure, the tripartite looks better placed. The dense network of cooperation it engenders may look damaging in the long run, and may very well be, given the likely harsh economic climate of the coming decade, but in buying immediate labor peace it has been worth the price, if the level of foreign direct investment in the Czech Republic can be taken as a sign of affirmation. However, provided the sense of betrayal groups like Solidarity and Podkrepa feel, in the face of legal reforms that have (they believe) curtailed their influence and potential power, does not make them permanently hostile to market economies, shattering nationwide wage bargaining is likely to bring clear long-term benefits. Firms will be able to reckon and control their labor costs at the factory level, not having to worry that higher labor costs from higher-cost regions will be imported to their firms because of a nationwide deal.

The reason behind the limits imposed on trade unions by both models of trade unionism is a classic dictum of democracy: Trust no one with excess power. Trust no single institution, either.

In most free societies, therefore, the great systems of economic life are placed in balance with and against one another, like the three points of a triangle: the state, employers, and labor. No person or party can easily master all three independent centers of economic power, and each has internal interests contrary to the other two. In the struggle for advantage and equilibrium among all three bodies, the hope is that none of the three will gain excessive power.

Trade unions, if given a viable structure and clear demarcation between their responsibilities and those of employers and the government, can liberate, empower, and protect their members. Already underway everywhere in Eastern Europe and the NIS, the revolution in trade union design must be accompanied by many institutional changes that seek to rid unions of the weighty dead hand imposed by socialism that so repressed the economic responsibility of millions of people. This political task, as we have seen, is immense. And the economic task, whereby unions become aware of the sometimes uncomfortable economic consequences of their actions, is of equal importance. Unfortunately, given the haphazard responses (by governments and bosses) to labor concerns evident throughout the region, it is obvious that few political or economic leaders have yet begun to imagine the full practical dimension of a vital trade union movement in a modernized economy. Despite the setbacks to union influence caused by the onset of either reform or economic decay (as in Ukraine), the labor movement in Eastern Europe and the NIS is beginning to take the broad shape that will carry it into the next century. Its leaders, like hard-pressed businessmen in a recessionary economy, are waiting for the upturn.

5

Capital Punishment

Inflation, Banks, and the Transition

In the communist era, the economies of today's transition countries were driven by aged politburos and five-year-plans seemingly written in stone. The regime's ersatz central bankers, credit directives in hand, sat obediently at the side of their printing presses, awaiting the commands of their political masters. Successive shocks in the transition to a free market—industries restructured, property privatized, prices freed, inflation rising—forced the new central bankers who came into being after 1989 out of such slavish passivity, often against their will. At times the financial world they confronted was lawless. Belarus, Kyrgystan, Latvia, Lithuania, Moldova, and Ukraine saw a wild, simultaneous circulation of their new currencies with old Soviet rubles; Croatia, Slovenia, and Macedonia witnessed their new national currencies trading side-by-side for a brief time with dinars from defunct Yugoslavia. From the Elba to the Urals, hyperinflation sometimes raged. So incompetent was Russia's Viktor Gerashchenko at his job directing the country's central bank that Jeffrey Sachs, formerly economics advisor to Boris Yeltsin, called him "the worst governor of a central bank of a major country in history."

After several years of hesitancy, incompetence, and rare boldness, many countries of Eastern Europe and the NIS came to grips with the debilitating legacy left by profligate communist financial systems. New two-tiered banking structures are rising on the rubble of the old unitary monobank systems (where all banking activities were lumped into a single state structure or a series of specialized state-owned banks for agriculture and industry). In the first tier are new central banks (many with formal independence from the ruling government of the day) with far-reaching powers over monetary policy and bank supervision; in the second tier are "new" commercial and savings banks carved from the old state banking monolith, as well as legalized private and foreign banks. The critical problem of inflation has been beaten back in a large number of countries, output decline in some (Russia, Kazakhstan, Lithuania, and Albania) is slowing, and some countries—notably Estonia, Poland, the Czech Republic, Slovakia, and Georgia—have indeed seen their economies grow, some relatively well.

Russia's "Black Tuesday" on October 11, 1994, brought even the wayward and economically illiterate Gerashchenko to heel. That day, the ruble crashed 22% in value against the dollar, after falling 29% in value from September 1 to October 10. Two days later, on October 13, the ruble rebounded by reclaiming 25% of its lost value, though a slow (and continuing) decline began once more in early November.

Central bank action (and inaction), and a realization that root-and-branch reform of national credit systems was needed, caused these wild swings. Through the first half of 1994, Russian inflation fell, due to tough decisions taken by Boris Fyodorov, then finance minister. Industrial subsidies—direct injections from the central bank—were slashed, and the brakes put to printing rubles. By August 1994, inflation had fallen to a monthly rate of 4.7%, a third of its rate eighteen months earlier. Behind this good news, dark clouds gathered. After Prime Minister Viktor Chernomyrdin sacked Fyodorov (and other reformers), the money supply expanded, averaging a growth of 13% per month in the first six months of 1994. Government borrowing zoomed to 18% of GDP by July. These actions precipitated the ruble's collapse, delayed only because Russia's precocious financial markets absorbed this infusion of capital. Russia's lag between expansions in money supply and rises in inflation had roughly tripled from five weeks to five months.

By early September, inflation was back up to 7.7% a month and to 13% one month later. Bloated agricultural and industrial subsidies were revived, and the state deficit mounted. Moreover, the central bank, after first defending the value of the ruble, began to talk its value down, withdrawing from trading in rubles on the Moscow Interbank Currency Exchange. This left Russia's domestic financial market confused and prey to rumors. On October 10, these rumors struck. Whispers were heard that the Russian central bank was selling rubles, thus pushing the currency's value down, and holders of rubles began to sell. The result?

A crash such as Russia had not seen before. Two days later, the central bank restored some of the currency's value through heavy buying of rubles, but the damage was done. A stunned President Yeltsin called for Gerashchenko's head and established an investigatory commission composed of national security officials, not bank and finance ministry bureaucrats. Abandoned by his patron, Prime Minister Chernomyrdin, Gerashchenko resigned, sparing new fights between Yeltsin and the Duma over his dismissal.

Gerashchenko's follies were different in degree, not necessarily in kind, from the mistakes made by many of the region's other new central bankers. Deregulation of prices, de jure and de facto, after communism's collapse incited monetary tumult everywhere. While new opportunities for small private businesses were created, for example, in Poland, life became difficult for big state firms. Many state companies found it hard to react to changing conditions. Confronted by an overnight loss of subsidies at the start of 1990, many Polish state enterprises, for example, raised prices and cut production, instead of cutting costs. As lack of demand further depressed sales, many industries stopped paying their bills. Debts piled up between companies. Although many state-owned enterprises (SOEs) were loss-making businesses, due to their inefficient management, large numbers of employees, and their provision of social services, these firms could not be closed or privatized readily. Loans from commercial banking entities—often tied to firms themselves in many Eastern European and NIS countries—were in reality thinly disguised state subsidies for the SOEs. Most of these were bad loans, but the idea of credit assessment was almost nonexistent. As under socialism, political interests continued to determine credit expansion, fanning the fires of inflation. Feeding on itself, monetizing state and industrial debt inspired hyperinflation in Belarus, Bulgaria, Serbia, and Ukraine and near brushes with it elsewhere.

As table 5.1 shows, by 1995, inflation was retreating in Albania, Estonia, Kyrgyzstan, Latvia, Lithuania, Moldova, Poland, Slovenia, Slovakia, and the Czech Republic, with central banks leading the battle for price stability. Elsewhere, too (notably Romania since the election of Emil Constantinescu as president in late 1996), virulent inflation is waning. Tough fiscal policies in Hungary brought inflation down to around 29% in 1995–96, but

Table 5.1

Changes in Inflation and Output 1989–1994

Inflation (Consumer Prices, Annual Averages)

	1989	1990	1991	1992	1993	1994
Albania	0.0	0.0	36.0	226.0	85.0	20.0
Belarus	1.7	4.5	94.0	969.0	1188.0	1500.0
Bulgaria	6.4	23.9	334.0	82.0	73.0	115.8
Czech Republic	2.3	10.8	56.7	11.1	20.8	11.0
Estonia	6.1	23.1	210.5	1076.0	89.8	47.0
Hungary	17.0	28.9	35.0	23.0	22.5	19.6
Kazakhstan	na	4.2	90.9	1381.0	1517.0	1100.0
Kyrgyzstan	0.0	3.0	85.0	855.0	1209.0	280.0
Latvia	4.7	10.5	124.4	951.2	109.0	36.0
Lithuania	2.1	8.4	225.0	1021.0	390.0	70.0
Macedonia	na	608	115.0	1691.0	244.0	70.0
Moldova	na	4.2	98.0	944.0	789.0	350.0
Poland	251.1	585.8	70.3	43.0	35.3	30.0
Romania	1.1	5.1	174.5	210.9	256.1	125.0
Russia	2.0	5.6	92.7	1354.0	896.0	300.0
Slovakia	2.3	10.8	61.1	9.9	23.2	15.0
Slovenia	1306.0	549.7	117.3	201.3	32.3	18.7
Ukraine	2.2	4.2	91.0	1210.0	4735.0	2000.0

Change in Output (Percentage Change of GDP from Previous Year)

	1989	1990	1991	1992	1993	1994
Albania	9.8	-10.0	-27.1	-9.7	11.0	8.0
Belarus	8.0	-3.0	-1.2	-9.6	-11.6	-30.0
Bulgaria	0.5	-9.1	-11.7	-5.6	-4.2	0.0
Czech Republic	1.4	-0.4	-14.2	-7.1	-0.3	3.0
Estonia	-1.1	-8.1	-11.0	-25.8	-7.8	5.0
Hungary	0.7	-3.5	-11.9	-4.3	-2.3	1.0
Kazakhstan	-0.4	-0.4	-12.0	-13.0	-13.0	-11.0
Kyrgyzstan	3.8	3.2	-5.0	-25.0	-16.0	-10.0
Latvia	6.8	2.9	-8.3	-33.8	-11.7	5.0
Lithuania	1.5	-5.0	-13.1	-37.7	-16.2	4.0
Macedonia	na	-9.9	-10.7	-14.7	-15.2	-8.0
Moldova	8.8	-1.5	-11.9	-25.0	-14.0	-3.0
Poland	0.2	-11.6	-7.6	1.5	3.8	4.5
Romania	-5.8	-5.6	-12.9	-13.6	1.0	0.0
Russia	na	na	-9.0	-19.0	-12.0	-12.0
Slovakia	1.4	-0.4	-14.5	-7.0	-4.1	1.0
Slovenia	-1.8	-4.7	-8.1	-5.4	1.3	4.0
Ukraine	4.1	-3.4	-12.0	-17.0	-14.0	-20.0

Source: EBRD, Transition Report, 1994; National Statistics; EIU.

chronic budget deficits trap its economy in a treadmill. Even Ukraine, after the longest period of hyperinflation in this century, is at last tackling its inflationary demons.

Darkness is lifting as governments and central bankers work to establish coherent monetary orders and stable currencies. Central bankers, indeed, often have no choice but to reform. Many Eastern European countries—as a shocked Gerashchenko discovered—now have "unofficial" governors, the financial markets, the strongest constraint on what a central bank can do. Faced with monetary and fiscal measures that they think will cause more inflation, financial markets (both official and black market) can push down exchange rates, or push up interest rates, or both, as Russia experienced. If Eastern Europe's central banks are now more concerned with monetary restraint, it is because financial markets have made them so.

The same is true about the concern over the health of national banking systems. Even when not directly involved in establishing the commercial system, central bankers cannot be indifferent to the changes being wrought: some of these changes have profound implications for the whole monetary system. Ukrainian banks set up by industrialists, for example, inappropriately lend massive amounts back to the same loss-making enterprise that established them. This phenomenon is not unique to Ukraine. After years of bungling its supervisory role, in 1995 the Bulgarian central bank restricted the banking license of the Bulgarian Business Bank after that bank was caught making large illegal loans to companies owned by relatives of the bank's largest shareholder and executive director, a Mr. Kitov. If central bankers are unable to put such practices to an end—and in Ukraine it appears that, into January 1995, they were not even trying—the banking system may very well collapse, taking the central bank with it. Indeed, so desperate did Bulgaria's finances become that in July 1997, it was forced to junk its central bank in favor of a currency board, the workings of which will be described later.

So central banks must get their hands dirty in overseeing the commercial banking system. Although it is not the purpose of this essay to look into reform of commercial banking systems, a quick look at the state of commercial bank reform is warranted. Look at table 5.2 to get a snapshot of how well Eastern Europe has been reforming its banking systems. The EBRD has graded Eastern Europe's infant financial systems on the quality of their efforts at banking reform. Countries with good marks happen to be those that enjoy low inflation and, more telling, independent central banks.

Many of today's new breed of central bankers, said the *Economist* on February 3, 1996, are blunt outsiders: Marat Sultanoz, the head of Kyrgyzstan's central bank, is barely in his 30's; Einars Repse, governor of the Latvian central bank, is reput-

Table 5.2

EBRD Grades Bank Reform

Albania	2
Belarus	1
Bulgaria	2
Czech Republic	3
Estonia	3
Hungary	3
Kazakhstan	1
Kyrgyzstan	2
Latvia	3
Lithuania	2
Macedonia	2
Moldova	2
Poland	3
Romania	2
Russia	2
Slovakia	3
Slovenia	3
Ukraine	1

Key:

4 = Well-functioning banking competition and prudential supervision.

3 = Substantial progress on bank recapitalization, bank auditing, and establishment of a functioning prudential supervisory system; significant presence of private banks; full interest rate liberalization with little preferential access to cheap refinancing.

2 = Interest rates significantly influencing the allocation of credit.

1 = Little progress beyond establishment of a two-tier banking system.

Source: EBRD, Transition Report, 1994.

ed to make Milton Friedman seem like a Keynesian; Hanna Gronkiewicz-Walz, one-time head of Poland's central bank, saw nothing wrong with running for the Polish presidency in her spare time in 1995.

Puzzling many, central banks assumed potent roles in the search for price stability even as they reinvented themselves as guardians of financial order. In Estonia and Albania, and even in go-slow Bulgaria, they have not had to wrest independence from reluctant states, the historical pattern in Western economies. Instead, politicians surrendered power over central banks, hoping that independence would permit the bank to impose monetary and thus budgetary discipline. Given uncertain economic conditions in Eastern Europe, considerable political and interest group pressure is aimed at central banks, usually to demand postponing interest rate hikes or to protest cuts in subsidized credits. These fights are the background to the campaign to determine how much independence central banks should have and the limits and uses of this independence. Should central banks be vested by law to achieve price stability, damn the political consequences? Should central banks be provided with the autonomy and freedom from government interference necessary to achieve this end? Given such freedom, can central banks be made democratically accountable? Answers to these questions will have a profound impact on the entire region.

5.1 Plumbers

Under socialism, central banks existed in name only. Credit was controlled and allocated by central planners, just like steel or any other commodity. Hungary, in 1987, divided its monobank into a central bank and five separate state-owned commercial banks, but credits never ceased to be centrally directed. Everywhere in the region, interest rates were set by official fiat, not by the market, and reflected the industrial and agricultural priorities of planners, not the availability of credit or the attractiveness of investments. Moreover, because profits were expropriated and capital markets were virtually nonexistent, firms almost exclusively used bank credit to finance investment. In fact, firms had an incentive to borrow indiscriminately as past borrowing and the right political connections were often used as a benchmark to allocate new credit. Since profits were calculated as a percentage of total costs, large finance costs served to increase the paper profits of a firm, making the temptation for industry to borrow from the state monobank nearly irresistible. As long as socialism lingered, the monobank system had as its primary duty the issuing of credit to meet government production schedules, not to establish a stable financial order.

Just a few years ago, administrative credit allocation remained as common in Eastern Europe as it was rare in modern free-market economies, though some countries, notably those in the Visegrad group and in the Baltics, began (for the most part) to wean themselves off the practice soon after communism's end. Banks are usually required to lend to "priority sectors," an expansive term that can include small farmers, large farmers, small businesses, state businesses, exporters, and others. Each group is deemed deserving enough to pay "special" (that is, subsidized) rates of interest.

This has two results: (1) central banks find it hard to control monetary growth; and (2) whenever central banks try to control growth, priority sectors run to friends in government to get their cheap credit restored. Confusion over who is in charge of monetary policy leads to price instability. The ravages of inflation have forced countries throughout Eastern Europe and the NIS—some reluctantly, some with evident enthusiasm—to reinvent their central banks in line with those found in capitalist economies, where the central bank usually has primary authority over monetary policy.

5.2 An Ideal World

In an ideal world central bank governors would be invisible. Just as John Maynard Keynes wanted economists "to get themselves thought of as humble, competent people, on a level with dentists," so central bankers would gain little acclaim if they managed decades of no inflation, low interest rates, and stable banking. Most come to the fore only when things go horribly wrong. A smoothly working monetary system, indeed, is like plumbing: you appreciate its value only when it leaks. Routine maintenance imposes on a central bank six key tasks:

1. *Control of monetary policy.* Central banks monitor and control changes in the money supply—the amount of money in circulation at any given time—and in the supply of credit available to firms and individuals.

2. *Banker to the government.* Governments are big business-es with huge budgets. In modern free-market economies, public spending on goods and services typically accounts for 20–30% of total GDP (much more if transfer payments—pensions, indus-trial subsidies, and so on—are included). A government deposits its revenues with the central bank and pays its bill with central bank checks.

Because central banks stand uncomfortably at the point where a country's fiscal and monetary policy meet, they must insure that government has the money it needs in order to pay its bills; in any one year, that can mean periodic borrowing whenever a country's revenue and spending patterns are not in balance. Most transition countries now regularly run budget deficits, and public debt is rising as a proportion of GDP in most of them. The size of a government's borrowing, and the way it is financed, affects the rate of monetary growth in a country. So the region's central banks face a tricky task: they must control growth in the money supply while also striving to finance large public-sector borrowing. In Western economies central banks finance government deficits in a variety of ways:

- *Tap.* Bonds are offered for sale at an announced price and yield; if they are not bought on the day of issue, the government holds on to them, selling them drip-by-drip. This involves the central bank judging what inter-est rate will appeal to the market; if it underestimates the rate, it may sell very little and eventually be forced to change the terms. If it pitches the rate too high, it will sell all the bonds but at an unnecessarily high cost to the government (that is, future generations of tax-payers will be forced to pay the interest).

- *Tender.* The central bank announces that it intends to sell a certain number of bonds on a particular day and invites offers. It then allocates all the bonds to the high-est bidders. This approach, widely used in the United States, has one obvious virtue: the government can always be sure of getting the financing it needs. But there is corresponding uncertainty about the price it will receive and therefore the interest rate it will have to pay; if governments have any interest rate objectives (if only, for example, not to cause wide fluctuations), they are unhappy with a tender arrangement. Britain tries to get around this by announcing a minimum price for a government bond. If the issue is oversubscribed, it will go to the highest bidders; otherwise, others are allocated their orders at the minimum price.

- *Underwritten Issue.* Halfway between tap and tender, this method requires some institutions that agree, for a fee, to take up (or "underwrite") any unsold government securities. (When companies issue shares, they invariably employ underwriters, usually investment banks, to act as "buyer of last resort.") The problem is that, even in the West, there are not that many institutions with the financial muscle—or the inclination—to do the underwriting job. Japan is the exception; its credit banks have a near exclusive "right" to buy government paper (a right which is also a duty that they cannot refuse). In return, they receive certain tax and interest-rate privileges.

The trouble with all three methods of financing government deficits through the sale of state bonds is that such sales may crowd out commercial bank lending to enterprises.

3. *Banker to the banks.* The central bank takes deposits from commercial banks and lends to them. This function is partly concerned with monetary policy, but also has a vital prudential aspect. The central bank acts as "lender of last resort," that is, it stands ready to provide any bank with cash should its customers want to withdraw their deposits suddenly. However unlikely this prospect may be (and it is less unlikely in the unstable atmosphere of Eastern Europe and the NIS), no bank could redeem deposits for more than a few hours unless it knew that the central bank would, as a last resort, provide it with emergency cash. (Nor, for that matter, would customers be prepared to put money into a bank unless they knew they could withdraw it.)

4. *Banking supervision.* Central banks usually have a major say over who can operate as a bank or other deposit-taking body. They check bank returns and, either by law or gentle arm-twisting, force financial institutions to meet standards that protect depositors. In some countries, the central bank is not the only (or even the main) body responsible for regulating commercial banks. The United States, for example, divides authority among the Federal Reserve Bank system (the central bank), the

Comptroller of the Currency, and the Federal Deposit Insurance Corporation; individual American states also have their own supervisory organs for banks chartered in the state.

5. *Currency issue.* Designing, printing, issuing, and withdrawing notes (and often coins as well) is usually the job of the central bank. Inflation increases this work: more notes must be printed and distributed.

6. *Managing foreign exchange reserves.* The central bank, often with the advice of the Ministry of Finance, intervenes in currency markets to affect the exchange rate of the national currency.

Many, if not all, of the transition countries' central banks are also burdened with a seventh key task: *managing relations with the International Monetary Fund (IMF).* Here the central bank sometimes seems caught in the middle of a never-ending dispute: it must convince the IMF that the policies it and the government are pursuing are serious efforts that will bring down inflation and thus are worth the IMF risking a loan to the country in question, but at the same time the bank must accommodate its own government, which would like to have more fiscal leeway than the IMF is willing to live with. Despite this dilemma, the matter of dealing with the IMF has enhanced the status of central banks because they often are the IMF's main negotiating partner.

It is not by chance that control of monetary policy leads the list of central bank duties: it is one that makes central banks powerful, and thus controversial, because they directly and indirectly influence the aggregate amount of money and credit in the financial system. But managing the money supply is also the most difficult of a central bank's tasks. As money comes in a variety of forms, even determining the money supply itself is a complex task (see box 5.1). Indeed, in a modern banking system characterized by a number of independent lending institutions, controlling the supply of credit is as much an art as it is a science. Moreover, there exist wide differences of opinion among economists concerning how the supply of money and credit should be managed.

Box 5.1

Measuring Money Supply

Circumstances in Eastern Europe make managing the money supply an even bigger headache for central bankers there than elsewhere. Russia, Poland, and Hungary, among others, were all saddled by the old communist regimes with huge foreign debt obligations. Since communism's fall, budget deficits have ballooned everywhere but in Estonia and the Czech Republic. So central banks have often been called upon to fill the breach.

Take the case of Hungary. Massively indebted to Western economies, burdened with huge transfer payments (for example, to pensioners), the Hungarian government's public-sector borrowing requirements dwarf the ability of the country's credit markets. But the government cannot borrow easily on international credit markets to meet its debt obligations—its bonds would be rated poorly and thus have to carry a crippling rate of interest. As a result, government covets all domestic savings and has little interest in stimulating commercial banking or equity markets that might emerge as rivals to it for credit. Given capital controls and a tiny public equity market, government bonds and bank deposits are, other than investment in one's own enterprise, the only repositories for savings. By putting pressure on banks to improve the quality of their portfolios, the state puts pressure on them to invest more and more of their capital in state obligations. The result? In 1992, Hungary's government absorbed 47.1% of all domestic savings, a figure even more daunting when compared with the 2.9% of savings that the Czech government absorbed.

Russia faces a similar fate. To finance huge budget deficits, its Ministry of Finance sold an ever-increasing number of state bonds. The revamped 1995-96 budget, for example, reading in the Duma, sought to finance future budget government deficits primarily through government bond issues, rather than the usual, and highly inflationary, device of borrowing from the central bank. Heralded as a major step in solving Russia's fiscal and monetary problems, such bond sales are usually of little help unless a government controls its spending and the central bank slashes monetary expansion. Similar to the situation in Hungary, Russian government bonds have continued to out-price other investments and thus soak up domestic savings.

As in Russia, bond issues are often not enough to satisfy other Eastern European governments' insatiable demand for money to finance their expenditures. They demand that the central banks directly fund their deficits; this "monetization" is the root cause of the high rates of inflation that brought such countries as Belarus and Ukraine to near ruin. To prevent this, for a time Bulgaria, Hungary, the Czech Republic, and Slovakia fixed central bank credits to the government at no more than 3-5% of budget revenues (although Slovakia's prime minister, Vladimir Meciar, put pressure on the Slovak National Bank to provide his government with cheap credits); the National Bank of Romania (NBR), was also not supposed to be a mere cash cow, but even under the fiscally wayward presidency of Ion Iliescu, credits to the state were supposedly limited by law not to exceed either 10% of the national budget or twice the NBR's operating capital.

Such roadblocks are readily circumvented. Indeed, says the Austrian economist Eduard Hochreiter in his study "Central Banking in Economies in Transition," the Hungarian parliament, in December 1993, raised the maximum legally permissible public debt ratio for 1994 from Ft 50 billion (4% of projected revenues) to Ft 80 billion and did something similar in 1995.

In Bulgaria, according to Hochreiter, "the Law on Updating the 1991 State Budget (July 18, 1991) provided that up to 50% of the 1991 budget deficit be financed through a National Bank credit in violation of National Bank Law provisions. The compromise decision through short-term advances extended every three months. At the end of 1991, the total amount of credit received was transformed into a credit with a 10-year term."

5.3 The Theoretical World: Monetarism

In recent times, debates about the conduct of monetary policy have been dominated by Milton Friedman and the doctrine of monetarism that is linked to his name. "True" monetarism boils down to three propositions:

1. *Fiscal expansion (that is, increased spending by government) has no independent effect on prices or on the level (as distinct from the composition) of output.* It has an impact solely to the extent that the central bank turns it into money (thus increasing the money supply). Not long ago this idea was economic heresy, for it was assumed that monetary policy has a permanent and profound effect on the day-to-day economy. In particular, it was believed that there was a permanent trade-off between the rates of unemployment and inflation.

2. *Monetary growth has only a transitory influence on output and employment but has a permanent influence on prices.* This means that you cannot increase the overall level of employment, over the long run, by the simple act of turning on the currency printing presses. Here is a lesson governments find hard to learn, for they are often interested in short-term effects and prefer to act in line with Keynes' famous quip that "in the long run, we are all dead."

3. *The velocity of circulation—the amount of spending financed by a currency unit—is stable, or anyway, changes at a predictable rate.*

Monetary growth comes about through a complicated interaction between the central bank, commercial banks, and the public. For example, suppose a central bank issues an extra amount of dollars, D-marks, or local currency. These are then deposited with a commercial bank. If the public demands it, this cash can then be on-lent and redeposited in a multiple monetary expansion constrained only by rules requiring banks to hold reserves against a certain proportion of their liabilities (that is, their loans). If, for example, this ration is 1:10, the banks may on-lend 90% of their deposits, and the total monetary expansion may be ten times the original increase in cash. So a bank's ability to "create" money is limited by its ability to secure sufficient reserves of the required type. Central banks manipulate the monetary expansion—this system of on-lending just discussed— by shifting the reserve requirements that banks must honor and by raising or by lowering interest rates they must pay the central bank to secure additional reserves. In the advanced economies, central banks can also alter the supply of money by buying and selling government securities through "open market operations." In Eastern Europe and the NIS, where securities markets are in their infancy and setting interest rates is very difficult, the favored option, up to now, is to manipulate reserve requirements, which is the most direct way of controlling the money supply.

The amount of money in circulation and its velocity help to determine prices. What monetarists argue is that, because changes in the money supply have no long-term impact on the level of output and employment and affect only the price level, any attempts by central banks to play with monetary policy will confuse financial markets and lead to unstable prices. Not trusting politicians or even independent central bankers, monetarists advocate strict monetary rules obliging central bankers to keep the money supply growing at a steady, unvarying rate, and certainly no faster than the economy's growth in real output.

Many outsiders assume that most central bankers are paid-up members of the Milton Friedman fan club. This belief has been extended to Eastern Europe, particularly in those countries that made fighting inflation a watchword. Some criticisms leveled at tight monetary policy advocates are usually exaggerated or unfair. Monetary policy becomes synonymous with monetarism and is equated with callous disregard for unemployment, bankruptcies, and high interest rates. Politicians make monetary policy a scapegoat for their fiscal failings. Businessmen and trade unionists would sooner blame central banks than reform labor markets. However, among Eastern Europe and NIS's central bankers and their advisors, the number of true monetarists is negligible.

On every point in the Friedmanite program, most economists would insist on caveats or flatly disagree. Some think that larger budget deficits financed by selling government bonds can expand economic activity, and even doubters concede that the initial boost to growth may last for several years. More importantly, some think that velocity shifts unpredictably, so a straitjacket of monetary rules will not lead to steady, inflation-free growth.

5.4 The Real World: Discretion

Indeed, rather than follow strict "monetarist" rules, most central bankers today practice discretionary monetary policy. The U. S. Federal Reserve Board is the best example of this. It switched from operating via interest rates to a form of monetary base control and back again; has introduced new targets for domestic debt (excluding financial institutions) and suspended old ones; pays attention to the real growth in the economy; and is painfully aware that American interest rates echo around the world. In most respects, but primarily because the U.S. dollar remains the world's predominant reserve currency, the Federal Reserve Board is the closest thing the world has to a central bank. (In Eastern Europe, Germany's Bundesbank, because many countries peg their currencies to the D-mark, often plays a dominant role.)

The Fed applies discretion to one issue in particular: the meaning of monetary statistics at a time of structural change in the world financial order. With new financial instruments invented almost daily, there is great uncertainty about the velocity of money and its consequent links with prices and output.

The fear is that monetary controls are no longer what they seem, and a central bank that does not use its experience to look beyond them may do its country no favor. But discretion is not secrecy, which is a problem almost everywhere in Eastern Europe. The Fed's great virtue is that it explains what it is doing and publishes the minutes of meetings of its open market committee, where policy on interest rates is decided. Financial markets are not kept in the dark, and what is sometimes criticized as Wall Street's obsession with monetary policy is better seen as healthy debate on a vital subject. In most transition countries, alas, the discretion of central bankers too often means that decisions reached by closed minds remain behind closed doors.

5.5 Monetary Restraint

Agnostic as they may be about choosing between monetarism or the discretionary path, Eastern Europe's central bankers must act to control the supply of money. Many in the region accept that inflation is bad for financial stability, probably bad for the real economy (especially investment in new business), and must be treated by monetary restraint. Raising interest rates is not enough, for rising inflation also pushes up interest rates, making it hard to judge whether monetary policy is really tightening or just reflecting past laxity.

The leading central banks in Eastern Europe—Poland's, the Czech Republic's, Hungary's, and those in the Baltics—therefore adopted targets for monetary growth, much in line with that prescribed by the monetarists. They may have doubted how easy it would be to hit their targets, and some central banks have preferred the vague term "guidelines" for this policy. But most acted as if they believed that formal policy restraints would both reassure financial markets (and the IMF) that inflation would not be allowed to keep rising and also persuade businessmen and workers to moderate their price- and wage-setting behavior because their excesses would no longer be financed by the central bank printing money.

Each country has encountered numerous difficulties in both defining and trying to hit its monetary targets. Which definition of money should it choose, and what to do if M1 and M2 and M3 are growing at different rates? (Indeed, when interest rates are rising, for example, bank deposits are switched out of low-interest accounts and into accounts that garner higher rates of interest.) And what to do when monetary control clashes with other objectives, such as a stable exchange rate? But, worst of all, in countries where inflation has become strongly embedded, what is to be done when, rather than prices taking the strain of monetary control, the quantity of production takes the hit, and a slump results, is prolonged, or deepens?

Monetarists believe that this will only be a short-term effect until price inflation subsides under the influence of firm monetary control. But where inflation is high—as in Russia, Belarus, Ukraine, and Bulgaria—and industrial lobbies can push the central bank into printing money to keep decrepit old industries afloat, the clash with monetary controls can be a painful one, or monetary control may break, as it did in Russia.

In Eastern Europe, only the Czech Republic and Estonia have come close to hitting their monetary targets, for reasons that will become clear later. Most of the others missed badly. This creates a problem known as *base drift:* if the money supply ends up above its target ceiling, what should be used as the starting point for the next target? Governments can either treat last year's excess in monetary growth as water under the bridge or scale down the percentage increase to be allowed in the next period so that growth over, for example, two years does not exceed the sum of the intended growth that was targeted for the two years at the start. Often targets are "rolled over" (expanded) before they reach the end of their natural life. But if the money supply is way outside its target range, "rolling over" the same growth target may amount to considerable relaxation of the original target. This issue is exceedingly relevant in Eastern Europe today. Russia's central bank under Gerashchenko set monetary targets of under 7% per month in 1994, for example, and this was lowered even more in 1995. But throughout 1994, monetary growth was more than triple the target level each month.

Base drift is one example of the difficulties postcommunist central banks experience in seeking to enforce monetary control. Throughout the region, month by month, the money supply moves erratically—sometimes falling below its intended floor (Albania in the spring of 1994, for example, or Latvia that summer) and then rising through its ceiling within the space of three months. In themselves, these fluctuations need not mean a failure of control, but they unsettle financial markets and make it difficult for central banks to judge how close they are to achieving their longer-term monetary goals. Hence, the intense debate in Eastern Europe and the NIS about the best methods of monetary control.

How effective central banks are in performing their tasks is largely a function of their relations to the central government. As we have seen, supporters of monetary targets claim that part of their value lies in limiting the discretionary power of central bankers and governments. The argument is similar to that made for written constitutions: "Better to have rule by law than by men." In fact, even with monetary targets, most central bankers—and postcommunist ones are no different—insist on using their judgment to interpret monetary developments, sometimes with startling results.

5.6 Set Them Free

Financial markets (always) and central bankers (sometimes) demand monetary restraint. Politicians are not inclined to listen, unless financial markets make them. How is it possible to insure that monetary policy is properly directed? As we have seen, openness about the goals of the central bank is one key; independence for the central bank is the other.

A study entitled "Modern Central Banking," presented in 1994 by the IMF's Stanley Fischer at a celebration marking the Bank of England's 300th birthday, makes the case that statutory central bank freedom to conduct monetary policy is a key to keeping inflation low. Briefly, here is Fischer's argument. Inflation higher than 1–3% per year carries a cost that demands action. Until inflation rises well above 5%, the cost to the economy is containable. But economic policy contains a bias toward increasing inflation. Governments can increase their purchasing power by coercing the central bank to print money. This increases the money supply and decreases the value of money held by the population. Thus, inflation is a form of taxation, and a stealthy one at that. For this very reason, it is also very attractive to governments: they can effectively raise taxes without unpopular legislation explicitly boosting the tax rates. Not surprisingly, such creeping taxation tends to be used to excess.

"Dynamic inconsistency," says Fischer, is another cause of inflation. By this he means the tendency of governments not to keep their promises. Suppose one promises to keep inflation low. If workers and enterprises believe it, they will set prices and conclude contracts accordingly. But after they do so, a government that wants to increase output has an incentive to squeeze a burst of temporary growth out of the economy by arranging an "inflationary surprise"; by spending more than it collects in tax revenues, the government can create additional demand and stimulate growth of output and employment. This may lead to a painful contraction later on, but governments often do not look past the next election. The story does not end there. Firms and workers understand that governments do not always tell the truth about their economic plans: firms and workers (particularly trade unions) anticipate these surprises and build them into their wage and price demands. The result is a self-fulfilling prophecy: with each additional attempt to squeeze growth out of the economy by turning on the printing presses, prices will rise faster and faster, canceling out any increase in growth through this upward ratchet to inflation.

Breaking the link between government and the creation of money through central bank independence weakens both of these catalysts of inflation. As Fischer makes clear, there is a problem. It may be true that in the long run it is impossible to secure higher output by tolerating higher inflation, but in the short run such a trade-off does exist. It is no good saying that in the long run this artificial growth evaporates. In the short run an independent bank makes politically charged decisions about the rate at which inflation should be brought down and the extent of the temporary losses in output and employment that may result from such decisions. But one thing is clear: countries that let inflation get out of control can expect large declines in output.

America's Federal Reserve and Germany's Bundesbank have shown that wide consensus can be built for the freedom central banks need to do their jobs right—and the economic benefits of central bank independence are clear. Establishing consensus in Eastern Europe and the NIS—countries that have been living with high rates of inflation and fear that mastering prices will boot masses of people out of work—has not been easy. Big enterprises consider the continuation of central bank credits a key to survival, but such credits are also triggers for ceaseless inflation.

Fischer measures central bank independence according to fifteen different criteria, including the length of the governor's term, whether the bank has a statutory or constitutional obligation to achieve price stability, whether it sets short-term interest rates, and so on. Evidence for the benefits of independence is overwhelming, as figure 5.1 shows. Such countries as Switzerland and Germany, which meet most of Fischer's criteria, have low inflation over the longest period; countries such as Greece, Spain, and Italy, which do not, are stuck with chronically high rates of inflation.

No European central bank asserts its independence more than Germany's Bundesbank. A law passed in 1957 gives it independence from the federal government in the conduct of monetary policy. The bank "shall be required to support the general economic policy of the federal government"—but only if this does not prejudice the performance of the Bundesbank's functions, which are to insure "stable prices, high employment, balanced foreign trade and constant and reasonable economic growth." The state secretary of Germany's Finance Ministry in Bonn sits on the Bundesbank's council and can order a decision taken by the central bank to be delayed for two weeks, but not longer. On the government's advice, the federal president appoints the Bundesbank's president (who can attend cabinet meetings), its vice president, and up to eight other council mem-

Figure 5.1

Inflation and Central Bank Independence

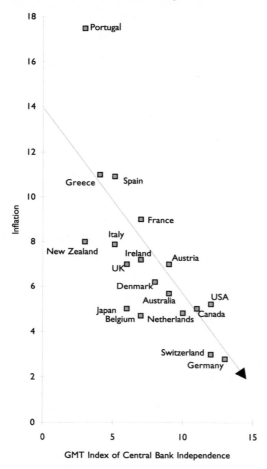

Source: Grilli, Masciandara, Tabellini: "Political and Monetary Institutions and Public Financial Policies in the Industrial Countries" *Economic Policy*, October 1994, pp341–392.

bers. The council's remaining eleven members are the heads of the regional central banks. All council members serve eight-year terms.

Germany's experience of economic collapse and hyperinflation in the 1920s and the Bundesbank's peerless record of keeping inflation in check after Hitler's war ranks the bank, after the Constitutional Court, as the second most respected in public opinion polls of the country's institutions. This, as much as its legal safeguards, insures the bank's vigorous independence. Governments are usually wary of challenging the Bundesbank and regret it when they do. In 1980 and 1981, the then chancellor, Helmut Schmidt, pushed hard to persuade the Bundesbank to lower interest rates—and failed. That failure went some way toward undermining Schmidt's standing in the country and contributed to his electoral defeat in 1983.

The Bank of England ran last when it came to central bank independence (until the new Labour government headed by Tony Blair reversed course and granted it full control of monetary policy in May 1997). Its relationship with the Treasury was best summed up by Prime Minister Thatcher's longtime chancellor of the exchequer, Nigel Lawson, in a statement to a House of Commons select committee in 1987: "I make the decisions and the bank carries them out." (That same Nigel Lawson, after watching inflation surge in 1988, spent his last year in office devising a blueprint for making the bank independent.) The act of parliament in 1946 that nationalized the bank empowered Treasury officials to direct it in the name of public interest. Over the next three decades, intervention in the Bank of England's affairs was an almost daily occurrence. The Treasury consults the bank before interest rates change, but the relationship is understood by both to be one of owner and servant. That perception contributed mightily to the high rates of inflation Britain endured throughout the 1970s and to the vastly high real interest rates that the Thatcher government had to impose in the 1980s in order to choke off inflation.

The rest of the European Union's central banks fall into two groups: those resembling the pre-1997 Bank of England in servility and those that fall between the English and German models.

5.7 The Currency Board Way

No transition country bet more heavily on the benefits of central bank independence than Estonia. Indeed, it went so far as to make the Bank of Estonia so independent that the bank's governor cannot tinker with monetary policy in any way at all. Estonia opted to transform its central bank into a *currency board* (a policy adopted by Bulgaria in July 1997), meaning that the central bank issues currency only in accordance with strict rules.

The currency board model of central banking adopted in Estonia makes the Bank of Estonia something of a machine: it can print money, but only under a commitment to *convert* the Estonian kroon, on demand, to D-marks at the fixed rate of eight kroon to one D-mark. To make this commitment credible, the Bank of Estonia holds reserves of D-marks equal to 100% of the kroons in domestic circulation at the fixed rate of exchange. The Bank of Estonia issues new currency only when there are enough D-marks in the bank's vaults to back it. Otherwise, the bank does little else: no open market operations, no lending to the government, no guarantees for banks. On this latter matter, the bank's founding governor, Siim Kallas, was blunt: "We know countries in which there is no end to 'subsidies' paid to commercial banks to keep them going. How long can a society put up with this? In any case, such long-term behavior is more expensive and painful for a society than a sharp and decisive cut." Cut he has: in 1993 and 1994, roughly half of Estonia's commercial banking sector, born in the frantic foreign-exchange dealing of Estonia's last months in the ruble zone in 1991, was shut down.

A farsighted ex-trade-union leader, Kallas sees several advantages in Estonia's currency board. First, its mechanisms are simple, a considerable allure given the paucity of real banking experience in ex-communist countries. Indeed, his confidence in the immutability of the bank's program allowed Kallas to make a (failed) bid to become his country's prime minister. (No small irony attends Kallas's attempt to take charge of Estonia's government: the independence he stood for as the bank's governor meant that no political grouping was loyal to him, a point made clear in the parliament rejecting his nomination to the premiership.) Secondly, a currency board forces the government to adopt a realistic fiscal policy. It has: in 1993 and 1994 Estonia had a budget surplus. If the government wants to run a deficit, it has to persuade private commercial banks to lend it money. Browbeating the central bank into printing money is not an option. Kallas insists that the currency board he initiated compels whatever government is in power to reckon its budget prudently.

Add cheaper money to the benefits Estonia gained from its currency board. As Ardo Hansson and Jeffrey Sachs have predicted, the credibility that a currency board brings soon lowers the cost of cutting inflation. Their argument goes like this: A government that intends to use a fixed exchange rate as an anchor against inflation (but without a currency board) needs to set interest rates at a premium because of the risk that the strictness of its policy will be jettisoned. Tie your hands with a currency board, and that risk of change is eliminated. Result? Lower interest rates result because no premium need be added.

Figure 5.2

Output Decline in the Baltics

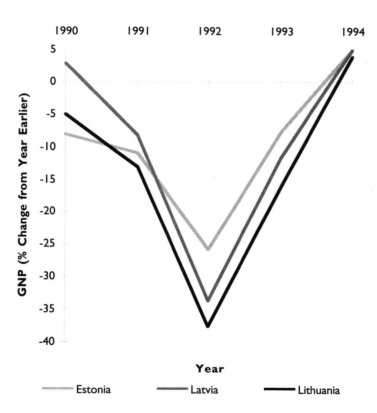

Source: EBRD, Transition Report, 1994.

To support their argument, Hansson and Sachs compare Estonia with Latvia and Lithuania, both of which have followed tight monetary policies without first establishing currency boards. They used floating exchange rates. Each essentially balanced its national budget. Real interest rates in Estonia have been lower, say Hansson and Sachs, because investors do not ask to be insured against the prospect of a currency devaluation. Lower real interest rates mean that there is a lower risk of bad debts, a smaller spread between borrowing and lending rates, and thus lower overall economic costs. The decline in output in Estonia, as figure 5.2 shows, has been lower than in either Latvia or Lithuania.

The rigidity inspired by a currency board creates its own problems. Prime among them is an overvaluation of the currency. As inflation throughout the Baltics is higher than in the home countries of the dollar and D-mark (though Estonia has now pushed its inflation rate a nudge below 10%), the currencies on which the Baltic currency boards are based, the Baltic currencies are appreciating in real terms. As a result, imports are increasing and exporters are suffering. There is no possibility of changing the exchange rate without jeopardizing the board itself. If the Latvian lat is becoming overvalued, then the solution lies in restraining prices and wages—politically, a far trickier problem and one that invites fresh government intrusions in the market in the form of controls on wages and prices.

Currency boards also put pressure on banking systems. Under a currency board, central bankers are restricted from pumping new funds into the financial system to keep suspect banks above water. The liquidity crunch that followed Estonia's implementation of its currency board saw a handful of weak banks go under. The damage caused by chronic bank failure was undoubtedly great. However, the benefits gained from tough monetary policies are certainly just as great. Estonian banks quickly abandoned their old habits and are learning to assess investments with a critical eye; people are encouraged to save as interest rates reach positive levels; and trade is booming as the exchange rate has been stabilized and foreign currency trading liberalized.

The risks posed by a currency board seem particularly great for large economies, and currency boards may, as Milton Friedman argues, be little better than "a temporary option." For, says Friedman, though a government establishes "what it regards as the equivalent of a currency board," it may not really be "willing to follow the fiscal policies that are required to make it effective." So unchecked inflationary pressures may "sooner or later make it impossible to maintain the fixed exchange rate" without resort to formal wage and price controls. This may be particularly true in large, insular countries, such as Russia and the other ex-Soviet states, where a smaller proportion of goods are traded internationally, and thus foreign competition is less likely to counteract the inflationary pressures that lead to currency appreciation. So it may be sensible to reject the currency board option as not feasible. However, it is at least as likely that the countries doing so are just not serious about balancing the budget and beating inflation.

5.8 Time to Peg

Another tool governments and central banks use to fight inflation is exchange-rate policy.

Exchange rates are managed in three different ways: They can be fixed; they can float; or they can be controlled in a way that combines these two devices, in what is known as a *crawling peg*. In a fixed exchange rate a currency's value is set in stone against another currency, as Estonia's kroon and the Croatian kuna are aligned with the D-mark. A floating exchange rate means that a currency is freely traded (continuously) on the foreign exchange markets, finding its own level, and perhaps changing its value, hour by hour. The major capitalist economies all operate on this system. A crawling peg combines the two systems. Here the rate is fixed officially but is altered regularly by small amounts to spread a devaluation (meaning a cut in its value) or a revaluation (an increase in a currency's valuation) over a longer period of time.

With a pegged rate, the goal of monetary policy becomes that of defending the exchange rate. When too many people, for example, sell their zlotys, the Polish central bank is committed to using its reserves of foreign currencies to keep the value of the zloty at the pegged value. To succeed at this, the government's monetary and fiscal policies must be believable: expectations of high inflation will make people fly from the zloty, foreign reserves will be quickly exhausted, and the currency will collapse. In contrast, when inflation comes down and confidence in the zloty increases, the money supply grows automatically as people convert foreign into domestic currency. Pegging the exchange rate is not a substitute for cutting budget deficits and keeping monetary policy tight, but it can be an important disciplining factor.

Heeding IMF advice, at the time of independence most countries of the former USSR let their currencies float. This meant that the government would not defend the exchange rate. In theory, they could still attack inflation through tight fiscal and monetary policies, a strategy known as "money-based stabilization." But, in fact, monetary policy was usually chaotic. Laxity incited by political pressure caused inflation to rise so staggeringly that people refrained from using the domestic currency; barter and hard currencies came to dominate trade and business. Such critics of the IMF as Jeffrey Sachs prefer what is known as "exchange-rate-based stabilization," which entails a fixed exchange rate as the frontline of defense against inflation. The record since 1991 suggests that this alternative is more successful.

If Ukraine or Moldova, Russia or Belarus had pegged their exchange rates to·a stable currency in the manner of the Baltic states, they would have had a fixed anchor against inflation. True, this would have meant putting national reserves on the line to support the rate, but that would in turn have forced governments to commit more completely to anti-inflation policies. Poland's stabilization fund, which allowed the Mazowiecki and Suchocka governments to peg the zloty to a basket of currencies, was never tapped because of the government's fidelity to its tight budget and monetary policy. When an exchange rate is pegged, prices of traded goods begin to stabilize because they are subject to competition from abroad at the fixed exchange rate.

Fixed exchange rates were a key ingredient to reform in Poland and the Czech Republic. From May to October 1991, the Polish zloty was fixed to a basket of European currencies. Annual inflation, which reached almost 600% in 1990, was down to 45% by 1992, and was half that again by 1996. To preserve its real exchange rate, Poland's fixed system was changed to one of "crawling devaluation" in October 1991. A 9-zloty-per-day devaluation was set, yielding a rate of 21% per year. In 1993, that rate was increased by 25%, to 12 and then to 15 zlotys per day. Although not explicitly, Hungary also follows a crawling devaluation. After a series of devaluations, in 1991, the Czech koruna was pegged at roughly 28 koruna to the U.S. dollar, where it remained within an allowed band until a balance of payments crisis in the spring of 1997 forced a devaluation. Inflation, which peaked at an annual rate of 56.7% in 1991 after price liberalization, stabilized at an annual rate of approximately 10%, among the lowest in the region. Huge capital inflows put heavy pressure on the inflation rate and the exchange rate and helped force the devaluation of the koruna.

Preserving the value of the zloty and crown forced financial discipline on governments that might otherwise have asked the central bank to monetize government deficits. Look to Romania for a telling example of what could happen to fixed exchange rates when a government relaxes its monetary policy. Romania's

Figure 5.3

Net Foreign Exchange Reserves, Romania (in Millions of U.S. Dollars)

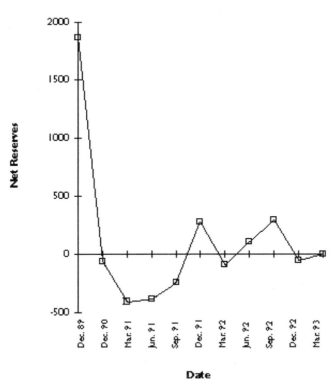

Source: National Bank of Romania.

attempt under President Iliescu to maintain the overvalued leu without curtailing fiscal excesses or reforming its exchange rate regime led to the depletion of its substantial foreign reserves (see figure 5.3). It was forced to let the leu devalue heavily, which led to increased uncertainty about inflation. Only when the new Constantinescu regime pegged the leu to the dollar and D-mark in late 1996 did the currency stabilize.

Pegged rates do create their own problems. Most transition countries ration foreign currency by exchange controls and import licenses, so there is limited market pressure for a devaluation. Only the black market shows what the exchange rate ought to be, and many governments, such as Romania and Belarus, so dislike its revelations that they, fine and imprison currency traders.

Also, because taming inflation takes time, there is a danger that the exchange rate can become overvalued. When domestic prices rise relative to foreign ones, a nation's real exchange rate rises. This makes imports cheaper and exports more expensive. If domestic prices and wages do not go down to meet the increase in foreign competition, declines in production and a rise in unemployment will follow. At some point, maintaining the exchange rate becomes untenable: this is one reason why Poland, for example, moved from a fixed exchange to a crawling peg regime in 1991.

To the surprise of a few lucky governments in Eastern Europe, fixed exchange rates may lead to problems when a country succeeds in attracting a lot of foreign investment. When the exchange rate is fixed, the inflow of foreign money augments the domestic monetary base and can create an inflationary pressure of its own. The Czech Republic was confronted by this problem for three years until it was forced to devalue its currency. Estonia, Latvia (where the flow of black market Russian funds is huge), Macedonia (because of capital flight from Serbia into its banks), and Slovenia also experienced similar difficulties.

To be sure, the influx of foreign investment may be easily neutralized by a process called *sterilization*. In order to prevent the real appreciation of their currencies, the central banks can sell government bonds to absorb the excess capital and thus remove the pressure on their currency.

For central banks, this strategy is costly for a number of reasons. In order to persuade investors to hold more bonds than they otherwise might, the central bank has to offer a higher rate of interest, which causes the bank to expend money and crowds out the market for private capital. High interest rates may very well attract more foreign capital to flow into a country, making matters worse. Sterilization could, in the end, become self-defeating. Indeed, countries that face upward pressure on their currencies often have little choice but to allow appreciation to occur.

5.9 One-Way Street

So inflation in the Baltics, the Czech Republic, Poland, and elsewhere has come down, and their central bankers can expect to be praised? Not likely. Most people in their countries are now more concerned about unemployment than inflation, and politicians who have harped about inflation have been regularly losing their jobs at the nearest election. Worse, many people are inclined to think that inflation has fallen only because unemployment has risen. Throughout the region, monetary policy is being blamed for higher unemployment when it might have expected to be praised for lower inflation.

Macroeconomic policy makers therefore face as harsh a dilemma as ever. The striking exception is the Czech Republic, which has kept a low jobless rate—it currently hovers at under 3 % of the workforce—through a combination of monetary tightness and fiscal ease, flexible labor markets, a huge surge of investment from abroad and tourism income, and relatively stable exchange and interest rates. However, recent events have demonstrated that this combination of policies is no longer a viable alternative, even for the Czech Republic. For other countries, macroeconomic policy is open to attack. And in some places those attacks are succeeding, at least at the polls. In Hungary, Poland, and, for a time, in Bulgaria, as well as elsewhere, former communists reclaimed power on a promise to reverse or at least soften the social impact of macroeconomic reforms that followed communism's collapse. (Hungary's current socialist government in fact promised both to deepen reform and preserve the social safety net.) For the most part, however, they have found options for change limited or nonexistent.

As grim as events seem in countries that have undergone the macroeconomic stabilization process, those that ducked anti-inflationary measures have done even worse. In the summer of 1994, the government of Prime Minister Viktor Chernomyrdin consistently gave itself higher marks for managing the Russian economy than its record deserved. The Moscow Interbank Currency Exchange (Russia's largest capital market) became cynical. On October 11, 1994, as we have seen, it corrected the grade and flunked Chernomyrdin's policies. With few exceptions, investors and holders of rubles felt they had been duped by the government long enough. Specifically, they no longer believed in the central bank's inflation figures and forecasts, for the monetary excesses of the summer had become widely known. The capital market therefore assumed its role as unofficial governor, and the young traders on the floor before their computer screens vetoed the policies of a prime minister and the central bank governor. Allowing inflation to run at a gallop did not prevent output from dropping precipitously and unemployment from rising, even if official statistics do not adequately measure the trend (see figure 5.4).

Figure 5.4

"Black Tuesday": Noncash Ruble-USD Exchange Rate

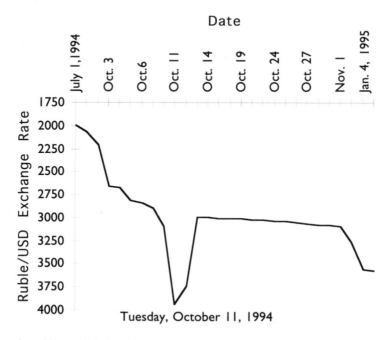

Source: Moscow Interbank Exchange.

The story in other NIS countries is similarly bleak, though the details vary. After Ukraine was kicked out of the ruble zone in late 1992, there was no check on the government's printing of money. Hyperinflation soon roared as parliament exercised its right to order the central bank to advance industrial credits at any time and in any amount. With its back against the wall by

Figure 5.5

Unstable Monthly Inflation in Russia, Ukraine, and Belarus

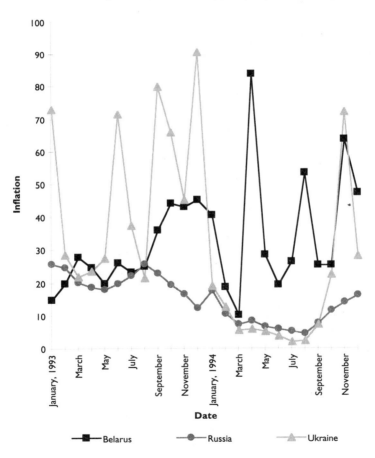

Source: National Statistics Belarus, Russia, Ukraine.

mid-1994, the National Bank of Ukraine began to rein in the printing presses. Viktor Yushchenko, the bank's governor, scaled back and delayed credits to convince parliament that "money is not something you wish for; it is something we must earn."

Yushchenko's lone efforts to restrain Ukrainian inflation bought some respite. By mid-1994, inflation was halved, but success was fleeting. Parliament balked at cutting agricultural subsidies, and by the time Leonid Kuchma was elected president in September, inflation had returned to its former high levels. Kuchma's election, however, was symptomatic of a growing realization in Eastern Europe, even among those hostile to reform, that inflation cannot be allowed to run out of control. More importantly, figures such as Kuchma exhibited some awareness that markets negate the supposed benefits of inflationary policies by pushing down exchange rates and forcing interest rates higher. Prices were always increasing sooner and by more than governments hoped, and real spending, which was intended to halt the steep falls in output, could not be propped up.

Central bank loans to banks servicing industry and agriculture are a root cause of continuing high inflation in the NIS. Indeed, throughout Eastern Europe, but most particularly in the NIS, most central banks are involved in providing the funds used by these banks. Even when it does not act as a bank directly, the central bank usually has a hand in deciding how commercial banks lend their money. Commercial banks in Russia, Belarus, Ukraine, Romania, Slovakia, and arguably Hungary are still required to lend to "priority sectors"; the term expands to include small farmers in Slovenia, large farmers in Lithuania, and state businesses and exporters everywhere. Each group is deemed deserving enough to pay "special" (that is, subsidized) interest rates (see figure 5.5).

This has two results: (1) central banks find it harder to control monetary growth; and (2) whenever they try to, "priority sectors" comes to mean those businesses run by cronies of the president or speaker of parliament. Ukrainians are so cynical about this process that one government was dubbed the "Zvahilsky Limited Company" (after a former prime minister) for its abuse of industrial lobbies. This cynicism is not misplaced. From May to December 1993, for example, central bank credits to industry shot up 577% and for agriculture, 524%. Indeed, a Rada (parliament) resolution opened an unlimited line of credit for collective farms. The same thing happened with industries and enterprises that needed foreign exchange, but with one difference: foreign exchange cannot be printed at home, so favoritism (and bribery) is even more the deciding factor in who gets what. Only Estonia and Latvia, with their currency boards, come close to eliminating this problem.

5.10 Watchdogs

Fighting inflation may be the most important, but it is not the only task of central bankers in the postcommunist world. They also guard the integrity of the financial system by imposing standards of prudent behavior on commercial banks and other lending institutions. Here central bankers face similar pressures to those encountered in their war against inflation.

Since gaining their independence, the Baltic states have discovered just how hard it is to make banks behave prudently. Estonia, Latvia, and Lithuania have all endured a banking crisis, the effects of which continue to be felt. Banka Baltija, Latvia's biggest private bank, was closed and liquidated in 1995. Early in 1995, nine small Lithuanian banks were shut down, and two big ones needed state help to survive. This shock pales when compared to the government's decision in December of that year to suspend the operations of the country's two biggest banks, Litempex and Innovation Bank, firms that, combined, hold over 25% of the country's total deposits. A political brouhaha followed when, it is said, Lithuania's then prime minister, Adolfas Slezevicius, was tipped off in time to withdraw $30,000 from his personal accounts in Innovation Bank before its doors were shut. A run on all Lithuania's banks was avoided when the government agreed quickly to guarantee most deposits and purchased Treasury bills back from wayward banks.

Financial health in Eastern Europe and the NIS requires that some banks go bust, but the commercial banking system must be able to withstand these failures and prosper. Central bankers are not particularly squeamish folk, but most blanch at the idea of blood being spilled openly on the bank floor. Everybody knows that a bank could not repay depositors if all the bank's depositors asked for their money back at the same time. People also know that banks make loans to each other, often heavily, so that trouble in one may mean trouble for all. The risk of a lot of financial bloodletting is therefore far greater in banking than in other businesses, which might suggest that no bank should be allowed to suffer even the slightest bruise.

Such cosseting would do more harm than good. Bankers would be exempted from the consequences of their follies, and therefore tempted to try anything—that is, until the costs became so high that no one could cover them up and the entire financial system came under threat. This logic would in fact require the banks to be nationalized, since private-sector rewards should only go to those who bear the full costs of private-sector risks, particularly the risk of going bust. But state bankers, as those in Ukraine amply demonstrate, pursue even wilder follies (or become more inefficient) when the public purse is open to them.

This dilemma can be managed but never solved. Central bank managers need to draw a bright line between protecting the financial system as a whole and protecting every crooked or incompetent banker. But if they draw the line too clearly, they reassure the incompetents; a bit of uncertainty is a useful spur to prudence.

Good central bankers ponder these questions, usually in private. They know that the surest monetary touch and the wisest exchange rate schemes would count for nothing if the banking system crumbled. They must therefore provide several lines of defense against this happening: (1) supervise the banks to ensure prudence; if that fails, then (2) persuade depositors that their money is safer in banks than under mattresses; and if that does not work, then (3) bail out the whole system. Since this sequence is not as clear-cut as it sounds, it would seem sensible for central banks to be involved at each stage. In Eastern Europe, not all of them are.

On April 15, 1994, signs reading "closed for technical reasons" were taped to the locked doors of Banka Bohemia, the Czech Republic's seventh largest bank. The day before, its assets were seized by the Czech National Bank after thousands of panicky depositors withdrew a total of 2.5 billion koruna ($85 million). The run was triggered after Banka Bohemia (which, according to its balance sheet, had deposits of 11 billion koruna) saw its license revoked by the CNB at the end of March. It was placed under administration by the CNB for issuing $1.2 billion of bogus securities, known as "prime bank guarantees."

Although the CNB has sole responsibility for licensing commercial banks, setting their reserve requirements, and debt/equity ratios, it did not uncover Banka Bohemia's fraud. The U.S. Securities and Exchange Commission (SEC), the stock market regulator, tipped the CNB that "possibly fraudulent" Banka Bohemia paper was flooding the market to the tune of over $400 million. While the CNB investigated, Banka Bohemia was put under the administration of Ceskoslovenska Obchodni Banka, a state-owned trade bank and a cofounder of Banka Bohemia. Most of Banka Bohemia's directors were forced out or removed. Unable to determine the full extent of Banka Bohemia's liabilities, the interim administrator (with CNB approval) hired an American law firm, White & Case, to sort out the mess. Depositors can rest easy. All accounts have been transferred to Obchodni Banka.

The Banka Bohemia incident prompted the CNB to tighten its grip. Following the seizure of Banka Bohemia's assets, the CNB hastily closed down two other small banks, AB Banka and Kreditni and Prumyslova (Credit and Industry) Banka, which had dubious balance sheets. Although depositors were not insured formally in any of the banks concerned, the CNB made certain that depositors received their money or had their deposits transferred to caretaker banks.

The Czech parliament, for its part, was also stirred to action in the wake of the Banka Bohemia closure. In July 1995, it passed amendments to the Banking Law that strengthened the CNB's hand in supervising the banking system. The new legislation secured the CNB's authority to issue and revoke bank licenses, to take over the administration of suspect banks, and to impose high penalties on miscreant financial institutions. Additionally, a new deposit insurance scheme was passed. Formerly, only the four large banks with state ownership stakes had their assets guaranteed by the state. Now, deposits in all commercial banks, including the big four, are insured up to 80% of their value.

This tumult was but the most recent chapter in a long, muddled story. In 1990, all Czech commercial banks were technically insolvent. To keep them afloat, the government created a "loan hospital" in the form of the state-backed Consolidation Bank, to which some former communist debts (equal to around 20% of the banks' total credits) were transferred and rescheduled. Meanwhile the main commercial banks were lumped with other

Czech enterprises in the country's mass privatization scheme. Thanks to recapitalization in 1992, a program supervised by the CNB, most banks now claim to be in solid health. The CNB reports that Komercni Bank, the largest commercial bank, has questionable loans equal to only 10% of its total.

Despite this history, signs of weakness are still not being addressed by the CNB. The overall number of bad debts in the commercial banking system remains huge: some assessments say over 35% of bank assets look dubious. The annual report of Agrobanka, the country's fifth largest, showed that it was technically bankrupt in 1993. But it was not the CNB that acted to save the day; the bank's shareholders (primarily the big Czech investment funds) injected more capital.

The CNB's deficiencies are not uncommon. Most of the region's central banks are too overburdened by the demands of maintaining the currency and controlling government debt to cock a watchful eye toward commercial banks. Responsibility for bank supervision is almost universally vested in central banks throughout Eastern Europe. In some countries, such as Belarus, Bulgaria, the Czech Republic, Latvia, Macedonia, and Russia, the central banks have sole charge of commercial bank regulation, but usually are dilatory in their oversight function. The Bank of Lithuania is, in theory, solely responsible for regulating commercial banks, but the Commission on Securities also has a say in determining a bank's capitalization requirements.

The Bank of Estonia keeps a beady eye on commercial bank loans and has the power to act quickly. In 1992, it shut down three large commercial banks. Within a year, more than a third of the country's commercial banks disappeared. "No doubt" the bank owners "were very angry," said Siim Kallas with more than a little sarcasm. But his refusal to help was not merely coldhearted; it was designed to discipline bankers who might assume that they would be rescued automatically should things go horribly wrong. Although the Bank of Estonia does not guarantee depositors, it can 1) call a three-month moratorium on a bank granting loans or engaging in foreign exchange trading; 2) impose restrictions on obtaining foreign loans; and 3) increase reserve requirements. Moreover, the bank can also call a preemptive strike: it has the right to publish a commercial bank's accounts at any time.

Bulgaria's central bank has sole authority to monitor commercial banks, but the government is reluctant to stay on the sidelines. Legislation passed under the government of Professor Berov initiated a program to help commercial banks clear their balance sheets. In a one-shot deal, the banks were given government bonds in exchange for bad loans of state-owned companies. Naturally, these bonds are not popular and so are traded only at a discount. These bonds are accepted in privatization transactions, however. In 1994, over 85% of privatized assets were purchased using such "bad loan" bonds.

In Poland bad debts haunt not only state-owned banks but new private ones, too. The country now has over one hundred private banks (not counting its 1,600 agricultural cooperative banks), and foreign ownership of banks (bringing new expertise) is growing. Though they account for only one-tenth of total Polish bank assets, about a quarter of them may well be insolvent. Improvisation is the National Bank of Poland's response to bailing them out. Some banks are recapitalized, others forcibly hived off to big state-owned banks. The state-owned agricultural bank, which has bad debts estimated at 20 trillion old zlotys ($900 million), poses a sticky problem. New capital has been injected by the NBP, but far more is needed. One of the coalition partners in the current government, the Peasant Party, insists that it be kept afloat.

State-owned commercial banks, nine in number, have been dealt with more systematically by the NBP. Unlike in the Czech Republic, bad loans have not been wiped off the books. Instead, two of the healthiest banks were privatized without requiring bailouts. The rest were recapitalized with government bonds worth 11 trillion old zlotys. To pay these bonds off, the banks had to establish special units supervised by the NBP. Most of the plans they came up with for ridding themselves of these bonds involved restructuring debtor firms and debt-for-equity swaps. Two advantages are evident in this method: first, banks must themselves tackle the problem of their bad loans, which should improve the ability to assess risks. Second, the scheme entices the government to privatize more banks: as each is sold, the government bonds used to bail out the bank are transferred to a fund financed by international creditors.

The Bank Slaski fiasco, however, halted this momentum. Major oversubscription, related to a speculative frenzy on the Warsaw Stock Exchange, and late delivery of its shares during privatization helped push up the share price to thirteen times its opening value on the first day of trading. Windfall profits were made, and the resulting political chill cost the finance minister his job and has frozen other planned privatizations, such as that for the big Bank Przemyslowo-Handlowy.

Hungary fragments its supervisory powers more than any other country in Eastern Europe. Perhaps this is a reason why it has been slow to clean out its banking Augean stables:

- The Finance Ministry's agency for State Banking Supervision (SBS) supervises the solvency of commercial banks and inspects and sets the ratio of capital to bank loans. It also vets the quality of a bank's portfolio, its income, and its monthly and long-term liquidity as well as its management. Among its powers it can: (1) issue decrees on banking standards, (2) remove a bank manager, and (3) restrict the voting rights of influential bank shareholders.

- The National Bank of Hungary supervises the day-to-day liquidity of commercial banks and oversees all foreign currency transactions. It shares the power to license banks with the SBS.

- A department to monitor banking has also been set up within the Ministry of Finance. Its tasks include preparing schemes to consolidate existing banks as well readying state-owned banks for privatization.

Sorting out this mishmash is difficult, though some streamlining is taking place. Before 1992, the NBH divided its supervisory activities among a number of departments, and these in turn all had to form working relations with the SBS. Since January 1993, a single department has taken command of all the NBH's commercial bank oversight duties. This department and the SBS seek to harmonize their functions. That collaboration stands a chance of working, but is complicated by the wider debate about state intervention over bank credits and what, if any, shares the government should retain in the private commercial banking sector.

According to the Bank for International Settlements (BIS, the club of the world's central bankers, based in Basel, Switzerland), Hungary's bank supervisors say that one of their main tasks is spotting early signs of financial weakness. This falls primarily to the SBS because it monitors long-term liquidity and portfolio investments. Ask SBS members what this means in detail, and they give a variety of answers. Certainly the SBS has taken number crunching to great lengths. It uses a rating system that has up to fifty ratios (on capital, asset quality, management, earnings, and liquidity). The NBH's supervisors, because of the need for daily oversight of the foreign exchange markets and the value of the forint, place greater store on personal contact with senior bankers, though recently it has become more quantifiable (perhaps also because three of the country's commercial banks originated within the NBH itself and were only hived off in 1986).

So oversight, though sometimes disconnected, is not the real problem behind the inefficiency of Hungary's banks; political intervention is. In 1990, the Antall government launched its first rescue attempt, underwriting some of the bad loans that the banks had been saddled with from the communist era. Then in 1992, another 105 billion forints ($1.3 billion) of dud bank loans were swapped at a discount for government bonds. In 1993, the government opened its purse again in a bid to boost commercial banking capital to the minimum levels recommended by the international regulators of the BIS. So far over 154 billion forints worth of government bonds have been thrown at bank balance sheets. The total in this bailout is now over $3 billion, almost 10% of Hungary's GDP. In the process the government doubled its domestic debt.

What was secured by this bailout? Almost all of the country's biggest banks remain in state hands: only the Foreign Trade Bank is partly privatized. The National Savings Bank and the savings cooperatives retain their monopoly of retail banking. Although there are plans to sell off Budapest Bank, one of the healthier banks involved in the current recapitalization effort, there is little sign of a coherent strategy for the others.

In the wake of the October 1994 ruble panic in Moscow, commercial bank supervision in Russia became up for grabs. Yeltsin's government blames inept central bank supervision for touching off the causes of the panic. Gerashchenko's reduction of interest rates at the nationwide savings bank inspired people to withdraw their savings and put them into currency speculation. A second catalyst to withdrawals were widespread reports that most commercial banks were failing to meet their reserve requirements. In October, withdrawals from Promstroybank were five times greater than deposits.

Blaming commercial banks for the ruble's collapse is not altogether misplaced. Heavy speculation in rubles by commercial banks inspired fear among government officials that bank speculators were deliberately seeking to drive the ruble's value down. An anonymous Central Bank official told *Nezavisimaya Gazeta* on October 13 that such vast trading by banks could be achieved only through a coordinated effort intended to "fulfill a special task—a collapse of the ruble." Sinister motives were also seen by Yeltsin's ministers, one of whom told that same newspaper that the ruble panic was aimed directly at the government. Debate on the new draft law for the central bank now centers on the powers of bank supervision: the Duma wants to retain oversight for itself; Yeltsin's ministers want to put banks under the watchful eye of the Finance Ministry. One thing is clear: neither political body trusts the central bank to do the job effectively.

No matter who is charged with the task, if commercial bank supervision is to work, supervisors must pay attention to three aspects of a bank's balance sheet:

1. *Capital.* In some countries banks have to keep their capital up to, say, 10% of their assets. However, supervisors often apply different ratios to different kinds of assets depending on their risk. In Poland, loans to the Polish public sector need not necessarily be backed by capital, though the NBP frowns on the practice; in Slovenia investment in property carries a capital ratio of 30%, and so on.

2. *Liquidity.* To avoid any mismatch of liabilities and assets, some supervisors specify how much a bank should keep aside to meet its short-term obligations. Poland's rules are flexible; depending on the type of liquid assets held, a bank must keep aside anywhere from 10% to 50% of its assets. In Bulgaria, one of the difficulties the Bulgarian National Bank (BNB) faced in organizing supervision of banking institutions was the vast number of small banks that emerged after 1990. Usually undercapitalized and saddled with nonperforming assets, most were former branches of the BNB that had been removed from BNB administration and, in some cases, nominally privatized. Linked indebtedness in portfolios meant that one bank's going under threatened the whole system. But unclear ownership structures made it difficult for the BNB to clean up the mess. Indeed, the main owner, the state, lacked any mechanism to administer its own stake in these dodgy banks. To put an end to this anarchy, the government created a Bank Consolidation Company (BCC) to

which all shares of state banks, held in state-owned companies and other state banks and institutions, were transferred. The idea was to put all the rotten eggs in one basket, where their numbers could be pared down or eliminated, thus at a stroke enhancing bank liquidity. With ownership consolidated (see figure 5.6), the BNB and the government moved to clean banks' balance sheets of bad loans and to privatize bank shares in a systematic manner. But the Socialist government inhibited this momentum. That work began anew in May 1997, after the Socialists lost power.

3. *Portfolio distribution.* Most countries now set a ceiling on how much a bank can lend to a single customer (save the government). It varies widely, from Poland (10% of a bank's capital) to Russia (20%), to the Czech Republic (35%), to Romania (65%). Ukraine does not lay down any limit, and some commercial banks are rumored to have lent up to 100% of their capital to individual firms. Many of these loans are reported to be share swaps so that, if and when privatization comes, Ukrainian banks are likely to become the biggest shareholders in the country's industries.

Figure 5.6

Ownership Structure of Bulgarian Banking Sector

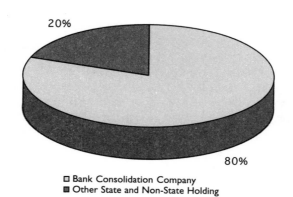

20%

80%

□ Bank Consolidation Company
■ Other State and Non-State Holding

Source: National Bank of Bulgaria.

As the Czech and Hungarian methods demonstrate, no supervisory system is infallible. Indeed, there are worrying signs that supervision can be abused to increase the state's role. In Poland, for example, a number of bank boards' members have been sacked by supervisors and replaced with political appointees loyal to the ruling government.

5.11 Insuring Stability

Suppose a bank is rotting from within: its managers know it; central bank supervisors may know about this weakness, too, if only intuitively; and stock market traders may be discounting the value of the bank's shares. What stops this business failure from turning into a financial panic is the calm of the bank's depositors. But they will stay calm only for one reason: even if the bank closes its doors for good, depositors will get their money back.

That was one of the lasting conclusions Americans drew from the financial panic of the early 1930s, known as the Great Depression, when an astounding half of American banks failed in a mere three years, four thousand banks in 1933 alone. Within a year, Congress established the Federal Deposit Insurance Corporation (FDIC). Professors Milton Friedman and Anna Schwartz, in their classic study "A Monetary History of the United States," called this "the most important structural change in the banking system to result from the 1935 panic and . . . the structural change most conducive to monetary policy since . . . immediately after the Civil War." After World War II, the number of bank closures in the United States dropped to a few per year, but in the 1980s and early 1990s bank failures exploded in the now infamous savings-and-loan debacle. Many attributed these bankruptcies to a combination of lax regulation and deposit insurance that created an essentially risk-free environment for the depositors and encouraged excessive risk taking by banks.

Today, most of the countries in Eastern Europe and the NIS are only fumbling their way to clear programs that insure deposits. Ad hoc insurance has dominated in Russia, with the central bank favoring depositors in banks with extensive loans to state enterprises. Depositors in Romania's twenty-five commercial banks, only seven of which are state controlled, are guaranteed against loss, but no time is set for repayment. Estonia's central bank shuns insurance altogether.

The attractions of insurance include:

1. *Discrimination.* Insurance aims to safeguard depositors, not managers and shareholders. Loose talk of a bank being "bailed out" usually implies that incompetent people have got off scot-free, which is what government ought to avoid; the Czech government seems to be obeying this maxim in the case of Banka Bohemia.

2. *Cheapness.* Deposit insurance may not cost the government a bean. Banks (and hence their customers) have to pay an annual premium set as a small fraction of their deposits. In Latvia, the central bank determines this figure, currently 1% of deposits. In Poland, the NBP and the Finance Ministry argue about who has responsibility. Slovenia, Macedonia, and Lithuania have their central bank contribute one-half the cost.

Strong though the case for insurance is in principle, any scheme for insuring deposits usually fudges the question of who is covered and for how much. Insured depositors are generally lazy depositors. They do not provide the market check on bankers that most central bank supervisors want to encourage. In advanced capitalist economies official insurers have tended to favor smaller depositors while facing the biggest ones with the possibility of loss. Britain's deposit protection scheme insures 75% of the value of deposits up to £10,000; the U.S.'s FDIC sets a cut-off point for insurance at $100,000. Besides, insurers argue, even 100% protection for everybody might not stop depositors from fleeing a particular bank if they knew they would face delay and hassle before getting their cash back.

In theory, the story of bank supervision could end here: any badly run banks that escape the watchdog's scrutiny could go bust, for their depositors are insured. Reality is different, and central banks have to get their hands dirty. All the more so in the case of Eastern Europe as central bankers have to deal with much more than simply bank supervision.

5.12 In the Engine Room

As awesome tasks still lie ahead for the central banks of Eastern Europe and the NIS, it may seem odd to ask why they are needed at all. Yet the question is not nonsensical. The duties of central banks could be performed by government departments: the finance ministry responsible for monetary policy, the industry ministry for banking supervision, and so on. With few exceptions, the infant market economies of the postcommunist world have chosen to have central banks, separately constituted and staffed. "History demands us" is the explanation of one of Slovenia's deputy central bank governors, but there are more compelling reasons than that.

Look at it from a country's standpoint, from some lofty notion of good government. It does no harm for one branch of government to be somewhat immune from the daily political fray. Without a politician at its head, always wondering where the next vote is coming from, the atmosphere in a central bank is vastly different from a finance ministry. It feels more detached, better able to take a longer view. This does not make central bankers wiser than finance ministries, merely different. Unless you believe that finance ministries have a monopoly on wisdom, that difference is a virtue.

Separation of powers is a vital principle in democratic governance; a detached central bank is part of the democratic, free-market brew. Skeptics wonder why politicians should establish independent central banks that might thwart their will and perhaps cost them votes at the next election. But look at it from a finance minister's point of view. Often he is isolated, besieged by ministerial colleagues intent on politically motivated spending, unable to talk to the private sector about market-sensitive subjects, perhaps uneasy about the advice he is getting from bureaucrats in his own department. The central bank governor may be the only person he can turn to for a second opinion. He may not like the opinion, he may choose to ignore it, but it may be comforting to know it is there. Moreover, the central bank can be an ally in government in-fighting: "I've taken advice from the central bank on this, and it is adamant that such an act would seriously harm the exchange rate/our credit rating/our national reserves," finance ministers can argue when confronted by disagreeing colleagues. Should things go wrong and interest rates jump, the central bank is the perfect scapegoat, as Russia's deposed Viktor Gerashchenko demonstrated. That said, politicians are usually keen to keep their scapegoats tame. Estonia is the region's one absolute exception, and it remains to be seen how independent the Bank of Estonia will be now that Siim Kallas, the bank's founding governor, has developed a taste for political power, having failed in his bid to be prime minister precisely because of his lack of a political power base.

Relations between central banks and their governments can be defined by statute, but the wider world has its say. Throughout Eastern Europe, pressures in the financial markets are coming to influence and, on occasion, to dominate economic policy, thus increasing the status of central banks relative to governments. Innovations by private moneymen pose challenges that central banks seem best equipped to meet. The whole business of finance, with its jargon and its billions and its unruly international pace, is one with which few Eastern European and NIS politicians feel comfortable. They may be relieved to pass the responsibility to central bankers.

They may pass them a message as well: BEWARE. Half a day with a history book would remind politicians how many big disasters have had financial roots. Political scandal often involves financial fraud. Raise interest rates before an election and a government can lose its majority in parliament. So the political reaction to financial matters may be instinctively cautious. And this puts Eastern Europe's central bankers in a bind. Although most have acquired more authority and autonomy (and some, like Estonia's, both) over the last few years, they have less dictatorial power than in the old communist days. Financial markets force disinflation on them; they cannot force-feed fiscal restraint on governments, still less on companies and workers to prevent them from pricing themselves out of business. As for international competition and the foreign exchange markets, technology alone assures that moneymen will always be one step ahead, producing bright new schemes that are hard to police.

Harder still is judging where the policing should end. If governments insist on total security for the financial system, they will soon achieve the security of the morgue. In the words of Latvia's central bank governor, Einars Repse, "supervisors must always be a day or two behind the bankers, otherwise innovation is being curtailed." Wise, or at least wary, politicians should agree with him—until that 24-hour difference allows some financial shenanigans to occur, when politicians will, invariably, leap to lead the mob of central bank critics.

Inevitably, central bankers in the transition countries will, for a long period, remain exposed to all sorts of hazards, both financial and political. By gaining more authority over national financial affairs, they attract more controversy. If they decide to support a troubled bank, they can be accused of bailing out their friends; if they decide not to assist such a bank, they risk being blamed for instigating a financial panic or, worse yet, a crash. They either fuel inflation or throw millions out of work; let criminals go free or squash entrepreneurial investments. Public spats about central banks are coarse, the language shrill, but that is what happens everywhere in the world when money and politics intersect. And if postcommunism's central bankers manage to keep control in the economy's engine room, they should not expect to be thanked. Politicians will be quick to claim credit for any successes that the bankers have—and, perhaps, begin to shout orders again.

6
Financing the Future
The Development of Capital Markets

Financial systems throughout Eastern Europe and the NIS have been changing before the eyes of the world as stock and bond markets spring up—seemingly overnight—in the former socialist countries. This headlong rush to establish the citadels of capitalism indicates that the old communist contempt, indeed hatred, for finance is becoming a thing of the past. Increasingly, transition countries discover that domestic savings are mobilized, and foreign capital attracted, only by modernizing and unleashing their capital markets.

"We're the revolutionaries now," quipped Igor L. Boutickov on closing Tashkent's infant stock exchange after its weekly midmorning session of trading one day in the summer of 1995. Almost stealthily, in a bland second-floor room crammed with a few dozen men and women seated before flickering computer screens, the Tashkent Republican Stock Exchange that Boutickov invented (though it trades shares in only a dozen or so semiprivate firms) is bringing to Uzbekistan the financial revolution now taking place, with varying degrees of speed and enthusiasm, from the Baltics to Bishkek. So keen is the Uzbek government headed by President Islam Karimov (a regime otherwise quite dilatory in its commitment to modernization of the economy) to promote activity and trading on the exchange that a three-year tax holiday on income from dividends and share trading started in July 1995.

Undoubtedly, this momentum is infectious. Voucher privatization turned millions of ordinary Czechs, Kazakhs, Latvians, Lithuanians, Moldovans, Slovaks, and Russians into sometimes enthusiastic and sometimes wary shareholders. In 1995 alone, new stock, bond, and commodity exchanges opened in Moldova,

Romania, Estonia, Kazakhstan, Kyrgyzstan, and Uzbekistan, while the prices of shares listed on established markets in Russia and Central Europe rode a roller coaster of prices. In the first half of 1997, for example, Russia's and Hungary's stock markets rose 124% and 49% respectively in dollar terms. The speed with which these markets grow owes much to the region's overriding financial fact: the huge capital requirements needed to restructure old industries and create new businesses, which is forcing dramatic changes in the ways governments and firms raise money.

Thirst for capital is obvious throughout the postcommunist world. Consider infrastructure needs alone. Long, almost venerable, waiting lists for telephones, power shortages, decrepit road and rail lines: all these pitfalls to economic growth are endemic to the region. Fixing these problems is vital because poor infrastructure inhibits business investment and hence imprisons growth. Moreover, yawning government deficits need to be met when governments cannot balance their books. Estimates of the capital needed to finance such investments between 1995 and 2000 range from $750 billion (the European Union, or EU) to over $1 trillion (the European Bank for Reconstruction and Development, or EBRD). In Russia in 1994, for example, government revenues were equal to 27.3% of GDP, but government expenditures equaled 37.3%, forcing the government to repeatedly visit Moscow's infant bond market, a pattern that has continued in the years since. These numbers look worryingly big, but that does not mean that the ex-socialist countries will need to raise all these enormous sums from foreign sources alone. Savings are on the rise throughout the region, meaning that it may be possible for much of the financing to be done domestically. But the demand for capital does mean that countries must compete for it by deregulation, scaling down exchange controls, and other forms of liberalization.

Capital thirst is not the only reason for the rush to capital markets. A recognition that the market must have a bigger say over credit allocation also plays a significant role. If firms are to become efficient, they must be weaned from easily available government transfusions, the old socialist standby, and increasingly turn to a more demanding (as well as more flexible) source of funds: private investors, both domestic and foreign.

Of course, there have been shocking instances of financial manipulation, but they are by no means specifically associated with a transition to free markets. Finance and fraud are not interchangeable terms: you can and usually do have one without the other. The kind of financial ruthlessness more properly associated with the transition is the sort of ruthlessness—to some people more cruel than the ruthlessness of communism—discussed earlier: the spontaneous privatizations and corrupt dealings that turned a class of seemingly disgraced apparatchiks into a new ruling class of parvenu millionaires.

There is a specific type of financial fraud commonly, but erroneously, held to come to the fore during the transition. This is the harebrained scheme, the fantastic game, the man who has a crazy promise that will bring any investor an instantaneous financial utopia. Briefly, in the early stages of the transition, such financial lunacy had its innings. But the transition to free-ish markets is a serious business, not to be diverted by eccentricities. Once a line of financial orthodoxy begins to be established—and although it is often a grim and rigid line, it is not a crazed and wayward one—the financial schemers and lunatics, mild or serious, begin to be put down by a state that can no longer risk the public backlash that inevitably accompanies the failure of these schemes.

Teething pains of this sort abound in the early stages of the transition within specific countries. A myriad of brazen flimflams throughout the postcommunist world convinced many ordinary people—at least at the start of the transition—that the dawning world of capitalist finance was nothing more than a casino, and a rigged one at that. Thousands of Russians and Romanians, to cite two notorious examples, lost their life savings in the MMM and Caritas scandals of the early 1990s, which were in essence variations on the pyramid schemes urban street con men have been running for generations. By some government reckonings in Riga, between 1991 and 1994, a third of all adult Latvians lost money in financial scams. Public cynicism in Latvia deepened when only three such financial crooks were arrested, and none jailed. The Bank of Latvia shrugged off its policing duties. "If someone does not observe the rules (of the road) and a car crashes," said Mr. Repse, the bank's chairman, "it is not the rule maker who is to blame." Political disdain of this sort, all too common in the region, incited formation of a "cheated investors" party with a one-note program: pay us back! But the indifference

169

that marked the government's response to the scandal infects voters also. During the first general election it contested, the new party failed to pass the threshold of votes needed to be seated in parliament and now wants to ally itself with the Luddite social democratic and labor parties, who remain ideologically opposed to any and all financial deregulation.

Less headline-grabbing flaws also hinder capital markets, particularly illiquidity (that is, the availability of buyers and sellers) and a lack of transparency. In some ways this lack of liquidity is structural: large markets tend to be more liquid, and at this point in their development the postcommunist stock markets are small. In 1995, Warsaw's bourse, the region's most active, approached the $10 billion mark in capitalization, a mere 6–7% of the country's GDP in that year. Budapest's market is even smaller, though the most popular shares do have a liquid market.

But buyers must beware: in most transition countries' stock markets, settlement of share trading is a nightmare, and laws regulating and taxing capital gains are either nonexistent or a muddle. Some of the bigger companies in countries such as Russia, where insiders are firmly in the saddle, still hardly seem to recognize that outside shareholders—local or foreign—have any rights whatsoever, and they try to keep them out as much as possible. For example, Purneftegaz, a big Russian oil company, purposefully keeps its share registry in an isolated village in the remote western Siberian marshes. Any would-be buyer of the company's shares must fly from Moscow to Surgut, catch a train to the sleepy provincial center of Khanty Mansiisk, and then drive for a few hours in order to register his or her shares (registration that can still be denied at the door), and thus make ownership legal.

Custody (asset safekeeping and accounting) is always a big worry for investors, foreign and domestic alike. They do not want to entrust their shares to fledgling brokers with scant track records. The problem is one of safekeeping. In the West, instead of keeping share certificates at home tucked under a mattress, most shareholders trust their brokers to hold their shares until they want to sell them. Because most brokers in the transition countries are new to the game and stock exchanges are untested watchdogs of broker integrity, investors do not have the same trust in the honesty and reliability of brokers and are left in the lurch about where to place their shares for safekeeping. Some foreign banks, particularly in Moscow, have been granted permission by governments to assume these custodial functions. But most are kept on a short leash, and access to them is denied to most average investors.

For mutual funds with overseas investments, custody is an especially serious problem. Because of a U.S. law designed to prevent manipulation, American mutual funds (which are the biggest) must place their shares with an "independent custodian" satisfying certain stringent integrity requirements that new domestic institutions in the transition countries are not likely to meet. This is one reason why Chase Manhattan, Citicorp, and Credit Suisse have all established custody businesses in Moscow. But Russia is huge, with a potential for huge profits, which means that Western brokers are willing to absorb the costs of such establishments in the hope of big profits to come. Other countries lack this lure. This is also why the laws of some countries mandating that shares be deposited with domestic custodians are potentially quite damaging. The problem is particularly serious in countries in which shares are "immaterial" (that is, do not exist on paper), and the only documentation of ownership is found in a company's share register. Such meager documentation makes it next to impossible for mainstream funds to invest, because the local companies could never be qualified as proper custodians.

Share registration, custodial duties—these are the scrivener's end of the world of finance: dull, but vital to efficient markets. By definition, capital markets involve transactions that are complete only at the point when the seller of a share or bond is paid by the buyer. Until that point is reached, there is a sort of financial limbo where all deals remain uncertain. Indeed, it is useful to think of the financial system as something akin to an inverted pyramid; it is seldom appreciated that every stone of that pyramid—that is, every transaction—involves some degree of uncertainty. The more primitive the financial system a country has—the more delay between the time a buyer agrees to pay and the moment payment is actually made—the greater and more damaging the uncertainty. A nightmare scenario in all financial systems is that an institution will go under, leaving huge bills unpaid in this limbo. Since other individuals and institutions proceed on the assumption that settlement will be made, they will be damaged not just by the direct loss of unpaid bills owed to them, but also by the extra business they already wrote for the next layer of the pyramid in anticipation of the revenues that will now not be received. Without reliable settlement mechanisms, a financial system is vulnerable to a domino effect that may start as only a little local difficulty.

But the most fundamental problem with investing (for locals and outsiders) in Eastern Europe and the NIS is that capital markets are virtually information-free. Managers in the insider-dominated companies of the region have a vested interest in not releasing information about their firms, even if they have it, which often they do not. According to a recent study by the World Bank and the CEU Privatization Project, an astonishing 49% of large outside owners of Russian companies report that they receive no financial information from most companies in their portfolio. Even when insiders do not block access, market institutions whose job it is to collect, interpret, and distribute this information are in their infancy. As a result, investing in the region is often more like playing roulette than making an informed choice about one's portfolio.

6.1 Place Your Bets

Although such figures are slippery, capital investment is growing fast despite the hurdles and worries that bedevil the region. In 1990, foreign direct investment (FDI) and portfolio equity investment were only about a third as big as development and standby loans from the World Bank, IMF, EBRD, and individual governments (see figure 6.1). By 1993, although official loans increased in absolute terms, FDI and portfolio investment were a bigger source of funds. Direct investment (meaning that one firm buys a stake in another and is active in exercising its ownership rights) in the region has waxed and waned, with Poland, Hungary, and the Czech Republic benefiting in the early 1990s, Russia in late 1993–94. Now, the Baltics, Ukraine, and even tiny Moldova (which saw FDI rise 75%—admittedly from a small base—in one year alone) are becoming somewhat fashionable, at least among swashbuckling investors.

If the early years of the postcommunist transition were the era of FDI, the next era looks as if it will be the age of portfolio investment. Daiwa Europe, a mutual fund subsidiary of the big Japanese investment firm, expects fund investment to top $1.25 billion in 1997. The coming of portfolio investment is important because portfolio investment forms the world's biggest source of capital. Portfolio investors—primarily such institutions as mutual funds and pension funds—buy shares not because they want to manage companies, but because they expect the companies in which they invest to grow, providing increasing share value as well as dividends. Such investors largely leave managers to run the companies as they see fit, monitoring them through their trading in the stock market, with share prices acting as a sort of approval rating. In 1992, to cite just one not atypical example, portfolio investment was almost nonexistent in Lithuania, while FDI stood at over $100 million. In 1995, however, portfolio investment reached $62 million, while FDI remained constant. The

Figure 6.1

Official versus Private Financial Flows to Eastern Europe, 1990–1994 (in Thousands of U.S. Dollars)

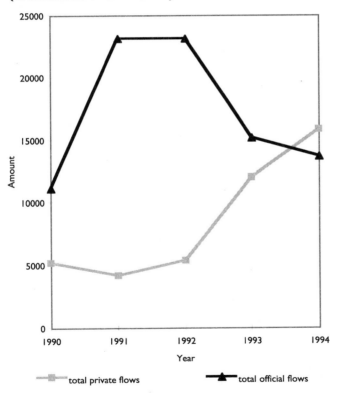

Source: IMF, IFC, EBRD.

EBRD reckons that between 1996 and 2000, portfolio investment in shares, bonds, and other instruments of East European and NIS firms will catch up to and surpass the level of FDI.

All this creates great excitement in the region's bourses, attracting domestic as well as foreign buyers. Russian, Polish, Czech, and Hungarian equity markets have risen to dizzying heights, only to collapse and regroup. Indeed, Russia's equity markets now act as political barometers much as they do in the West, as the wild swings in the market during the presidential contest between Boris Yeltsin and Gennadi Zyuganov in the spring and summer of 1995 demonstrated. Despite the ups and downs, Hans-Joerg Rudloff, once king of the Eurobond market and, as the first head of CS First Boston in Europe, the man who led the world's charge into the Russian market, said in late 1995 that "if everything comes together—capital market development, economic growth with lowering inflation, an increase in liquidity—it is conceivable that the region will be able to meet damn near all of its own capital needs." Rudloff is putting his money where his mouth is; he left CS First Boston to set up his own investment bank specializing in East European and Russian equities.

But if growth of investment is to continue, functioning capital markets must become permanent pillars on the financial landscape. Even in the most free-market-oriented countries of the region—Estonia, the Czech Republic, Poland, and Slovenia—companies continue to rely heavily on bank finance. As a result some banks are enjoying wide margins and fat profits. Now these countries need to free corporate borrowers from reliance on costly bank lending and direct them to the emerging capital markets where they can raise capital by selling shares in their firms.

Capital markets are needed even more urgently as catalysts for growth in such countries as Belarus, Ukraine, Romania, Macedonia, Kazakhstan, Uzbekistan, and Bulgaria that came late to the reform table (or have not even arrived yet). In all seven countries, state banks show little interest in profit and loss, and huge rafts of companies continue to depend on state handouts. How to allow useless companies to go bankrupt is a knotty problem that no one in the region has yet solved. But for profitable enterprises, developing capital markets means that access to money need not be dependent on the goodwill of bureaucrats. Investors who provide the alternative sources of cash may be more demanding about the kind of information and accountability they expect from companies. That, in turn, should only encourage firms to become more efficient.

Dynamic new intermediaries to facilitate financial transactions must emerge if capital markets are to function. Some are doing just that and, at times, in the most unlikely and infertile of terrains. FICO, a financial firm with headquarters in Minsk, Belarus, grew in a short two years from a tiny three-person currency exchange tucked away in a faded Minsk hotel into a 200-employee company with a turnover of $10 million a month and ownership stakes in twenty biggish privatized companies. "When we started," says Natalia Shevko, FICO's shrewd general director (who borrowed $40,000 in Moscow to get the firm running), "nobody knew how to deal in currencies or trade shares. We borrowed some books and tried to implement the Western experience here." Despite murky laws and political hostility, the firm is positioned, says Tom Jenkins of Coopers and Lybrand, "as a full-service merchant bank" that mediates for institutions as varied as Belarusian state banks and the Exarchate of the Russian Orthodox Church in Belarus.

Although the increasingly repressive government of Belarus has cracked down hard on FICO, the fact that robust financial activity is underway in the scorched economic climate of Belarus points to a lesson for most policy makers: the region's thirst for capital, both domestic and foreign, means that those countries that want to succeed must produce competitive financial markets as well as competitive financial products to market. To meet this goal will mean significant changes to stock markets, bond markets, banks, and, most importantly, in the way governments themselves do business.

6.2 All About Bourses

Stock and bond markets exist primarily to introduce those with capital to businesses that need it. Their second function is to provide an after-sales service, a market in which shares and debt instruments can be easily and reliably traded. (The two goals are not unrelated: the more liquid the markets, the more easily people invest in securities traded on them without fear of being locked in to their holdings.)

Differing national traditions affect the relative strength of stock and bond markets, as Western experience amply demonstrates. Shares in many German companies, for example, are privately held, which means that relatively few are traded on the Frankfurt Stock Exchange. Companies instead secure capital through the close, long-term relations they have with German banks. These companies, like those in Japan, also raise a lot of cash by selling corporate bonds. Such long-term government bonds are popular with those financial institutions that have long-term liabilities, for example, insurance companies and pension funds committed to paying out predetermined amounts to individuals many years ahead. In the West, an ever-increasing portion of private personal savings is managed by these institutions. The United States and Britain, however, possess highly developed stock markets, and companies use them widely to raise capital through floating shares.

Stock markets channel money into existing companies and into new ones. The former get the lion's share, primarily because their reputations have been tested over time, so the risk in investing is diminished. But there are many ways in which a company can issue new shares. One way is for an already quoted company to offer shares to its own shareholders. In such a "rights issue," shareholders subscribe for new shares in proportion to their existing holdings at a discount to their market price. If they do not want to exercise their rights, they can sell them to others who want to buy the company's shares.

The most common method for companies to "go public" is an "initial public offering" (IPO), in which a company first sells shares to an intermediary (an "underwriter") that specializes in issuing new shares, such as an investment bank or a stockbroking firm. These shares are then sold to the public, usually at a small premium. A key feature of this "flotation" is the publication of a prospectus outlining the company's record and prospects. It has to be vetted by lawyers and auditors and, in some countries, advertised in the press.

Less common in any stock market is an issue by tender, in which shares are not offered at a fixed price. The prospectus that the company publishes to announce its arrival on the market quotes only a minimum price, and investors must name their price and the number of shares they would take. Allocations are made at the highest price that will clear the issue. Small issues can also be accommodated by a "placing," where investment banks sell the shares to their clients, normally pension funds and insurance companies.

Because in many countries new issues must be registered with a special government agency, such as the American Securities and Exchange Commission, and must comply with various special requirements of the exchange on which they are to be traded, legal and auditing fees make going public a costly proposition. Underwriters also charge a commission amounting to at least $1\frac{1}{4}\%$ of the proceeds in exchange for their obligation to take up any shares the public does not buy.

Small, cash-strapped but innovative companies can avoid some of this cost by tapping the alternative "unlisted securities market." These markets are tailored to allow people to invest in fledgling companies that would have flinched at the cost of a full listing. The costs of going public here are smaller because the exchange listing requirements are less demanding.

The United States has long offered alternative routes to capital for small or new companies. The New York Stock Exchange (NYSE)—the only exchange actually located on Wall Street—is the senior market, founded in 1792. It overshadows all other exchanges around the globe in terms of the capital assets listed on the exchange. The much smaller American Stock Exchange (ASE) operates a nursery for small and mid-sized companies. There are also fourteen regional exchanges. Last but not least, there is the over-the-counter market, NASDAQ, that has no trading floor but operates via a network of computer screens. Here shares are traded without most of the demanding listing requirements of the NYSE. NASDAQ, for the most part, is a market for companies that may not choose or be able to meet the strict criteria for a quotation on the formal exchanges, although America's biggest high-tech companies, such as Intel and Microsoft, who began their existence on NASDAQ, remain listed on the exchange.

Trading on most American stock exchanges works on the auction principle, in which securities brokers arrange trades by competitive bidding. Responsibility for keeping an orderly market rests with specialists, to each of whom a certain number of stocks are assigned. A specialist's job is to buy or sell for his own account in order to maintain a continuous market if there is an imbalance in supply and demand. He also maintains a book of so-called limit orders, that is, orders to buy or sell a share at a preset price or a better one. If these orders cannot be satisfied immediately, they are entered in the specialist's book in order of time and price. When market prices match specifications, the order must be executed before other business and before later orders at the same price. For his troubles the specialist collects a floor brokerage commission.

Not all bourses use specialists in this manner. Some exchanges, such as the French, which is a model for many transition countries, make all trades within a (computerized) central system. All bids and offers are collected by licensed brokers and processed by the central exchange. After a certain time, prices are fixed by a computer that matches bids and offers. Although there are some disadvantages to this system when large blocks are traded, it solves one problem endemic to developing markets: low liquidity is dealt with as bids and offers can be collected over a longer period of time than that allowed in the American system. Consequently, it has strong appeal in Eastern Europe, where the Lithuanian, Latvian, Romanian, Polish, Czech, and other bourses mimic the French model.

In the United States, unlike most other countries, customers can buy shares "on margin," which means by paying only a percentage of the cost, with the balance advanced on credit by the broker. (Margin trading allows the investor to leverage his own funds and thus make money more quickly. But the reverse is also true; when a speculator makes a wrong bet, losses may be lightning-quick and devastating.) Since 1934, margin limits have been set (and varied) by the Federal Reserve Board, the American central bank. In addition, exchanges have their own margin requirements. Since margin players can lose more money than they invest, they may be required to top up their margin (put up additional money) from time to time if prices move against them.

Official margin limits were established in response to abuse and widespread speculation in the 1920s. This also resulted in the creation by legislation of a formal watchdog, the Securities and Exchange Commission (SEC). The SEC has become the model for regulatory bodies around the world, including Eastern Europe and the NIS. It has regulatory powers over all the leading U.S. stock markets. All new issues must be registered with the commission, which scrutinizes the registration statement for errors and omissions. The SEC and individual investors can sue the issuer, the underwriters, and sometimes the lawyers and accountants for any misrepresentations.

6.3 Privatization by Trading

To novice privatizers, flogging state industries on a stock exchange seemed like a perfect device to kill two birds with one stone. Companies are sold, not given away, thus in theory raising revenues and minimizing complaints of corruption from the public. Moreover, the mass issue of shares means that a stock exchange is kick-started. Every transition country government that tried this gambit, however, has gotten scorched.

Hungarians and Poles were the first to be taught this harsh lesson. The much-vaunted "First Privatization Program" in Budapest was supposed to be a model for the sale of a large number of state firms. Twenty companies deemed the "flagships" of Hungarian business were chosen for the first sale. Foreign investment banks and consulting firms advised the State Privatization Agency (SPA) in the process, and elaborate plans were made to prepare the companies for privatization and to design the postprivatization ownership structure. Following French methods, a strategic investor was to be found for each company, and a portion of the shares was to be floated on the Budapest exchange (sometimes together with Vienna's bourse) in a series of IPOs.

What was projected as a way to usher Hungary into the family of Western nations turned abject failure as no chosen company was sold for several years. Instead, with managers firmly opposed to SPA-led sales and Hungary's economy worsening daily, the firms languished in an ownership limbo until the program was quietly abandoned.

Poland's "capital privatization" was more successful in creating a lively stock exchange in Warsaw, but not in making a dent in state control of most Polish industry because the number of companies floated in this matter was very small. One reason for the Warsaw's bourse's dizzying rise in 1993–94, indeed, was that a mere twenty-one companies were listed on the exchange, meaning that there were not enough shares to go around to meet demand, thus artificially inflating prices. More issues are traded now, but they are still a mere fraction of Polish firms.

The problem with using stock exchanges as a vehicle for privatization is that the process is far too cumbersome. Preparation of the companies for such sales, involving a valuation and a changeover to a new system of accounting, is time-consuming and very costly. Too many government agencies—finance ministries, privatization agencies, securities commissions, central banks—dip their hands into the pot, and the officials in charge of the flotation quickly learn that they can rarely lose or be attacked politically for not selling, but can very easily be accused of corruption if the selling price is too low.

Take the case of IBUSZ, a Hungarian company privatized on the Budapest Stock Exchange (BSE) by Hungary's first postcommunist government. The company's IPO soared at first, from Ft 4,900 to Ft 12,500 within days. Political attacks about squandering state assets soon popped this balloon. From success story, IBUSZ became a scandal of profiteering. The head of the privatization agency (SPA) was sacked, damaging and delaying the entire privatization process and the BSE. Much the same happened in Poland when Bank Slaski was privatized through a sale of shares. A political firestorm erupted, with cries of corruption and ministerial sackings convulsing the privatization program.

The lesson that IPOs are a suspect and difficult way to privatize and that they do little toward the creation of a functioning capital market is apparently a difficult one for ministers and politicians, let alone ordinary people, to learn. Consider the case of Macedonia. Feuding erupted between the country's Privatization Agency and its Security Commission in February 1995, when the latter denied the former permission to open a stock exchange, which the country lacked. The Privatization Agency wanted to use the exchange to flog the 50% of company shares that were transferred to it in the chaotic early days of Macedonian independence in 1990–91. (Macedonia's state pension fund was to receive 15% of the shares for its capitalization.)

Legal and policy reasons could be marshalled to support the commission's obstruction. The Security Commission's charter calls for Macedonia to have a stock exchange initiated by the private sector—banks, savings institutions, investment funds, brokerage houses—not by the state. Moreover, the Privatization Agency favors insider privatizations, a method distinctly unfriendly to the needs of a developing capital market. Managers, who like to keep company information close to their vests, are able to buy their firms by putting down as little as 10% of the company's book value and promising to buy up to 51 % within five years. Insider buyers have a ready-made interest in suppressing share prices, not maximizing shareholder equity.

Beaten but not broken, the Privatization Agency tried to start a spontaneous market for shares by offering the 5% of OTEX (a textiles company and one of the country's few commercial success stories since the breakup of Yugoslavia) it held to banks, savings institutions, and individuals that registered with it. Television, newspaper, and radio advertisements touted the sale. Nevertheless, the sale flopped, as only seventeen shares were sold on the first day and only two hundred more in the month that followed.

Similar efforts in Belarus and Latvia incited similar fates. When the Belarusian authorities sold shares in PromStroi Bank, one of the country's largest, prices at the bank's initial public offering in October 1993 scarcely reached $.17 per share. Since then they have fallen to $.052 per share. To be sure, rampant inflation pushed the share price (as measured in dollars) down, but economists at the EBRD reckon that the bank's managers also played a sinister role in suppressing the value of shares as they were buying out the bank's nationwide network and extensive property on the cheap. Latvia's Privatization Agency doomed its two attempted IPO's to failure by concocting a confusing scheme that fixed a ladder of different share prices for different categories of bidders.

6.4 Too Much of a Not-So-Good Thing

Mass privatization is another way privatized firms emerge on infant equity markets. Problems that bedevil countries that went this route are the opposite of those that privatized by using sales: a surfeit of companies not ready for public trading makes for a very spotty market.

The Prague Stock Exchange is proof positive of the fact that even strong economic growth and government encouragement are not enough to insure that investors in stocks will make money or that new capital will be raised. Five years after their establishment, Czech stock markets remain sleepy backwaters of little importance in the country's growth. Blame for this must go, in part, to the country's rapid privatization. The market remains indifferent to most of the hundreds of issues that flooded onto it. Moldova, which used a variant of the Czech mass privatization scheme, faces similar problems. Of the six-hundred-plus joint-stock companies created during privatization, a mere twenty-five have been able to complete shareholder registration, the first step toward listing on Moldova's stock exchange.

As a result of mass privatization, in the countries in which the method has been used it is hard to trace who owns what shares, and what stocks are being bought and sold. Traded companies in the Czech Republic are not required to disclose much information about themselves and so do not, and the market lacks a strong supervisor to deter insider trading and other abuses. Concentration of ownership among a few investment funds means that most trades are struck privately, at unpublished prices and off the Prague Stock Exchange. Banks and investment funds, indeed, tend to sell shares to each other in private. Perhaps 90 % of all share trading is conducted in this secretive way. The Prague stockbrokers Wood and Company have argued that such off-the-exchange trading is a key reason why the Prague market has the lowest ratio of turnover to market capitalization in the world.

Public and private officials are not blind to these flaws. "I am not enthusiastic when I read in the foreign press that the difference between the number of companies traded in New York and Prague is very small: five hundred to six hundred companies," says Kamil Janacek, chief economist at Komercni Banka, the big Czech commercial bank. The problem is that "there are many companies that in normal economies would be either not tradeable or not joint-stock companies at all." Only two hundred companies should be on the exchange, says Janacek. "Our main problem is how to get 'nonstandard' shares" off the exchange and "not damage the rights of existing shareholders." Jiri Skalicky, the minister of privatization in 1995, agrees: "Step by step," he says, we must push "many joint-stock companies off the capital market." The first step in this direction was taken late in the summer of 1995, when the exchange separated all the listed issues into three distinct investment categories, effectively downgrading most of the ineligible stocks.

Equally at fault in stunting the performance of the Czech capital market is the performance of privatized firms themselves. New owners are mainly investment funds, many run by banks with little experience in restructuring companies. So long as a bank fund's own loans to a firm are being paid, the fund representatives keep their mouths shut at board meetings. But foreign investors have bought Czech shares at high prices in the expectation that private ownership and a growing economy would spark strong growth in profits. They were wrong.

Such mistakes are likely to be repeated in Kyrgyzstan as it transforms bodies built with privatization duties in mind into everyday financial institutions. The coupon exchange, where privatization vouchers were traded, was recast as the Kyrgyz stock market. Investment funds became brokerage houses. Certainly isolated Kyrgyzstan, as part of its bold liberalization of the economy (daring, particularly in comparison to its richer former Soviet neighbors Kazakhstan and Uzbekistan), pushed privatization farther and faster than anyone expected: by 1995, 55% of all industry was in private hands. So speedy was the privatization process, however, that investment funds (as in the Czech Republic) had little time (and often less incentive) to engage in industrial restructuring. Because they needed to gain managerial support in order to secure employee coupons, it is said in Bishkek that relations are far too cozy between managers of privatized firms and investment fund bosses, and that this stifles business reform.

Though privatization may be no cure-all for existing capital markets, it remains the best catalyst for getting a capital market off the drawing board. Even in slow-moving Romania, the expectation of the (long-postponed) mass privatization program created powerful inducements to create new financial institutions. Romania's central bank made registration of investment funds far easier than that of banks, with a corresponding ease in regulatory oversight. Banks themselves ran fast into this loophole, with Dacia Felix and Credit Bank opening their own investment funds that used bank facilities for selling certificates and giving loans as well as for holding fund deposits from ordinary Romanians. Although these funds were, under President Iliescu, restricted from getting involved in Romania's coupon privatization program, they eagerly awaited the time when coupons could be exchanged for shares in Romanian companies, at which point they envisioned becoming a major player on the market.

Despite the open hostility which was often shown toward them by the Iliescu government, competition among Romanian investment funds was fierce. By 1996 the biggest were fast approaching the country's big six banks in terms of size. Hoped-for profits were such that a number of foreign financial groups leapt into the Romanian market. Austria's Creditanstalt-Bankverein, for example, has formed two local companies to tap this burgeoning field: Creditanstalt Financial Advisors acts as an investment bank, advising and financing those who want to enter the mutual fund field, and Creditanstalt Invest Romania directly provides management skills to Romanian funds. The director of both firms is Sorin Dan, who is also a director of Proinvest, which administers Dacia Felix Fund. Not surprisingly, he began to push for "future cooperation between Proinvest and Creditanstalt Invest Romania on administering together the Dacia Felix Fund." That sort of cooperation may be the best hope for turning investment funds into the catalysts for restructuring that they are meant to be.

6.5 Run, Don't Walk

With the newly privatized companies as the sole supply of the region's equity trading, East European and NIS exchanges operate in what can only be called a black hole of financial information. It is in fact next to impossible for outsiders to work out what is going on inside most of the region's traded companies. Managers, either because they are protecting their backs or are behaving in the high-handed way they always have behaved, are usually loath to give information to outsiders. Socialist accounting standards, still in use in many companies, largely ignore costs and thus leave a firm with little idea of whether its declared profits are real or figments of the imagination. Companies that are making money do their best to hide their profits so as to ward off the tax collectors and to make profitable side deals possible for themselves.

Stories about abuse of shareholder rights abound. Most firms, for example, do not pay dividends. Those that do often issue dividend statements that bear little or no relation to a firm's profits. Some also issue new equity to their managers' friends without shareholders' consent. In 1994 in Russia, for example, the Primorsky Shipping Company actually doubled its share capital by making an unauthorized issue of the company's shares to a subsidiary.

Even when investors want to buy shares, it can be a daunting task. Foreigners seeking to invest in Lithuanian banks must ask permission first of the bank, then of the central bank, and finally of a number of ministries. People who want to buy shares in the Russian energy giant Gazprom must do something similar.

If they later want to sell the shares they have purchased, Gazprom has first refusal and can buy back its shares at a discount. Small wonder that Gazprom shares are rarely traded.

Pricing share issues under these conditions can be a nightmare. In Russia, for example, brokers try to gauge the value of oil companies by the clumsy means of dividing a company's market capitalization by its proven reserves of oil and gas. In 1995, this method valued most Russian oil companies' reserves at a piddling five cents a barrel, less than 1 % of the amount at which similar assets would be valued at in the West. But asset valuations are also unreliable because they tell investors nothing about a company's ability to generate cash. A company can have great assets, but if it offers no hope of future profits, then it is a waste to buy shares in it.

Given this absence of information, the level of share prices and trading over the next few years at least is likely to be heavily influenced by capital flows, not by the value of underlying assets. However, when the fundamentals cease to matter, markets tend to become excessively volatile. Speculative fever can indeed make the region's markets hair-raising places. Poland, Russia, and Hungary all saw investment bubbles inflate and burst in the early 1990s.

Lack of liquidity is also a bane. In Lithuania, bid-offer spreads as wide as 100 % are not unknown. In Ukraine, there is no market at all in the shares of the few privatized firms that now exist. The only way to invest in them is to plunk someone outside a factory gate to hold a sign offering to buy a worker's shares. In the spring of 1996, a NASDAQ-style centralized computer system was established in the country, but with most shares in the hands of employees and managers, this system offers little hope of enticing the sort of share trading that will generate pressure on managers for reform. Moreover, lack of actual share certificates in most countries also poses a big headache. Usually the only proof of ownership is a company's share register. Even if new investors insure that they are on it, they are not safe. Companies in Kyrgyzstan, Latvia, Moldova, and Slovakia are known to arbitrarily strike off unwelcome shareholders. In Slovakia, indeed, this can be done for political reasons.

Political turmoil incites further gyrations. Although some countries, especially those that expect to enter the European Union in the near future, have settled into some sort of democratic consensus; in others, the specters of runaway inflation, political unrest, interventionist backlash, authoritarianism, or even civil war are never too far below the horizon.

Politics aside, there is also an exchange risk. Foreigners invest in dollars or D-marks, but a power plant, airline, or telecom facility in the transition countries will be earning forints, kroons, lats, lei, rubles, or tollars. If the Slovenian tollar were suddenly to depreciate in value against the dollar, would payments be guaranteed? And how is the currency risk balanced between borrowers and lenders? Questions like these are most prominent in Russia, where the ruble is not yet convertible but the need for infrastructural and other investments is gargantuan. Then the question is whether access to foreign exchange can be guaranteed at all.

Only Estonia, because its currency board system of national finance maintains an unbreakable link between the kroon and D-mark (eight Estonian kroons equal one D-mark), has escaped this snare. Currency stability allows Estonians legally and confidently to invest abroad through the forty-two mutual funds offered by Hansapank and Forekspank, two of the country's biggest financial concerns. Foreign funds, such as the London-based Baltic Republic Fund, also attract $30 million to Estonia from overseas investors.

But no amount of uncertainty seems to stop the urge to gamble on the market. In Moscow and St. Petersburg, brokers' offices are crowded with investors staring at flickering price screens. In Poland, during the wild bull market of 1993, amazed traders swapped stories about cab drivers and pensioners clutching lists of shares. In the spring of 1995, billboards in Maribor, site of one of the three Slovenian stock exchanges, touted brokerage houses and the latest share offerings.

6.6 Gold Rush on the Vltava?

Still, "here today, gone tomorrow" bourses and widely fluctuating prices are no way to encourage the foreign investors who have spotted, among many other opportunities, the massive infrastructure demands of the transition countries and want to invest in such projects through national capital markets. Such uncertainty means that these investors often prefer to give the stock market a miss and buy directly into companies that will satisfy these needs.

When the Czech government announced that a big chunk of Czech Telecom would be sold, a global scramble was set off. AT&T, British Telecom, Deutsche Telecom, Koninkilijke PTT, Swiss Telecom, and others rushed for a piece of the action. Bids arrived despite fears that the company's books were a mess. Such enthusiasm makes some people worry. A French banker involved in the sale compared the rage for telecom investment in the Czech Republic, Hungary, and even Russia to the mania for investing in American railways in the nineteenth century. Miles of track were laid, but investors in railroad companies often came up losers. Something similar may now be happening with modern-day equivalents: telecoms in Ukraine and Belarus.

America's AT&T in Ukraine and Britain's Cable and Wireless in Belarus both made big bets that telecom investments were no-lose propositions. Their certainty is waning, not because demand for improved communications is not there, but because bureaucratic mazes make fulfilling investment plans a nightmare. The problem goes beyond today's politics. Investors in communications want a reasonable return on their investments, but in both countries (as elsewhere in the region), telecoms are heavily regulated and prices controlled. Investors will put in financial capital only if they can be sure that government will in return commit its political capital to the tricky business of phasing out such controls. Even the free-market Estonians and Czechs have found this a bitter pill to swallow.

Just how tricky the investment in regulated businesses can be was illustrated by the spat between the Czech Republic and France over an investment in CSA, the Czech state airlines. The Czechs fretted about raising fares and cutting costs, two reasons why the deal unraveled. The episode set investors thinking. If plane fares for affluent travelers are politically vulnerable, how viable will other infrastructure investments that touch the wider population be? And if fares, communications, or electricity tariffs are subsidized, can investors rely on governments (which may disappear by the time of the next election) to make up the revenue shortfall?

Balancing these concerns makes negotiating infrastructure deals vastly more complicated. Haggling between governments, ministries, contractors, and bankers over billion-dollar projects like the Czech and Ukrainian telecom deals can take years. In the tug-of-war between investors and host countries, investors hold a trump card. The longer that transition countries wait, the more pressing their infrastructure needs become. And international financiers have a queue stretching from Asia through South Africa to Latin America of potential clients competing for their capital.

6.7 Silver Lining

Foreign direct investment (FDI) is important, both as a source of capital and a transfer of expertise. But FDI is limited as an engine of capital inflows because investors must not only send money, but also stretch their organizational capacities and scarce managerial resources (which, moreover, may be less valuable in the unfamiliar environment of the postcommunist countries than in their home market). Very large companies competing for a share of world markets can perhaps cope with being extended in this way. But the capital needs of the countries in transition go beyond the huge infrastructural projects and other plums of the domestic market. To generate sufficient resources for broad economic growth, they must attract international portfolio investment and tap domestic savings. For this, well-functioning capital markets are the best hope.

On this front, despite birth pangs and uncertainty, the record is cautiously encouraging. Although the market fever of 1993 and 1994 was overdone, it was not necessarily an aberration. Despite the subsequent falls on the Eastern stock markets, these years marked an important step forward: international investors discovered the region. Mutual fund interest in Russia, Poland, and the Czech Republic was especially marked. In 1993, capital inflows tripled; most of this cash was distributed among Russia, Poland, Hungary, and the Czech Republic.

In the first six months of 1994, despite an uncertain political situation marked by the rise of Vladimir Zhirinovsky and his ersatz "Black Hundreds," portfolio money flooded into Russia at the rate of $500 million per month, according to the then privatization minister (currently first deputy prime minister) Anatoli Chubais. That figure slackened in the second half of 1994, remaining flat for most of the next year, though the market began a sharp and steady rise after Boris Yeltsin's reelection in 1996. Russian companies are tapping this market with new offerings. Lukoil raised hundreds of millions of dollars by selling a 15% stake to foreigners.

Nothing succeeds like success: Warsaw's bull market of 1993 inspired many companies to swallow their doubts and list new issues on the exchange, doubling the number of shares on offer. Indeed, new issues such as Efekt, Bank Rozwoju Eksportu, Bank Inicjatyw Gospodarczych, Universal, and Exbud all saw their IPOs sold out fast despite lacking underwriters. Bank Slaski, Powszechny Bank Gospodarczy, and Bank Rozwoju Eksportu became Poland's first domestic underwriters when they purchased the unsold shares of Polifarb Cieszyn later that year.

This ability to tap domestic savings is essential because any market that depends for its long-term health on foreign money will inevitably collapse when it goes out of fashion. Here there are some encouraging signs, in Russia and elsewhere. The introduction of positive real interest rates in Russia in the autumn of 1994 led to a sharp increase in saving. Capital flight is by definition impossible to track with accuracy. However, signs abound that it has stopped in some countries and is slowing elsewhere. Estonia, which uniquely permitted its investment funds to shift their money abroad, now reckons that money is returning from places like Germany. Russia's securities commissioner, Sergei Vasiliev, believes that much of the foreign investment in Moscow securities that arrived in 1995 was in fact flight capital coming home to roost.

6.8 No Pain, No Gain

Behind the din of financial boom and bust and the shrill calls of "I told you so" coming from old-fashioned socialists in the region, large, impersonal forces are at work. The explanation for this bustling activity is that many stock markets look poised to become something more than the street bazaar they appeared to be (rightfully in most cases) just a scant year or two ago. Eastern Europe and the NIS stock exchanges are in the midst of a long-term spurt in growth. In 1993, stock markets in the ex-socialist countries had a total market capitalization of a few billion dollars at most. Today the same markets are capitalized at twenty times that amount.

A mixed brew of private and public forces fuels these developments. Russia's story is not atypical. It has two very different types of equity markets comprised of 200-odd stock exchanges. The first market trades bearer shares which were issued by the likes of MMM and Russki Dom Selenga. Most of these are more con than company, having few real assets beyond their ability to dupe investors into believing that their share price will rise indefinitely. The other market is in the registered shares of 17,000 privatized companies. This market is growing fast, and its rules are tightening.

Russian companies had to issue audited accounts in 1995 for their annual general meetings. These give investors some idea of a company's worth and allow them to make rough comparisons with businesses in other countries. On this basis, most Russian shares still look dirt cheap. Take Gazprom: it has proven gas reserves of 44 trillion cubic meters, produces 29% of the

Figure 6.2

Market Capitalization in Selected Markets, 1995 (in Millions of U.S. Dollars)

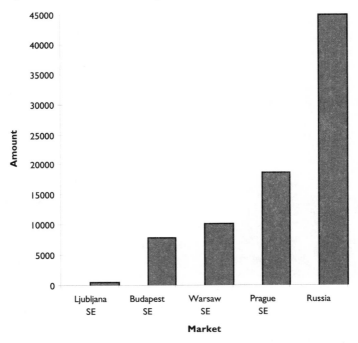

Source: National Banks, National Bourses.

world's annual output of natural gas, and exported gas worth $6.7 billion in 1993. But its shares are still traded mostly on a gray market (see figure 6.2).

Reasons for this disparity are also not hard to find. Gazprom is technologically antediluvian and monumentally mismanaged. Even apart from this, the managers, protected by the highest Kremlin powers, are so securely in the saddle that it is not clear ordinary shareholders will ever see any return on their investment.

The riskiness of transition country investments may shrink, however, as markets mature and market regulators find their bearings and gain confidence. Emerging markets are volatile for good reason. Investors are groping for fair values, small investors and syndicates often dominate at the expense of more stable institutions, regulation is weak and exchanges are vulnerable to manipulation. Under the conditions of the postcommunist transition, many problems are exacerbated by bad old habits and powerful vested interests opposed to ownership by outside investors. As markets grow up, these characteristics are likely to fade.

Tutoring helps. In the past three years, Russia, Slovenia, Romania, Moldova, Latvia, Lithuania, Kyrgyzstan and Uzbekistan have all established securities and exchange commissions, which are battling to bring some order to their respective markets. In Russia, Moldova, and Kyrgyzstan, these regulators are learning from the U.S.'s NASDAQ and New York Stock Exchange. The French bourse has played a big role in restructuring securities oversight in all three of the Baltic countries. Estonia, Latvia, and Lithuania are all learning how to police their markets without the dead hand of regulation killing off trading vitality and to encourage securities firms to set up compliance departments. (Adopting outside models can, however, breed confusion. Officials at Hungary's State Securities and Exchange Commission, which is also based on the American model, find it hard to apply American legal tools in a wider Hungarian legal system based on German principles.)

The development of institutional investors should bring added stability and reliability. Although some investment funds established as tools of mass privatization failed outright—a number of Russian fund managers vanished with shareholders' cash or were jailed for fraud—others grew into reputable and established institutions. Along with new private pension funds (in the

Czech Republic and Estonia) and mutual funds (such as Poland's Pioneer and Korona), these institutions may be less skittish than individuals and may carry more clout in pushing for reform.

Those brave enough to buy are already being better protected through several initiatives:

1. The Warsaw Stock Exchange requires that shareholder registers be kept by independent brokers, not by the firms themselves. Brokers, in turn, maintain accounts with the National Depository of Securities. Moreover, to build public confidence, Warsaw stockbrokers are forbidden from offering investment advice to customers. And, to enhance transparency, companies must publish monthly earnings reports—an even more exacting standard than the quarterly reports that are the norm in the West—and are banned from explaining their affairs privately to potential investors. Indeed, all price-sensitive information must now be published.

2. Kyrgyzstan requires listed companies to submit audits that may be vetted by the Ministry of Finance. Fiddling the books can be penalized by fines and/or prison sentences.

3. Hungary's BSE demands that all brokers settle trades within a day.

Although reforms such as these are tremendously important, they need to be backed by strong and continuous growth. However, the correlation between growth and rising share prices is not perfect, as Slovakia is now demonstrating. Its economy is growing at a robust 5.8% per year, but share prices are flat on their back due to the widespread perception that the government headed by Premier Vladimir Meciar is moving the country away from a free economy. Speculative booms a la Poland and Russia, indeed, can in the short run boost prices to unsustainable levels (something the region is likely to see time and again in the foreseeable future). Economic growth can also divert money from stock markets into fixed investment. But in general, fast-growing economies will have better performing stock markets.

6.9 Competition, Regulation, Supervision

The biggest threat to the official exchanges comes from the growing number of shares that are traded privately and the inadequate oversight of this trade. In Slovakia, for example, over 90% of all share transactions are said to be conducted off the two Bratislava-based exchanges, and often at the behest of the

Figure 6.3

**Turnover on Selected Stock Exchanges, 1994
(in Millions of U.S. Dollars)**

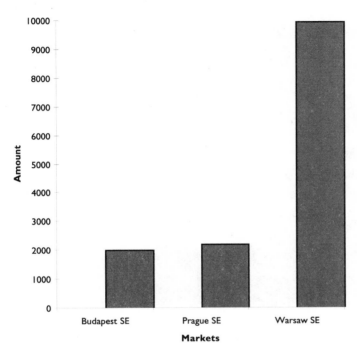

Source: National Banks, National Bourses.

state. The Prague Stock Exchange's record is not much better. Ceska Sporitelna, the big Czech savings bank, reckons that where 39% of Czech shares are traded on the Prague exchange, 60% are dealt elsewhere. (Other observers put this figure even higher, at 80% or 90%.) When Lithuania tried to stop such deals, trading in all shares came to a virtual halt as fears of heavy-handed government regulation were reawakened. One near-term goal of Hungary's SSEC is to bring the country's off-market trading under its umbrella; indeed, it wants all exchanges to be regulated by the same law, whether they trade in goods, securities, or futures (see figures 6.3 and 6.4–6.7).

193

But off-market trades have a good side too. The dominance of private sales and the growth of unregulated over-the-counter markets keep the official exchanges on their toes as they push stock markets to compete for customers by providing a reputation for reliability and integrity. As major stock exchanges strive to provide the things that private trades cannot, they improve their reliability, integrity, transparency, and enforcement. Competition among bourses also breeds better bourses. A report written last year for the EU by Graham Bannock and Partners, a British consultancy group, shows that exchanges that lack competition fail in their function. They overregulate, and they impose far too complex listing requirements; consequently, they inhibit development of an equity culture among investors.

Figure 6.4

Warsaw: Stock Exchange versus OTC Trade

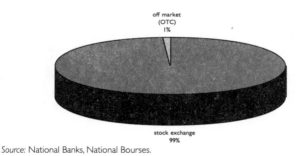

Source: National Banks, National Bourses.

Figure 6.5

Budapest: Stock Exchange versus OTC Trade

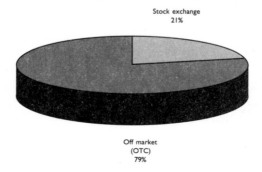

Source: National Banks, National Bourses.

194

Figure 6.6

Prague: Stock Exchange versus OTC Trade

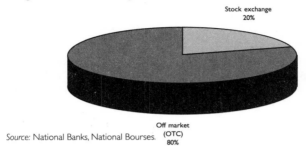

Source: National Banks, National Bourses.

Figure 6.7

Bratislava: Stock Exchange versus OTC Trade

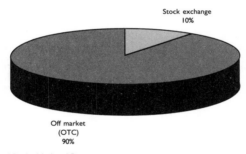

Source: National Banks, National Bourses.

Imposing order on chaotic exchanges may not be a bad thing. Bulgaria's government, for example, now requires that exchanges meet a minimal capital requirement of 100 million lev ($1.8 million) in order to trade. Dozens of impromptu exchanges have shut in the face of this, leaving only the Sofia-based First Bulgarian Stock Exchange functioning. But one pernicious problem identified in the Graham Bannock report occurs when established national exchanges boss second-tier bourses. Bigger bourses are reluctant to let smaller cousins flourish for fear of losing business to them. That fear certainly exists in the transition countries, particularly in those countries where the state played a strong hand in creating the market and where bourse regulators try to restrict big institutional investors and banks from pouring money into rival exchanges.

Many regulators in Eastern Europe and the NIS have not yet grasped this concept. Bulgaria's SEC imposes disclosure requirements for a prospectus that make the rules of the London and New York stock markets look loose in comparison. Lithuania, where many chaotic but lively financial exchanges sprang up in the private sector after 1991, now insists that only the government-sponsored National Exchange of Securities (NES) is authorized to trade in shares and bonds. Saying it wanted to root out firms privatized under suspicious circumstances, the government also ordered that all currently traded issues (over 2,000) be reregistered with a state-run central depository. Because of political interference in 1995–96, that depository is not yet fully functioning, so brokers are faced with ugly choices: stop trading until the depository is working or risk having the government nullify deals as illegal.

An extremely ripe example of this trend is also found in Slovakia. Its BOB Bourse, a derivatives market—unique in the region—is under pressure from the Ministry of Finance to merge with the bigger Bratislava Stock Exchange. Because the BOB competes against the main stock exchange, government regulators cracked down hard. Trading on the BOB began to fall in the wake of new restrictions. Investors in the exchange, however, may not lose their shirts if it is swallowed by the BSE. Stockholm's Options Market owns 30% of the BOB, and the Swedish government is taking an active hand, directly and through the EU, in protecting its citizens' interests.

Official zealousness, usually accompanied by its twin, bureaucratization, indeed may be the biggest threat to capital market growth. In searching for financial order, governments are constantly tempted to lay down commandments that are far too restrictive for financial institutions. Economic growth requires finance as its lifeblood, and capitalist finance in turn is born in risk. No matter how cleverly designed, any scheme to create a risk-free financial environment will stifle economies.

Disclosure of the information investors most need and self-regulation by financial firms, not heavy-handed administration, are the best ways to nurture capital market growth. A good supervisory approach has a core of rules to do with transparency, capital ratios, avoidance of over-concentrated lending, insider trading, and the like. But is based on a basic recognition that both established and budding financial firms cannot be shackled by an overly complex regulatory scheme. Provided that a financial company plays by certain simple rules and that its customers know what is going on, supervisors should not be able to stop it from innovating by imposing all sorts of petty regulations.

Regulators in the transition countries will find this hard. A penchant for butting in and devising detailed rules is addictive. Moreover, "discretion" for government regulators is usually an invitation for firms to curry favor and bureaucrats to meddle invidiously. State regulation also inspires the dangerous notion that financial safety is merely a matter of obeying the rules. If left to governments, capital markets will usually be run by the worst sort of combination: a politician's timidity and a policeman's nightstick. Disclosure by financial firms and building independent capital market bodies with reputations for trust will get to the heart of the matter. And trust must be informed, not blind. Transparency inspires belief in the honesty of deals; private-sector oversight bodies within capital markets will build on this, not through law, but through self-regulation that polices the integrity of markets.

6.10 Banks: Godfathers of Finance

In April 1995, a consortium of the nine main pillars of the Russian banking industry made the Chernomyrdin government an offer the banks thought that ministers could not refuse. They offered to lend the government 9 trillion rubles if it let them set up a trust to manage for the next five years the state's remaining stakes in Russia's biggest firms. Under this plan, the government would repay the loan from the proceeds when the shares were eventually sold (by the banks) on the stock market.

The bankers' motives were not hard to see. Before 1995, making money was easy pickings for Russia's bankers. They could borrow rubles from the central bank at interest rates lower than the prevailing rate of inflation. They could swap these rubles into dollars, sit back while the ruble fell, and then use some of the dollars to buy just enough devalued rubles to repay the central bank's loan. The dollars left over were pure profit. Since the rate at which the central bank lends to other banks is now consistently above inflation, life for bankers has become hard. Shakeout and consolidation are making banks more aggressive. Many have already been lapping up shares in big companies, not just because shares were cheap, but also as a way of forcing the firms to buy their services. This wheeze would have accelerated the process. The bankers also clearly hoped to end up as owners of the shares under their management.

For the Russian government, the proposal had one big attraction: it would allow the government to raise cash immediately, with the prospect of more money if the eventual sale of shares went well. But it would also have given control and perhaps eventual ownership of large swathes of Russian industry to the big banks, many of which, it is feared, are linked to organized crime groups. The banks, moreover, were demanding fat fees to perform this service. That the government took the plan seriously, indeed allowed the big banks to gain strong footholds in industry, testifies not only to its hunger for cash, but also to its fear that the banks could kick up a hornet's nest of political trouble.

In Germany, banks control large share holdings in industrial enterprises, owning some of the shares outright and voting an even greater part on behalf of their trust account clients (who empower the banks to exercise their stockholders rights). In Japan also, banks are important shareholders, often leading a group of large stakeholders dominating most Japanese companies. This model has been much praised for having forged strong and stable relations between banks and companies. These, in turn, are often said to provide reliable monitoring of the management and shareholder support for a long-term view of the company's interests. The success of the German and Japanese economies is sometimes linked with this system.

There is another side to the same coin, however. Both banks and companies pay a price for this intimacy because it makes each the hostage of the other. However, sometimes a strong and stable relationship can turn into a calamitous liability, as when the failing fortunes of industrial companies result in the near-collapse of a big bank. The huge bailout necessary to keep France's second biggest bank, Credit Lyonnais, afloat is testimony to this. Even that paradigm of universal banking, Deutsche Bank, screws up at times. Its recent failures to spot looming disasters at Metallgesellschaft, one of Germany's biggest industrial groups, and Schneider, a property group, cost the bank dearly in both cash and reputation.

German companies, too, take a hit. It may help them to have the solid support of a loyal bank, but they surrender freedom in return. Deutsche Bank owns a large stake of Daimler-Benz, voting more than 40% of its stock, making it the car maker's biggest and controlling shareholder. Although Deutsche Bank says that Daimler-Benz is free to shop around for its financing needs, it insists on being the lead manager for all big transactions such as rights issues.

All over the ex-socialist world there is a move afoot toward such "universal banking." One reason banks become shareholders is coldly practical: it makes sense in countries with weak bankruptcy laws to own shares in big firms in order to force them to repay their loans. But no matter the reason, governments might cock a wary eye at the trend. This is one reason why Anatoli Chubais, Russia's first deputy prime minister, rejigged the proposal by Russia's big banks to try and keep the banks in line, but without success.

6.11 Taming the Leviathan

It will be hard to keep banks from dominating finance in the emerging markets of the postcommunist world. To begin with, their political importance gives banks big advantages as capital markets are formed. For when banks dominate business, it is easy for governments to intervene in commercial decision making, whether by owning banks directly (as in Belarus, Poland, Romania, Slovakia, Ukraine, and Uzbekistan) or by steering the lending decisions of those banks supposedly in private hands (Albania, Latvia, Lithuania, and Slovenia). Banking is also too concentrated. In Uzbekistan, for example, Uzpromstroybank and Uzargoprombank issue about 90 % of all industrial and agricultural credits. Such monopolies can be challenged only by licensing new competitors, which is what is happening in Tashkent as new banks like Tadbirkor move aggressively into the big banks' turf.

Banks were often further strengthened by the mass privatization programs in Eastern Europe and the NIS because they were best positioned to form voucher investment funds and gain control over most of the equity of the privatized firms. This happened in the pioneer country of mass privatization, the Czech Republic, where banks control eight out of the ten biggest investment funds, and in Kazakhstan, where banks dominate the country's one hundred fifty privatization investment funds. Kazakhstan's big banks also established the country's unitary capital market, the Central Asian Stock Exchange (CASE), by first forcing a merger of the rival Almaty and Kazakh commodity exchanges, and then expanding the new market's focus to include securities, including privatization investment coupons, the Kazakh equivalent of vouchers.

In Hungary, banks have also managed to break into securities trading. At its reestablishment in 1988, the Budapest Stock Exchange blocked commercial banks from trading in government securities. BSE stockbrokers feared competition from banks, and they reiterated their opposition at the BSE's general assembly meeting last July. Fearing that it would lose such trading to the over-the-counter market, and possibly its leading role in Hungarian finance, the BSE decided to let banks in. Banks can now deal in government securities and financial derivatives (which they use to manage currency and interest rate risks) on the same market.

Bulgaria's government, too, has run up the white flag. It tried to shiver commercial banking from other financial services, but failed. Banks, however, must now register with the Securities Commission and play by the same rules as other financial groups. In particular, they must disclose more details of their activities than required by the banking regulations. The government has also opened the once exclusive domain of commercial banking to other financial intermediaries.

Kazakhstan also took steps to open up the banking sector. It intends to sell its shares in sixty-two state banks on the stock exchange, attempting to assure that broad ownership will prevent too much cross-ownership. Foreign banks are allowed to compete on a nearly equal footing with the national ones. Thirteen have accepted the challenge, including Chase Manhattan, ABN AMRO, and Bank Austria, as well as the Bank of China and Industrial and Commerce Bank of China.

Elimination of state-directed lending will also help to keep banks in line. As economists might have predicted, the heavily state-directed credit systems of Belarus, Kazakhstan, Romania, Ukraine, and Uzbekistan fostered inefficiency and weakened the emerging capital market system. Other countries such as Estonia, the Czech Republic, Latvia, and Russia are growing with relatively freer banks; one result is that their banks are starting to sort out their balance sheets while banks in Slovakia, where bureaucrats continue to direct bank loans, are mired ever deeper in debt.

Such differences are narrowing as deregulation spreads. In Estonia, Latvia, Lithuania, Poland, and Slovenia, liberalization of interest rates has happened or is beginning. Liberalization was one reason for the shakeout in Latvian banking that took place in the summer of 1995, when one-third of the country's banks shut their doors. In Romania that year, new bank licenses were granted for the first time since communism's fall. Economic necessity is driving these changes. As Siim Kallas, formerly the governor of Estonia's central bank and architect of the country's financial system, argues: "Yes, state-directed credit has brought economic growth in places like Asia. But this comes only at the early stage and at a high long-term cost. After this first burst, it acts as a permanent barrier to growth, so it is better to avoid it from the start." Many transition countries have reached that point. "I want markets to allocate credit," says Kyrgyzstan's finance minister, "not the government."

Even in Ukraine, where banks suffered from years of nationalization and state direction, things are changing. Forced to lend to sick industries, banks are sick. Under Leonid Kuchma's government, on this issue banks are at last being reformed. They may even be partially privatized. New licenses have been given out for private banks; the emphasis on lending to sick industries is being reduced.

Competitive pressure on banks is also the key ingredient that vital capital markets can provide. Here the magic word is "disintermediation," a term with which bankers in the United States and Europe are wearyingly and sadly familiar. If companies have the ability to borrow directly from capital markets and investors can put their money directly into stocks, bonds, and commercial paper (short-term company securities), banks lose their captive audience.

Disintermediation poses two potential threats that grow as this practice does:

1. As banks are cut out of some business, they may be tempted to take bigger risks. Banks should take risks, but they must know how to price them correctly, as part of a balanced portfolio. In seeking new businesses to replace disintermediators, a banker may not be as good at pricing risk, at least at the start. Worse, government action may make them see themselves as immune from such risks.

2. For supervisors, disintermediation is tricky. If they extend their knowledge and power to nonbank institutions that are assuming some banking risks, that could overstretch them. They would be right to wonder where the process would end because experience in the transition countries shows that inventive businessmen can push disintermediation a long way. Foolish business-to-business lending may cause ongoing financial damage if it builds up such an interwoven system that a loss anywhere hurts financial confidence everywhere.

Slovenia faces that prospect. When it cleaned up the banking sector's massive debts in 1990–91, assuming bad loans on the books, the government issued an unlimited guarantee for savings accounts. That promise was the catalyst for a vast inflow of savings that had been spirited abroad (primarily to Austria), which contributed to a 40% rise in the real value of the Slovene tollar in 1992. But such a guarantee leaves bankers feeling invulnerable, meaning that risk assessment is likely to be neglected because the government will pick up the tab for any losses incurred by banks.

6.12 Bonds that Free

Publicly, governments that have allowed capital markets to grow insist that they will not interfere in their management too heavily. But the debate between those who are in favor of an interventionist domestic financial policy and those who argue for a hands-off approach has only just begun. As governments scramble to meet their financing needs, the temptation to shape capital markets to meet short-term state budget needs will grow. The region's emerging bond markets provide an important test of a government's reformist credentials.

Nobody disputes that, except for the Czechs and Estonians, governments in the region have huge budgetary headaches. According to the EBRD, Hungary's deficit was 55% of GDP in 1994, Poland's 50%, Kazakhstan's 11% (in 1993, but probably higher since), Kyrgyzstan 19%, Romania 16%, and Russia 37%. Keeping national savings captive is a way that governments try to meet their debt obligations. In Uzbekistan, individual firms (state-owned or not) cannot float their own bonds to compete with the government's paper. Latvia thought banning commercial banks from reselling state bonds would maintain their value, but this discouraged banks from buying state paper in the first place. Coming to its senses, the government lifted that ban in April 1994.

Lithuania sugarcoats its bid to keep banks as a captive market for state bonds. Interest paid on government securities, both municipal and national, held by banks are not taxed. But there is a catch: tax-free status comes only if a bank holds a government security until maturity. If it does not, regular business tax rates apply. This inhibits the growth of a secondary market for state securities, a check likely to cripple Lithuania's prospects for developing a vital bond market.

In many transition countries the domestic bond market is still too often treated as a means of generating forced savings, as much as a mechanism for raising capital. A number of governments make purchase of state securities compulsory for banks and other financial institutions, often at below market rates. Belarus wants to extend forced purchasing to individuals, which turns the bond market into a form of taxation rather than a form of savings.

Slovak investors fear that the Meciar government may extend this bullying to bonds issued by state firms. With an equity market in the doldrums due to the hostility it faces from the Meciar government, investors are left with few choices as to where to put their money. They can keep them in savings accounts that pay a negative rate of interest, or they can buy state bonds or the bonds of state companies like Slovenske Elektrarne. Either way, the Slovak government keeps its hand on the financial rudder.

In the end such policies will turn out to be short sighted. State expenditures must be brought under control, and markets can help in disciplining their growth. Governments, being the most secure debtors, already have an advantage in the bond market, and trying to increase it by bullying tactics can only lead to squeezing out private borrowing. Active primary and secondary markets in government and corporate bonds are more likely to succeed in financing both the reasonable requirements of the state and the private sector when governments stop forcing people to buy their debt and allow the market to determine its value.

Some governments see the point of this: since 1995, the price of Kyrgyz, Latvian, Moldovan, and Polish government bonds are set by auction on the open market. Other governments may follow these examples. When and if they do, they open the door a bit wider to would-be corporate bond issuers as well. Many global bankers are anxious to show the way.

Bond financing seems the best bet to meet the region's immediate infrastructural needs. Although bank and equity finance play a role in financing infrastructure development, bond markets—which specialize in the long maturities of fifteen or twenty years demanded by infrastructure projects—should eventually bear more of the strain. Gaining the confidence of international bond markets is particularly important here in order to supplement domestic sources of capital.

The Czech Republic and Poland (which started from a very low level) have gone a long way toward making their bonds viable. Standard and Poor's and Moody's, the two premier rating agencies, gave the Czechs investment-grade ratings for their state bonds. Moody's also gave Poland an investment-grade rating. Other countries are also improving their positions sufficiently to sell bonds on the international markets. Slovakia received an investment-grade rating from Moody's based on its strong growth between 1993–95. Slovenia has been told by Standard and Poor's that it will receive a positive investment-rating whenever it asks. Estonia, too, is knocking at the door, ready for a positive rating, and may do so not because the government needs to borrow money to pay its bills, but because it wants to set a national rating that will in turn help companies sell their bonds. Citing these reviews by reliable rating services, bond buyers are gaining evidence that economic success is no flash in the pan. That growth in all of these countries (save Poland) comes linked with low inflation gives them an edge in competition with others in the region, particularly Russia.

Infrastructure projects are not the only likely source of new bond business. A broader market in corporate debt securities, especially those of private sector companies, is of great import as well. To global investors, the comparative balance between debt and equity markets in Eastern Europe and the NIS is a big indicator of the scope for future development. In the United States, 45% of new company funds are raised through corporate bond markets; a somewhat lesser figure tends to be the rule in Western Europe. In the transition countries the figure was less than 2% in 1995.

The belief that economic development will necessarily lead to the development of vibrant corporate bond markets is challenged by the German and Japanese experience, where banks have a lock on corporate lending. The same may happen in Eastern Europe and the NIS. Also, because of the morass of interfirm debt that followed in the wake of communism's collapse, there is today a bias against firms in the transition countries saddling themselves with even more obligations. Furthermore, inflation led to very high interest rates in many countries, and that makes borrowing extremely risky. Not surprisingly, therefore, companies prefer to raise funds through share issues, rather than debt. But a change in psychology may be fostered by the realization that continued issuance of shares onto poorly performing or flat stock exchanges will end up diluting a company's ownership.

From the investor's point of view, corporate bonds are safer bets than equities. Though Estonia mimics Germany in most things, its banks avoid taking equity holdings. This is one reason that the initial public offerings of such firms as Tartu Congress Center and Lekto failed in the market. Estonian banks prefer to buy bonds from creditworthy firms, which for now are few in number. But those firms that are creditworthy can clearly benefit from the emerging bond markets. Baltika, for example, raised 5 million kroons through a bond tender with an annual interest of 12%, some 4–6% less than it would have had to pay for a bank loan. Levi, a start-up firm that specializes in the risky business of installing cable television systems, also tapped the corporate bond market, although at a higher interest rate. Most company bonds come from big concerns such as Esti Gaas and ETK.

Innovation is a sure sign of a maturing market. In August 1994, a new type of security, called a KWIT (Komercyjny Weksel Inwestycyjno-Terminowy, which translates as Investment Term Commercial Bills of Exchange), similar to corporate bonds, appeared in Poland. These bills harken back to an interwar piece of legislation, the Bill of Exchange Law of 1936. This law has particular appeal for investors, as it is quite demanding in its disclosure requirements. ING Bank Warsaw has parlayed this transparency into a vibrant trade, issuing a dozen KWITs in 1995.

More progress is clearly expected in the future, at least by some. The potential for East European and NIS bonds has moved Moody's, Standard and Poor's, and IBCA to deepen their presence in the region. Unsolicited, Moody's has been issuing ratings for banks in the region, having already issued a few in Poland. Following the lead of these agencies, Slovenia is trying to transform Sluba Drubenega Knjigovodstva, the old monopoly bookkeeping agency for industries under Tito's social ownership regime, into what it hopes will be a national rating agency. This body's ties to the government may crimp its prospects. Because it must compete, however, with the private sector rating agencies developing within Slovene banks and investment funds, its ratings will have to be reliable or risk being dismissed out of hand. Skepticism dominates rating agencies. "Just because a company has glossy brochures, and an impressive board, doesn't mean we know anything that really matters. There may be ties and obligations that we can never find or understand," says one Moody's executive. Even so, the increasing activities of these agencies reflect the growing interest of their clients in the region's bonds.

6.13 Take the Offensive

Dizzying rises and falls in stock prices, bond issues that go unsold, financial scandals that leave thousands grumbling: all are likely to continue for some time in the transition countries. But after the cheats and profiteers have their day in the sun, financial mania may gradually, if haphazardly, mutate into productive investment. In the meantime, it should be realized by all that the crashes and uncertainties that occur are natural and cleansing and serve to sort out the wheat from the chaff in finance and business. Postcommunist governments must steel themselves to withstand these eruptions, realizing that their cleansing effects can be healthy. Good capital markets understand that investment is based on continual change and its anticipation.

So enthusiasm for capital markets should not be ruptured by scandals or brutish government responses to them. Overregulation is dangerous because it revives fear of state-directed finance at a time when the region's capital markets are just beginning to modernize. As Harvard Business School's Michael Porter argued in his book *The Competitive Advantage of Nations,* successful industries tend to emerge in places where intensely competitive rivals push each other to excel. Too tight an oversight of the emerging financial world will deprive financial firms of their incentives to innovate. Worse, if the health of infant markets and financial firms deteriorates, governments might be tempted to drag these entities even closer into the state's embrace.

Better for governments to shun pleas that capital markets need minute-by-minute policing. Better still, they should heed the message that finance in the region needs ever increasing levels of competition, not less. It needs market-based supervision, not excess or ham-handed state regulation. That means, among other things, finishing the legal infrastructure for capital markets as soon as possible and setting firms free to compete—both companies listed on the exchanges and the financial services firms that make the stock exchanges go. Once this infrastructure of laws is defined and on the books, there will be fewer places for cheats to hide. Governments must also resolve not to sacrifice long-term economic gains to ease short-term political pains.

The problem is that when governments fret about financial stability, they are usually worrying about rogues and crooks. They ought to spot the mote in their own eye. The biggest danger to financial stability is economic instability, particularly inflation, which is a child of bad fiscal and monetary policies by government. As the nations of Eastern Europe and the NIS continue to reform, the capacity of governments to cause harm will be greater than it is now.

Capital markets will need to prove themselves to be more than a here-today, gone-tomorrow fad if the transition countries are to insure their continued progress along the road to prosperity. If the region's infant stock, bond, and commodity markets do stabilize and mature, this could produce beneficial effects far wider than governments anticipate because effective capital markets impose their discipline on governments as well as on businesses. Where the boom and bust cycles of sovereign debt lending once depressed development in other regions of the world, private debt and equity investment can provide the transition countries a lasting solution to their economic woes by channeling funds to business leaders in companies rather than to bureaucrats in a labyrinth of ministries. By acting, indeed, on the assumption that power in the region once more belongs to capital, reformers are paying a backhanded compliment to their old nemesis, Karl Marx.

7
Social Insecurity
Pension Systems under Fire

In the wake of the vast economic, social, and political transformations underway throughout the postcommunist world, it is more than pardonable for East European and NIS finance ministers to think that restraining public spending as they reform their economies is a vexing job. Their successors will one day envy them if a budgetary time bomb facing each government in the region is not defused. Governments are barely managing to meet the lavish pension obligations imposed by the deposed communist regimes. Soon the cost of these benefits will be too much for national budgets to bear. Keeping the promises made to pensioners during the communist era will turn the children of pensioners gray.

The cast is the same, though the backdrop varies, in little scenes of human anguish playing daily from Riga to Tashkent. Slack-shouldered men and women, old at sixty, gather in small groups at a loss what to do, missing their work almost as much as their pay. Such visions of breadline poverty haunt old and young alike, whether in the decaying high-rise flats of Bratislava and Kiev or outside Chisinau and Brest in the acres of low wooden huts. Old folk in the region are by no means whatsoever the poorest in the world; in fact they are often housed and clothed no worse than the rest of the population. Sometimes, indeed, they do better: the number of automobiles among the retired population in Poland rose by 96% between 1990 and 1994, while the corresponding rise for the general population was only 39%.

Under communism, however, today's retirees were told time and time again throughout their lives that the future would be better, only to see that illusion disintegrate along with the communist system beginning in 1989. Politically, it seems, the

Table 7.1

Incidence of Social Incomes by Activity of Head of Household
(Percentage of Households in Which the Given Income Exists)

Types of social income	Czech Rep.	Poland	Hungary	Slovakia	Germany
Head of household active					
Sickness benefit	29	8	12	18	9
Pension	13	45	22	15	8
Family allowance	66	25	45	60	45
Unemployment ben.	4	10	7	5	21
Social assistance	7	5	8	4	2
Any social income	81	64	65	73	55
Head of household not active					
Sickness benefit	7	2	2	5	3
Pension	92	82	81	82	76
Family allowance	14	11	16	24	7
Unemployment ben.	4	16	12	6	25
Social assistance	6	7	14	10	4
Any social income	97	86	91	95	83
Households, total					
Sickness benefit	21	6	7	14	7
Pension	43	59	50	37	43
Family allowance	46	22	32	48	25
Unemployment ben.	4	12	9	5	23
Social assistance	7	6	11	6	3
Any social income	87	72	78	80	69

Source: World Bank.

Table 7.2

Population Density of Pensioners

	Czech Rep.	Poland	Hungary	Slovakia	Germany
% of pensioners within population	20	23	25	16	26
% of households in which the only income source is pension	19	16	23	13	27

Source: World Bank.

209

despair of old and oldish people is more potent than if they had never hoped at all. In 1996, Bulgaria and Estonia became the latest—after Lithuania, Poland, Slovakia, and Hungary—to see the votes of disgruntled pensioners be decisive in returning ex-communists to power. And pensioners provided the biggest bloc of support for the communists in the Russian presidential elections of June and July 1996. It is small consolation to say that the old are not victims of the region's infant market economy (as many mistakenly but bitterly and emphatically believe), but of an economic storm that usually drowns out realistic ideas about pension reform (see tables 7.1–4.

Despite feeling discarded, pensioners pose a threat to both the success and the continuance of economic reform. Governments are bent double by the weight of transferring resources to retired people. As economies shrank between 1990 and 1994, pensions bit deep into national budgets. Ministers confronted with the task of discovering means and mechanisms to meet these obligations peer into a fiscal black hole. Poland's pension bill rose from 7% of GDP in 1989 to 16% in 1993. By 1995, 20% of Hungary's national budget was going to pensions, 25% of Ukraine's; the figure was 28% in Slovenia. Only Uzbekistan, with its burgeoning young population, has seen real pension expenses hold steady since 1991. Between 1990 and 1994, spending on social protection (with pensions claiming the lion's share) doubled in Moldova and Kazakhstan. Indeed, according to a study from the Vienna-based Institut fur Wissenschaften vom Menschen (IWM) entitled *The Social Costs of Transformation in Central Europe,* "close to 80% of all households" in the region "get some social income, around 70% if the head is actively employed, and 90% if not."

As the following figures and tables show, share of budgets and GDP in the postcommunist world devoted to pensions is vast—and rising everywhere in the region. Moreover, despite tax regimes specifically earmarked for pensions, governments must dip into their general revenues to meet their obligations to retirees. These subsidies run from a low 10% of the pension budget in Slovenia and the Czech Republic to almost 60% in Kazakhstan. By 1995, indeed, all the monies taken in each month by the Pension Fund of the Russian Federation were being disbursed immediately to pensioners, eliminating even the possibility of the government building a nest egg for future payouts. On top of that, between 1–3% of Russia's national budget was going to subsidiz-

Table 7.3

Percentage Distribution of Pensioners

Age group of pensioners	Czech R.	Poland	Hungary	Slovakia	Germany
under 55	11	26	22	17	5
55–59	12	15	16	17	14
60–64	19	15	17	23	25
over 65	58	43	46	43	56
total	100	100	100	100	100
Thousand number of pensioners	582	801	705	528	658
% of pensioners within population	20	23	25	16	26

Source: World Bank.

ing pensions. Governments can't even raise taxes fast enough to keep up: Albania has been boosting its social tax bills by 3-4% per year since 1991. Expenses, however, are rising twice as fast.

Everywhere in the region the army of old-age pensioners is huge: 13.5 million people out of a population of 52 million in Ukraine; 2.4 million out of 9 million in Bulgaria; 327,000 out of 1.5 million in tiny Estonia. In Poland and Hungary, says the IWM, some 15% of the prime age earning group of people aged 25–54 already claims a pension (see table 7.5 and figure 7.1). Eight factors swell the ranks and cost of pensioners:

1. The age at which people become eligible for pensions is often absurdly low. Women usually retire at age 55, men at age 60. Because life expectancy is generally low (perhaps as low as 59 years for men in Russia, as compared to well over 70 everywhere in the West), these low retirement ages may seem a reasonable policy option. But pensions are not a free lunch; they are a real budget item, so retirement ages must be fixed at levels where the cost is affordable without stifling economic growth.

2. Even earlier retirements than the standard low retirement ages were encouraged in the first years of economic reform. Slovenia's government, supposedly to combat unemployment, lowered its retirement age a full four years: to age 56 for men and 51 for women. Macedonia, which had realistic retirement ages (65 for men; 60 for women), knocked five years off these standards at independence. The next year (1991), there were 14,102 new pensioners, double the expected increase. In 1990-

Table 7.4

Ratio of Pensioners within the Male, Female, and Total Population, by Age Group

	Male	Female	All Pensioners	Total Population of Pensioners (in Thousands)
Czech Republic				
25–54	4	6	5	1222
55–59	27	76	52	134
60–64	88	100	95	118
65 and over	98	99	99	338
total	25	38	32	1812
Poland				
25–54	12	17	14	1451
55–59	62	77	69	178
60–64	75	86	81	152
65 and over	96	93	95	364
total	32	42	37	2145
Hungary				
25–54	11	14	12	1193
55–59	61	91	76	144
60–64	93	92	92	130
65 and over	98	91	94	342
total	35	42	39	1809
Slovakia				
25–54	4	8	6	1446
55–59	31	85	64	137
60–64	90	95	92	133
65 and over	97	98	98	236
total	22	31	27	1952
Germany				
25–54	2	4	3	1049
55–59	34	44	39	237
60–64	78	84	81	206
65 and over	94	97	96	383
total	32	38	35	1875

Source: World Bank.

91, the first year of Poland's stabilization effort, 400,000 workers took early retirement. In 1992, more than half of Slovakia's 45,816 new pensioners were early retirees. In the West, by con-

Table 7.5

Pension Expenditures as a Share of GDP, 1992

Slovenia	13.0
Poland	11.4
Hungary	9.7
Czech Republic	9.5
Bulgaria	8.4
Romania	6.7
Albania	6.3

Source: National Statistics, World Bank Estimates

trast, retirement ages are starting to rise, reflecting the slowly emerging will of governments to tackle the cost of pensions before it is too late.

3. The old communist habit of granting generous early pensions to people in favored groups or industries—say, miners or military officers—cut the average retirement age even more, to 57 for men and 53 for women, says the World Bank. Some Albanian women could retire on a full pension as early as age 40. Old habits die hard. One early act of Lithuania's first postcommunist government was to carve out a special pension for ex-political prisoners—including a number of members of the government.

4. Privatization, and the industrial restructuring that sometimes follows, increased the number of early retirements. Hungary's Employment Fund picks up 100% of the tab for early retirement if a firm ceases to exist; 50% of these costs are picked up by the fund if a firm cuts its workforce 25% or operates at a loss. Early retirees are generally allowed to draw their pensions and continue to work. Had governments put them on the dole (given them unemployment insurance), instead of on pensions, government handouts would stop when such workers found new jobs.

5. Because monitoring of pension systems is lax or nonexistent, pensions are never taken away from those who skirt the rules, nor are people effectively required to quit their jobs upon retirement. In Russia, 20% of pensioners continue to work in their old jobs. To buy peaceful privatization, Latvia allows pen-

sioners to double-dip in this way. In Slovakia, one-third of all old age pensioners remain working and may legally do so up to an income of 22,000 korunas.

6. Lax regulation of disability pensions is also a cause of bloated pension budgets. Polish doctors usually rubber-stamp bids to receive disability pensions. Various studies estimate that 40% of Poland's disabled pensioners are suspect. Jiri Kral, the Czech minister of pensions in 1995, reckons that despite tougher

Figure 7.1

Pension Expenditures as Share of GDP, 1992

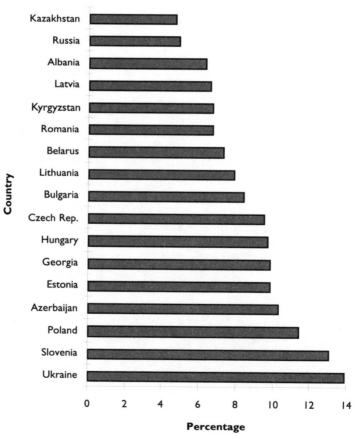

Source: World Bank

medical vetting than in Poland (Czechs see an independent state-registered doctor, not their own physician, when making disability claims), disability pensions still account for 18% of pensioners.

7. Peasant farmers get a free ride on pensions. Because no "employer" pays the social security tax, farm pensions usually come directly from national budgets. Poland's government subsidizes 95% of the budget of the Social Insurance Fund for Farmers (KRUS). Between December 1989 and December 1992, the number of KRUS pensioners grew 43.8%. Only Latvia fixes a realistic pension tax on farmers: 18.5% of gross income.

8. Pension provisions are absurdly generous. Russian, Hungarian, and Lithuanian pensioners receive a maximum of 75% of their average wage in their best five years of employment. In Slovenia, the average pension is 85% of the average wage. Macedonians with a pension based on 40 years' work now receive 10% more than the average working wage. Most absurdly, in 1993, the average Belarus pension was more than the average wage for workers. To be sure, in most countries, inflation

Table 7.6

Pension as a Percentage of Average Wage, 1992

Slovenia	85
Poland	74
Albania	55
Latvia	52
Czechoslovakia	49
Hungary	49
Romania	43
Uzbekistan	43
Belarus	42
Lithuania	41
Kazakhstan	39
Bulgaria	34
Kyrgyzstan	34
Ukraine	34
Estonia	33

Source: World Bank.

Figure 7.2

Pension as a Percentage of Average Wage, 1992

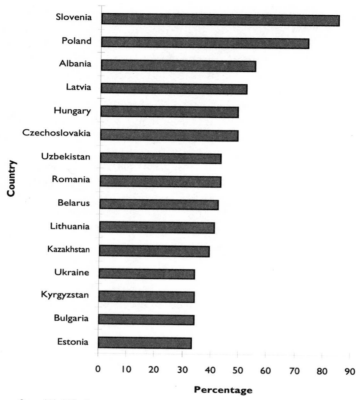

Source: World Bank.

eats away the value of pensions. In Russia, half of all pensioners receive the minimum pension; the figure is 70% in Kyrgyzstan. Yet pensions are indexed in the most inflationary way possible. They are linked, not to prices, but to wages. This, perhaps, made a degree of sense at the beginning of the transition, when real wages were falling. In the long run, as economies grow (or wage pressure intensifies, as it already has in the Czech Republic), this type of indexation always proves more costly.

While the number of pensioners is rising (see table 7.6 and figure 7.2, and table 7.7 and figure 7.3), the number of people paying into pension schemes is falling. Some workers lose jobs as factories close; others go to work for small businesses in the private sector and master the art of tax evasion and avoidance. Every fourth Pole is retired or gets a disability pension. The IMF's Xavier Marate reckons that by 2020 there will be 1.38 workers for every Polish pensioner. In Albania, Belarus, Bulgaria, and Romania, contributors are nearly equal to the number of pen-

Table 7.7

Pension as a Percentage of Average Wage, 1994

Slovenia	85
Poland	70
Hungary	67
Czech Republic	50
Slovakia	46

Note: Slovak figure from 1993.

Source: World Bank, National Statistics.

sioners. Alexi Saci, Moldova's pensions czar in 1995, reckons that there are two pensioners for every person with a productive job in his country.

This demographic picture is growing bleaker. With communism's end and the trauma of transition, a demographic cataclysm has hit the region. Birth rates collapsed and death rates soared, most strikingly among teenagers and young adults, the very people who are expected to contribute the most to national pension schemes. According to a spring 1994 report in the journal *Europe-Asia Studies,* between 1989 and the first half of 1993, the birth rate fell by over 20% in Poland, 30% in Romania and Estonia, 35% in Russia, and an incredible 45% in Belarus and Ukraine. Only in the Czech Republic, where the shock of transition is mild in comparison with the rest of the postcommunist world, is the birth rate somewhat constant. Indeed, a May 1995 report by the demography department of Prague's Charles University reckons that Czech births and life expectancy were back on the rise by the end of 1994.

Figure 7.3

Pension as a Percentage of Average Wage, 1994

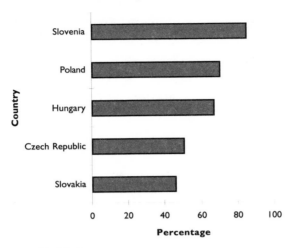

Source: World Bank.

Cynics also note that death rates are rising among old people as well, perhaps reducing the budgetary burdens. Murray Feshbach, of Georgetown University in Washington, D.C., says the death rate in Russia, for example, rose 30% between 1989 and 1993, to 14.2 per thousand. For men aged between 16 and 59, it rose by 30% between 1992 and 1993 alone. On today's trends, a 16-year-old boy in Russia has only a 60% chance of surviving to the age of 60. Indeed, Feshbach estimates that life expectancy at birth for men fell by three full years, from 62 to 59, between 1992 and 1993. That puts Russia one year behind India in the worldwide life expectancy tables.

Demography, however, need not be destiny. For Eastern Europe and the NIS, these social trends may suggest a deepening pension crisis as fewer and fewer working people support a reserve army of the old. Yet the history of social science extrapolation tempers the conclusion that calamity is inescapable. Parson Malthus predicted demographic disaster for Britain almost two centuries ago: at the dawn of the wrenching transition of the industrial revolution, he feared there would be too many people, not too few. Those modern-day Malthusians, the Club of Rome, warned in 1971 that because of population and economic growth the world risked exhausting its natural resources: in real terms, commodity prices have remained low in the two decades since.

Faced with harsh and divisive political choices, the almost natural propensity of democratic governments is to please the largest number of voters. It is always easier to obtain votes for state-dispensed benefits than for cuts in government services, for appropriations than for taxes, to facilitate consumption than to stimulate production, to protect a market than to open it, to inflate than to deflate, to borrow than to save. The pressure of a democracy's electorate is normally to opt for the soft side of these equations, which gives rise to a tendency for governments and societies to be drawn downward, as if by gravity, towards fiscal erosion and crisis.

Pressures and pressure groups agitating for reform also exist, so governments need not throw up their hands in surrender. Indeed, as we will see, Moldova, the Czech Republic, Slovenia, and Estonia are grappling in a variety of ways with the thorny issue of pension reform. Three forces propel them to act. First is the insatiable demand of pensions on national budgets. This is changing the way pensions are funded. As people realize that they can no longer count on a state-financed safety net, they begin to increase their personal savings. Second comes the need to secure and enhance the value of these savings against inflation in the form of private pension funds. As these are built, domestic savings are mobilized and directed, leading to a third force for economic change: an urgent necessity to revamp capital markets and banking systems so that capital accumulated in pensions can be invested reliably.

7.1 The Old Wave

As everywhere else, it is wise to treat generalizations about the former socialist world with caution. While the Austrian head of a private Slovene pension fund grapples with the impact of the latest fad in Asian stock markets, his counterpart in Ukraine struggles to introduce the idea of private pensions. Yet because of the legacy bequeathed by socialism, it makes sense to think of the pensions crisis in a comprehensive way. All current pension schemes in the region were inherited as state monopolies; nowadays all are expensive and inefficient. The insurance principle on which these pensions were in theory based never meant much except in terms of jobs for the motley army of bureaucrats who pile up employer contribution records. And the jumble of taxes and benefits that remain in place from the socialist era to fund pension schemes hits some people in unintended ways.

A root problem of this crisis is that national pension funds—created to pay for state-mandated pensions—are not real funds at all. No communist-turned-postcommunist country built up contributions to cover future claims. From the beginning, the costs of pensions were not fully linked to any direct contributions by employees or employers. Today's existing schemes also suffer from a fusing after 1989 of the insurance principle with the state's duty to engage in the relief of poverty. No benefit could realistically be based on an actuarially fair return on past contributions and simultaneously meet the needs of pensioners in a time of high inflation. The problem was compounded by the fact that concepts of poverty rose in line with economic reform. Pensions were indexed not to prices, but to wages, so that envious pensioners could feel they were keeping pace with their neighbors. Overlapping the goals of pensions and poverty relief, however, caused ruinous inefficiency and the anomaly that too much money is handed to people (aged 50–65) who should be working, leaving too little to meet the real needs of pensioners over age 65.

Reform of pensions is never easy. Pensions are often regarded as the electrified "third rail" of politics: like the cable that powers subway trains, touch it and you die. Even when government has a gun at its head, systematic reform is elusive. An example: in the autumn of 1991, Poland's pension system faced meltdown. A mere five days of reserves to meet pension obligations were on hand. Here was the moment to turn crisis into opportunity. Wojciech Topinski, Poland's first postcommunist social security administrator, tried to seize it, pushing a supposedly tough-minded reform government into root-and-branch reform of the pensions system. Use part of the monies realized from privatization of businesses and supplement this with state debt to transform the state pension system into a real self-financing fund, independent of the national budget, he argued. Raise retirement ages immediately, Topinski advocated. Apply harsh scrutiny to bids for disability pensions.

Brave on macroeconomic stabilization, the government led by Premier Tadeusz Mazowiecki flinched on pensions. Government printing presses bailed out the pension fund with a fresh tranche of zlotys. In November 1992, Finance Minister Leszek Balcerowicz received a special credit from the central bank to keep the fund solvent well into the next year. Topinski resigned, kicking up a short-lived tempest in the press. Poland's economic recovery since 1992 has made the situation less apocalyptic to manage, but what will happen to the country's pensions budget when recession eventually hits? No less a figure than Balcerowicz acknowledges what was lost. "Avoiding pension reform," he says ruefully, "was my greatest error."

The main question facing governments is how to cope with the consequences of the existing pension systems for taxes and public spending. So strapped was Macedonia for cash for its pensioners that, in 1993, the government simply skipped two out of the twelve monthly payments due pensioners. Terrifying though the prospect of paying for the old generation sounds, constructive thinking can indeed make it manageable. Five major reforms will be needed:

1. Restricting the size of, and easy access to, state pensions so that the official pension scheme becomes a true safety net for the old and not a social welfare or unemployment program. State pensions should be made simple and earnings-related features eliminated so that they provide a basic level of security, to be supplemented by savings and voluntary pension schemes. The three Baltic countries have contained their exploding pension budgets by curtailing pension hikes. Coupled with inflation, the effect of restricting increases in the value of pensions has been to level pensions to a basic rate.

2. Carving off the national pension fund from the regular budget so that pension trustees can gauge the taxes necessary to meet the long-term promises made by the system. In turn, this reform requires that pensioners be made aware of the costs of their pensions. Most pension taxes in the region are paid solely by employers, so the cost of pensions is obscured to the workers, who bear the burden of the tax through lower wages and thus not through a direct deduction from income. The system should also move away from pay-as-you-go schemes (to be explained below) that provide the. illusion of national savings, but really hide the true cost of national pension bills.

3. Starting private pension funds that allow people to supplement the limited state scheme. Privately managed but publicly regulated, these will allow individuals to save effectively for their own retirements. But state control must not be heavy-hand-

ed. Poland's first law on private pensions initially authorized a National Insurance Fund to levy a charge on the country's ten private pension companies, in order to guarantee 100% of pension savings against loss. The charge was so high that it discouraged formation of new funds. Besides, such guarantees are a bad idea: they make pension managers lazy and careless, and they take away the incentive of the pension account holders to monitor the performance of the fund. (Sensibly, Poland junked this guarantee in November 1994.)

4. Phasing out or eliminating all special retirement schemes and raising the age at which all pensions are claimed. The scale for savings here is vast. An example: perhaps one-third of all Bulgarian pensioners took advantage of such schemes. Because many early retirement programs allow for workers to leave ten to fifteen years before what should be the normal age (65) for claiming a pension, a phase-out of these perks is necessary. Rapid boosts in retirement age should occur for those sectors favored with youthful pensions; slower rises for those entitled to retire at age 60. (Of course, some schemes carry enormous moral weight, for example, the unique Chernobyl benefits created in Belarus after the nuclear disaster of 1986. An 18% tax on wages was imposed to cover special disability pension costs for people with radiation sickness. To try to cut the 30% bonus pensions given to workers involved in the Chernobyl clean-up would be morally wrong and politically foolhardy.)

5. Restricting disability pensions to the truly disabled. The World Bank's senior health economist, Alexander Preker, estimates that eliminating the abuses of disability pensions and early retirement will save up to 40% of state pension budgets throughout the region.

The rest of this essay looks at: (1) pensions systems in the West as they seek to reform themselves and what these reforms may mean in Eastern Europe and the NIS, and (2) a variety of reform efforts now underway.

7.2 A Global Problem

Pension finance is one area where Eastern Europe is now on a par with its neighbors to the west. Social security systems in Europe and the United States also face crisis and eventual breakdown. Politicians in these countries, too, scramble and manipulate so as to avoid a reckoning. Many, however, are inching toward creating private pensions to bridge the gap between the needs of the elderly and tight national budgets.

Industrial countries usually choose to finance their pensions on what is known as a pay-as-you-go basis. This means that the taxes paid by today's workers are used to pay today's pensions, instead of being saved and invested. Pay-as-you-go schemes are popular with politicians precisely because of their "chain letter" distributional effects. In the early years, beneficiaries (small in number) of the schemes pay little or nothing in contributions compared to the benefits that they consume: their pensions come as a sort of gift from the state. Only a few generations later, however, the costs of this windfall to early retirees in the scheme come home to roost, particularly as governments lure votes by expanding benefits to offer similar largesse to each generation.

For most of the post-World War II era in the Western democracies, demography allowed the pay-as-you-go system to flourish. The baby boom that ran from 1945 to the arrival of the birth control pill in the 1960s created a big cohort of workers who could pay pension taxes for retirees. Roughly half of all workers are now in that phase of life—age 35 to 55—when they save most in order to buy homes, educate their children, and, above all, anticipate old age. With plentiful labor and a large pool of savings, economies through most of these years could hardly fail to grow. And with relatively few old people, the burden of social security payments, and the taxes needed to pay them, were relatively light for decades.

Everywhere in the developed world this fortunate bonanza is running out. Early in the twenty-first century the vast baby boom generation will begin to retire, carrying with it pension expectations spawned in the fat years of the 1960s. Every worker will then face the prospect of having to support through taxes an ever-increasing number of elderly dependents. In 1965, for example, a third of West Germans were under 25. In the year 2000, only a quarter of Germans will be, and a fifth will be over 60. In the wake of reunification, Germany has raised unemployment insurance premiums, and pensions are nowadays reckoned on net, not gross, pay. All the same, German workers, like workers everywhere, will be poorer unless higher productivity permits wages to rise sufficiently to make up for the increased social security tax burden.

Moreover, savings rates will fall as retired baby boomers consume their nest eggs of retirement savings. Fewer workers means less abundant capital, which means that growth may no longer be taken for granted. Indeed, demography may depress growth just as growth is most needed to meet the rising cost of pensions and the health costs of the elderly. Higher taxes to pay for grandparents may dampen incentives to work and save, making the baby bust even worse.

This pattern will affect just about all the rich economies, but at different times and with varying force. It will therefore shake up international competitiveness. Some countries are especially vulnerable, for they have few savings set aside in pension funds. Those that do have funded pension schemes are protected somewhat, but not as completely as they hope.

Figure 7.4

Rapid Aging: Percentage of Population over 60 Years Old

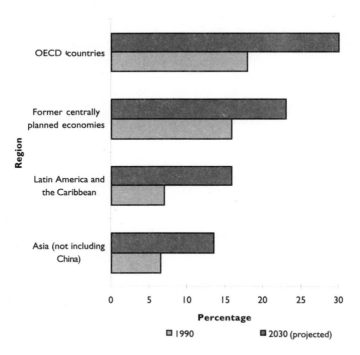

Source: World Bank.

In the West, the main difficulty in pension finance will arise when the bulge of babies born in the late 1940s reaches 60 and 65 early in the next century, just when the drop in births after the 1960s will be reducing the working population. But demography is expensive today, too. In almost every industrial country, live births rose from 1895 to 1914 and then soared briefly after 1919. As better health and nutrition keep old people alive for longer periods of time, the ratio of the number of retirees to workers (known as the dependency ratio) has been increasing in most rich countries (see figure 7.4).

The cost of a rising ratio of beneficiaries to contributors in existing state pension schemes varies from country to country, but a common theme is clear: with present arrangements, spending will eventually become insupportable.

In the United States, the dependency ratio is expected to rise from around 21% in 1990 to 23% by 2000, to 33% by 2020, and to 42% by 2030. By 2055, the ratio could be more than 50%—just two workers for every pensioner. To pay the current level of benefits given by government to pensioners, the social security tax would have to rise from today's nearly 15% of payroll (one half paid by employers, one half by employees) to something like 40%, a sure recipe for killing job creation.

In Germany, the retiree-to-worker ratio reached 45% by 1980, probably the highest in the world. By 2010, it will be 60%, and by 2030, around 90%: roughly one pensioner for every worker. Karl Heinz Juttemeier of the Kiel Institute for World Economics and Professor Hans-Georg Petersen of Kiel University reckoned a few years ago that, to maintain current benefits, the Bonn government would need to increase its payroll tax (as in the U.S. it is divided equally between workers and employers) to around 32% of gross wages. That would push overall marginal tax rates for many middle income families to above 80%. Even these studies optimistically assumed that Germany's real output would grow at 3.5% a year to 2000, and at 2.4% from then until 2030. In the face of this evidence, the generosity of German pension schemes was curtailed somewhat in 1992. Yet the trends have not been reversed. Many pensioners continue to have higher real after-tax incomes than they did when they were at work.

225

Britain's demographic outlook is less frightening: the ratio of pensioners to working people was a high 35% in 1981 and is expected to rise to about 45% in 2030. For a time around the turn of the century, however, the ratio should fall to a low point of 33%.

France, Italy, and Spain, unlike the U.S. or Britain, pay nearly all pensions to the old directly out of money earned by the young. Aging will make this unsustainable. A French government paper recently predicted that, if the value of pensions remains unchanged, contributions will leap from the current 20% of payroll to between 31% and 42% by 2040. Italy is still more vulnerable. It spends nearly 15% of GDP on pensions now, up from 5% in 1960.

Table 7.8

**Projected Public Pension Spending by Region, 1990–2050
(Pension Spending as Percentage of GDP)**

Region	1990	2000	2010	2020	2030	2040	2050
OECD countries	9	9.7	11.6	14	16	16.2	16.4
Former centrally planned economies	7	8	8.6	10.3	11.2	12.5	13.7
Latin America and the Caribbean	2	2.2	3.1	5	7.1	9.4	11.7
Asia (not including China)	1.6	1.9	2.2	3.8	5.7	7.6	9.7

Source: World Bank.

Japan is experiencing the most dramatic aging. Between 1970 and 1990, the number of people over age 65 increased 86%, from 7.4 million to 13.8 million. Between 1945 and 1960, the average number of children per family fell from 4.5 to 2.0 and then declined again to 1.4 by 1988. As a result of these changes, the ratio of beneficiaries to contributors in the state pension scheme rose from only 8% in 1976 to 23% in 1990 and is projected to soar to 63% by 2020. Even allowing for predicted changes in coverage in the main state pension scheme, such figures—similar to those in Eastern Europe today—would spell ruin if Japan financed its pensions in the manner of East and West Europeans (see table 7.8 and figure 7.5).

Figure 7.5

**Projected Public Pension Spending by Region, 1990–2050
(as Percentage of GDP)**

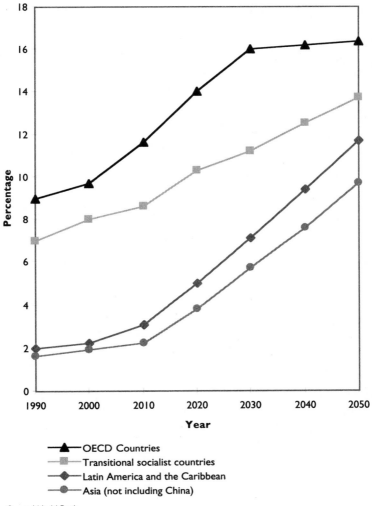

Source: World Bank.

But there is a silver lining in all this gloom. In the United States, Britain, and Holland the soaring stock markets of the 1980s and 1990s put many private pension funds in the happy position of having more than enough money to meet their future pension promises. As a result, some firms have taken contribution "holidays"; despite generous provisions, pensions nowadays add nothing to the cost of an American-built Ford or GM car. These burgeoning private funds have an enormous impact on the wider economy as they plough their riches into stock markets, pushing up share prices and making equity finance cheaper. At the same time, the funds contribute to dramatic financial innovation, making equity more convenient, and still cheaper, for firms. It is no coincidence that financial market sophistication is concentrated where there are privately funded pensions. Rich economies without independent pension funds—Germany, Italy—have primitive stock markets. Big German and Italian firms can get around this problem by raising money in New York or London, but for smaller ones, the cost of equity finance is higher than it might otherwise have been.

Configuring private pensions to make them more efficient is a tricky business. Tax rules in Germany and Japan create new pension headaches because these rules encourage firms to promise pensions without creating special funds to pay for them. Instead, firms save for their employees' retirement by making reserves. German firms can deduct their contributions from taxable profit; Japanese firms can write off part of them. Reserves have a great attraction: rather than entrusting them to an independent investment or pension manager who merely tries to earn a good return, employers decide how to use these monies. The result: German and Japanese firms use them in ways that further their immediate business plans. One frequent ploy is to buy stakes in friendly companies, which makes Germany and Japan dominated by families of firms that hold stakes in one another. This web of cross-ownership shields firms from hostile takeovers and breeds strong relations between producers and suppliers. Moreover, such funds are like putting all your eggs in one basket. Pensions are too closely tied to the health of employers. If a company goes bad, workers are either out of luck or the government is forced to pick up the tab for their pensions.

By some reckonings, German firms are short in these reserves anywhere up to 50% of promised pension benefits. So far, companies have been making up any shortfall out of their cash flow. As the population ages and more Germans retire, this will become harder to handle without crimping needed investments.

7.3 The Price of Pay-As-You-Go

In Eastern Europe and the NIS, as in most industrial countries, governments usually chose to finance pensions on a pay-as-you-go basis. Benefits mushroomed and everyone was happy. But this seductive cycle is reversing. Steady or falling working populations and growing numbers of old people mean that painless and steadily expanding transfers between generations cannot continue indefinitely. Soon workers will be asked to pay their social security taxes into schemes that are actuarial loss makers. That will strain the implicit contract that binds contributors and beneficiaries in pay-as-you-go schemes. Once governments decide that tax rates have reached their ceiling, adverse demographic trends mean that benefits, or other kinds of spending, must fall. This, in turn, demoralizes today's contributors, who see that they will never receive the same benefits as their parents (for which they are now paying).

Because Japanese pension benefits are paid for on a funded rather than a pay-as-you-go basis, the depth of the crisis facing its government as the population ages is less dire. In a funded system, the contributions of current workers are invested, rather than paid out to current beneficiaries, and the benefits paid to each retired person depend on the financial return of their contributions, rather than on levels of present taxation. So the main state scheme, the Kosei-Nenken-Hoken (KNH), has built up a large funded reserve which, assuming normal rates of return, will be enough to meet future commitments.

To see the advantages of funding over pay-as-you-go, compare Japan's tax system under the two regimes. The tax rate needed to provide present benefits to today's pensioners in a pay-as-you-go system would be a low 3.9% of gross earnings. Assuming no growth in real earnings, however, the required pay-as-you-go rate would soar to well over 30% by 2025. Even with growth in real earnings of 2.5% per annum, the tax rate would have to rise to 25%.

Under Japan's present funded system, pension contributions in 1989 were 10.6% of gross earnings. Today's workers are thus paying for the higher demands that they themselves will make on future social spending. Furthermore, if the funded system is well run, the current reasonable tax rate need not change. Funded systems are in this way immune to demographic pressure; since each person saves for his own retirement, the appropriate level of contributions depends only on the scale of benefits and on the real interest rate earned by the fund. However, there's the rub: governments rarely run their systems well. Japanese government policy is to use the KNH reserves for infrastructure projects such as road building; in return it pays an interest rate that is fixed below the market rate. In some recent years the effective interest rate has been negative, so government interference is eroding the value of the fund. By the time Japan's demographic crunch arrives in the next century, the government may already have been forced to either pick up the tab or switch to a ruinous policy of pay-as-you-go.

Many economists reckon that funded schemes have a number of other advantages over pay-as-you-go pensions. Neither is really "cheaper" than the other, they argue, because the true cost of both is equal to the resources eventually transferred to pensioners. However, funded schemes gradually place a smaller burden on contributors because they encourage higher rates of economic growth. The argument goes like this: in a growing economy, a funded pension scheme must accumulate assets to meet future commitments which are rising in line with total income. If the reserves are held in equities, the government will have effectively raised the national savings rate—as compared with a pay-as-you-go system, where there is no accumulation of assets—thus increasing the resources available for new investment that will produce faster growth.

The growing burden of pensions poses yet another threat to economic efficiency: lowering work incentives. The projected increases in social security taxes will raise the proportion of after-tax income that an unemployed person receives as compared with those who work. This causes a risk of greater voluntary unemployment, creating a vicious cycle: even fewer workers, even greater strains on social security budgets, this time from higher spending on unemployment insurance. And if the higher tax rates squeeze more economic activity into the unrecorded or "black" economy, the tax base will shrink as well.

7.4 No Way Out

Even if politicians can be persuaded to think ahead ten or twenty years, the options that they face are painful and limited. Switches from pay-as-you-go to funded schemes are politically and economically difficult. So extensive are the Russian government's raids on the state pension fund that in the months of January to February 1995, it owed the fund 10% of its total holdings. In 1992, Latvia's reforming government swallowed the pension fund within the national budget merely to milk a temporary surplus (2 million lats) in the pension accounts. Romania pulled much the same stunt. In June 1993, its Ministry of Finance and the National Bank of Romania agreed to consolidate the social insurance budget within the state budget in a special account at the National Bank. This allowed for money to be easily shifted from one account to another. A codicil to the agreement allows the NBR to place the social fund surplus in commercial banks paying a higher rate of interest. However, surpluses are often diverted to cover current government expenditures.

Such deceptive maneuvers should not be surprising, nor are they unusual. In monitoring the expenses of the Belarus social insurance fund, the government's watchdog control agency discovered that, in 1991, 291 million rubles had been spent on all sorts of construction schemes by unions and enterprises. The temptations of a huge funded reserve, when held by the state and available to finance more spending, is great. The United States surrendered to this urge in the mid-1980s, when an increase in social security taxes (intended to pay for the pensions of the baby boom generation) was used to fund the nation's growing deficit. Japan's experience shows that even efficiency-minded governments nibble away at funded schemes.

Most governments prefer to tinker with the problems, rather than face them head on. Here are some of the things they are doing:

Trimming the fat brings savings, as Moldova discovered. By threatening to break the postal monopoly for delivering pension checks, pensions director Alexi Saci cut in half the 3.5% of the pension budget devoted to postal fees. A tax agreement with Russia pushed payments of some military pensions onto their big neighbor. Slashing central administration saved another 6%. But such tinkering is not enough. Saci's ambitions extend beyond cost-cutting. Real savings, he says, can only come through hard choices: "cutting benefits, raising taxes, and privatizing pensions."

Decentralizing is another relatively easy option. It is hoped that dividing the system will lessen political pressure, allow for experimentation, and bring greater administrative efficiency. Some, like Saci, even hope that regional pension systems will become the foundations for independent pension funds that compete for the savings of the elderly. But decentralizing is no cure-all, particularly if regional managers remain pawns of the center or are an added layer of bloated bureaucracy. Wearied by the muddled and fragmented pension system of the Tito era, one dominated by workers' councils, Slovenians are nervous about any new division of their so-called Pension Community. Albania grafted regional and communal administrations onto its national pensions administrations. Now, reckons a European Union study, pension requests in Albania take ten months to be reviewed instead of four.

Russia's Federal Pension Fund is, like Moldova's, divided into regional branches. With some regions doing better economically than others, the Federal Pension Fund orders innovative and prosperous regional funds—such as those in Bashkortostan, Samara, and elsewhere—to send to Moscow any surpluses that remain after monthly pension obligations are met. (Russia's Federal Pension Fund is probably the most efficient of the country's tax collectors. It harvests 88% of taxes due it, while other federal authorities are said to lose as much as 40% of their intended revenues.) Samara's regional pension authorities stall in sending in their funds as they are hoping to capitalize their pension system through the investment of surpluses. Bashkortostan turns over its surpluses, but has added a special 1% regional pension tax that it wants to use to help make its fund self-financing.

Raising taxes is also a common stop-gap solution. Such taxes are now pressing against the limits of public tolerance and are past the bounds of economic efficiency. Romanians pay between 25% and 35% of their gross wages in pension contributions, with an added 3% going to a fund for supplementary pensions. Poland's social security tax, paid by employers, tips 45% of gross wages. High rates also prevail in Hungary (44%, with 38% from employers and 6% from employees), Latvia (38%), Moldova (41%), and Kazakhstan (58%). Depending on salary, Bulgaria's tax ranges from 35% to 50%. Macedonia has kept its tax rate of 16.5% of total payroll steady, but has watched the deficit in its pension fund soar to 20.7% of government revenues. Such punitive social tax rates have three debilitating effects:

1. Labor costs become uncompetitive internationally. As low labor costs are supposed to be among Eastern Europe's main comparative advantages, this is a dangerous side effect.

2. Employers think twice before hiring new workers, discouraging job creation.

3. Tax avoidance is encouraged as employers hide the number of employees and evade payments. As this practice gathers pace, the government's tax base shrinks.

Romania is a good example of this last dynamic. Its national bureau of statistics, in a survey conducted in March 1994, concluded that 45% of all employees now work in the underground labor market. As many other employees work under so-called collaboration contracts, which allow employers to treat workers as subcontractors and thus not make any social tax payments, the percentage of workers actually contributing to the state insurance fund may well be less than half of the working population. To combat this drain on revenues, the government has empowered the Ministry of Labor and Social Protection (MLSP) to make direct raids on company accounts. The MLSP can issue a direct order upon a company's bank account. If there are insufficient funds, the ministry takes partial payment and orders the bank to pay up as more money is deposited. Facing similar problems, Poland responded by amending Article 282 of its Labor Code to permit the Finance Ministry to impose harsh penalties on employers who avoid paying pension taxes. A special article (190) in the code allows for imprisoning particularly recalcitrant employers for up to three years.

Finally, levels of benefit are sometimes reduced. If a government breaks the informal and formal links between pensions and earnings growth—a feature of all the schemes—and replaces it with a link to prices, which grow more slowly in the longer term, some savings may be achieved. Estonia and Latvia have bitten that bullet, while Macedonians index pensions 2.5% less than the prevailing average rise in wages in the overall economy.

No amount of cost-cutting, decentralizing, and benefit trimming will be enough to revitalize the region's existing pension systems. Painful root-and-branch reform is demanded.

7.5 Bitter Medicine

The switch from a bloated, state-directed pension system that mortgages the future to a funded one that encourages savings and investment requires, indeed demands, new ways of thinking in ministries, in the national pension fund, and in private firms. Pension funds need credit analysts and actuaries; companies that will become investment vehicles for retirement savings need to produce decent accounts. Government bureaucrats used to dishing out orders must learn to let pension fund managers think for themselves. New regulations combined with old ways of thinking—or the reverse, old regulations governing new business ideas—can make a dangerous brew.

Bulgaria's experience offers a lesson in the latter. Its 1994 income tax code allows a person to deduct 20% of the minimum wage from his taxes if the money is used to fund a private insurance or pension plan. Employers can reduce their payroll tax up to 10% if they offer such schemes. However, companies that give employees private pensions run into another law: it is illegal to deduct pension contributions directly from salaries. Moreover, although the monies accumulated by private pensions are not taxed, pension funds cannot invest these monies on their own. So the funds are deposited in banks, which in turn are required to invest 85% of their capital in shares and bonds whose redemption is guaranteed by the state. But Bulgaria has been plagued by banking scandals and bank collapses. The country does not have enough pension supervisors and auditors to cope with the new system. Bank managers who take on pension funds can be leaned on by powerful people. Such teething troubles may take years to sort out. Parliament keeps promising to produce a regulatory regime for pensions, but in the three years between 1992 and 1995, no such bill was ever posted for debate.

In most transition countries, moreover, pension funds—both public and private—are too often treated as a means of generating forced savings for the state's coffers, rather than as mechanisms for insuring security for the old and raising capital. Most governments make purchases of their securities compulsory for both the state pension system and whatever private pension funds and accounts exist. Sometimes, as in Ukraine, these purchases are compelled at below market interest rates. The Kazakhs have been thinking of extending the forced purchase of state securities to individuals who establish their own private pension accounts, which turns pensions into a form of taxation rather than saving.

This policy is wrongheaded in a number of ways. Government bonds are likely to succeed as attractive investment vehicles for pensions only when governments stop forcing people to buy state debt and instead allow pension fund managers to rely on the market to determine the value of such investments. Some governments are seeing the point of all this. The Czechs, as we will see, realize that forcing pension funds to purchase government paper only drives up inflation as too much money chases too few notes. Lithuania plans to experiment with auctions in which insurance companies will bid on government bonds in the open market. Whether or not behind-the-scene arm-twisting will take place remains an open question.

State-directed credit allocation through pension funds also delays modernization of financial markets. Pension funds can become a key source of competitive pressure for the investment funds that now dominate trading in shares. If pension funds can invest directly in companies, investment funds will lose their solitary role as overseer of capital markets. Many countries in the region are riddled with powerful webs of cross-ownership: investment funds own large chunks of shares in banks, for example, and banks own shares in each other. The theory is that these links provide informed relations looking toward the long term. However, such stability may not be a virtue if it allows managers to become complacent. In the United States, the behind-the-scenes advocacy exerted by big pension funds on corporate boards has become a powerful tool in making managers more accountable to shareholder interests. Calpers, the California Public Employees Retirement System, is perhaps the most powerful institutional investor in America. It regularly battles with the boards of corporations that it believes are underperforming and thus depriving Calpers' pensioners of a maximum return.

If the problem of compulsory purchases of state securities was merely a technical one—a question of reforming the laws and regulations, for instance—then it would fade with time. But there is more to the problem than this. Such compulsory purchases go to the heart of the most difficult economic and political challenge facing all governments in the postcommunist region: allowing huge state enterprises to go bankrupt. Anxious lest they throw thousands of people out of work, governments as hard-nosed as the Czechs and as indecisive as the Hungarians are reluctant to cut off credit to big loss-making state enterprises. Compulsory purchases of state bonds risk making the state pension system (as well as private funds) the biggest captive buyer and, in effect, a hidden source of subsidies for loss-making state enterprises. The lure of these cash cows means that large state enterprises do not pay market rates for the money they need, and the financial system is stunted in its growth.

To avoid these problems, state pension funds must be separated from the budget, and their managers must be made independent. This is where the hard part begins. Breaking the back of state control of pensions is notoriously difficult as governments chafe at losing a captive source of revenue. Consider the example of Slovakia. In January 1995, its social fund was split in two, with the Social Insurance Company taking responsibility for pensions and the General Medical Insurance Company for medical affairs. Both bodies were intended to act on the insurance principle. The road to state intervention, however, is paved with good intentions. Although these bodies are supposedly independent—of their twenty-one member board the state has only seven nominees—insurance entities are effectively shackled. Standards for when and how people draw their benefits may be set by the boards, but it is ministers who control the purse strings, set the contribution rates, and determine how pension funds are invested. And employer and employee contributions flow into the central budget, not the funds. This is accountability without responsibility.

The board of Slovenia's Pension Community must also fight off constant ministerial pressure to direct the fund's investment into government-favored assets. So far, as only one-third of board members are appointed by government, it has held firm against such control.

Independence also has its dangers. Hungary's Social Insurance Fund formally became a separate entity in the national budget as far back as 1989. This change was intended to bring more transparency and accountability into national pension finance, with self-governing Social Insurance Councils created as watchdogs. However, without control over finance, these councils were dogs without teeth. In 1991, the self-governing bodies of the Social Insurance Funds were strengthened, but in the worst possible way. Trade unions assumed an absolute majority of the fund's sixty-member board. As the May 1993 union elections produced a landslide victory for the old state union, the MSZOSZ, and its allies, control was vested in a body that viewed saving jobs, not solid investing, as its duty. Because the funds are backed by a state guarantee, this is a recipe for irresponsibility as union-controlled funds try to preserve jobs by using the fund's resources to shore up industrial white elephants cut off from state subsidies. Even the socialist government of Prime Minister Gyula Horn seemed to recognize this: in November 1994, it hinted that the state guarantee was not ironclad. Hints, however, are not correctives.

But the lesson of the Hungarian and Slovak experience is not that you are damned if you grant independence from tight government oversight to pension funds and damned if you don't. It is that independent oversight boards that react to market forces, not government or trade union whims, must be crafted and then set on their way. An ideal system of management for state pensions would do several things. It would, first, give administrators enough freedom to manage well. It would insure that they use that freedom to make certain that long-term obligations are in line with the fund's long-term revenue expectations. If promises have to be curtailed, it would allow managers the freedom to tinker. In such a system, pensioners would know that someone was looking after their basic level of pension security without regard to immediate political needs, and state pension managers would have the power to act decisively if benefits and revenues got out of whack. The system should keep pension funds sufficiently distinct from government coffers to insure that, if the government borrows from it, it pays the market rate of interest to the fund.

This may be too much to ask of any state institution, to say nothing of the weak postcommunist states. Indeed, as the architects of Chile's revolutionary system obviously believed, nothing short of complete privatization, with each working person having a vested account in one of many competing independent pension funds, may ever make the state system truly efficient (see box 7.1). Here is one more argument why mandatory state pensions should be limited to providing only the most basic level of security. Additional levels of benefits should be provided by private, voluntary schemes.

Box 7.1

Pensions, Pinochet-style

On pensions, the most daring reformers are not looking to Europe, the United States, or Japan. They are studying in the transition countries the pension experiment underway in distant Chile, a country that also has a recent history of dictatorship. A succession of Chilean ministers and consultants have visited countries as disparate as Estonia and Kyrgyzstan, Albania and Moldova. And visiting politicians and bureaucrats from Eastern Europe regularly arrive in Santiago to see what they can learn and emulate, and what they should be doing next.

Like many countries of Latin America—and like those in Eastern Europe—where pensions have traditionally been both promised and managed with carefree abandon, Chile found that its pensions system was heading for trouble, if not bankruptcy. Accordingly, under the military government of General Augusto Pinochet, which seized power in 1973, the state pension system was privatized, meaning that the pay-as-you-go system run by the government has become one in which workers contribute to private funds (13% of their income, as opposed to the 20% of salaries commandeered by the old state pension system) in the expectation that they will get their money back, plus the fruits of its investment, when they retire.

The new system is still untried in its ultimate ends, in that the current contributors have not yet started to retire. The state system stopped taking new contributors in 1983. But the dozen new private pension funds are now big: together they hold assets of about $22 billion, roughly equivalent to about 50% of Chile's GDP, and are growing fast. They take in about 4% of GDP each year. Estimates hold that by 2005 the funds will top out at 100% of Chile's GDP.

This is helping to turn Chile into a nation of little capitalists, with workingmen in bars discussing the performance of pension funds along with news from the soccer fields. Private pensions gave a stake in free-market capitalism to millions of ordinary Chileans, thus making the reform difficult if not impossible to reverse. The national savings rate has risen from under 3% in 1974 to 24% of income today. About three-quarters of Chilean workers are now involved in the new pension system, which means that each receives a regular statement of his individual account; if he or she does not like the performance of the fund where the pension is invested, he or she can switch to another. The funds need to diversify their portfolios and are now allowed to invest abroad, though so far only in such safe assets as United States Treasury bonds.

Paying off the pensioners already in the system was the biggest problem Chile faced. Resources gained through privatization covered some of these costs, but the bulk has been paid out of the national budget surplus the country has been running after closing inefficient industries and dramatically scaling back industrial, agricultural, and social subsidies that had abounded in the old days.

7.6 One Way Ahead

No East European or NIS government has been as bold as Chile's in shifting pension obligations into the private sector. But with more than a few caveats, twists, and moments of handwringing, a few governments in the region are encouraging private pension schemes as a complement to the rickety state pension systems that now dominate their economies. Still, most governments lag behind the market as spontaneous generation of pension funds is taking place, even though there is scant legal authority for their existence. Take the case of Russia: many big corporations and joint-stock companies—RAO, Gazprom, Avto VAZ, Menatep Bank, Tokobank—have established their own pension plans, sometimes in collaboration with in-house trade unions, sometimes not. Even the Russian Orthodox Church started a small fund, open to priests and laity. In 1995, these funds banded together to fight the State Budget Law, which would have forced private pensions to buy state securities. The private pension funds won.

Russian Policy, a fund established by five people in 1994 with an initial investment of 200 million rubles, offers a typical investment strategy: 35% of its monies are in short-term state securities. The rest are deposited (and reinvested) by friendly and reliable banks. It is too soon to tell whether or not the investments will meet future promises, but first returns are not bad. In the last quarter of 1994, the funds were paying a yearly dividend of 121%, compared with the 96% annual interest available in most Russian banks. These funds promise to become one of the most powerful financial forces in Russia. As they grow, the pool of domestic savings mobilized for investment will likely quadruple within four years, reckons the IMF. Such funds will alter the financial landscape—that is, if governments grant them sufficient freedom.

Improvised pensions are not unique to Russia. Estonia saw six private pensions begin taking deposits before the government got around to writing a legal code for their activity. (This said, only one has survived. The others left the business and are waiting for the proper legislation.) Lithuania opted for German-style company pensions, but beyond expressing this preference the parliament has offered companies little guidance, or restriction. Most companies take advantage of this laxity to require employees to make personal pension contributions, which may or may not be matched by the company itself. These funds are then used by managers to further the interests of the company, not the security of the pensioner. In Bulgaria, big state enterprises, not private companies, have been the quickest to take advantage of lax rules on forming collective pension schemes. Where these funds are invested is a mystery to most Bulgarian analysts.

239

By mandating that only individuals, not organizations, may start private pension schemes (it takes as few as fifteen people banding together), Hungary appears to have avoided the employer domination of pension funds. Look again. Roughly one-third of the country's forty-five licensed pension funds are organized by employers. Bosses usually make most of the contributions to these funds, deducting 100% of such outlays as a business cost. Individuals are allowed a 50% deduction against income tax. And where money goes, control follows, allowing employers to direct the funds' investments.

Drawbacks abound in employer-backed schemes, as the German experience is now demonstrating. Employers take on long-term pension costs that it would be wiser to disperse among diversified investments. They also tie an employee to his job—employment-related pensions are not often portable, that is, carried by the worker from job to job—and may thus distort the labor market by making workers immobile. Governments also have to be wary: regulation of such plans needs to be meticulous so that the state does not end up bailing out promises that firms, either through bad investment of pension savings or a failure to save at all, do not keep.

Hungary's Aranykor Fund, under the control of Ilona Hardy, the former president of the Budapest Stock Exchange, specializes in avoiding these pitfalls. Aranykor's specialty is in offering pension plans for employees of companies that lack the skills to do the job. To limit their risk, she farms out key areas of fund management to an impressive team: Austria's Creditanstalt performs all banking duties; Hungary's MHB Bank is detailed asset management; and the accountants Ernst and Young keep the books and administration. So far, Aranykor's membership is slight, but, as some pension fund sources expect the national market to grow from 10,000 participants in 1995 to almost 200,000 by the turn of the century, such gilt-edged service may stand out.

Determined to deal with all its pension problems at once, Poland's government procrastinates with writing laws to regulate its emerging private pension schemes. Undeterred, the big Polish mutual fund Pioneer (an offshoot of an American parent with the same name) has rushed into this vacuum, offering long-term investment vehicles it markets as retirement plans. The scheme is based on monthly automatic payroll deductions. Contributors (1,200 in number today) buy shares in the mutual fund (see box 7.2). Benefits are then paid out either in a lump sum or in monthly installments. And Pioneer is not alone, although its investment vehicle is unique because no other mutual fund offers such a plan. Poland's life insurance companies—Powszechny Zaklad Ubezpieczen (PZU) has 94.7% of the market—are offering traditional fixed benefit plans. Grace Zrodlowski Kabat, of Britain's Sedwick group, reckons that 1,284 million zlotys ($526 million) were invested in life premiums in 1994, a 45% increase over 1993. As the government now allows employers to deduct premiums from taxes, the amount invested in such schemes is certain to grow even more dramatically this year.

7.7 Two Ways Ahead

Starting from different points, the Czech Republic and Slovenia have gone the farthest distance along the road to vital pension reform. Removing legal barriers to the formation of private pension funds has unleashed in both countries a proliferation of new pension products.

"A man must be responsible for his life, he must be responsible for his future," Premier Vaclav Klaus told the Prague daily newspaper *Lidove noviny* in late March of 1995. Such strong rhetoric is not unusual for the Czech prime minister. Neither is the fact that the program that has emerged does not match his rhetorical flourish. It is instead a messy fusion of pay-as-you-go and the insurance principle that, despite its complexity and government intervention, seems to work. For the Czechs have not junked their state pay-as-you-go system; they have transformed it. By the turn of the century, it will be merely a social safety net for the old, expressing the solidarity between old and young. The pay-as-you-go system will be funded by continued levies on wages. If pensioners want more, they must invest their own money in any of the forty-eight private pension plans now fiercely competing for savings.

To encourage such investments, the government promises to match part of the pensioners own savings. Say a pensioner invests 100 korunas per month in a private pension plan. Once the pension fund managers list this investment with the Ministry of Finance, the state budget transfers an additional 40 korunas into the pensioners account. Bigger investments by pensioners yield larger state contributions, up to a maximum of 120 korunas per month on an investment of 500 korunas. In the first

Box 7.2

How Pension Funds Work

Inflation and taxation make it hard for people to build up retirement savings. But there is a variety of ways in which people try to beat both.

There are three main ways in which most savers accumulate capital for retirement: through life insurance policies, through employer-based pension plans, and through individual investments.

Life insurance is much the same the world over. The saver (or the insured) pays a sum of money (a premium) to the insurance company each week, month, quarter, or year. In return, the life office undertakes to pay him certain predetermined benefits. Benefits depend on both the size of the premiums paid and on the type of policy taken out. The most popular form of such policies used as a pension is the endowment policy. Here premiums are paid for a prearranged term, usually between ten and twenty-five years, and the sum in the endowment is paid out at the end of that term if the policyholder survives (or on death).

There are two types of endowment policies that determine the sum in the endowment: with- and without-profits. For a without-profits policy, the company's in-house crystal-ball gazer (the actuary) works out from well-thumbed life expectancy tables how long the premiums are likely to be paid. He then takes a guess at the minimum return the company is likely to make on the money, deducts a healthy slice for expenses and guarantees to pay out the rest (the sum assured) at the end of the period. Thus the company guarantees to pay out a specific sum many years hence, on the basis of premiums received over many years. The rates of return on money invested will therefore vary enormously, and the actuary always makes pessimistic assumptions about how much those premiums will earn. If things work out better than he guesses (which they invariably do), the excess returns will go into the company's reserves.

With-profits policies also guarantee a fixed sum at the outset. This is usually lower than the guaranteed sum under a without-profits policy. However, because the with-profits policyholder is entitled to annual bonuses (that is, is allowed to participate in full in the income his money earns for the insurance company), the maturity value of his policy quickly overtakes that of the without profit policyholder. He does not actually receive the profits on his own individual premiums but gets what the company's actuary considers his share of the returns of the entire life fund (that is, all policyholders' cash, including part of the excess returns from without-profit policies). Endowment policies are a reliable and, in many countries, a tax-efficient way of investing because premiums are often tax deductible from income.

Employer-based pension plans are the primary vehicle for private retirement savings. The traditional form of employer-based plan is known as a defined benefit plan. Under this type of plan the employer makes regular tax deductible contributions to the plan and pledges to pay beneficiaries a fixed and predetermined monthly benefit upon retirement. The employer either manages the plan or hires a money manager to do the job. In either case, the employer has a fiduciary duty to the plan beneficiaries. The employee pays no taxes on the contributions made on his behalf or on increases in the value of these "savings" that may be generated through capital gains. Only at retirement do an employee's monthly benefits become taxable as ordinary income.

A newer form of employer-based pension plan is known as a defined contribution plan. Primarily because it is less expensive for employers the defined contribution plan is becoming the dominant form of employer based pension in the United States. Under this type of plan, the employee becomes directly responsible for directing how his retirement savings are invested, and his eventual retirement benefit will depend upon the performance of his individualized account. This account is funded from pretax contributions by the employee and optional contributions by the employer. These contributions can be invested among a choice of mutual funds. Although the employer does not make investment decisions under a defined contribution plan, it retains a fiduciary duty for the administration of the plan. Prior to retirement the employee is not taxed on any appreciation in the value of his or her account, and after retirement mandatory withdrawals are taxed as ordinary income.

In addition to relying on employer based pension plans, a growing number of people save for retirement on their own. The primary vehicle for these savings are mutual funds which provide the small investor with diversification and professional management at relatively low cost. Mutual funds are professionally managed investment pools which invest in equities, bonds, commercial paper, and real estate. Investment objectives vary widely among funds and range from capital preservation and the generation of regular income to aggressive capital appreciation. Mutual funds now hold a third of the total equity in U.S. stock markets.

quarter of 1995, it has been estimated that the government deposited 1 billion korunas (approximately $50 million) into these private accounts.

Such government sponsorship is important, but it needs to be supported by economic growth. Belief in the economy's continued strong growth, says Jiri Doubravsky, head of the association of Czech pension funds and president of the Podnikatelsky Penzijni Fond, is the key behind the decision by over one million Czechs to open private pensions in the first year of the system. "To be sure, the government subsidy makes these plans a viable savings option, a much better one than the traditional savings account. But for the majority of the investors in my fund the belief is that only a pension that grows as fast—or, we hope, faster—than the economy will satisfy their retirement needs."

The correlation between growth and rising pension savings is not perfect. In an advanced economy with developed financial markets, there always exists a wide variety of publicly traded securities (both equity and debt instruments). Pension funds can easily diversify their investments across many firms and types of obligations. Unless they are mismanaged, their performance will rarely, if ever, fall below that of the economy as a whole.

This is not the case even in the more advanced economies of Eastern Europe, where only a few companies are publicly traded. Next to government interference, the scarcity of suitable investments is the biggest obstacle to the growth of reputable private pension funds. Pension monies must not be invested in too speculative instruments, such as unlisted securities: although it may be possible to diversify over a large number of unlisted firms, supervision of funds that invest in such businesses is too difficult. This type of aggressive investment may be good enough for more speculative types of funds, but not for the nest eggs of small investors.

In the absence of efficient capital markets, the development of pension funds is not easy. One way is to allow them to invest abroad, as Slovenes do, but most countries shy away from such free capital movements. Another is to restrict most of pension funds' investments to government bonds (with all the potential for political abuse this entails) and allow them to use a small portion of their funds to be placed in more speculative instruments. Finally, government may (and probably should) opt for allowing slightly higher levels of risk in pension funds than would be normal in more advanced economies. (Hungary, indeed, now permits a maximum of 30% of pension funds' assets to be invested in local equities.) Although it is certainly possible to go too far, timid East European politicians are likely to err in the opposite direction. And the degree of risk should quickly diminish. As companies compete for pension capital, this may spur the development of capital markets and gradually result in greater supply of less speculative investments. Relatively safe debt issues of the better domestic producers might perhaps lead this development. But for a time, the returns obtained by pension funds may have difficulty matching the growth of the economy.

In any case, competition among pension funds is crucial to enhance both returns and accountability. Czech funds now compete fiercely for the loyalty of pension account holders, who can switch funds with ease. The result is that fund managers are quickly learning to measure their performance. One criticism of this competition for pension accounts has been voiced by the Ministry of Finance, which argues that competition will induce pension fund managers to boost their immediate performance by seeking short-term gains at the expense of long-term prudence. This is a key reason why the ministry bans direct investments by funds in Czech equities, as well as restricting to 10% the amount of a pension that can be deposited with any one Czech bank. Such short-term thinking, responds Bohumil Dolejsi, head of the private Penzijni Fond, the country's fourth or fifth largest, is "a game only the stupid play."

Dolejsi and other fund managers chafe at the restrictions the government puts on their activities. Although they expect to profit handsomely from Czech pension reforms, they fear that government ideology is restricting their business, to the detriment of themselves and the Czech market. Their biggest complaint is that Prime Minister Klaus has created such a bogey out of the idea of the corporatist state that he blocks companies from offering pensions as a perk of employment. No specific law prevents companies from offering such pensions, Dolejsi is quick to point out, but the fact that the government refuses to treat them as tax-deductible expenses means that "they are never more than a dream." Unless these restrictions are loosened, the funds are afraid to lose their edge.

Although most Western countries allow corporate deductibility, Klaus' policy is also understandable. Corporate tax deductions, in addition to deductions from individual income taxes, are a form of subsidy favoring pension funds in which employers have greater chance of domination. Severing that link may contribute to a shift of power away from corporate insiders and, as truly independent pension funds begin to look over managers' shoulders, toward greater corporate accountability.

Fund managers such as Dolejsi also believe that equity investments would enhance returns and reduce the risks of holding only government paper. If restrictions are lifted, pension account holders will demand higher returns. Businesses will compete for this capital, improving the transparency and efficiency of financial markets. It will also force the government to put in place rules that deter insider trading in shares and to devise means whereby minority shareholders (such as pensions, which normally cannot hold too big a slice of any one company) are protected from being cheated. They argue for a bolder, more permissive (and riskier) regulatory policy.

The potential advantages of deregulation are even more obvious for pension funds in Slovenia, where a combination of economic growth and a hands-off government fosters the development of powerful pension funds. Under Tito-style socialism few places in the world could have matched Slovenia's pension funds in the arcane art of paper-shuffling. Today competition is fierce and international, forcing old ways to be abandoned.

Despite the usual parochial hang-ups and fears of capital flight, Slovenia's government opted to open its pension markets to foreign firms and to allow its domestic pension funds to invest abroad. These outward thrusts will continue. They are strategic, not tactical, in intent and are based on the view that international competition and investment not only diversify risk, but prepare the Slovene economy for incorporation into Europe. They also bring about rates of return on pension fund capital that will ease the pressure on the government budget.

Austrian-based pension/insurance groups such as Merkur Versicherungen AG of Graz (which owns the private Merkur Ljubljana pension fund in Slovenia) and Grazerwechselseitige Versicherung (which owns Prima Maribor pension fund), as well as investors such as Michael Rostaher (an Austrian who owns a Maribor-based insurance and pension group) were the first to make the running, but the move into the Slovene pension market has become so popular that Safeinvest, another Austrian firm, has carved out a profitable niche for itself marketing a wide variety of international pension plans to Slovene citizens. (The Austrians, of course, are not the only foreigners taking an interest

245

in providing pension funds in the region. Emerging market pensions are becoming fashionable across European insurance. According to the European Federation for Retirement Provision, more than three dozen European insurance firms have opened individual or joint venture pension plans in Eastern Europe.)

Competitive pressures are forcing Slovene pension funds like Ljubljanska zavarovalnica, wholly owned by Slovenia's big SKB bank, to become more efficient. The armies of scriveners huddled over ramshackle piles of paper, which typified the old pension system (itself a ramshackle structure, with layers upon layers of commissions and institutions administering the so-called Community of Pension and Invalid Insurance) have given way at Ljubljanska zavarovalnica to aggressive young men and women riveted to their computer screens. By comparison with other industries, they are well paid for their devotion. Statistics on profits are hard to come by, but the funds must be doing well if people employed in Slovene insurance companies earned an average $13,000 in income last year, $5,000 more than the national average.

The problems Slovenes face are rather different than those faced by their Czech counterparts. There are hundreds of quoted companies in which to place pension investments, but this edge is dulled by the absence of reliable trading, which leads to nightmarish settlement problems on the Maribor and Ljubljana exchanges. Complicated manual checks are required, and share ownership must be registered with the central bank. Many of these trades are rejected because of some defect in the paperwork. As a result, pension funds can go days and even weeks without knowing precisely where their money is invested. This worry incites more international activity as funds prefer to trade in foreign shares or in the few Slovene companies listed on the Vienna exchange. The problem is that such trading is more expensive than domestic trading, and listing abroad, which is expensive for Slovene companies, is thus feasible only for a few. As a result, smaller Slovene companies may not be able to attract pension fund capital, which means that they may fail to benefit in the near future from the modernization of finance that pension reform is bringing.

In the long run, Slovenes are likely to resolve these problems. Although there is no published data on the number of participants in Slovene private pensions, $45 million in gross premiums was paid into such funds in 1995. In a country of only 2 million people, this is not small potatoes. And according to the Slovene Central Bank, this money earned a real rate of return of 8% in 1995, a more than respectable result in a time of transition.

Foreign pension fund managers are attracted by the growth prospects for pensions in many East European and NIS countries, but are still put off by the high risks and heavy government regulation. Only Slovenia grants pension funds a free hand to invest their monies at home or abroad, though in late 1994 the government passed a law requiring that pensions active in the country incorporate themselves within Slovenia. Investment in the region's emerging stock markets is volatile, which comes as a shock to pension fund managers accustomed to sleeping soundly. The apparent riskiness of managing pensions in the region will decrease as the pension and capital markets themselves mature. Emerging markets are volatile in their early years for good reasons. Investors struggle to establish fair values; small investors and syndicates dominate at the expense of more stable institutions such as pension funds; regulation is weak and small exchanges are vulnerable to manipulation. But as markets get larger these characteristics will fade.

Responding to these fears, Slovenia established an Office of Insurance Activity Supervision within the Ministry of Finance last year. The Czech Republic, Hungary, Estonia, Latvia, and Lithuania are following this lead, establishing pension oversight commissions that are battling to bring some order to their respective markets. These new regulators are learning from their counterparts in France, Germany, Switzerland, and the United States how to police a market and to encourage pension funds to set up compliance departments. The development of pension funds as institutional investors in turn will bring about more stable oversight of the emerging capital markets as fund managers press their governments for active policing.

7.8 The Greatest Prize of All

Can the Czech and Slovene experiences be replicated elsewhere? Baltic private pension funds are showing some success both in attracting foreign participants (Estonia) and in the growing numbers of company-based plans (Lithuania). Given the huge bureaucracies—the antithesis of nimble private pension fund management—that now govern state pensions in most ex-socialist countries, the chances of success seem slim elsewhere in the near term.

Russia is the most alluring prospect for pension reform, yet it poses the biggest question. So large are the sums Russians are now saving—according to the OECD, Russia's national savings rate is approaching 20% of income, a figure that would do any Asian tiger proud—and so undeveloped is the domestic private pension industry, that the question should not be if change will come, but when. Today, a private pension fund industry that effectively manages personal retirement savings scarcely exists. This is one reason why, soon after relinquishing his post as privatization czar to become deputy prime minister in 1995, Anatoli Chubais put a team together to begin the process of codifying what promises to be a huge growth industry.

What money will these funds be chasing? To start with, company pension accounts. Many of Russia's emerging private-sector firms are awash with liquid assets. The result is that they are beginning to park some of their cash in company pension accounts that can be set against tax liability and also invested. The problem is that such pension investing, because of a lack of regulation, is accomplished in a gunslinging manner. The funds engage in a lot of speculative trading, with shares in the "hottest" companies being traded (and commissions generated) almost daily. Big businesses, such as the huge Lukoil energy concern, like this sort of investing because the tax exemption granted to pension funds enables them to convert capital gains into income free of tax. In a rising market, this formula works. But what happens when the market falls?

This type of investment is not only important as a more extreme example of today's fever for financial assets in Russia. It is also acting as a catalyst for the development of the pension management business. When the inevitable crash comes, it will draw attention to the dubious activities of many of today's pension managers and demonstrate the need for a more professional pension management industry. Today, pension account trading is good business. It pushes share prices higher. But as a source of security, this is pension management of the worst kind. Loosely regulated company pension plans are a sort of ice cube money. They melt easily.

According to the Association of Non-Governmental Pension Funds, by 1994 there were more than 1,000 private pension schemes, most acting like cowboy investors. Moreover, the system of pension fund accounting is arcane. The investment performance of a pension fund is calculated by book value—what the fund paid for a stock or bond, not on its current market value. All unrealized gains or losses are simply ignored. The total investment return, in the sense of what has gone up and down in value, is deemed irrelevant. And in many cases a number of company and individual funds are pooled into one big account, making it even harder for companies to demand accountability.

This system is acceptable only because the pension business is still not regarded as tremendously important by enterprise managers and owners. The person responsible for supervising the pension fund tends to be a minion. This issue may come to a head only when the ratio of contributions to payouts becomes less favorable, which in most cases is still years away. Opening salvoes in the coming war to discipline pension funds, however, have been fired, not only by the formation of first deputy prime minister Chubais' exploratory commission, but by the Moscow National Pension Bank, which aims to position itself as a reliable and conservative pension fund manager. Their cause is helped by foreign actuaries and pension fund consultants (some of whom, like Britain's David Calland, have the ear of President Yeltsin) who are setting up in Moscow to preach their gospel of performance measurement for pension funds.

Many of Russia's biggest and best-run companies are (if only gradually) becoming aware of their pension obligations, and they are growing concerned about actual investment performance and reliability. This is not yet a pressing problem. Most company pension plans in Russia remain "young," with contributions far exceeding payouts. This is one reason why they are growing so fast. In the past two years, one EBRD economist reckons, Russian company pension funds have been growing at a compounded annual rate of 22%. It is this pile of money on which pension fund managers, and the ever-watchful Chubais, are setting their sights.

Competitive management of pension accounts is on its way in Russia. But, despite the tremendous pressure, liberalization of the pension market on the Slovenian model, in order to allow international competition and also international investment of pension fund capital, may not come that quickly because the

Russians want time to build up their own expertise and also want to see the country's swelling savings accounts used to invigorate Russian securities.

The virtue of today's myriad experiments throughout South American, Europe, the United States, and Asia is that Russia as well as other governments in the region have so many different (and often successful) experiments on which to draw. The Czechs, Slovenes, Estonians, Latvians, and Russians have been inspired along the path of pension reform by the success of the Dutch, British, Chileans, and Americans in their private pension plans. As East European and NIS countries compete for the capital they need to further their growth, they will discover that pension reform breeds financial vitality in sorely needed capital markets. This, as much as the specter of budget deficits, is the best hope that countries other than the Czech Republic and Slovenia will grasp the nettle of pension reform. Those countries that fail to establish responsible, capital-generating personal pension plans will find themselves behind in the race to prosperity.

8
The Trade Winds Shift

As communism fell apart between 1989 and 1991, its trading system, Comecon, collapsed with spectacular speed—a decline and fall that was not at all unexpected by outside observers of the region, but which stunned local officials (both reformers and their opponents) and business leaders alike. In response to this rapid transformation of the regional trading environment, dozens of countries scrambled for new markets even as their economies, battered by external competition and the freeing of domestic prices, went into early free fall.

Economic slump and trade protection are macroeconomic pathologies that usually feed on each other, as hard-pressed governments look inward, not outward, for economic salvation. The surprise has been the pronounced talents that many transition countries have demonstrated in reinventing their trade policies and reorienting their international trading relations within a relatively short period of time. A half-decade into the postcommunist transition, the trade winds are blowing briskly across Central Europe and Central Asia. And no country in this region—no matter how hard or desperately it tries—has shown itself able to withstand their force (see table 8.1).

A little worldliness is, perhaps, an advantageous thing. Ion Ciolu, a former trade union boss in a Dacia automobile factory's export division, is the sort of exporting entrepreneur pushing the postcommunist countries into the maelstrom of world trade. Soon after Nicolae Ceausescu's fall, Ciolu formed his own private trading company, Regent Group, which barters Dacia parts for imported color televisions. "It was unthinkable that a private company could buy parts from a state-owned company and then sell them abroad," says Ciolu. So unthinkable was this notion indeed that, kowtowing to Dacia's hidebound managers, prosecutors in Bucharest investigated (unsuccessfully) Ciolu and his

Table 8.1

Export Reorientation of Transition Economies

	Value of Total Export (US$ million)		Index	Share of Inter-Republic Exports		Change in Share (%)	Non-agricultural Exports to OECD (US$ million)		Index	Share of OECD Exports in GDP 1994	Index of Export Re-orientation
	1991	1994	1991 =100	1990	1994		1991	1994	1991 =100		
Baltic States											
Estonia	2,624	1,103	42	98	34	-66	150	479	320	19.4	26
Latvia	4,171	1,101	26	97	52	-46	107	334	311	27.4	39
Lithuania	5,556	1,686	30	94	55	-42	138	445	322	31.8	35
Central Asian NIS*											
Kazakhstan	13,191	8,339	63	89	84	-6	65	177	272	2.3	49
Kyrgyzstan	3,493	817	23	97	86	-11	1	11	1,309	1.2	50
Tajikistan	2,310	660	29	82	52	-37	1	15	2,413	9.1	36
Turkmenistan	5,029	3,049	61	96	88	-9	6	6	97	5.9	47
Uzbekistan	10,485	4,030	38	89	57	-36	3	26	960	5.9	47
European NIS											
Belarus	21,638	8,018	37	92	87	-6	100	387	386	2.3	49
Moldova	2,732	1,342	49	93	91	-2	11	36	323	2.0	45
Russia	168,455	84,351	50	68	44	-35	4,937	4,195	85	7.5	48
Ukraine	51,647	20,535	40	83	77	-7	682	1,279	187	3.3	52
Transcaucasian NIS											
Armenia	1,954	453	23	97	91	-6	8	39	501	0.6	50
Azerbaijan	6,654	1,094	16	92	67	-27	6	11	179	2.9	65
Georgia	2,493	404	16	91	79	-13	8	6	78	2.1	68
Central and Eastern European Countries											
Bulgaria †	5,230	3,500	67	53	33	-38	545	1,117	205	19.7	31
former CSK †	11,330	15,700	139	37	15	-59	3,457	9,237	267	30.7	18
Hungary †,‡	9,672	10,000	103	41	23	-44	2,558	5,159	202	19.9	22
Poland †,‡	14,670	16,970	116	41	13	-68	2,955	8,730	295	14.5	21
Romania	4,571	6,120	134	25	15	-40	1,895	2,812	148	14.2	37

* Newly Independent States.
† share of CMEA exports in total exports.
‡ the reference year for the share of the CMEA and value of total exports in 1989.
Source: UN Comtrade.

dealings for many months in hopes of finding a way to crimp his dealings by legal means. None were found. Years after the fall of the Berlin Wall and the Soviet Union's breakup, trade reorientation, often inspired by men like Ciolu, had delivered goods from around the globe to where Comecon's dreary writ once ran supreme. Import substitution rather than foreign products, protection of domestic industries, artificially high exchange rates:

these were the policies to which Comecon rigidly adhered, no matter the damage they inflicted. The demise of Comecon's system between 1989 and 1991 was followed by a period of chaos in which most factories were left without markets and to their own devices.

Many enterprises, in the wake of Comecon's disintegration, stood idle or went bust. Firms that struggled on needed to sell anywhere to anyone—and often at any price. Passports in hand, new trade entrepreneurs exploited private contacts, often acquired by a person who had been an official in, say, the ministries of trade, foreign affairs, or energy that handled socialist contacts with the outside world, for all they were worth. And for some traders, early actions have paid long-term dividends. Soon after the failed August coup of 1991, Moscow faced food shortages due to chaos in Russian transport. Bartimpex (a private Polish food exporter) earned the lasting loyalty (it still gets contracts) of Moscow's powerful city-hall machine by delivering food on credit to the city.

8.1 Opened by Force

Many postcommunist economies opened themselves to international trade because they had little choice in the matter. "Fraternal socialist trade," as it was once known, was disintegrating long before communist governments fell. One such case is Bulgaria, which in 1991 was trapped in a typical socialist trading triangle: Russian arms sales to Iraq were to be repaid by Iraqi oil exports to Bulgaria, which were in lieu of payment for Russian imports of Bulgarian goods. When trade sanctions were imposed following Iraq's invasion of Kuwait, however, the deal boomeranged horribly, and Bulgaria found itself without oil or payment from Russia.

The sheer incompetence and bureaucratization of such trade deals set in motion the breakdown of state trading monopolies even before communism's collapse. At the time of Mikhail Gorbachev's fall, Russia possessed only a few dozen state bodies authorized to trade outside the socialist camp; now, at least 150,000 firms and individuals are engaged in import and export deals. "One day," says Yuri Yaroslavtsev, former head of state trading house Loexport and now a foreign trade consultant, "we received a call from a furniture factory. They wanted to export.

'Tell us exactly how we can get to the world market. What are the practice requirements?' We tried to propose ourselves as consultants. No success. Everyone wants to trade on their own."

Foolhardy or not, import-export wanderlust is catching on everywhere. Consider one convert: Rosvooruzheniye, Russia's state arms export agency, says export sales in 1995 were 40 higher than the previous year. It predicts this will double in two years' time. No less than eighteen different Russian arms firms competed to sell Russian fighter jets to Malaysia. Russian business gossip suggests that many enterprises prefer to export, charging prices lower than domestic ones and thus incurring paper losses, for the simple reason that foreigners pay cash where Russians only promise to pay.

Consider now the money involved, for such trades are but the tip of the iceberg. Poland, the Czech Republic, Hungary, Kyrgyzstan, Moldova, Slovenia, the Baltics, and Russia all have the foundations of an open trading system in place. Their trade is shifting fast into the private sector and toward the West. Poland's infant private sector accounted for a mere 4.9% of exports in 1990; four years later it claimed the lion's share, 51%. In 1989, 48% of Czech exports went to Comecon economies and 37% to developed economies. Three years later, only 18.5% of exports were going to former socialist countries (and the bulk of these to Slovakia), and 67.6% to developed economies, with the EU claiming a whopping 56% of this trade. Bulgaria almost turned its trade upside down: in 1990 Comecon countries got 80.1% of Bulgarian exports, and OECD countries 9.0%; by 1995 OECD countries claimed 51.8% and Comecon 33.0%. Romania is a special case. Slow to reform, it expanded imports sharply at first as new foreign debt was taken on. Only since 1994 has import growth been supported by rising export revenues.

Because the trade links with the nations of the former USSR were severed, Kyrgyzstan's trade volume was 35% lower in 1995 than in 1990. This collapse would have been catastrophically worse if new markets had not been opened elsewhere in Asia, particularly with next-door China, long shut off from even the most basic trading relations. What is happening, says Arthur Dunkel, a former director general of the General Agreement on Tariffs and Trade (GATT), the predecessor to today's World Trade Organization, "is the greatest injection into the world trading system since the Asian tigers began to modernize thirty years ago."

254

Sometimes reorienting trade is more than a matter of economic necessity; for Macedonia this scramble for markets has been a matter of life and death. Through little or no fault of its own, Macedonia, since becoming independent, has been rocked by four brutal trade shocks:

1. war in Bosnia and Croatia cut access to Macedonia's traditional neighboring markets;

2. UN sanctions blocked sales to Serbia, where a majority of Macedonia's exports went when it was part of a united Yugoslavia;

3. Comecon collapsed;

4. a unilateral trade embargo was imposed by Greece in February 1994 (lifted at the end of 1995), which prevented landlocked Macedonia from exporting from the nearest world-class port, Salonika.

With its back to the wall, Macedonia maintained its exports at roughly 1990 levels through a near-desperate search for new trading partners. For example, exports to Comecon fell from 30% of total exports in 1990 to 19% two years later. Sales to other former Yugoslav neighbors fell by 40% over the same period. Total Macedonian exports did not collapse because new markets were developed—despite the Greek blockade—in the EU, Bulgaria, and Turkey. Macedonia may have the last laugh. Having found Bulgaria's port of Burgos an attractive and economic alternative to Salonika, Macedonian trade is likely to continue to flow through it.

Macedonia learned its trade lessons the hard way, but the lesson is unchanging across the region: the transition economies will tend toward inefficiency unless compelled to compete and excel. Even when industries are privatized or deregulated, prospects for increased efficiency are scant without healthy drafts of foreign products and business practices pushing managers and workers to improve productivity. The chairman of Tallinn's port decided in a matter of days in 1992 to allow private Finnish shipping companies equal treatment with Estonian firms—healthy competition which, he reckons, has increased the productivity of Estonian shipping and transport firms. If the port had remained under direct ministerial control, bureaucrats might still be pondering this decision. Almost to a man, managers who have crossed the divide from state to private industry say that both the prospect and reality of opening economies to imports and foreign competition works to improve domestic business performance.

8.2 Trading Up, Trading Around

The political will to make trade reform a national priority is the first condition of successful entry into world markets. But other political, historical, and economic factors also matter. For the Visegrad countries of Poland, Hungary, the Czech Republic, and Slovakia, as well as the Baltic states of Estonia, Latvia and Lithuania, the end of communism brought the end of Russian domination and the start of their return to the European fold. Indeed, the Czechs, widely regarded as model reformers, have been so successful in opening up their economy that they are now encountering the problems that come with too much of a good thing: a huge influx of foreign currency, both in payment for exports and direct investment, is putting upward pressure on the koruna. For most of 1996 the Czech government resisted this pressure (not least because it faced parliamentary elections in May). The government of Premier Vaclav Klaus feared that a revaluation, by making Czech goods more expensive, would hurt employment and thus cost votes. That delay, it now seems, only made matters worse when a mounting trade deficit forced a devaluation in May 1997.

Hungary, by contrast, exemplifies the problems associated with a gradual opening to trade. It started trade reform with singular advantages, as the "goulash" socialism of the Janos Kadar era allowed for far greater exposure to international trade than elsewhere in the Soviet world. (By 1985 trade was no longer a state monopoly, with 259 state farms and industries, as well as 38 special trade organizations, allowed to trade with the rest of the world.) It also received the greater part of foreign investment in the early reform years. But a somewhat complacent trade posture has made it probably the weakest of the Visegrad countries in terms of removing remaining barriers and has left its balance of payments chronically precarious.

The Baltic states came to trade reform only in 1991. Animated by a desire to put their enforced membership in the USSR behind them, each embraced radical programs of trade deregulation. Estonia razed its trade bureaucracies, and all three Baltic states have over the years introduced stable, convertible currencies. Slovenia and Macedonia, despite difficulties related to the disintegration of Yugoslavia, were also in a privileged position as each gained from the relatively open trading structures bequeathed by Tito's somewhat more lax socialist regime. As in Hungary, though, complacency is likely to hinder continued progress in international trade.

After these front-runners come a second tier of trade reformers: Bulgaria, Romania, Croatia, and Albania. Each has been torn between eastward habits and westward yearnings, for differing reasons: Bulgaria because it was especially dependent on Soviet trade; Croatia because the Tudjman regime has militarized state administration; Romania because civil society had been so completely enfeebled by the Ceausescu dictatorship that when communism collapsed, large chunks of the old elites were able to hold their places atop state trading agencies. Albania has made significant progress in opening itself to trade with the wider world, but because of the devastation wrought by the paranoically hermetic Enver Hoxha regime, it started well behind other players in the region.

The political priority given to rejoining Europe by the Baltic and Visegrad states has greatly influenced the speed, scope, and institutional shape of trade reform in these countries. New trade laws are being written to be compatible with EU legislation. Some of this is clearly helpful: Poland, for example, made life for importers and exporters easier by adopting the EU's "Single Administrative Document," cutting back the time businessmen waste filling in stacks of forms and applications. Moreover, new institutions are being shaped that look like continental European ones. Bad bits of the EU, however, are being copied, too: Hungary's agricultural support system, for example, looks like, and is as noxious for agricultural trade as, the EU common agricultural policy.

Of the former Soviet republics, the best reformers are those who are most hard-up—driven by desperation as much as anything else. Landlocked, wedged between Russia, Kazakhstan, and China, highly agricultural Kyrgyzstan embraced free trade with a vengeance. Like the Baltic states, its opening to the world followed immediately after its decision to leave the ruble zone. Finding new markets has not been easy, but the mountainous eastern part of the country has now established firm trade links with China (prompting protectionist cries in Bishkek that cheap Chinese beer is killing the domestic variety). With Iran, Turkey, and Pakistan competing to establish trade links in Central Asia, the Kyrgyz people look set to rediscover their roots as traders along the ancient Silk Road.

8.3 Late Arrivals

Brooding about the degree of independence from Russia they really want, other NIS states—Belarus, Ukraine, Kazakhstan, Moldova and Uzbekistan—have dithered about trade; in this confusion, they have wound up holding tightly to the restrictive regimes of the past. These countries have been the slowest to free their prices and to introduce predictable customs regimes. Most continue to subsidize farms and factories to such an extent that protectionism follows naturally. Each of these countries regarded itself at independence as rich or potentially rich, and thus succumbed to the temptations of behaving accordingly, deferring reform by living off present or anticipated sources of wealth. Uzbekistan, in particular, did not think it necessary to push for export earnings because it could use gold to pay for its import needs.

Many of the former Soviet republics were at a disadvantage, at least when compared to the more fortunate countries and economies of Central Europe. Hungary, Poland, the Czech Republic, Slovenia—each could call on a history of strong foreign trade relations that the long years of communist autarky had never really erased. In particular, Hungary and Slovenia had acted as windows on the West during much of the Soviet era. The countries of Central Asia, however, had been isolated from the world for generations and lacked the political resources and networks of personal contacts on which to draw in confronting the world market for the first time.

When the leap into the new world of international trade is not made wholeheartedly, old ways of thinking tend to linger. Listen to the voice of Cristian Ionescu, a former Romanian minister of trade, when asked to explain why state trading companies lose money: "Profit emerges from productive activities." These enterprises "have zero profit because they have no production of their own. Profit out of what?. . . . As for the private trading companies, we support their profit out of our own pockets." Here is nonsense worthy of that great Romanian master of the absurd, Eugene Ionesco.

Fear of open borders is another symptom of the old ways. Politicians in the region often attempt to exploit anxieties born out of the competition from foreign goods. International trade usually tops the standard list of scapegoats for economic woes, and protectionism usually follows in lock step. In Poland's last government the Peasant Party agreed to maintain the minister of privatization in office only if his powers to privatize certain industries, particularly cigarette manufacturing plants, were sharply curtailed. Tobacco farmers fear that former owners will import tobacco.

Such lobbying sometimes cuts two ways: in Lithuania, for example, a hide and fur processing plant in Diauliai works short hours because tariffs imposed at the behest of domestic lobbies have made it impossible to import the materials it needs. This raises the hope that the scales of lobbying power will become more balanced. In Russia, for every Avtovaz (the decaying giant automaker whose boss, Vladimir Kadannikov, replaced Anatoli Chubais as first deputy prime minister for a time in 1995) lobbying for trade protection, there are emerging forces arguing against it. Gazprom secured for itself an exemption from all import levies, and the mayors of major cities like Moscow, which depend on imported food, fight tooth and nail against high import tariffs for agriculture.

8.4 The Advantage of Comparative Advantage

From the start of the reform process, reformers were of two minds about liberalizing international trade. Radicals saw it as essential if the inflation unleashed by liberalizing prices was to be tamed by the whip of competition. Gradualists, on the other hand, wanted trade reform to be staggered, adopted piecemeal. They worried that a sudden opening of decayed economies to global competition would lead to unnecessary social, political, and economic strains. Outright opponents of reform (mimicking protectionists around the globe) were more blunt: free trade, they shouted, means lost jobs.

Opening to foreign trade does impose short-term costs. Some domestic industries, especially the old dinosaurs, are bound to suffer, and with them the jobs of their employees. But there is a reverse side to this state of affairs: foreign competition is often the main spur for internal enterprise reform. Without such pressure, talk about restructuring often turns out to be nothing more than talk: old firms carry on as inefficiently as before. When foreign goods arrive, however, bosses are forced to respond. Foreign trade is also the best way to eliminate domestic monopolies. While domestic antitrust policies are seldom effective, foreign trade by definition makes competition a reality.

Foreign trade delivers other immediate benefits. Shortages disappear overnight (as they did throughout Eastern Europe in 1990–91) as importers look abroad for low-cost and high-quality goods. These imports mean that consumers are no longer forced to settle for shoddy products. Moreover, business can acquire capital equipment with which to modernize production without the endemic delays such imports faced in the past.

The biggest mistake of the opponents of free trade is to fear that foreign competition will lead to long-term decline in domestic production and employment. "If we fully open our market, our industries will be hammered from two directions," says Eva Radeva, legal advisor to Bulgaria's Ministry of Trade. "Quality products from the West will destroy our industries; low-cost goods from Asia will kill off the rest. To shoot yourself in one foot, maybe; but to shoot off both feet at one time must be madness." Fears like this are based on a fundamental misunderstanding of two concepts: *absolute* and *comparative advantage.* An assumption is often made that a country must be better than others at making certain goods to be able to specialize in the production of such goods and to profit from foreign trade. Some countries do indeed have such "absolute advantage." But economists since David Ricardo have recognized that a country need not have it to benefit from trade.

A much weaker condition, called "comparative advantage," is sufficient. Think of, say, Germany and Poland. Germany probably has an absolute advantage in the production of both cars and textiles. But as Germany faces choices concerning future expansion, it has to decide whether to produce more cars or more textiles. If Germany's absolute advantage in car manufacturing is greater than in textiles (that is, its cost effectiveness is greater in cars than in textiles), German producers will find it more profitable to make more cars instead of textiles, and leave the latter to others. This is because car exports will bring greater returns, more than covering the cost of textile imports. This means that Poland (and countries like it) has an opening here: its *comparative* advantage in textiles to Germany—that is, if Germany keeps its markets open to foreign trade from poorer countries.

In the early stages of transition, many postcommunist countries may in fact have an absolute advantage in the production of certain goods because their labor costs are still quite low. This is probably one of the reasons why trade reorientation in many East European countries has been so successful. As the living standards in transition countries improve, however, labor costs will go up. Some countries will still find niches in which their absolute advantage may be preserved. Once given up for dead, Szczecin Shipyard in Poland, for example, seems to have found a profitable market for its cargo ships. But because of the importance of comparative advantage, *all* countries stand to gain from trade in the long run.

8.5 Jobs Will Come

Theory is one thing, policymaking is another. Whether radical or gradualist, the move into global markets was made against severe short-term hardships. All postcommunist countries suffered deep recessions in the first years of the transition; trade among them collapsed and, as prices were freed, the population became generally poorer, at least according to official statistics. Much of this hardship, to be sure, was the legacy of communism's failure, not the product of the arrival of international competition. But governments found this a hard argument to make to a citizenry struggling to adapt to a fast-changing world.

Open markets encountered much early skepticism. Few people, whether in the former communist countries or in the West, believed a quick economic turnaround possible, or that new export markets could be discovered and cultivated without painstaking effort. Judging by the speed of the recoveries now underway, many of the countries that moved fastest and furthest with radical trade reforms have come out best.

Some parts of the trade reform agenda are relatively standard, though they inevitably prove to be more difficult and time-consuming for liberal governments to enact than other aspects of a liberal trade regime. Anyone, for example, can eliminate complex licensing procedures or lower tariffs, given the political will. It takes a fair degree of expertise, however, to negotiate and reach trade agreements with other countries, reform customs police so that bribes are not front and center when a businessman looks abroad, and establish an orderly settlements process for payment of import or export deals. Irresolute governments find it easy to get bogged down in all of these things.

The bottom-line question facing politicians as they ponder reform is this: Is the potential gain from liberal trade worth the present pain? Advocates of open economies can name the advantage of free trade: more goods at lower prices. They tend, however, to feel slightly embarrassed when asked to quantify them: the gain in terms of money saved by a huge army of consumers sometimes looks too small for all the pain that can be inflicted on the workers in an industry adversely affected by trade. Consumers often don't remember that they bought this car or that coat at a lower price because the government opened the economy to world trade; those few who lose their jobs because of foreign trade, however, are sure to remember come the next election. So the political risk of freeing trade is high.

In a paper titled "New Gods, Old Theory, and the Welfare Costs of Trade Restrictions," Professor Paul Romer of the University of California at Berkeley suggested that all such calculations underestimate the true benefits of free trade. His point is simple but profound: tariffs, quotas, and other forms of protection do more than raise prices at the margins; they may prevent a particular economic good from ever appearing within an economy. Modern economics has devoted a lot of effort to theorizing about such "discontinuities" in other parts of the discipline. But the implications, Romer argues, have not been incorporated into the debate over trade. If a tariff (or other protectionist policy) prevents a new good from ever appearing, the loss for the whole economy is multiplied well beyond a mere price increase.

To illustrate his point, Romer sets out a model of an economy that uses labor and many different kinds of imported capital to produce goods. Tariffs reduce both the amount and the variety of capital available to domestic producers. The run-on effect of such policies is to greatly reduce national income. For developing countries, these policies can be almost catastrophic. Such countries do not use smaller amounts of the full range of goods available in rich countries; they use smaller amounts of a much-restricted range of goods. According to Romer, "a rough guide to the welfare losses in any country will . . . be the difference between the range of productive inputs that are available there and the range of productive inputs that could be put to use there." Seen this way, the costs of protectionism in the transition countries—meaning not just high tariffs and the distortions that inevitably result from them, but also the non-availability of many goods of all kinds—look vast and long-lasting.

Estonia's rapid progress is largely due to a textbook application of monetary conservatism and free trade, but explicit in this program is a recognition of the correctness of Romer's thesis. According to the OECD, imports of new technologies have had a dramatic effect in jump-starting Estonia's economy. Its first post-communist government introduced almost completely free trade, a stance its successors have grumbled about consistently. Their inaction speaks louder than words, however, as Estonia continues to march on to the beat of free trade.

To be sure, more than economics motivated this plunge into world trade. Estonians believe the biggest threat to their continued success comes from Russia. The best protection against this ancient threat? "Integration with Europe is the guarantee of our economic sovereignty and our security," President Lennart Meri repeats like a national mantra. Trade is one way to get close to Europe, and Estonians have pushed this neighborliness faster than even the most starry-eyed optimist could have expected in 1991. Then, over 90% of its trade was with the nations of the USSR. Now, almost three-quarters of its trade is with countries of the European Union. Some industries, of course, have been hit and hit hard—agriculture in particular, as Estonia is one of the countries with the freest trade in foodstuffs anywhere in the world. But in a small country, foreign competition has been decisive in pushing businesses to reform quick and to keep prices low.

To get along with their new trading partners and so deliver the inputs needed to modernize their economies, Estonia and the other success stories of trade confronted the task of bringing their production standards up to world levels. When communism collapsed, few managers in the region had heard of the International Standards Office (ISO). Today, thousands of firms from the Baltics to the Balkans clamor for a positive rating from it. The ISO rates a company's trading reliability: quality control and a company's record for completing and paying for transactions are two key elements of this rating system. Given the paucity of brand-name recognition for transition country products, and the socialist era's reputation for shoddiness dogging the region's firms, such validation is indispensable. In 1989 electrical machinery producer Rotomatica became the first company in Slovenia to get an ISO rating. A British partner insisted on it.

Rotomatica's managers claim, most of its European trading partners insist on seeing the ISO certificate before ordering more goods. So important has a positive rating become in Slovene trade that the Ministry of Science and Technology now actively works with firms to upgrade their processes so as to meet ISO standards.

8.6 Chelnoks Show the Way

Not surprisingly, retail was the first area opened to international trade in most transition countries, because communism failed to provide what people wanted, and reformers knew instinctively that people would respond positively to a flow of once-forbidden goods. Three things, above all, made this possible.

Borders were thrown open. Unlike under communism, when unofficial travel was considered subversive, once the transition began, people could get passports and go abroad. Anyone who owned a truck or even a car in Poland, for example, could go to Germany or Austria to do some private trading. Geographic proximity to the West gave a natural advantage to some countries such as Poland, which borders on Germany. The Baltics, with their ferry connections to Scandinavia and strong economic growth, quickly became destinations in their own right for their eastern neighbors, like Belarus and Ukraine. Even in countries without easy access to global trade, like Russia or Kazakhstan, local traders seized the advantage of cheap fares on state airlines and started to wander the globe in search of cheaper goods for resale back home. Kyrgyz traders have turned trade with mainland China over the Tien Shan Mountains into a billion-dollar industry.

Under the old regime, private economic activity (including trading) was almost always criminal, and private foreign trade (possible only via smuggling) was a crime akin to treason. Access to foreign goods was a privilege accorded only the most loyal among the nomenklatura, who could shop in stores restricted to their brethren in the communist elite. The breakdown of these prohibitions opened the floodgates to private trading.

Currency convertibility enabled masses of people to participate in the benefits of trade, both as consumers and as traders. Although the official exchange rate was devalued, the black market rate (which had been the only relevant one for most people) tumbled and the currencies appreciated in all countries that implemented macroeconomic stabilization programs. Under the old regime, an average Pole earned $10 to $20 a month at the black market rate; today his wages are over $300. This made many foreign goods affordable for the first time, and the demand for them skyrocketed.

Chelnoks, as they are known in Russian (from the word meaning "to shuttle"), the motley army of grandmothers, ex-physicists, low-level apparatchiks, and young street toughs, became the shock troops of the postcommunist world's entry into world trade. Many chelnoks begged, borrowed, and saved to take newly available cheap flights to China, Turkey, and elsewhere, in order to bring back as many consumer goods as they could pay for and carry back for resale, usually in impromptu kiosks or large flea markets scattered throughout urban centers. In Kazakhstan, estimates of the size of *chelnok* trade remained as high as $250 million in 1995, a tenth of the country's total foreign trade that year. Covetous of tax revenues, indeed, the Kazakh government imposed special customs rules for *chelnoks.* "But you can always find someone to bribe," says one Kazakh *chelnok;* "that is always cheaper than paying to the state."

From such humble beginnings, fortunes can be made. Starting with a dilapidated sidewalk table selling imported lipsticks, chewing gum, and Mars bars, Yuri Geller, a Ukrainian *chelnok,* expanded in less than two years into owning a string of hard currency shops, warehouses, and over one hundred kiosks that sell everything from English whiskey to Korean compact disc players. Today's owners of Kyrgyzstan's biggest trading companies were yesterday's solitary *chelnoks.* On a bigger scale, the same entrepreneurial spirit helped new Slovak trading companies, such as Sipoz Holdings and Chirana Export/Import, challenge the dominance of former state trading houses, eventually breaking their iron grip on the export of goods produced in state-owned firms.

8.7 The Old Boy Network

Despite this burst of entrepreneurial energy, the ghosts of the old monolithic communist trading structures have continued to haunt the economic landscape. Poland's half-dozen foreign trade organizations (FTOs), which once held exclusive powers to trade Polish goods internationally (including foodstuffs produced on supposedly private farms), are trying to reinvent themselves as

Japanese- and Korean-style trading houses, expanding (and owning stakes) not only in the companies they once represented overseas, but also in banks and other firms. Once the sole international marketer of Polish household goods, Universal Trading Company, for example, now owns the country's biggest condom manufacturer, a former communist newspaper, and a variety of shipping and other transport companies. From its base in exports of electrical goods, Elektrim has expanded into banking and even yoghurt making. Agros Holdings continues to dominate food exports and imports, where it plays a powerful role in fixing prices, as farmers must negotiate with it rather than with ministry bureaucrats. Mostostal, which specialized in selling construction materials (and hiring out Polish construction workers) throughout Europe, now also sells textiles.

History rather than coherent business planning accounts for the rise of these conglomerates. The first postcommunist devaluation of the zloty was a boon to FTOs; they where among the few enterprises in Poland to hold large tranches of foreign currency. Despite the loss of trading monopolies, windfall profits arose in the first years of transition because of currency dealing. Many FTOs ploughed these profits back into buying up ownership of the companies they once represented abroad. Added profits were also made during the Warsaw stock market boom of 1993–94, when shares in companies FTOs had bought cheaply from the state were sold off.

But expansion into other industries only distracted FTOs from their core business, foreign trade. One of the seven banks owned by Elektrim went bust and another had its license suspended, thus ending Elektrim management's dream of using the banks to finance group activities. At the same time, FTOs use their old political connections to keep rivals at bay. Elektrim and Universal have pushed for official certification requirements that block competition to some of their goods. In another part of the world, Kazcontract, heir to Kazakhstan's state committee on supplying material resources, has transformed itself into a joint venture but retains its old communist-era boss and got the government to sanction its near-monopoly control of mineral trading as well.

Given that change in the official structures is slow in coming, it is no surprise that much of the region's international trade began in *chelnok* suitcases. *Chelnok* trade also flourished because it could get around unpredictable lurches in trade policy during the early transition years, while larger export and import business lacked a bedrock of stable laws and institutions. No one trusted anyone. Corruption was (and remains) rife. Without international agreements, stable currencies, and binding legal contracts, long-term trade relations were hard to establish. If trade were to grow beyond the one-man or one-woman operations of the *chelnoks,* government needed to play a walk-on role.

8.8 Back to Barter

Of course, when governments get into the business of international trade, the chances are high that they will get it wrong. A strong theme runs through the history of state efforts to manage trade: national liquidity and the question of whether there is enough of it to finance international trade without further inciting inflation. Moreover, as hard currencies like the dollar and D-mark come to dominate the settlement of international transactions, countries also became quite choosy about the money they accept for their exports. Russia, for example, shunned Ukrainian coupons as payment for exports of natural gas; Moldovans balked at receiving Romanian lei; the first Central Asian state to bolt from the ruble zone, Kyrgyzstan, spurned Uzbek and Kazakh rubles. In this hothouse atmosphere, finance to expand regional trade simply evaporated.

In a knee-jerk response, many transition countries resorted to barter, what economists call countertrade. This seemed almost natural. Communist barter was a central planner's dream because it dealt in quantities at fixed prices. In general, barter flourishes when finance fails to oil the gears of normal commercial trade. Estimates from the World Trade Organization, the Economist Intelligence Unit, the OECD, and elsewhere suggest that various forms of countertrade still account for at least one-third of all transition country trade.

The true size is probably impossible to measure accurately because standard official statistics on international trade do not differentiate countertrade deals from the rest. The proportion of these rose sharply in the early 1990s because many NIS countries were willing to barter their souls for energy. Only the truly naive could doubt the reason for countertrades' sudden proliferation. Locked into the Soviet energy distribution system, Ukraine, Belarus, and even Estonia lacked the hard currency to purchase oil or natural gas on the world markets. For a while, Russia

267

extended unlimited credit. Eventually, the Kremlin demanded to be paid: the favorable settlement Russia reached with Leonid Kuchma's government, for example, on ownership of the Black Sea naval fleet is widely believed to be a barter deal for the continuance of Russian energy exports to Ukraine.

Barter is also resorted to for political reasons. In Slovakia, since the return of Vladimir Meciar to power in November 1994, there has been a strenuous effort to restore trading links with Russia. The Ministry for the Economy, for example, issues licences for the export of strategic goods to Russia and specifies that a fixed percent of this trade must be conducted through barter deals. Why? It wants to keep inefficient Slovak state companies going. The only markets for these industrial dinosaurs are the ones they have always had, in Russia. Even there, selling is not as easy as it used to be; Russian consumers nowadays are more demanding. Still, given the shortage of finance, companies will barter goods that each might use in-house, even if they would not buy them in the open market.

As a means to exchange goods, however, barter is exceedingly inefficient. As a mechanism for matching goods and purchasers it is extremely costly and time consuming—after all, money was invented thousands of years ago to get around exactly this problem. The special danger barter poses in the transition countries is that the only people who can cut down on its cost somewhat (for they were the trade matchmakers of the old regime) are the members of the discredited nomenklatura, who can preserve in this way some of the value of their old connections, both domestic and foreign.

This is why barter, once it has become established, is hard to call off or scale back. Latvia's Commodity Exchange Fund was given sole regulation of barter trade in the hopes of stunting it; no luck, at least insofar as trade with NIS countries is concerned. One minute Hungary's government tried to curtail the cutting of barter deals; the next it tried to foster them in order to pay for imports of Russian energy. Between 1991 and 1994 Poland tried to limit barter trade by administrative fiat: all barter deals needed permission of the Ministry of Co-Operation with Abroad. Despite these hurdles, barter trade with the NIS persisted. In 1992 it covered 22.7% of Polish exports to Russia, 22.5% to Belarus, and 8.9% with Ukraine. Only when the Polish government, in late 1994, lifted all official restrictions and got out of the barter business did barter trade decrease. Once again, the market showed itself to be a better regulator than bureaucrats.

There is also a strong prima facie case that the state is the biggest beneficiary of the fad for barter. Documents involved in barter agreements are far more complicated than in any normal commercial deal, where money changes hands and that is that. How should goods be valued? What penalties should follow any delay? How should contracts be implemented? How can buyers be compensated for unexpected shoddiness or nonperformance? Every question is a bureaucrat's delight, and those delights do not come without enormous inefficiencies (including a new spate of regulations) imposed on business.

The fatuousness of barter is well captured by a simple Russian joke. Vladimir, a dog owner, told his friend Igor that he was planning to sell the animal. "How much?" asked Igor. "Two million rubles," replied Vladimir confidently. "You must be joking," said Igor, "that mongrel will be lucky to get 10,000 rubles." A few days later, Vladimir met Igor again and told him that he had sold the dog—and for two million rubles at that. Igor was stunned. "Nothing to it," said Vladimir. "I went into a pet shop and the man there happened to have two cats for sale at a million rubles each. We exchanged."

8.9 Banking on the State

Yet the problem of financing trade is no joke. Ask exporters and importers from Tallinn to Bishkek to identify their single biggest headache, and the answer will be the same: persuading banks to lend them money to finance their deals. Ask how finance for trade can be secured and the words "government export/import banks" will be mouthed immediately. From the biggest free trading countries (Albania, the Czech Republic, Estonia, Kyrgyzstan, Slovakia, and Slovenia) to the laggards in trade (Belarus, Croatia, Ukraine, and Uzbekistan) it has become conventional wisdom that the state must act to fill the gap. But this popular remedy may be no cure at all.

One reason why banks—state and private—are wary of lending to exporting and importing firms is that receiving payment for trade is often a nightmare. Two-thirds of all trade deals with Ukraine in 1993, says the EU, became barter arrangements after Ukrainian firms failed to pay in hard currency. Imports are perceived to be risky as well, and many countries worry about the stability of their banking systems. So worried was Kazakhstan's government that it forbade Kazakh banks from lending more than 30% of the value of an import deal; the rest can be paid only after goods cross into Kazakh territory.

The lack of trade finance also seems to be in part a consequence of the region's robust push into world markets. When trade relations are expanding quickly, competition for finance becomes keen. The shortage is aggravated by the fact that banks in the region rarely lend solely on the basis of hardheaded assessments of the reliability of a loan. Personal ties, corporate links, and political nods also play a large role, thus misallocating whatever export/import finance is available.

Although it is tempting to blame the banks for the scarcity of trade finance, other significant factors are surely the region's history of government mismanagement of trade matters and the unstable rules of the game. In Belarus, Ukraine, even Latvia, bureaucrats have imposed heavy and unforeseen taxes after imports have arrived. Place enough of these burdens on those who borrow from the region's weak financial institutions—increasing the likelihood that trade credits will not be repaid—and there is little wonder that bankers fear getting into the export game.

Government-backed export promotion is fast becoming the politically expedient answer to the drought in trade finance. As in the West, governments want to use state guarantees, credits, and insurance to push their nation's exports into markets and sales they fear domestic companies would otherwise not secure. But this worry is not as dire as businessmen and ministers would have people believe. When a country has something others want to buy, finance is rarely a problem. Many Slovenian companies, for example, have found it easy to secure foreign finance for their trade deals. Indeed, in order to reduce pressure on the tollar caused by such capital inflows, in February 1995, the Bank of Slovenia imposed special restrictions on foreign-funded loans: 40% of the loan must be deposited in a Slovene registered bank. Despite all this, Slovenia established the Slovene Export Corporation, 83% of which was owned by the Ministry of Finance, to push Slovene exports into risky markets such as those in Iran, Sudan, and Algeria.

Poland is also constructing a labyrinth of state institutions to grease the gears of export finance. Its Corporation for Export Credit Insurance (KUKE SA), with a capitalization of 3.1 billion zlotys, supposedly insures exporters against both commercial and political risks. This insurance takes a unique form: KUKE requires that the party importing Polish goods open a fixed line of credit. Only when this is done will KUKE issue its insurance. These sums KUKE uses as its guarantees are derived from loans that KUKE gets, interest-free, from the Polish Treasury. If an importer defaults, the KUKE loan is automatically remitted by the treasury.

The danger in such credit guarantees is not merely that of delinquent debtors. Businessmen push to have their exports insured against currency losses and fluctuations as well. The new Polish Guarantee Fund looks most likely to assume this role, as its primary duty is to promote trade, particularly for mid-sized Polish firms, with former socialist countries. Polish businessmen also see these guarantees as essential if they are to bid on long-term contracts—for building a dam or a chemical complex, for example—without worrying that a change in currency values will leave them with tremendous losses. Guarantees are also extremely popular not only with exporters but also, of course, with importers whom they protect (indirectly) against foreign exchange risks as well.

Because every businessman likes to make one-way bets, governments everywhere are being pushed to open export credit agencies. Albania, Slovakia, Estonia, and Romania are following Poland's lead. Slovakia's Export Support Fund is to focus on small- and mid-sized companies, and will not only give them credits and insurance, but will also solicit business on their behalf. Its Export Credit Insurance Corporation is extremely active, insuring 25.7% of all exports to Germany, 12.7% of exports to the United States, and 5.0% to Poland. The Czechs, too, are dipping their toes into the waters of subsidized trade, allocating $53 million to the Czech Export Bank in 1994, which will only grant credits if they are guaranteed by the state-owned Export Guarantee and Insurance Company.

So far, most export credit and insurance agencies in the transition countries have followed risk-averse strategies. What is worrying for the future is that, as solid export deals find their credits privately, state agencies will push their activities into unstable parts of the world, or to shaky or shady customers. If these groups abandon or delay paying their debts, taxpayers in

271

the region will have to pick up the costs. Already there are signs of this, as Slovakia's Export Support Fund has allocated $1 million to promote trade with neighboring Ukraine (which is chronically unable to pay). Such programs pose an additional risk: governments are dragged into haggles over the terms of credits and guarantees in any particular deal.

Taken together, governments might conclude that the benefits of getting into the trade finance game are outweighed by the risks. Mounting evidence that international trade has been growing without official financial support and guarantees (40% of all Romanian exports, for example, find private domestic finance) should cause governments to think hard before they get any deeper into subsidizing international trade. The truth is that export credits are rarely about business (in Slovenia the SEC covers a mere 4% of exports); they are about politics. Ministers love them because they can be used to keep failing industries open by subsidizing exports that otherwise make no business sense.

8.10 Muddle and Meddle

Customs regulations are another means of ministerial meddling. Belarusian *chelnoks* complain that special tax collectors visit their market stalls, insisting that import duties be paid on the spot, even if they were already paid at the airport on arrival. More sophisticated squeezes also exist. In Slovakia, for example, exporters and importers (save for a few select industries) are automatically granted licenses to conduct business. Sounds good, but look closer. When applying for such licenses at the Ministry of Economy, the businessman must submit details about foreign partners, the agreed price, the contract's length, and so on; bureaucrats instantly become as informed as insiders in the deal.

Everywhere misuse of such insider information is rife, as bureaucrats sell their knowledge to competitors or line their own pockets. "I work two days a week for reporting to my boss," says one Kyrgyz customs official, "other days I work for my pocket." Small wonder then that customs police are among the owners of new dachas springing up around Bishkek. Everywhere, indeed, corrupt customs officials are the butt of popular jokes. One circulating in Sofia goes like this: "Is it true that there are one hundred new millionaires in Petrich?" one businessman asks another. "More than that, for there are at least one hundred twenty customs agents there."

Fiddling with customs remains a stock-in-trade of transition governments. Latvia's customs regime has zigzagged wildly. In 1992 its temporary tariffs distinguished among currencies in setting customs duties on imports and exports: settlement in hard currency generally secured a lower rate; settlement in rubles often yielded duties of up to 100%. Slovenian customs are more direct: if a good is manufactured in Slovenia, tariffs are high; if no domestic industry in a particular good exists, imports enter tariff-free. No matter how clear customs regulations are, enforcement is usually inconsistent: in Latvia last year, when customs service auditors replaced customs officers at their posts, sums equal to the weekly collections of the regular customs police were accumulated within hours. Customs agents are now forbidden to carry more than five lats when on duty. Everything above this is presumed to be a bribe.

Given all the pressures, governments are of two minds about what to do. They want tariff and customs revenues to fill depleted state coffers, but many also want to promote the growth of trade. Uzbekistan's policies are not atypical in their confusion. After years of timid reform, in 1994 it suspended all customs duties on imports and slashed the number of exports subject to licensing from seventy to eleven. One might think that daring, until realizing that two of the restricted exports (cotton and gas) account for over half of the country's nongold exports.

One motive for this incoherence is pretty much the same everywhere. So desperate is Lithuania for its customs revenue that the government insists that importers pay duties (18% of value, on average) and taxes in cash on the spot. Carrying such sums is usually considered unsafe, but prepayment by other means is virtually impossible, due to exchange rate fluctuations and a primitive banking system. Fearing that such roadblocks stunt growth, reformers often urge that tariffs be lowered and customs regulations unified and made transparent.

More generally, with trade regulation in flux, another, far more insidious, danger lurks: that lobbies will capture the state institutions governing trade, and shape the permanent structures and regulations to their will. Such "regulatory capture," as economists call it, poses long-term threats to the health of the international trade. World Bank economist L. Alan Winter suggests that transition country trade institutions are "particularly vulnerable to the special interests represented by a highly concentrated group of several large producers, whose common interest is to block or at least impede the inflow of foreign produced goods."

8.11 Role Reversal

A mirror image of these fears about trade can be found in Western Europe. Promises to expand the European Union, or at least make it increasingly hospitable to trade with its eastern neighbors, have begun to sound a bit hollow, as the increase in imports from the East began to generate hostile political reaction at home. Transition country economies are now seen as villains, not victims, and many in the EU fear that the success of their new Eastern competitors can only come at their own expense. They allege, for instance, that the wages of EU workers will be ruthlessly undercut if markets are opened wide to transition country goods.

Worries about competition from low-wage countries are as old as trade itself. What is different for Europe this time is the sheer weight of the new competition, particularly as many transition country workers are educated and capable of operating even very complex machinery. The emergence of a pool of cheap, educated workers, with access to first-class technology, it is argued, means that workers in Europe will be coerced into settling for ever-lower wages (though wages in the East have been rising fast, by 9–10% in 1995–96 in the Czech Republic and Slovakia, for example). One particularly prominent Euro-pessimist is Maurice Allais, a French Nobel laureate in economics. He claims that free trade with the EU will lead to mass unemployment and huge wage inequalities, as production and jobs flee east. The result, he says, will be a social explosion in Europe. The way to avoid it? Restrict imports to keep out competition and thus prevent a social explosion, he suggests.

Fierce competition from lower-wage and lower-cost countries, it is claimed, will "steal" jobs, thanks to "unfair" advantages of lower costs. When Russian aluminum exports to the EU increased five-fold in 1993 alone, EU commissioners charged Russia with dumping. Russia was forced to impose so-called voluntary restrictions on its exports (which are only slightly less onerous than the mandatory ones the EU would have imposed had the Russians not scaled back exports on their own). Such restrictions are becoming routine as the EU labels all sorts of products "strategic" and thus subject to tight import controls: lumber from Belarus, Estonia and Poland; tomatoes from Albania; goose livers, wine, and steel from Hungary. Squeezed the most has been Bulgaria, as over 50% of exports intended for the EU have been classed as "strategic" and thus effectively blocked. The EU is not alone in its protectionism. American trade barriers against Russian uranium, says Deputy Foreign Trade Minister Nicolai Drostov, cost Russia $150 million to $170 million each year (see table 8.2).

As explained previously, fears that trading with the poorer nations to the east leads to these countries stealing EU output and jobs are based on the misbegotten belief that any increase in one country's export level must be at the expense of the importing country's output. A second's thought should show that this is a rank fallacy. Increased exports give the developing post-communist economies more money to spend on imports, which they certainly do. Most of the transition economies, indeed, are spending all the hard currency they can lay their hands on to buy imported capital equipment and brand-name consumer goods, mainly from the EU. Those in the EU who clamor for protection rarely mention that EU exports heading east have been growing at an even faster pace than imports—indeed between 1990 and the end of 1994, EU exports to the East grew by 80%, while imports increased by only 40%—and that the EU's overall of balance of trade with the East is strongly positive. So any trade war with the East would be greatly to the EU's disadvantage.

If the EU stands to gain so much from open trade with the East, it may be asked, why do governments impose a variety of self-damaging protectionist restrictions? The answer is simple, say the theorists of modern democratic politics. The opponents of free trade—those who produce goods that may not withstand foreign competition—are easy to organize, because they are easy to identify and their losses are immediate. Those who stand to gain from free trade—the people who might gain jobs in the future and future consumers of lower-priced goods—are not. They are a diffuse constituency and politicians are famous for their short-termism. (This is also an insight the postcommunist countries would be wise to attend to as the siren's song of protectionism is increasingly heard in the East.)

Table 8.2

Trade Balance of Eastern Europe and Russia

	1991	1992	1993	1994	1995*
Eastern Europe					
World	-3.8	-6.3	-12.9	-10.3	-8.9
Developed Market Economies	-1.4	-4.7	-10.2	-9	-6.7
Russian Federation					
World	6.4	5.4	17.5	21	14.1
Developed Market Economies	2.9	1.5	10.2	13	6.8

*Data is for the period January-June 1995
Source: UN Commission for Europe

Foreign Trade by Destination (Percentage Change)

	Exports			Imports		
	1993	1994	1995*	1993	1994	1995*
Eastern Europe, to and from						
World	-0.1	46.4	26.8	10.4	9.9	37.7
Transition Economies	-7.3	5.2	23.3	4	-1.6	37.4
Developed Market Economies	1.2	24.5	31	12.9	16.6	39.5
Russia, to and from						
World	4.5	8.4	38.5	-27.5	5.2	16.8
Transition Economies	-10.6	-14.9	28.5	-32.3	-15.8	7.8
Developed Market Economies	7.6	21.7	30.8	-29.6	20.2	19.9
CIS, to and from						
World	-14.8	13.1	32.5	15.5	17	20.3
Baltic States, to and from						
World	44.3	13.2	32.9	75	28.1	24.9
Transition Economies	43.6	-1.3	3.1	73.2	1.6	-2.6
Developed Market Economies	39.7	47.6	76.3	76.9	75.2	52.5

*First half over same period 1994
Note: Data for Russia excludes intra-CIS trade ($U.S. billions).
Source: UN Commission for Europe.

The fact that people in rich countries fret about transition country success, not poverty, is itself a remarkable tribute to the success of trade reforms of the postcommunist economies. Indeed, faster trade growth in Eastern Europe and the NIS ought to be welcomed by everyone. Not only will it help to create new wealth and jobs, it also provides businesses with golden new

Figure 8.1

**Trade of FSU to Non-FSU Countries
(in Millions of U.S. Dollars)**

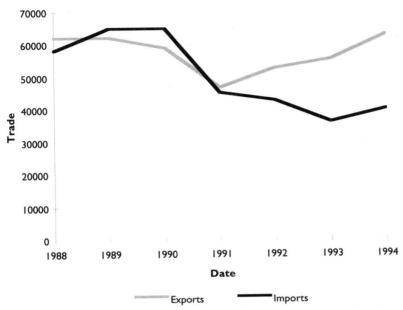

Note: the former Soviet Union (fSU) includes Belarus, Estonia, Kazakhstan, Kyrgyzstan, Latvia, Lithuania, Moldova, Russia, Ukraine, and Uzbekistan.
Source: UN Comtrade.

opportunities. Some companies already know this: Volkswagen has invested millions transforming a decrepit Skoda plant in Slovakia into one of its most efficient manufacturing sites anywhere; Daewoo and Samsung, originally attracted by the large Korean community (600,000 strong) in Uzbekistan, have committed over $1 billion in factories designed to capture auto and electronic trade in Central Asia for decades to come.

Trade in general is no zero-sum game. Elcoteq Baltic Ltd., for example, is one of Estonia's leading industrial exporters, selling 573 million kroon ($52 million) abroad in the first half of 1995. Two years ago it had thirty workers; today it employs eight hundred forty and is planning to take on four hundred. Elcoteq is a subcontractor for its Finnish parent Elcoteq Oy. Does this

277

Figure 8.2

Total Volume of Foreign Trade by East European Countries (in Millions of U.S. Dollars)

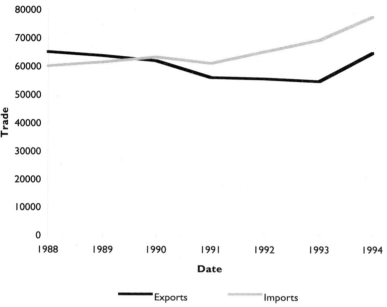

Notes: East European countries include Albania, Bulgaria, Czech Republic, Hungary, Macedonia, Poland, Romania, Slovakia, and Slovenia.
Source: UN Commission for Europe.

mean that Finns are losing jobs to Estonians? Not according to the parent company's annual report, which argues that only through such subcontracting has the firm remained competitive in the EU computer market of which Finland is a part.

Linkages among investments (such as those of Elcoteq Oy), trade, and jobs are complex, but it is highly likely that a growing proportion of transition country trade will take place within multinational firms, taking the shape of sales between affiliates and the parent company. In today's system of modern production, different parts of the manufacturing process are spread all over the globe, allowing companies to carry out each part of their operations in the most competitive country. Giant Tashkent Electric, for example, with its 12,000 employees and vanished Soviet markets, might appear ready for the scrap heap of economic history, but its managers have done wonders in reorienting sales: three years ago, over 90 % of its electrical units went to NIS countries; today 63 % go to the Middle East and Southeast Asia. That overseas presence delivered more than survival; visibility attracted the attention of Korea's industrial giant Samsung, which is considering making the firm a subcontractor in its global production web (see figure 8.1 and 8.2).

Specialization of this sort, because of the increased investment and productivity it brings, improves the living standards of both parties to a transaction. The case for free trade with the transition countries is no different. If Slovenia makes shoes and other leather goods more cheaply, then it makes sense for Italy (no matter that a few old ladies in Trieste and Rome want to reclaim Istrian villas nationalized fifty years ago by Tito) to open EU trade to Slovenia so that people can buy shoes with money made selling sophisticated consumer goods to Slovenes.

Overall, the trading partners of transition countries will gain through growth in their own economies. Faster growth in the emerging Eastern markets is already providing powerful stimulus to growth in specific European industries. One Commerzbank study, indeed, suggests that one-third of the growth in exports of German *mittelstand* machine tool makers since 1992 came from exports to postcommunist economies. The value of Estonia's imports from OECD countries rose 81 % in 1994 alone. From January to September 1995, total Estonian imports grew at a rate of 12 % and exports at 4 %. Turkey's exports to Central Asia doubled between 1992-94; 3 % of Turkey's total exports now go to this region. Such growth is convenient because it seems likely to arrive at a moment when Europe's domestic markets would otherwise be entering a period of lower growth. Moreover, as the post-transition recession begins to fade in more countries, import demand will continue to mount for the capital goods needed to assure that productivity increases as wages rise.

8.12 Neighborhood Trade

Positive (if unintended) side effects result from the developed countries' raising of import barriers. Because the EU has been slow in lowering its official trade barriers and has at times been replacing or supplementing them with unofficial ones such as more rigorous customs inspections, a big trend in transition country trade recently is toward regionalism and the return of economic geography. After several years of decline, trade among the former members of Comecon began to grow again by late 1994.

Old habits alone are not responsible for this emerging reality; market forces, too, are driving regionalism forward. Businesses in Central Europe, for example, are taking advantage of their low labor costs—workers in Poland, Slovakia, the Czech Republic, and Hungary cost, on average, less than a fifth of their counterparts in Western Europe—to become very competitive in nearby continental markets. Benign regionalism, however, needs to be distinguished from the autarkic sort practised by Comecon. Although Comecon was a discriminatory trading bloc, it was not a customs union or free-trade area because tariffs were irrelevant to its trade decisions. Nor was Comecon a common market, because prices were rigged through bilateral governmental negotiations and differed crazily from one Comecon member to another. Finally, Comecon was in no way a payment union because national currencies were never a part of Comecon transactions, which usually relied on barter of the fictitious "transferable ruble."

Thanks to the lower transport and transactions costs associated with the proximity of trading partners, neighborliness matters hugely in trade. This is why Canada is by far the United State's largest trading partner and Mexico its third biggest, and why Germany's top three partners are nearby France, Italy and Holland. Such high trading volume at lower cost is the productive face of regionalism: voluntary exploitation of local trading opportunities rather than the compulsory restriction practiced by Comecon (and nostalgically desired by the advocates of a restoration of regional exclusivity, such as President Lukashenka of Belarus). Throughout Eastern Europe and the NIS an open-minded economic geography is struggling to emerge against the old tried-and-failed regional autarky of the past.

Part of the problem facing the NIS countries is a structural one. Although less burdened now by transactions directed from the center and covered by subsidies, trade relations in the region continue to mimic a structure that presupposed the existence of an empire. With that empire gone, in country after country whole cities and industries have no reason to be where they are, or doing what they are doing. Only managed trade, bureaucrats appear to believe, can save them.

Except for Kyrgyzstan and Moldova, every NIS country (including Russia) continues to have huge foreign trade bureaucracies with turf to defend. The existence of these bureaucracies complicates trade because, due to the morass of deficiencies in settling import and export deals, trade among NIS countries is often conducted on a bilateral government-to-government basis. The only people who win in this game are those who know how to procure cheap credits and special export privileges. Restored to their old glory, they are not easily shoved aside.

The heart of the NIS is, of course, Russia. Half-blessed, half-cursed with rich natural resources, Russia mistakenly thought it could afford to sustain half-hearted trade reform. In 1996 its trade account was in surplus (some $20 billion by Moscow's reckoning, and $12 billion according to most Western estimates) as Russia sold mineral resources to developed countries and restricts imports according to the political preference of the day.

Russian businesses involved in international trade are in fact tugged in two opposing directions. Those that deal with the developed world work in a relatively open trading environment. Import tariffs have been lowered and unified, increasing transparency and predictability. Even the notorious "special" (read corrupt) import/export exemptions granted to such bodies as the National Sports Foundation (linked by America's CBS News and the German news magazine *Der Spiegel* to the illegal export of enriched uranium) and to energy companies such as Gazprom are being clawed back, ever so gradually. For businesses trading within the NIS, however, all is opaque. Import and export tariffs in the customs union of Russia, Kazakhstan, and Belarus for example, are in theory supposed to be unified along Russian lines. But the absence of a working payment system and the growing indebtedness of NIS countries to Russia ($9 billion and growing) push businesses into seeking ad hoc government support, both to cut deals and to secure payment. To find a way in this Byzantine maze can be a very daunting task for both Russians and their counterparts in the "near abroad." Imposition of the Russian system throughout the union also typically disadvantages smaller members. In July 1995, for example, Belarus agreed to import Hungarian meal, which previously had no import duty under the joint customs regime the 10% Russian tariff was imposed, however, thus scuttling the deal.

The CIS customs union also sets quantitative targets for both imports and exports for its members. The trickle-down effect from this is pernicious: export and import controls are revived. Here Ukraine is backsliding big time. Three years ago, 100% of Ukraine's trade was subject to export controls; by mid-1994 it had fallen to 60%. Now that figure is creeping back up, says Ukraine's central bank, with nearly 80% of all international trade in the second half of 1995 conducted under strict licensing regulations. Canada's huge Seagram's, famous for their whiskey, invested $150 million in Ukraine to produce vodka for export. When the first bottles rolled off the assembly line, however, Kiev bureaucrats ruled that they could not be exported, in order to ensure that Ukrainian domestic demand would be met.

Compared to the secrecy-enshrouded NIS customs union, the regional trade pact uniting Central Europe is a model of clarity. Scratch the surface, however, and the muddled motives and ambitions behind the Central European Free Trade Agreement (CEFTA) are revealed.

CEFTA was formed by Hungary, Poland, and the Czech Republic in 1992 (Slovenia joined in late 1995) and aimed at becoming a free-trade zone by 2000 (2002 in the case of Poland). Talk to its advocates and all is rosy. The Protocols of Budapest, signed in 1995, made half the trade between members duty free. Bulgaria, Romania, Croatia and the Baltics are clamouring to get in. CEFTA promotes itself as a 100-million-person free-trade area for the new millennium.

Talk is cheap. In reality, CEFTA is tugged in several directions at once. Outward-looking Slovenia and the Czech Republic see the pact as nothing more than a free-trade zone. Hungary is tempted by the notion of making CEFTA a more protectionist pact that could then be used as a wedge with which to pry open membership in the European Union. Poland and Slovakia want what Budapest wants, but they would also like CEFTA to be a bridge to maintain trade links with other postcommunist countries further to the east.

One reason why CEFTA members cannot decide whether their club is designed for free trade or to attain entry into the EU is because, save for the special case of Slovakia and the Czech Republic, members trade far more with the EU than with each other. Inter-CEFTA trade, indeed, accounts for less than 10% of the total trade of any member state. By contrast, the EU now accounts for half of each CEFTA member's trade.

A lot of tariff cutting is needed if CEFTA members want to increase trade among themselves, but that will not be easy. CEFTA members produce many of the same goods and recoil from the prospect that open trade between the member states will force uncompetitive players out of business. Poles fear, for example, that in a liberalized trading environment high-quality and low-priced Czech ales will flood in and drown Polish brewers. Domestic tractor manufacturers are protected in Poland because a 26% tariff is put on Czech-made imports. Hungary guards its pharmaceuticals industry with an 8% import tax. The Czechs, Poles and Slovaks erect tariffs ranging in size from 9% to 45% to keep out Hungarian sunflower oil and seeds. Slovakia slaps a 10% tax on all imports, but keeps promising to remove this tariff soon.

8.13 Handle with Care

If postcommunist governments fail to press for continued trade liberalization, all the ingredients for a rapid deterioration in the region's trading accounts are in place: the inclination to protectionism, the practices and disputes that could ignite an explosive mixture, could draw down the curtain on the region's move into international markets. There can be little doubt about the far-reaching domestic effects that a retreat into protection would incite, given the precarious background of all transition countries. Once the perverse logic of protectionism takes hold, its discord would likely echo through the newly privatized sectors, infant private firms, and state industries as well.

The good news is that, in just a few short years, the transition economies have become so integrated into regional and global trade that it would be almost impossible for governments to close their doors and survive—though the Lukaschenka government in Belarus is giving this myopic policy a good try at present, and with dire results. Elsewhere, too much money and too many jobs are now at stake in even the most backsliding country for the political process to sustain a complete trade stonewall. Besides, having unilaterally liberalized their markets over the past few years, most countries would find it impossible to hold on to their gains if they reversed course.

If transition governments sustain the responsible and reasoned self-interest that many have demonstrated in opening their markets to international trade over the past six years, the trading system is likely to remain an ongoing engine of growth and new jobs. But that can be assured only when both governments and ordinary citizens recognize the logic of international trade. Recent evidence suggests the first hints that even the most isolationist regimes will be forced to make progress (for example, Uzbekistan appears to be abandoning its policies of autarky, as its president, Islam Karimov, inches his way toward liberalization of the entire economy). More, of course, must be done, and continuously, for that is the nature of the trading system. Those who countenance trade closure and failure are likely to become the first victims of their own narrowness of vision. The pain, however, will not be limited to them.

9
The Power Brokers
The Politics and Economics of Energy

When the world's energy brokers ponder developments within their industry in the postcommunist world, many "experience a worrying sense of deja vu," a British Petroleum representative in the region once said. Little more than two decades ago, in the early 1970s, the world's energy consumers woke up to loud rumblings as the oil-producing nations—mostly in the Middle East—quadrupled oil prices overnight. Every type of energy source, and every link in the chain of supply and demand, trembled from this shock from one sector of the world's energy market. It took more than a decade, a second politically inspired oil price rise a mere six years later, and raging inflation accompanied by global recession before the industrialized economies were able to adjust themselves to the end of cheap fuel and a new world energy order (see figure 9.1 and 9.2).

Today, the economies of Eastern Europe and the NIS are experiencing an energy shock equally traumatic and demanding. The cozy subsidized world of socialist energy vanished along with the Soviet Union in 1991. Nowadays, the type, shape, and size of energy consumption in the postcommunist countries is more often determined by the world's energy markets than by ministers and bureaucrats who, mimicking King Canute, nonetheless try to hold back the tide. Just as it took the developed world a wrenching decade of change to come to terms with a global energy marketplace, so too the shift in energy supply and demand in the transition countries may not be fully sorted out until the twenty-first century.

Debates about energy in the transition countries are fierce and ongoing. How far and fast has energy consumption fallen? How much have the components of that consumption changed?

Should prices be freed for everyone and every industry? What is the proper trade-off between reliable energy and a clean environment? For a while, after communism's collapse, to cite one example, it was believed that energy consumption was in free fall alongside industrial production. Now, according to papers presented at an OECD conference in Paris in May 1996, evidence suggests that energy use did not decline by anything like that dark assessment. Moreover, as economies in the region begin to grow, energy consumption too is on the rise once more.

Figure 9.1

Ratio of Energy Intensity per Unit of GDP

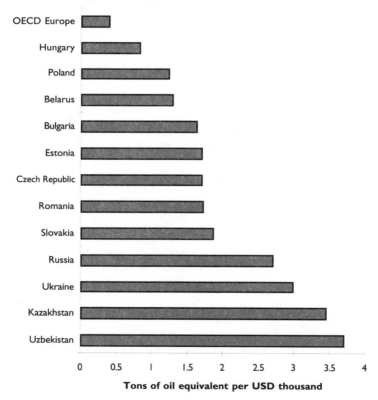

Tons of oil equivalent per USD thousand

Source: EBRD Transition Report, 1995.

Figure 9.2

Total Energy Consumption per Capita

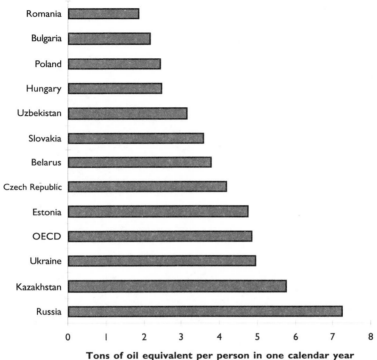

Tons of oil equivalent per person in one calendar year

Source: EBRD Transition Report, 1995.

Development—more accurately, redevelopment—is a cata-lyst spurring renewed energy consumption everywhere in the postcommunist region. Here, indeed, the process of restructuring is helped, not hurt, by rising energy prices; for the easy availabil-ity of cheap power was one of the primary forces that distorted industrial development under communism. Huge factories, pro-ducing unwanted goods, could be built, often in the middle of nowhere, because they were charged next to nothing by the state for the vast quantities of energy they consumed. Entire industrial sectors, indeed, not just individual factories, were permanently geared to receiving energy inputs at costs substantially below world market levels. Once the onset of the postcommunist tran-

287

sition deprived them of cut-price energy, however, these industrial behemoths were revealed as the gross value-subtractors they were from the start and remain today (if they are operating at all). Breathing a little easier, perhaps, from this forced restructuring are the citizens of the region, who benefit because usually the greatest polluters were also the factories most addicted to cheap energy, many of which are nowadays shut down.

Growth of a modern urban economy is a secondary aspect of this redevelopment. Today, it is debatable whetherany country in the region has fewer than a fifth of its population working on the land or in villages. In developed economies, however, the pattern is that most countries have only 5% (or less) of their people working in agriculture. As today's rural consumers of non-commercial, sometimes scavenged fuel—firewood and peat remain important sources in Albania, Latvia, Belarus, Moldova, Bulgaria, and Ukraine—move more and more into cities and towns they will consume coal, oil, and natural gas. Take the case of that Mitteleuropean boomtown, Prague, where the influx of rural Czechs (and displaced industrial workers from failing provincial factories) contributes 20% to the city's growing energy consumption, says the OECD. Indeed, some economists at the International Energy Agency (IEA) argue that, if the proportion of the population living in cities increases by only 10% in the coming decade—and Czechs are flooding into Prague much faster than that—energy demand will be one-third higher than it is currently, even if national income and population levels remain relatively stable.

Increased energy consumption may also produce rising emissions of carbon dioxide and other pollutants, which bring with them the risk of further poisoning of the already toxic landscape inherited from socialism. Today's infant, at times rather quaint, and usually ineffective efforts to restrain dirty emissions in the region are a response both to the filth belched into the region's air for decades by Stalinist heavy industries, and to pressure from European Union officials who are demanding that East European governments begin to clean up their industrial act before discussion of possible membership in the EU can properly begin. Such attempts at cleaning-up may be simply overwhelmed by the millions of extra tons of coal, fuel, and diesel fuel (ownership of cars is mushrooming everywhere in the post-communist world) that transition countries will burn in the coming years.

Rising consumption and the breakdown of the old socialist systems of energy delivery and subsidized pricing means that all transition countries are engaged in rebuilding their long-neglected energy sectors. The huge amount of capital required to finance these long-postponed investments is forcing reform upon monolithic state energy industries. In Poland, for example, 50% of generated power comes from equipment exploited for over twenty years, twice the EU average. In Ukraine, high and ever-rising extraction costs—primarily for coal—exist because investment basically stopped twenty years ago. In Poland, indeed, by 1989 the cost of mining a ton of coal was twice the price the coal fetched on the world market, costing the government an annual 3.5 billion zlotys in losses. So decrepit is Moldova's state power monopoly, Moldenergo, that energy production has fallen two-thirds since 1990, as electricity imports from Russia and Ukraine rose 40% to make up for an equal decrease in domestic power generation.

Complacent countries in this battle for energy savings are in for nasty surprises and chronic problems. Their confidence in stalling reform rests upon two doses of self-delusion: 1) a belief that energy use has fallen so sharply in their respective countries that there is little worry about supply being sufficient in the future; and 2) a conviction that oil and natural gas from the former Soviet Union—Russia, Azerbaijan, Kazakhstan, and Uzbekistan—will soon flow abundantly through pipelines that have yet to be built under contracts that have yet to be signed in countries (Georgia, Armenia, Azerbaijan, Serbia, Croatia) that remain highly unstable.

9.1 Where to Begin?

The starting point for governments in undertaking reform of their energy sectors must be in recognizing the growth and unpredictability of demand for energy. Indeed, even though the amount of energy used to generate a given level of income, what professional economists call "energy intensity," usually falls—often dramatically—as economies modernize and new technologies come on line to replace the old ways of doing things, the speed of decline in any one industry does not usually keep up with the increase in a country's overall appetite for oil, natural gas, and electricity. Because the postcommunist economies began their transition to the market numbered among the world's most energy-inefficient places, optimists inside and out-side the region maintain that there is vast scope for improve-ment in how effectively energy is used, developed, and priced (see figure 9.3).

A 1993 study of South Korea conducted by the World Bank shows just how rough it is for countries to adjust to energy price shocks, even when governments, businesses, and individuals act decisively and do everything right. South Korea, the study argues, survived the ballooning foreign debt, inflation and politi-cal instability imposed by the oil shocks of the last twenty years only by pursuing a policy of remorseless structural adjustment.

Figure 9.3

Power Tariffs

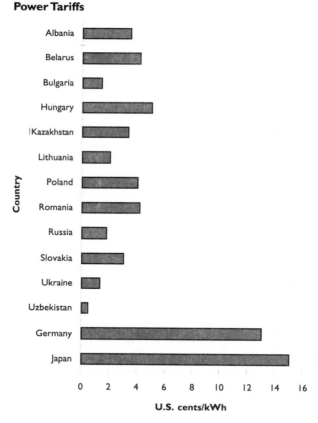

Source: EBRD Transition Report, 1995.

Instead of shielding industry from the ravages of higher energy costs, every bit of energy prices was, as part of a deliberate government policy, transferred to industrial and individual consumers. This, in turn, forced demand to adjust among both consumers and industrial users. Moreover, industrial subsidies that had been lavished in the 1960s on the *chaebol,* South Korea's industrial conglomerates, were slashed ruthlessly. Were all governments capable of such disciplined and far-sighted management as that practiced in South Korea (which at the time was a military dictatorship that did not have to factor public approval into its policy equations), the energy shock of the postcommunist transition could be weathered. That may be too optimistic an assumption, and besides, most governments in the region lack the political clout to force through such tough changes.

In some postcommunist countries the problem of energy adjustment is double-edged: not only must industrial and individual consumption patterns be radically altered by freeing pieces and removing state control from energy industries, but domestic energy producers must also be restructured to begin to conform to world standards. If hiking the prices charged to foreign energy customers were all that was needed to make energy firms efficient, Russia's notoriously wayward oil and gas giants (Lukoil and Gazprom, among others) would be world champions instead of the bloated, antediluvian monsters they are today. After all, rising world prices for oil, natural gas, and other energy products have been supplying an ever-increasing share of Russia's export earnings. Instead, Russia's energy giants have done little or nothing to modernize and bolster their efficiency.

According to the Russian Federation State Customs Committee, for example, the average dollar unit value for Russian fuel exports to non-NIS markets increased by 14% between the first half of 1995, with increases in unit values for oil equal to 17–18% and natural gas unit values increasing at half that rate. Oil production between 1990 and 1995 was barely a third of production of the previous five years, and the largest deposits at Mamontovsky, Samotlorsky, and Fedorovsky in western Siberia, as well as the Urals deposits of Arlansky and Romanshinsky, are near to exhaustion. The continuing decline in energy production in Russia means that production figures, nowhere near what they should be in any case, will continue to decay unless dramatic changes are made, for new finds are not coming on line to replace the old. Between 1986 and 1990, 515 new oil and gas deposits were discovered, including 46 large fields. Since the USSR collapsed only 215 new discoveries have been made, with only seven promising large reserves.

Proud and often reluctant to seek or accept outside help, Russians nonetheless hope to make some gains in their existing industry from new technology. At present 90% of the oil produced in Russia is recovered through a method called "water injection," which means pushing the oil out of the rock by pumping water in. This old-fashioned technique allows recovery of around 40% of the oil in place. Demand for oil to meet production schedules, however, often leads to excessive water flooding. Much of the extra technical equipment for more efficient production will have to be imported. Low-cost American-made semi-submersible pumps have already made a contribution to the removal of water from oilfields. But Russia, like all the other transition countries, cannot pin all its hopes on quick fixes and economizing. It will have to invest heavily in oil and other forms of energy as well as establish and support a truly free domestic energy marketplace.

It is nearly certain that this cannot be done without foreign investment and some element of foreign control over energy firms—and this thought does not please most managers of large energy concerns such as Lukoil or Gazprom, who would like to lock up their control of the tremendous wealth of these giants for themselves. Their priority, therefore, is to make sure that privatization "sticks," providing them with solid title and permanent, unassailable control before any foreign investors are let in on the scale that is needed. To maintain unchecked control of their companies, these politically influential managers have kept their books secretive and tried to shut out (for the most part) any and all outside interference, whether from abroad or closer to home in the guise of domestic Russian investment funds. Foreign money is in principle welcome, of course, but not any say in corporate matters. Lukoil, for example, has sold over $200 million in what are called "depository rights" (financial paper somewhat akin to a share certificate) on Wall Street and London. In October 1996 Gazprom, too, dipped its toes into these financial waters by selling $350 million worth of such depository receipts (a mere 1% of the firm's worth, according to observers). But these events have had minimal impact on management behavior.

Isolationism, however, is breaking down, as shown in the case of Surgutneftegaz, one of Russia's other privatized energy companies. Because the firm was oriented toward domestic sales, not exports, it was the energy company least likely to look outward for investment and assistance. Recently, however, Vladimir Bogdanov, Surgutneftegaz's president, has been taking the company out of its shell, opening talks with Elf-Aquitaine on a project to jointly supply natural gas to Germany. It is also moving rapidly into setting up its own retail distribution system to compete in the St. Petersburg region with the Finnish concern Kirishi, which has been growing by leaps and bounds in the western part of Russia. (The petrol retail industry, indeed, is the most competitive energy sector in the region, as foreign firms muscle their way into the market. In Bulgaria, despite the fact that the government keeps a lid on price increases, the one-time state monopoly Petrol now has less than 50% of sales because groups such as Royal Dutch Shell are building petrol stations in the country as fast as they can.)

Foreign investors are drooling at the prospect of developing the vast energy resources of Russia and Central Asia. The rewards may one day be sky-high, which is one reason why the American oil giant Chevron has already sunk $1 billion into Kazakhstan's vast Tengiz field. But the odds of getting burned by such investments may be nearly as high, not only because of the schemes Gazprom and others have developed to ward off outsiders, but because governments continue to make life difficult for investors. Indeed, only shortly after Boris Yeltsin's reelection as Russia's president in July 1996, the communist-dominated Duma flexed its xenophobic muscles by voting down a bill to give legal footing to production sharing contracts in energy. Russian reformers were hoping that such a law would unlock more than $20 billion in stalled Western investment.

Even if Russia's production sharing law is eventually passed or a presidential decree allowing the same freedom is promulgated, the legal basis for outside energy investment in the country will remain unpredictable. Taxes are often hefty, change chaotically, and are collected willy-nilly, at times at the barrel of a gun. An additional disincentive comes from the fact that Russia's extensive oil pipelines are run by Transneft, a graft-riddled state-owned monopoly (in 1995, bribes for access to its pipelines were said to run at about $3 to $4 per ton of oil). Moreover, oil and gas investors in Russia, Kazakhstan, or Uzbekistan will be taking on huge environmental liabilities along with any ownership stake they may acquire.

Still, some way of bringing foreign investors into resource-rich countries such as Russia, as well as energy-deprived places such as Moldova, will have to be found before the energy sector in the postcommunist world really takes off. The main problems arise from the fact that transition country economies find it hard to lay their hands on sufficient capital to build and rebuild the infrastructure they need to both supply and consume available energy. CS First Boston, one of the most active banks in the post-communist region, puts the overall capital requirements for power, oil, gas, coal, pipelines, electricity grids, and refineries in Eastern Europe and the NIS over the next decade at $1 trillion. Nowhere will this problem be greater than in the generation of electric power (nuclear, coal-fired, hydro-electric) and in oil and natural gas field development—the most capital-intensive sources of energy and also the ones most desperately in need of fixing. Changes in the structure and incentives of the energy industry will be needed for repair on the vast scale required to take place.

9.2 Breaking Up Is Hard to Do

Disentangling the old socialist energy system to create a market-friendly energy sector is a nightmare. Governments nonetheless want to do so for two important and related reasons: political and economic independence. Latvians, for example, remember darkly the winter of 1991 when the Kremlin, in trying to dampen Lithuania's bid for independence, hit all three Baltic countries hard by slashing energy supplied to the entire region, and Latvians (rightfully or not) fear that such politically inspired energy blackmail could be used again one day. Ukraine has had to compromise with Russia on some of its most cherished national political goals, such as complete control of the Black Sea fleet, because of the billions of dollars in debts it has run up on gas and oil imports from Russia since 1991. Pressure to close the decaying Chernobyl nuclear plant, though at times it provides a valuable diplomatic bargaining chip for the Kiev government, is also a threat to its economic sovereignty.

Ukraine is merely an extreme example of the threat that incoherent and outdated energy policies pose to national independence. Even in the peaceful divorce of Czechoslovakia, which was smoothed somewhat because the sources of energy supply had long been divided between the two nations, a gas transit pipeline from Russia was a long-running headache. After an agreement was reached, dividing the fees on gas transit at 2:1 in favor of the Slovaks, these funds did not reach the government in Bratislava, which ultimately insisted on a final breakup both of the pipeline company and the Czechoslovak federation. (A contributing cause of the breakup of Czechoslovakia was the decision of the first postcommunist government in Prague, one containing a number of prominent environmentalists, to slash aid to coal mines, causing a one-third fall in production and rising unemployment. That this government also wanted to hit two other areas of Slovak power generation—a proposed extension to the nuclear power plant at Mochovce and the hydroelectric dam across the Danube—gave strong economic arguments to supporters of Slovak independence.)

Despite this threat to the independence of the newly free states of the region, elements of the old system are showing a remarkable tenacity everywhere in the postcommunist world, and with good reason. Except for Russia, Kazakhstan, and Uzbekistan, transition countries do not have much oil or natural gas. Less than 5% of the oil produced in postcommunist countries last year came from outside Russia and Central Asia, and most of this 5% came from Romania's declining oil fields. The countries of Eastern Europe are certainly rich in coal, yet throughout the 1980s most had been moving away from this source of energy. Coal production in Hungary, Bulgaria, and Slovakia, to cite three rather typical examples, fell by 50% in just five years.

Between 1980 and 1990, says the IEA, the share of oil and gas in the region's energy consumption increased from less than a third to more than half, thus deepening dependence on Russia. During that same decade rapidly expanding energy consumption ran parallel to an industrial strategy that emphasized energy-intensive industries (for example chemicals, steel, and aluminum). The result was a rapid increase in energy use: up 6% per year during the decade in Romania and Bulgaria, 5% annually in Poland, 4% in Hungary and the Czech Republic, and 3% in Slovenia. Much of the blame for this change in energy policy can be placed on Russian geopolitical strategy. Two-thirds of its oil exports in these years, priced at only 40% of the world price, went to "fraternal socialist countries"—who became dependent on the source of cheap energy.

Even before the perestroika era began, Russia came to see that it could no longer afford such ideologically inspired generosity. Oil exports to noncommunist countries accounted for the bulk of the USSR's hard currency earnings. As the economy decayed, these funds were needed to pay for vital imports, including grain and Western technology. So the Kremlin restricted the level of oil and gas exports to socialist countries and began to raise prices incrementally toward world levels. Because Russia's East European allies were made in these years to invest in the construction of nuclear power plants as well as in oil and natural gas field development in Russia, the effect of some of these price hikes was delayed, and even now many transition countries continue to receive guaranteed supplies of electricity at somewhat lower than world prices. But as these agreements begin to run down (most will conclude just before or after the turn of the century), the transition countries will either have to pay the higher prices Russia will demand or look for other sources of supply.

Russia's energy price ultimatum of the 1980s, seen from a distance of years, may now seem a blessing, preparing the transition countries somewhat for the hammer blow of rising energy prices that came after 1989. Indeed, imports from Russia have slackened almost everywhere in the region, for one bad reason—recession and a corresponding inability to pay—and for two good ones: greater efficiency, and substitution of domestically available sources of energy for Russian oil and gas.

9.3 Where to Go?

The most important way of reducing dependence upon imported Russian oil and gas in many postcommunist countries appeared at first to be to find methods to reduce the share of oil used as fuel and to switch back to coal. Coal industry problems, however, are probably worse than any other in the energy sector. The older coal basins in Central Europe (as well as in the European part of Russia) are often nearly depleted, and construction of deeper mines is needed to get at less accessible coal beds. This is a costly, lengthy, and often an unpopular operation, as mining investments stir up the region's infant (but increasingly vocal) environmental groups. Strip mining of lower grades of coal—a cheap but environmentally damaging source of energy—is being used in Ekibastuz in northeast Kazakhstan, but few other places are suited to this form of mining, though the governments of Ukraine and Belarus say they want to pursue it.

The problem with both improved efficiency and better utilization of domestically available substitutes is that a rational energy policy requires a rational system of pricing. Niko Martinec, secretary to the energy division of the Slovene Chamber of Commerce, argued at a World Energy Council (WEC) meeting that a shift in the relative prices of different energies acts like a glacial drift: it is not perceptible to the human eye in the short run, but is irresistible in the long run. The glacier starts to move only when higher prices for energy are actually pushed through to final users, that is, businesses and households. In most postcommunist countries, that ice jam is only now beginning to break, sometimes freeing prices for industry, sometimes for households, rarely in any one country for both at once.

Energy options outside the old socialist energy network are also often costly to develop, and breaking the old ties is a time-consuming process. Engineers from Russia are needed everywhere to run and maintain the nuclear plants built during the socialist era. Governments are reluctant to offend Russian ministers one day in fear that they will need to call in Russian experts the next. The countries that declared their political independence most emphatically are the Baltic states of Estonia and Latvia, who look for foreign energy contracts (with Norway, Finland, or, for natural gas, with far-away Algeria) even though Russian imports remain the best buy. Bold talk of independence, however, often turns meek where energy is concerned. Both countries remain ensnared in the old socialist power grids. Despite the fact that most of its domestic electricity consumption is met by domestic oil shale and hydropower, Estonia's debts on natural gas imports allowed Gazprom to acquire a 30% stake in Estonian Gas, the monopoly gas distributor. Other countries are in even deeper thrall. In Moldova, Gazprom has grabbed 51% of the equity in the local gas pipeline monopoly, Moldova-Gaz.

Gazprom's activities in the region, indeed, are a rogue factor in all energy calculations. "Sometimes Gazprom acts purely as an energy company, and we know its motivations and how to respond to them. But at other times it acts like an arm of the Russian government—and the imperial arm at that," says a

Bulgarian diplomat at the United Nations. In Lithuania, for example, Gazprom has done more to determine the players in the domestic gas industry than the government in Vilnius. In December 1994, for example, Gazprom cut its ties to SAF, its longtime affiliate in Lithuania, in favor of a new, more pliable company, Stella Vitae. Cloak-and-dagger tales surround the change, with the president of SAF, it is said, briefly placed under arrest in the city of Kaunas just before he was to negotiate a new import and shareholding agreement with Gazprom. In his absence, Gazprom and Stella Vitae cut their deal. With payment arrears on gas purchases continuing to mount, Gazprom's influence in the country is only likely to increase, particularly as the government has been unable to cobble together a program to meet these debts and has built up no energy reserve against a cutoff in supply.

Throughout the Baltics, links are deep and cumbersome: over 80% of total Baltic energy needs are met by imports from Russia and other Soviet successor states. As we have seen, the connections are not just commercial; cross-boundary ownership and organizational links mean that local energy companies become parts of larger regional structures outside national control. Latvia's Baltija Center, for example, manages the flow of electricity for a number of generating plants throughout Belarus, western Russia, Estonia, and Lithuania. This means that management and reform of the electricity supply becomes a diplomatic issue, and efficiency is often a forgotten consideration. Latvian consumers, for example, do not get the cheapest available electricity—which is produced at the Ignalinas nuclear plant in Lithuania—because the differing national generating components in this network all want a share of the more lucrative peak charge contracts with Baltija's central distribution authority.

Hungary is also having trouble distancing itself from reliance on Russian energy sources. Some 75% of Hungary's crude oil imports come from Russia and the NIS. Only the Adria pipeline through Yugoslavia offered an alternative, but it has largely been inoperable since 1991 due to the Balkan wars. In natural gas, Russia dominates, too. Hungarian work in building the Orenburg-Iamburg pipeline was paid for in Russian gas—2 billion cubic meters annually until the end of 1997.

The natural gas agreement contains a renewal clause for Hungary to continue purchases at a fixed price. Russia, however, wants to cut a deal more to its liking and is using Hungarian energy sector reforms to do so. Mineralimpex, the company that long handled these gas imports, was merged into the Hungarian Oil Company (MOL) by its owner, the State Privatization Holding Company. Instead of recognizing that the gas rights were transferred from Mineralimpex to the new company, Russian energy suppliers attempted an end run by dealing with Panrusgaz, a joint venture previously established by Mineralimpex and Gazprom, with the apparent aim of excluding the Hungarian-controlled MOL from the lucrative gas importing business.

Not everyone, however, is keen to keep Russia at arm's length. Moldova needs good relations with Russia because 86% of its total generating capacity is located in Transdniestria, a region dominated by ethnic Russians who have sought to break away. Macedonia also yearns (with good reason) for a Russian energy connection. Twice since independence Greece closed Macedonian access to Salonika, through which Macedonia receives its oil imports. Deprived of energy, factories closed and houses went without heat. Now Macedonia is pushing hard for a pipeline to be built across Bulgaria that will connect the tiny republic to Russian gas supplies.

The problem is finding the money to build both the pipeline and a distribution system for gas in Macedonia. Albania, too, has dreams of securing Russian gas by connecting to this same hoped-for pipeline. And Lithuania's huge electricity plants at Elektrenai and nuclear power plant at Visaginas were built with distribution to the Soviet Union in mind. What would happen to them if power were no longer exported to Kaliningrad, Belarus, Russia, and the rest of the Baltics?

9.4 The Politics of Power

Second to assuring (to the greatest possible degree) independence, the need for capital is the lead force driving much energy sector reform. Loss of control is the price governments and state-owned utilities must pay for it. Private participation may be conceded grudgingly by governments, but it still forces reform upon utilities. Caught between governments no longer able to hand out large subsidies and local and international investors who demand a decent return on their investments, utilities and energy companies have little choice but to try to begin making a profit. If they fail, less investment will flow and demand will remain unmet, inciting popular discontent which, in turn, will inspire a return to more political control.

That is risky, as, with trade restrictions lowered, there are more gadgets to plug in, and more cars to drive, and demand for power is soaring. In Russia, Slovenia, Romania, the Czech Republic, and Albania demand for petrol is growing at twice the rate of the economy. In Poland and Estonia, increasing electricity demand exceeds GDP growth. ABB, a Swiss-Swedish power equipment maker, reckons that 20% of worldwide electrical equipment orders will be coming from the postcommunist world by the end of the century, and so it is investing heavily in the region. If electrical demand in Eastern Europe, says the World Energy Council, were to grow over the coming decades as fast as the economies of the best-performing countries in the region, say, 4.5% per year, the region would need to open a mid-sized power station every month. The need, according to Alexandru Stanescu, Romania's minister of industry with responsibility for national energy policy during the Iliescu era, is staggering, for the necessary investment would cost an estimated 2% of GDP each year. Transition country utilities, however, like those in developing countries everywhere, don't have the money to go on such a building binge.

In trying to meet these needs, regional energy companies are in a three-way vise: they lack capital; they suffer from inadequate technical and financial management; and they are under pressure to do something about the vast amounts of pollution they cause.

One of the reasons why utilities are starved for capital is that throughout the region, they continue to charge too little for the power they generate. Take the case of Poland, where a ladder of prices differentiating individuals and consumers continues, despite a variety of government reforms. Indeed, government regulation consistently pushed energy price increases well below inflation, a full 5% less in 1995.

Government subsidies and red tape are endemic, and the market is not allowed to operate. Electricity prices, and often petrol prices, in the region are consistently less than those charged in the OECD. They may rise with government budget deficits, says Plamen Denchev, head of Bulgaria's parliamentary committee on energy and energy resources, for the simple reason that the governments may not be able to continue to run such big debts in the future. The need to attract investors may also push energy prices upward. But in the meantime politics trumps economics. Sometimes the subsidies that keep prices low follow an explicit policy: large industries are favored in Romania, Slovakia, and Bulgaria (where petrol prices are fixed so artificially low that production hardly makes sense, and managers at NeftoChim, Bulgaria's biggest oil refiner, are running their plant at less than half capacity); households are favored in Latvia, the Czech Republic, and Albania. But most often, across-the-board subsidies result from a simple accounting failure: inflation is not factored into energy prices.

Household energy subsidies, says the World Bank, accounted for 5% of Russia's GDP in 1995 (one reason these subsidies came under attack by Russian deputy prime minister Boris Nemstov in 1997) and 5–6% of GDP in Ukraine in that same year. Although the natural instinct of politicians is to soften the blow of sharp energy price increases—twenty years ago America's supposedly conservative Nixon administration embraced energy price controls and rationing as its response to the first oil price shock—these decisions, in maintaining inefficient habits, have harsh economic consequences. Developing an efficient energy industry means raising household energy prices, with perhaps explicit subsidies to the truly needy. Hungary, for the most part, has bitten this bullet, with charges for electricity already covering economic costs. These price increases were necessary to guarantee foreign investors an 8% return on capital. But a World Bank study of Poland's household energy pricing suggests that an 80% rise is needed for heat, gas, and electricity—a tough pill for any government to swallow—if Poland's energy prices are to come up to world levels. One suggestion the World Bank makes frequently to governments in the region is for them to adopt something called "lifeline" pricing of energy, meaning that a low price for energy is charged to meet a subsistence need, with full costs charged for additional consumption.

Industrial price increases have also varied between countries even more than they have among types of users, and most often they have lagged behind the market. Estonia has led the field among price liberalizers, with gas prices rising 700% between 1990 and 1996. Bringing up the rear, Belarus's prices remain in a straitjacket of state regulations, though how long Russia will continue to subsidize the rampant economic nonsense of the Lukashenka government is an open question. In August 1995 the Kremlin balked at forcing Gazprom to continue to extend Belarus gas on credit.

9.5 Set Them Free

Some power companies try to fight back against the pauperism imposed upon them by their own national governments. Geoplin, Slovenia's monopoly gas distributor, took the government (its majority owner) to court in 1993, complaining about the low prices the government forced on it. The court's ruling went against Geoplin, but there is hope that this may be a tactical loss but a strategic victory. Ever since that decision, the government has eased up on its regulation of Geoplin's prices and settlement agreements with big gas users.

Not only are prices held artificially low, but utilities also cannot make their customers pay the bills for energy already consumed. In 1993 Latvenergo, Latvia's monopoly energy producer, had accounts receivable equal to 31.7% of its turnover. Two of Macedonia's biggest utility deadbeats, the metals industries Jugohrom and Fenzi, consume on their own 20% of total Macedonian electricity production, prompting cynics to suggest that the firms are, in fact, a secret electricity reserve. Shut them down, they say, and a large pool of energy will become available for others to use. In some countries, local utilities are imitating Gazprom's practices and trying to take over their deadbeat customers: Bulgaria's Multigroup, for example, has been accepting share capital from companies that can no longer pay their gas bills. In this way Multigroup has acquired big stakes in two of Bulgaria's most important firms, Kremkovtsi steel and Chimko, a producer of urea.

Governments hold the line on freeing energy prices in part because state ministries and industries are usually the biggest consumer of power and they have difficulty paying even at the present rates. Near-disaster can strike when firms, mostly electrical utilities, try to coerce ministers in to paying back their debts. In 1995, for example, the Kremlin was stunned to learn that Russia's strategic missile forces had been deprived of electric power because of the military's failure to pay its power bill for over two years. Lithuania's military commander ordered a house-to-house search for electricity company executives when they dared shut off power to a number of his bases earlier that year. Both the Russian and Lithuanian governments immediately ordered restoration of electrical power to their militaries—a sheepish Boris Yeltsin having first called President Clinton to promise that oversight of nuclear weapons would never be jeopardized in that way again. But neither government came up with the funds to pay the electricity bills owed by their armed forces, meaning that utilities and their consumers have to subsidize the most primary of state functions.

Getting tough with delinquent payers, however, can backfire. For example, NEC, Bulgaria's electricity monopoly, tried to punish the Kremikovtsi steel mill by cutting off its power for a mere half-hour. Even that brief shutdown caused serious damage to the plant's furnaces, and now NEC finds itself locked up in a nasty court fight over who will pay the bill for this.

Theft is also a persistent problem, amounting to 12–13% of total electricity revenues in Lithuania, for example, and billing is chaotic. A threat to cut off supply could be a potent weapon to force customers to pay their bills, especially since getting reconnected is usually a nightmare. But the risk of disconnection is not great: only 14,000 out of 1.2 million electricity users were cut off last year in Lithuania, because the government pushed Lietuvos Energija into tolerating debts, even if the subsidies it offers equal little more than a quarter of the total outstanding debt.

Collecting receivables and freeing prices is but the tip of the iceberg in the restructuring ahead for most countries in transition. In 1995–96, Romania and Bulgaria suffered from 15% and 18% shortages, respectively, of base-load electricity and 25% shortfalls at times of peak demand; some say that Ukraine, Belarus, and Moldova are in far worse shape. Sudden winter power cuts and brown-outs are common in many countries. From 1993–1996, indeed, electricity and heat were regularly cut off for up to twelve hours a day in Moldova. According to the EBRD, the value of lost industrial output throughout the transition countries is roughly five times the value of lost power. One conservative United Nations Economic Commission for Europe estimate suggests that the loss of income across the postcommunist world due to inefficient energy use and production is equal to at least 1.5% of GDP.

Knock-on effects of this inefficiency abound. Private investment, for example, can be diverted wastefully because of the failures of utilities. Fluctuating voltages damage motors and turbines, which must be replaced more frequently than would otherwise be necessary. Businessmen are forced to invest in voltage stabilizers and backup generators instead of in more profitable equipment. In Kiev, where shortages can be severe, the capacity of private generators is the fastest growing part of the energy sector.

Financial and institutional barriers to greater efficiency form a nearly impenetrable thicket. Even though it would be far cheaper to repair power stations than build new ones from scratch (though nuclear plants should perhaps be exempted here), ministers prefer to initiate glamorous new projects than to overhaul existing plants. However, Hungary, at present, seems to be something of an exception. Grand investment schemes rampant everywhere else in the region have recently given way in Budapest to more modest programs designed to lure outside investors. One of the current strategies of the Hungarian Electric Works (MVM) is to refurbish existing plants as the cheapest available way to generate more power. The Dunamenti central heating plant, which is being fitted with a dual-use turbine, is a very good example.

9.6 Capital Power

Radical change is thus needed throughout the region: private capital, more to the point, foreign capital. But politicians and economists find it hard to drown out the hoary old socialist mantra of energy independence. Professor Anatoli Aleksandrov, then president of the USSR's Academy of Sciences, claimed in 1981 that foreign investment "will warp and destroy national development." Now, however, some ministers see it differently. "Private power," Anatoli Chubais told the Davos conference in 1997, "is not a gimmick. It is a real solution to our problems."

In 1991, the number of nonstate energy businesses engaged in the region could be counted on one hand. These firms, mostly small local hydroelectric companies in Slovenia in the former Yugoslavia, were anomalies and posed little threat to state utilities. Today's push to privatize power does pose a threat, because it comes on a far vaster scale and invites foreigners to play a key role in determining the shape of an industry closely associated with national security and independence. The mere presence of foreign investment, indeed, is often enough to move a plant or industry in new directions.

Even if the transition countries were to fully understand the need for foreign investment, there are other specters to haunt them. Memories of the Third World debt crisis of the 1980s, for example, make many investors jittery. Perhaps 40% of the capital invested in developing countries during these years was supposedly for energy projects. Investors today demand more information about where their money is going. Governments are also wary about assuming debts that they will later decide are unbearable. But such problems are being lessened to some extent because such multilateral agencies as the EBRD and the World Bank usually take small stakes in big power projects in order to provide extra clout for investors in any dispute, and also to provide political protection for governments. A seismic financial collapse of private sector power projects is made less likely by such steps, but there are other worries as well. Fear of inflation, for example, and of depreciating exchange rates, which might occur over the twenty-year life usually associated with energy sector investments, are common among would-be investors.

Even confirmed reserves of natural resources are not enough. No one doubts that Russia, Kazakhstan, and Uzbekistan have plenty of oil and gas; the problem lies in getting it out. In Russia there is persistent legal and political chaos—in 1995, the Duma balked at legal reforms that would have guaranteed the rights of foreign energy investors—that makes even hardened veterans of oil and gas exploration think twice about investing the huge sums needed to turn the industry around. Investments in Kazakhstan and Uzbekistan are equally uncertain. And if oil and gas start to flow only when Russia settles down into a growing normalcy, the reduction in exports might in the meantime create difficulties for other transition countries. Russian demand slumped along with production in the early years of transition; it is now recovering with economic revival, thus limiting the amount of oil available for export to the rest of the postcommunist world.

In Central Asia, prospects are clouded even if political stability arrives. Whichever way they turn, engineers designing new pipelines face high hurdles, both natural and political. To the west lie the unstable regimes of Azerbaijan, Armenia, Georgia, and the Kurdish region of Turkey. To the south lie Afghanistan and Iran, with their Islamic fervor, and a Pakistan riddled with political turmoil. To the north is a Russia determined to hold onto its great-power influence and to profit from the region's oil and gas riches.

9.7 Monopoly Prophets

The primary need in energy generation is for transition governments to distance themselves from their utilities and energy suppliers. So long as power supply and generation remain primarily a political question, prices will be too low, grand schemes will take precedence over basic maintenance, and overmanning will persist. There must also be recognition that in order to create a competitive market in energy, there are costs to be paid; consumers who have been paying next to nothing for heat will have to begin to pay market prices, and industries will have to make do without the luxury of cheap energy inputs.

Privatization, to be sure, would be the most dramatic way to create the necessary distance. But state energy enterprises now headed for the marketplace include the politically sensitive electricity grids, power stations, and oil refineries and distributors once considered unsuited to private ownership. Even Western advisors to transition country governments have argued that energy companies and power utilities, being so-called natural monopolies, cannot be sold off in a way that will bring the benefits of competition to bear. The argument is that the structure of the energy industry requires that utility firms control all aspects of energy production from, say, extraction of oil from the ground to the sale of petrol for automobiles.

Moreover, governments worry that competition in energy will mean that firms in search of profits will cherry-pick the most profitable customers, leaving small consumers or those in remote areas without supplies. Therefore, a single buyer and seller, supporters of this position argue, is an essential instrument of national energy policy. In the interest of the environment or national independence, to cite two examples, the single buyer can opt for more expensive but perhaps either cleaner or politically less-sensitive fuels.

Countries are therefore not eager to privatize. Fearing, for example, the sort of stealthy takeover of local power companies by Gazprom (made possible because of the debts the local firms have run up with the Russian giant), Lithuania now balks at any divestiture of its energy companies. Even the giddiest of privatizers, the Czechs, are at times wary of selling energy industries. "It would be premature to rush into abandoning the role of the state in the energy economy," says Vladimir Dlouhy, a former minister of trade and industry. To be sure, the Czechs did not completely shelter their energy concerns from the privatization winds. In the first mass privatization wave, forty-seven state fuel and energy enterprises—seventeen coal, four gas, four uranium, and twenty-two energy distributors—became partly private joint stock companies, but with one big caveat: in companies of so-called strategic significance—CEZ Refineries, Czech Gas—the state retained at least a 51% controlling share. Other companies, such as Transgas, remain 100% state-owned. Although the state plans to reduce its holdings gradually by making small share placements on the Prague bourse, investors suspect that the regulatory regime being developed for the energy sector will allow the state to maintain its tight control.

Advocates of division and competition retort that the statist policies pursued by most countries in the region are incompatible with developing an efficient energy sector. Subsidies, for example, can still be used to promote security of supply and clean power generation. The difference between covert and overt state intervention is that, when private industries are supported out of the state budget, the subsidies become explicit (and thus more difficult to abuse) in an otherwise competitive market. Britain, for example, has recently been subsidizing both nuclear power and renewable energy through a non-fossil fuel levy, a 10% surcharge on everyone's electricity bills. Government intervention can also make certain that there is universal service in a competitive market: customers in remote areas, for example, could be subsidized through the tax system.

Despite these reservations, some countries are going ahead and selling their energy industries anyway, sometimes as a whole, sometimes divided into constituent parts. Hungary has gone farthest along this road, but not for energy-related reasons alone. Its socialist government sold off big sectors of energy generation capacity to close the country's yawning budget deficit. Privatization, however, came at the end of a series of sterile energy-sector reform efforts typical of the region.

Under socialism, MVM controlled all trade within the electricity sector in Hungary, a monopolization that yielded, as everywhere in the region, a cat's cradle of cross-subsidization. The accounting system made it impossible to identify how much of the income of profitable suppliers was spent subsidizing wastrel power stations. Moreover, the state forced MVM to subsidize coal mining hugely. Instead of ending these practices, the postcommunist government extended them even further, an

307

effort that almost wrecked the attempted reforms. Thus, in 1993 the government integrated coal mines and power stations into the MVM holding system. MVM began to purchase coal from mines it already owned at prices exceeding world market prices. It was even ordered to buy coal from mines that were not part of the integrated system, at prices and volumes fixed by the government. No surprise then that when privatization first was attempted in 1993 it failed very quickly, as bidders were prepared to pay only about 6 % of MVM's nominal value.

There were other problems as well. Objections by local governments in Hungary to privatization schemes in the energy sector forced the national government to offer a guarantee to foreign investors of 200–300 billion forints ($2–3 billion). (This promise kicked up a hornet's nest in Budapest, as legal experts reckon that the privatization minister was not authorized to make any such promise without the consent of the finance minister, permission currently missing from the guarantee documents.) The battles between the national government, industrial lobbies, and local political leaders are likely to force more alteration of the energy privatization program this year. When a new tender for MVM is solicited, the Paks nuclear plant is likely to be hived away from the offering and sold separately, like all other power plants (and, eventually, all electricity suppliers), but with a controlling state "golden share" (shares with enhanced voting rights) in each plant.

The Horn government remains cautious about dividing the various energy monopolies into competing individual firms, and also of turning over most control of the power supply to investors, particularly foreign ones, before it has to face the voters again in 1997. But its ultimate vision for the turn of the century is a bold one: electricity, gas, and oil industries sliced both vertically and horizontally. Generators would compete with each other to supply both industrial customers and households, and distribution will be split among a number of regional firms, who will compete to supply domestic customers.

9.8 Regulating Power

Still, even a complete transfer of legal property rights to private investors does not end the matter. The question that will remain after privatization is the way in which utilities will continue to be regulated by state oversight bodies or the government itself. That energy suppliers need some form of regulation is clear: somebody has to prevent a private owner of a monopoly energy supplier from awarding himself monopoly profits. But how to design a rational system of regulation, especially in the context of transition, when the government needs as much reform as the industry, is a big question.

One approach to this is the legalistic approach which lays down strict rules for regulated companies to follow and leaves relatively little leeway to government officials in implementing the regulations. Another way is more political: make the newly privatized companies directly accountable to parliament or to a government ministry for the charges they make and the performance they demonstrate. A more bureaucratic variant of this involves making utilities subject to an independent regulator with plenty of discretion.

Too much discretion, say critics of political bureaucracies. Businessmen fret that such a system is unpredictable, because it depends too much on the idiosyncrasies of individual regulators. In Britain, this system is accused of being too hard on some utilities and—worse—too soft on others. British Gas, for example, has lowered its prices 20 % in real terms since privatization in 1986 (while its bosses have personally fallen out with the regulator); electricity prices have increased by 4 % since 1990. In Japan, one regulator takes a dim view of environmental measures, another demands them. In Norway, while the electricity regulator declines to tamper with the government-developed formula for setting prices, the water regulator has found a way to stick to the formula but to revise prices all the same. The uncertainty in all this, critics argue, is unjust and expensive.

So what is a transition country government to think? On their own, conflicts between the regulator and the regulated are not conclusive evidence that a regulatory system does not work; it would indeed be suspicious if a would-be monopolist were always on friendly terms with the person responsible for restraining profits. The charge that cannot be evaded, and poses the greatest risk in the transition countries, is that too much of a regulatory system is subject to personal whim.

Much of this problem can be avoided if monopolies are broken up before they are privatized (which, however, involves many potential delays and offers multiple ways for the opponents of genuine privatization to stall the process) or if entry to new firms (especially foreign ones) is not restricted, so that the market works and detailed regulation can be avoided. Contrary to popular belief, not all of a utility needs to be part of a monopoly: in electricity, for example, distribution may be part of a monopoly, but generation need not. Still, even pared-down monopolies are likely to be too large in many postcommunist countries for any sort of reliable competition to emerge, and their privatization may be a serious burden on regulators who have to decide how far to distort a market in order to arrive at a price that is fair and efficient.

The problems of regulation are made even worse if, in their eagerness to attract investors, countries do not take the time to lay down a convincing legal-cum-regulatory framework for privatized and private power and instead cut ad hoc deals with foreign investors. "Special deals are bad for everyone," says Kathy Krumm, a chief World Bank economist for the region. Governments that favor them run the risk that companies will exploit the terms of their contracts in unexpected ways. It might then be hard to confront the offenders without threatening future investment.

Regulation also poses a risk to outside investors. Companies fear that governments might tear up their contracts or squeeze them into some new regulatory code; this is one reason why most outside investors look for influential local partners. And both sides suffer because special deals make the negotiations for each project very delicate and lengthy. Panic spread among potential Hungarian investors during the privatization of the energy sector each time the government attempted to toughen its terms. Much the same happened in the Czech Republic, despite the reputation that Premier Vaclav Klaus holds in international financial circles.

In fact, the sheer complexity of signing a contract for private power means that only a handful of investments are beginning to go on line, despite a welter of proposals. The dogged negotiating needed to conclude a deal is part of the reason why Poland's former industry and trade minister, Klemens Scierski, does not believe that private power's greatest contribution will be the kilowatts or the heating supply it produces. More valuable will be the discipline that the introduction of private power will impose upon local utilities and energy producers, a catalyst driving the reform of what used to be treated as an noncommercial, indeed a social, activity.

So the lesson for transition countries is to get the structure right from the start: wherever there is room for competition, it is preferable to government regulation. Where a supposedly impartial regulator is needed, the independence of the regulator must be tempered by the type of accountability which comes only when rules are relatively simple and applied equally. It has long been argued that the greatest threat to any system of discretionary regulation is what economists call "regulatory capture." Here an industry's regulators are subverted by the lobbying of big industries. The most dangerous type of regulator—that is, the one most susceptible to regulatory capture—is one that is charged with all sorts of oversight duties for an industry. Here the Czechs, so often pathfinders, may be heading down the wrong road. They envision a state energy agency that will not only be vested with the power to see that energy consumption develops along lines laid down by government, but also with environmental oversight of power generation, too. Ministries bogged down in too much legal red tape, however, can be pulled under and drowned by the lobbying force of big industries; superior resources usually give the industry the edge when regulatory decisions are challenged in court. Independent regulators administering a clearly defined and well-publicized set of rules remain the best defense against this sort of capture.

Thus price regulations, as well as any subsidies demanded by government and earmarked for a particular industry, must be transparent. Only that discipline will assure that energy producers do not become slack and politicians are not able to wield undue influence, lowering prices for favored industries or to appease the voters at large. Discretionary regulation without such clear boundaries can work, but is usually successful only in places where the state is well established and can call upon a long tradition of probity in the civil service. Because bureaucracies in the transition countries remain somewhat unstable, discretionary powers are unlikely to effectively serve the long-term interests of either an industry in need of clear guidance or a general population in search of reliable sources of clean power.

9.9 Keeping Them Leashed

Recoiling before the loss of power which privatization means, and fearful of the public resentment that foreign ownership of energy companies would incite (a fear that the Hungarian experience appears to demonstrate is more imaginary than real), most countries prefer a half-way house between direct state control and privatization. In essence, this process involves turning state-owned utilities directly managed by ministries into independent corporate entities. But does such restructuring by "corporatization" do any good?

Although Poland was one of the first to realize that ownership reform was an essential ingredient to increasing energy efficiency, it is also the clearest example that half-way measures bring lackluster results. Reform began rather quickly and sensibly after communism's collapse. In 1990 Minister of Industry Tadeusz Syryjczyk approved a plan that would divide Poland's state energy monopoly into three independent sectors—energy production, transmission, and distribution. In time, each of these sectors gradually would be divided further into distinct firms in competition with each other. A National Power Office was to oversee the process. By 1993 it and the government were prepared to move on to the second stage:

- Nineteen heat and power stations and thirty-three energy distributors were transformed into so-called State Treasury joint stock companies. Four brown coal enterprises became, in theory, independent firms, but because coal mines remain tied to brown coal power stations their independence is in name only. Black coal mines were grouped into six joint stock companies, with a further eleven incorporated into a single holding company—"all the rotten eggs in one basket," says a representative of the EU's Coal Commission.

- Heating supply was decentralized into 473 district enterprises, owned by a curious mixture of municipalities, private investors, and housing cooperatives.

- Ownership of gas was retained in a state monopoly, while oil was broken up into a number of partly privatized importers competing against the state's huge Nafta Polska SA. All petrol retailing remained in the hands of the state distributor, CPN.

Some degree of competitiveness was certainly introduced into the system by these reforms, particularly in the field of petrol sales, where foreign and domestic firms compete fiercely for the loyalty of the country's multiplying army of automobile owners. More importantly, perhaps, the state's Polish Energy

Network (PSE SA) now offers long-term contracts to its customers and the most reliable and efficient suppliers. Revenues from such long-term contracts and from outright state subsidy now form the basis upon which power generators and energy distributors are able to offer guarantees for their new borrowings. Indeed, in late 1994 the PSE succeeded in securing a $113 million credit (with no state guarantee attached, a first for Poland) from a consortium of banks including Creditanstalt and the EBRD. This loan was guaranteed by a long-term contract to export energy to Austria. The credit was in turn used to fund capital investments, with $75 million used to improve transmission lines and $38 million used to upgrade the Bielsko-Biala heat and power generating plant.

Although this contracting system stimulated market forces as power generators competed on price and reliability for the first time ever, failure to address other vital issues of the energy sector minimized the gains. Charged with guaranteeing energy supplies to distribution companies, the PSE, in tandem with the government's Energy Regulatory Authority (ERA), smothered the additional devolution of the energy sector because it feared that more competition would only disrupt supply. So the contract system, which seemed tailor-made to usher in privatization of individual power plants, was instead used as a blocking device, with the PSE disciplining plants to remain in the system through the use of its contract power.

Moreover, the manner of PSE's privatization is unlikely to bolster a vibrant energy industry. Other companies participating in the energy trade will be banned from bidding for ownership of or stakes in PSE. So, too (investors suspect) will foreign companies. The treasury instead intends to sell its shares directly on the Warsaw bourse, hoping for a wide distribution, but also weak shareholder oversight over management. The government's caution in delaying its reforms may be understandable; after all, the proposal has been the only thing to bring the country's four strongly antagonistic trade union federations—OPZZ, Solidarity, Solidarity 80, and KONTRA—together, as each participated in mass demonstrations against energy privatization and corporatization in May 1996.

Russia's electrical industry has followed a similar limited decentralizing pattern (with privatization thrown in), yielding similar centralizing results: an independent state agency with only limited interest in spurring energy market development.

Privatization in Russian electricity created one giant, the Unified Energy System (UES), and seventy-two local providers, called *energos*. UES owns all high-power transmission lines, the largest generating plants (26 in all), and the central distribution system. Since privatization, UES has cunningly gained outright ownership of nine energos and holds 49% stakes in sixty of the others. So UES continues to control over 60% of Russian electricity production and distribution. Yet it is unable to push through higher prices, let alone monopoly pricing, because the Federal Energy Commission is as manipulative of pricing as in the socialist era. These controls mean that UES shareholders do not get anything near value for their shares. UES assets are currently valued at a mere $2.5 billion, whereas Czech Electric, a company not even a tenth the size of UES, has a market capitalization of $1.7 billion. (A planned sale of $350 million worth of UES American depository receipts—ADRs backed by equities in the firm held on deposit by banks—to international investors may boost the value of the firm's assets.)

Czech Electric's high capitalization, however, does not mean that privatization has delivered the goods in the Czech energy sector. When Czech Energy Plants (CEZ) and Gas Production (PP) were split into distinct state joint stock companies and a number of regional distributors, there was no agreed mechanism to share the revenues from sales. Consultants suggested a 75:25 ratio in favor of the two giants but, unsatisfied with this lion's share, CEZ used its muscle to insist on an 86:14 breakdown in its favor.

Such monopoly power is crippling innovation and price reform. When regional distributors seek out cheaper sources of electricity supply, through its absolute control of the transmission lines CEZ prevents these outside supplies from entering the system. And because CEZ is pursuing an aggressive investment schedule (126 billion koruna—over $5 billion) to be spent over the next five years, it is likely to do all it can to protect its turf from cheap competition. The cost of such protection is high: CEZ told the country's electricity regulators that it cost them 240 koruna to produce 1 megawatt hour; CEZ's competitors say that actual cost is only half that, meaning that consumers are picking up the tab. Says Petr Karas, CEZ's chairman, "The idea of a free market is very strong. But sometimes it is in contradiction with reliability of supply." And when it is, Karas leaves no doubt about where he stands.

9.10 Saving Power

Getting national energy policies on structure and ownership right is not enough. Aware that energy imports, particularly oil, drain foreign exchange reserves, countries are trying to curb consumption. Indeed, in late August 1996 Romania faced the prospect of shutting down large swatches of its industry because it could not pay its oil bills. Anticipating such dire emergencies, Hungary, the Czech Republic, and Slovenia have all saved thousands of barrels of oil per day by using gas instead of oil to generate the steam needed to run boilers. Extensive mass transit systems, one of the few legacies of the socialist era of substantial benefit today, help to cut gasoline consumption, and privatization of tram systems will help to assure their long-term survival. Urban planning is beginning to take hold in a few cities, such as Prague, Budapest, and reform-minded Odessa. But even the most expert planning can only nudge the growth of demand. Ethanol, electricity, and other new fuels offer little hope of cutting the pollution and high costs associated with the masses of new cars crowding urban centers today.

For some industries, dearer power—primarily higher-priced electricity—has attacked every line on their balance sheets and made slabs of machinery redundant. For others, it has been more of a marginal imposition. The different impacts depend on energy's share in an industry's total costs. These are often 30% or more for such heavy industrial users as iron and steel, paper and pulp, and cement; for others, it can be as low as 10%. The larger that power costs loom in total costs, of course, the greater the rewards in saving it.

The chemicals industry uses hydrocarbons not merely for energy but as the actual raw material for about 60% of its output, and also foots a fuel bill that would bankrupt a fair-size country. Chemicals firms have suffered a double blow:

1. Their cost structure has been transformed. Before the late 1980s, the total cost of running a petrochemical plant in Central Europe was split 65-35 between fixed and variable costs. With the rise in hydrocarbon prices, the ratio has shifted to 30-70. The result: break-even capacity has fallen sharply. Running plants at high loading no longer makes sense if the extra output is simply sold off below cost.

2. Geography now works against the chemical industry. Before 1989, socialist governments always sited plants close to markets rather than to feedstocks; as a result transport costs are high from the start.

Conventional steel plants are another drain on energy. These often obsolete factories have always wasted energy by reheating the metal at each stage of the process. The biggest waste in bulk steelmaking remains the production of ingots, which then have to be reheated for rolling into finished steel. The remedy is continuous casting, invented in Britain in 1952 but pioneered by Japanese firms such as Nippon Steel, the world's biggest steelmaker. This method of casting involves pouring molten steel straight into a dish from which great slabs, ready for rolling there and then, are cast. Continuous casting saves 5–10 % of energy costs, depending on the quality of the steel. The problem with such innovation is cost: no steel company in the region has the capital to try this. Instead, steelworks in Romania, the Czech Republic, and Hungary are trying to improve their blends of ore, coke, and limestone. Governments are reluctant either to close obsolete steel plants or to invest sufficiently to modernize the few that can be made competitive on the world market.

9.11 The Nuclear Option

Throughout the region there are early hints of improvement due to structural energy sector reform. Prices have started to increase, albeit too slowly. Partial privatization in Russia, Hungary, and the Czech Republic and demonopolization in Poland, Estonia, and Slovenia mean that energy concerns are daily operating on a more commercial footing, with some plants beginning to increase their capacity through greater efficiency. Everywhere there is talk of savings to be made from running utilities and energy concerns as real businesses. Laggards, too, are becoming slightly more disciplined. Romania's RENEL, the state-run electricity monopoly, is telling the government that it can refurbish old power stations to create new capacity at a quarter of the cost of building new stations from scratch. But getting the structure of ownership and finance right will not on their own solve the energy problem. All transition countries will have to increase production of a variety of energy sources while they also broaden the types of energy they use.

Ten years ago, "going nuclear" was the popular choice of governments. Nowadays, that choice is looked on warily by most populations and treated antagonistically by neighboring countries. Moreover, nuclear power programs are notorious for falling behind schedule—in transition countries for industrial reasons rather than the regulatory or environmental problems common in the West, although these latter problems are also growing in frequency.

Blame for this can be laid at the feet of the Chernobyl nuclear power plant meltdown of a decade ago. The political fallout from that disaster means that nowhere in the world has the nuclear industry reclaimed its previous status. In the transition countries, moreover, the nuclear industry is saddled with the added burden of local reactors built according to Soviet designs: the VVER (basically the same type as the most common Western model, the pressurized water reactor built by such groups as Westinghouse and Framatone) and a unique Russian design, the graphite-moderated but water-cooled RMBK, which is the curious hybrid that failed at Chernobyl.

Many of the nuclear plants built in the socialist era are near densely populated areas, which increases their unpopularity. They were located at these sites in order to be incorporated as nuclear central heating plants for urban areas. Today, indeed, in Ukraine and Russia nuclear power heats many flats through centralized district-heating networks. Coupling nuclear steam-generating reactors to them was a simple technical feat achieved in the 1980s, but it meant that nuclear plants were placed even closer to populated areas than were nuclear power stations. Such plants now fuel Voronezh, and Nizhny Novgorod in Russia, and Odessa in Ukraine.

Despite their newness, nuclear plants are as much in need of investment as any other in the region. Few countries, however, have a coherent strategy for developing their nuclear programs. Indeed, Hungary's plan is the most coherent: abandon ship. As of now, the government plans to dismantle the Paks nuclear plant, which also happens to be the country's most efficient producer. Managers of the plant must create a reserve fund that will be used to dismantle the plant sometime between 2010 and 2015. (As no one has ever taken apart a working nuclear power station, the costs of doing this can only be guesstimated, but in 1996 a figure of 100 billion forints, or $1 billion, was envisioned.) Prices for everyone will need to be raised if anything like this sum is to be gathered.

The situation in Slovakia is more typical of events and attitudes in the region. Nuclear power—an existing station at Jaslovsk-Bohunice and a partly completed station at Mochovce—supplies the bulk of the country's electricity. Completion of Mochovce alone requires 5.6 billion koruna. Although 50% of this financing was to come from government subsidies, it never came. This unwillingness made domestic and foreign banks wary of added investment in the venture, even though one of the plant's four production centers was 90% complete and another 80% ready.

In stepped Electricite de France, which planned to use its technology to make the older Soviet design safer and more efficient. By demonstrating this means to improving nuclear energy, Electricite de France hopes to pick up contracts to restore Soviet-era plants throughout the region. A joint venture was formed, with Electricite de France assuming 51% control, and Slovensk Energetick Podnik 49%. With heavy French government backing, the European Bank for Reconstruction and Development provided one-third of the finance needed to complete Mochovce according to French design schemes. Additional finance came from Bayernwerk, Preussen Elektra, and Framatome.

Not even an increasingly authoritarian government like that of Vladimir Meciar can ram through a nuclear program unchallenged. Here Slovak environmentalists received a leg up in their protests from the EBRD, which insisted that the public be allowed to comment on the project. Local environmentalists, supported by groups in Austria, were powerfully energized by this opening.

9.12 All That Gas

Both the IEA and the WEC expect oil and coal to become less important in transition countries, although they disagree about how quickly this will happen. Even if oil prices increase 20%, the IEA supposes that oil demand will grow by 10% in the region. Coal demand will grow by under 2% a year. The WEC, however, sees coal demand shrinking in absolute terms by the turn of the century and beyond.

Nowadays, hope for a reliable energy future rests primarily on natural gas. Because it is plentiful, clean, and, more importantly, because it is cheap, natural gas is likely to crowd out other fuels, particularly as it offers a partial solution to the region's endemic air pollution problems. The sulfurous pall choking urban centers is a serious issue throughout the region. The United Nations Environment Program estimates that pollution inflicts billions of dollars of medical bills each year on national budgets. On some winter days the smog blanketing Kiev and Prague is between six and twenty times the highest levels in the West. The situation will worsen before it will improve.

Improve it most likely will. Cleaner air begins to become a priority once GDP reaches something like $5,000 per capita. There are no shortages of technical fixes for smog and automotive pollution, although they come at a price. And the pressure groups and public awareness that will help bring about a cleaner environment in the postcommunist world are being organized. Local protesters have forced Slovenia's government to think twice about new hydroelectric plants. Prague's city council is studying the ways cities such as Rome and Paris regulate traffic to control auto emissions. Poland is likely to require lead-free petrol within a few years.

Natural gas can also help, perhaps more than any government fix. When gas burns it releases less carbon than oil or coal; it contains virtually no sulfur; and with well-designed machinery, it also releases fewer nitrogen oxides, a particularly pernicious problem in the industrial heartlands of Central Europe and the NIS. When it comes to generating electric power, burning gas can be used to drive a turbine: the heat contained in the exhaust then makes steam that drives a second turbine. This arrangement, known as the combined cycle, has raised the proportion of gas's heat that can be transformed into electricity from below 40% to above 50%. Only the higher gas prices expected in the next century are likely to ever nudge gas from its present charmed position in the region.

Russia has huge reserves of natural gas and is well placed to exploit it on the basis of existing technology. In contrast to oil, gas reserves are not scattered throughout waterlogged forests but are concentrated in a few giant fields. True, they are not always easy fields to reach. Some of the best ones suffer from difficult Arctic conditions. There is also an abundance of gas in Kazakhstan and Uzbekistan and in Yakutia in eastern Siberia, but the six giant fields of western Siberia will continue to provide the bulk of production. Moreover, gas has relatively low capital costs, power stations that use it can be built rapidly, and it is efficient. Today, indeed, Russia's big energy companies, as we have seen in the case of Gazprom, are struggling to establish footholds in the fast-growing markets immediately to their west. Russian financiers, as well as Western ones, are striving to satisfy their critical need for capital.

The importance of gas in the thinking of governments in Eastern Europe and the NIS can be gauged from the fact that in the Czech Republic, Romania, Bulgaria, Albania, and Ukraine over 60% of estimated increases in fuel consumption is meant to be covered by natural gas. There are ambitious proposals for pipelines from Russia across Poland and Slovakia; from Central Asia across either Russia or Turkey; and from the Mediterranean across the former Yugoslavia. These ambitions make sense, a representative of Gaz de France told a gathering of regional energy ministers in 1995, because "gas is likely to be able to be used wherever it is found; it has low capital costs so that power stations that use it can be built rapidly, and it is efficient." Taking the hint, Russia may begin to liquefy gas and ship it to market, though that usually makes gas more expensive.

9.13 Upward

In 1920 Lenin defined communism as "Soviet power plus the electrification of the whole country." Communism's supposed potency was, in theory, to be revealed by this image: communism, working through all the technology of modern power—electricity grids, mammoth coal pits burrowed deep into the bowels of the earth, giant hydroelectric dams, nuclear power stations—would lift the so-called masses into modernity in one great leap forward. As events of the past half-decade have shown, Lenin's metaphor can be stood on its head, for building a power industry to support today's market-based growth and tomorrow's free-market-based prosperity in the transition countries is turning out to be a potent catalyst for stimulating capitalism. International and local investors have been recruited to supply desperately needed finance and expertise. Slowly if not surely, they are beginning the process of transforming state-owned utilities and energy systems. Where once energy was simply an aspect of social policy, managers of and shareholders in energy firms now demand profit; where once energy companies employed vast numbers of superfluous workers for the sake of creating jobs, everywhere in the region there is talk of efficiency. In a growing and promising number of cases, there has been privatization and outside investment on a large scale.

When transition countries began to confront the reality of world energy prices after communism's collapse, however, governments put too little faith in the market. By continuing to insulate consumers from higher energy prices, they slowed industrial restructuring as well as efforts at individual conservation. In energy, the pendulum may now be starting to swing the other way, as much of the load and hope of power generation in the region slowly begins to shift from public control to private initiative.

10

Struggling to Escape

Infrastructure in the Transition

Many of the countries of Eastern Europe and the former Soviet Union are increasingly blessed with entrepreneurs who inspire rates of growth that approach those found in the "tiger" economies of Southeast Asia. But the transition countries are also cursed with infrastructure that works against this budding private sector dynamism. Weakness in such vital areas as roads, rails, ports, and air transport means that economies are subject to crude shocks when, not if, overburdened systems of infrastructure fail. Businessmen throughout the region are caught in this web of sagging infrastructure that saps their resources. Big and small firms, governments too, are struggling to escape.

Today, indeed, the transition economies resemble nothing so much as rush-hour traffic in Moscow, Prague, Budapest, and Warsaw: no suburban stop-go crawl, but sudden bursts of exhilarating acceleration alternating with massive, fuming jams. Like the tiger economies of Southeast Asia, some transition countries are now pushing hard against structural impediments to accelerated growth.

Until recently, the biggest economic cloud hovering over the region was inflation, which between 1990 and 1992 reached peaks not seen in Europe since Germany's Weimar Republic. However, since late 1994, almost all of the transition economies have cut their inflation rates dramatically (as in most things, Belarus lags sullenly behind) and now seem to have got the situation more or less under control. Here the best performers—the Czech Republic, Estonia, and Slovakia—are nearing the low inflation levels found in OECD countries.

Meanwhile, the most dynamic portion of business in the transition countries is being done in international trade. This very success is making life more difficult for exporters and importers alike. Inadequate infrastructure is beginning to choke and, at times, strangle the region's trade expansion, and thus prospects for overall growth. Infrastructure is the economy's skeleton; on it, almost all commercial and government activity hangs. Transport, for example, vitally affects the ability of businesses to buy and sell; the availability of water and sewers determines human health and prospects for increased agricultural production.

So desperate is the need for improved infrastructure that a lot of unplanned and sometimes barely legal competition for dozy state infrastructure companies is emerging. In Ukraine, for example, 40% of all business mail is handled by a private Ukrainian-Canadian venture. As no specific law authorizes such activity, the firm's managers live in constant fear of the government calling a halt to their booming business. The Belarusian state owns 86% of all freight trucks in the country, yet the remaining 14% carried 71% of all the goods shipped by road in 1993, the last year for which such statistics are available.

The World Bank has long argued that there is a binding link between growth and innovations in basic infrastructure. Improved infrastructure has an energizing impact all its own; and lack of infrastructure, or inadequate infrastructure, can help to reignite inflation. Securing, for example, access to foreign markets for local products and the entrance of foreign competition at home can be done only by enhancing physical access to and from these markets. And when infrastructure resources are stretched to a breaking point, the costs they begin to impose—directly in terms of higher prices for the services they render, indirectly in delay or opportunities for bribery—can act as catalysts for a new round of inflation.

In most countries the problem is not that basic forms of infrastructure are lacking (though Albania ranks with the poorest of the poor in terms of households with access to piped water and other basic modern infrastructure services). Instead, infrastructure in the region was designed for a centrally planned economy. As a result, says the EBRD in its 1996 Annual Transition Report, government policies ignored questions of productivity, and "infrastructure services were supplied to enterprises with little regard for their costs of production, including consequences for the environment."

In general, governments shortchanged infrastructure (save for that geared to military use) in favor of industrial investment. Hungary is a good example: between 1980 and 1990, total investment in that country grew 42%, but transport investments grew only 8%. Infrastructure services to consumers, such as civil aviation and city streets, were the most neglected. When forced to spend on infrastructure projects, central planning emphasized industrialization at any cost, and capital projects, such as freight rail lines, were often overbuilt in out-of-the-way locations for isolated industries that were the only ones to use them. Nowadays, with many of the factories that had been located in rural areas shut down, such rail lines crisscross landscapes with little or no need for them.

10. 1 Stuck in the Past

The heritage of price controls and a misplaced faith in central planning is hard to get rid of. For example, even today postcommunist governments continue to favor cheap transport: it helps to keep city folk quiet, and allegedly allows low wages, so that industry can grow. The result: six years after the transition began, most transport services in the region cannot recover their costs. Thus they cut back investment, blighting hopes for a better economy. In the early years of the transition, with production tumbling everywhere, these failings had little impact as demand for infrastructure services collapsed, too. In Moldova, for example, total freight shipped within the country collapsed by over 70% in 1992 alone.

Was this a golden opportunity for scaling down inefficient use of infrastructure resources and for reform? In theory, perhaps. In practice, during the first years of the transition, some countries in the region began to expand, not contract, many old infrastructure industries. But instead of doing this in preparation for future growth, governments have used infrastructure firms as public works projects. When domestic demand (and the employment it secured) declined, railways, trucking firms, and ports had their payrolls padded by ministerial decree. In Lithuania, for example, railway employment has grown, not fallen, by 15% since 1993, despite a 38% decline in freight carried and a 23% decline in passenger traffic.

So much of the region continues to be marred by backward, bloated, and often wrongheaded infrastructure: Bulgaria with its huge and heavily subsidized Black Sea ports at Varna and Burgas constructed for a Russia trade that nowadays scarcely exists; Slovenia with freight rail links to Serbia for commerce (nonexistent for almost five years), instead of to Italy and Austria, where trade is booming; Hungary with regional airports that serve few passengers, and an international airport in Budapest that cannot handle today's mushrooming traffic. Where infrastructure is improving, change is often painful and slow. The end of cheap fuel supplies should help infrastructure to become more market friendly. In Bulgaria, for example, trucks carried 87.7% of all freight in 1989, but now carry only 47.7% because of the rising price of fuel. But this forces businesses to rely on Bulgaria's subsidized railways, which rarely—if ever—complete a run on schedule. In most cases, socialist-era distortions thus remain in place, and conditions are growing worse.

While some sectors are dominated by useless overbuilding, others are plagued by shortages. Interconnections between traffic-clogged cities are often worse than the chaos within them. For every 1,000 kilometers of land, Russia has just 148 kilometers of road and 19 kilometers of railways; the comparable figures for the United States are 640 kilometers of road and 51 kilometers of rail. Only 16% of Poland's roads are reckoned to be equal to Western standards; indeed, there are only 257 kilometers of so-called express roads in the entire country, a number not even suitable for tiny Macedonia.

Because infrastructure improvements have traditionally been seen as the province of the state, you would think that governments would act to address these failings. You would be wrong. Most governments, when faced by a budget crunch, slash capital expenditures on infrastructure projects (see figure 10.1), even as they try to pad employment. As this chart shows, capital investment plummeted in the first years of transition. Although that decline has slowed as economies stabilized and budgets have come into balance, real growth is still not here. With social spending on health care and pensions, to cite just two examples beginning to mount, room for state investment in infrastructure remains thin.

Figure 10.1

Government Capital Expenditures by Countries' Stages of Transition (Percent of GDP)

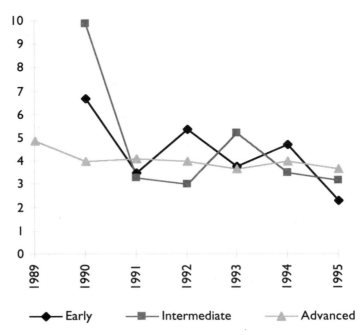

Note:

Early: Azerbaijan, Belarus, Tajikistan, Turkmenistan
Intermediate: Albania, Armenia, Bosnia, Bulgaria, Georgia, Kazakhstan, Kyrgyzstan, Macedonia, Romania, Russia, Ukraine, Uzbekistan
Advanced: Croatia, Czech Republic, Estonia, Hungary, Latvia, Lithuania, Poland, Slovakia, Slovenia

Source: EBRD Transition Report, 1995

This indifference, and the backwardness it yields, has a high price. It costs more to ship a container by rail and road from southern Poland to Gdansk than to move it from that Baltic seaport to anywhere in Europe. Economists in Moldova's transport ministry reckon that the cost of poor infrastructure is equivalent to a 30% tax surcharge on all businesses. So dubious are promised deliveries of shipments that most manufacturers in the region regard the very idea of Japanese "just-in-time" production methods (which Korean firms are trying to institute in their

Polish and Uzbek plants) as something of a joke. Indeed, the problems posed by poor infrastructure concern not only getting goods to their destination, but producing them in the first place.

Sooner or later, the gripes of individual business people will incite wider economic effects. Cries about inadequate infrastructure are today raising strong pressure for more interventionist industrial policies. Some firms argue that governments need to copy Korea, Indonesia, and much of the rest of Southeast Asia, where governments that are usually gun-shy about increasing the size of the state have spent billions of dollars nurturing infrastructure development, spurring local construction and other employment with huge public orders. Poland's big three trade unions, which dominate infrastructure employees, agree that it is up to government to think up and pay for ambitious infrastructure projects. Others, who would like more private enterprise, worry that large state infrastructure projects, which put control over huge contracts in the hands of politicians, will put the state back in control of much of industry as a whole.

10.2 Challenge to Change

According to economists at the World Bank, meeting the infrastructure needs of the transition countries (not counting telecommunications) over the coming decade will take an investment of at least $500 billion. So great are the region's infrastructure needs that companies from all over the world salivate at the thought of juicy construction contracts. Many of the world's engineering and construction giants—ABB and Bechtel, among many others—have offices scattered throughout the countries of Central Europe. In the next decade, according to the UN Economic Commission for Europe, investment needs in road, rail, and airport construction of the countries of Eastern Europe and the NIS are likely to be four times as great as those now planned in all the nations of the EU combined.

Investments and changes in infrastructure are expensive and have to be paid for, but this is less of a problem than it was. Or it should be less of a problem. The global capital market is a fact as well as a cliche. Governments, companies, and investors in the transition countries now have access to it on commercial terms—that is, if they present investments that make sense. In short, there is nothing endemic to the transition countries, as such, that denies them access to either the capital or the technology they need to bring their infrastructures up to date.

Infrastructure know-how, moreover, is more readily transferable across borders than ever before. Much of the rich world's transformation during the past twenty years has been the result of increased competition in such infrastructure sectors as communications, rails, roads, and air travel. And it is often a feature of today's dynamic infrastructure changes that they are simpler for the transition countries to adopt than living with the techniques that are now in use (compare the crisp, modern efficiency of Poland's more commercially oriented LOT airline with that of neighboring Belarus and its slipshod, state-controlled Belavia.)

If the huge sums of capital needed to finance such development are ever to be raised, however, governments in the region must begin to rely to a much greater extent on private capital. The World Bank estimates that, today, only 7% of investment in infrastructure in the developing world comes from the private sector, and estimates for such investment in the transition countries are even lower than that. Compare this with the role that private capital plays in infrastructure investment in advanced countries, where 20% of infrastructure investment comes from the private sector. Are the countries of Eastern Europe and the NIS ready to move decisively in this direction?

Not without a change of hearts and minds, for thinking about infrastructure in many countries (including the transition countries) is still largely dominated by outmoded ideas. It used to be a cliche in economics some twenty or thirty years ago that infrastructure industries were so-called natural monopolies. Unlike in other areas, where several producers can easily compete with each other, it would be wasteful, it was thought, if two railroad lines or highways were to be built along the same route. Also, industry as a whole was thought to profit from good transport links, but it is often difficult to charge all those who benefit from good roads or city streets, especially those who benefit indirectly. As a result, the argument goes, private parties will either underinvest in infrastructure (if they cannot charge those who use it), or they will charge too much (if they are allowed to become monopolists).

So, traditionally, governments have stepped in. The pattern goes something like this: where private investors begin to provide infrastructure services, as happened in the rail business in the nineteenth century, prices of such things as freight rates, shipping charges, and so forth, become progressively regulated. Companies are told to provide services, for example, rural train routes, where they cannot recover their costs. In exchange, they are allowed to charge more on other, more popular routes. In time, regulation becomes so pervasive that costs skyrocket, services decline, and the financial position of many infrastructure companies deteriorates. In the end, the state simply nationalizes and begins to run these enterprises itself. In other areas, private providers are not even given a chance. Until recently, the state simply built most roads by itself, and private investors have been precluded from the airline business in many countries.

State involvement was also rationalized by military concerns. The importance of infrastructure for defense is taken for granted: road building was a military necessity long before the advent of the automobile and the phenomenal increase in individual travel. While this concern exists everywhere, the communist economies were more militarized than others, and moving tanks always seemed more important than moving people or goods. Indeed, the Soviet Union became notorious for hiding the existence and layout of much of its road links, with maps being either secret or intentionally falsified to mislead potential enemies. That this also made them unusable to domestic nonmilitary consumers seemed of no significance.

As long as all industry was in state hands under communism, there was nothing unusual about infrastructure. But since the regime fell, it has been widely assumed that most industries should be privatized, except for "monopolies" and firms with "special significance for national defense." Under these rubrics most infrastructure industries are often kept under the state's thumb without much debate.

10.3 Marching Backwards

There is a price to this reflexive reaction. A glance at most international airports or capital city train stations in the transition countries conveys two messages. The first is of mounting activity. The imitation Irish pub within Kiev's Borispol Airport is a hive of individual traders lugging imports from Turkey and China for resale back home; Ljubljana's central train station is jammed with Italian, German, and Austrian tourists. The second message is of rampant squalor and inefficiency. Rude immigration officials or rail officials, little changed from the communist era, stand next to ticket offices filled with flickering computers. Training for Bulgaria's gruff rail porters (no surprise here) remains in the hands of a military department. Indeed, the official title for Bulgarian railway employees is "railway troops of the Ministry of Transport."

Militarization of infrastructure is a nagging problem in other countries as well. In Russia, control of aviation remains in the hands of the military, which continues to insist that all flight plans be filed and approved three days before a planned takeoff. Although charter companies are often able to escape these strictures, with airport authorities winking at flights that are not formally approved, military control is harmful for investment prospects as companies balk at constantly seeking military approval for their expansion plans. (Things may be changing for the better. The U.S. Federal Aviation Administration (FAA) has been working with a new Russian Interstate Aviation Committee to develop a distinct civil aviation administration.)

The military and technological significance of an industry are often ill-defined and provide a rarely examined screen protecting it against public scrutiny. On the simplest level, an airplane, road, or train can be of concern because it may be needed to ferry troops or materiel in an emergency. But there are other levels of concern, too. Aircraft, train, even bus manufacturing involves a complex interplay of technologies, from design teams to computer software. Few governments want to risk being seen as abandoning such "strategic industries." All these concerns blend with financial worries and a desire to protect the state's coffers. Hungary's government, for example, wants to go slowly on privatizing both urban and intercity bus routes for fear that contracts for new buses might no longer all go to the powerful Ikarus company—one the government hopes will make a killing when fully privatized. Such a mix of economics and politics is apt to do a lot of harm.

Subsidization of inefficient infrastructure companies is a whole separate chapter. Where direct subsidies used to be doled out in such places as Belarus, Romania, Albania, and Ukraine, hefty credits to infrastructure firms seem to be the rage today. In Romania, for example, since 1991 more than a dozen laws gave special credits at state-controlled banks to rail, road, and shipping firms. Borrowing soared, helping to push up the country's money supply and fueling inflation. Romanian infrastructure, indeed, was charged an average negative real interest rate of 5% on loans while growing businesses were starved of capital. The central bank tried to slow down this rush of credits, but its measures to cool the process were, says a senior bank economist, "subverted within the government."

Even when private enterprise is allowed, regulation is stifling, and like all regulated industries, infrastructure firms are continually subject to political abuse. For example, Palair Makedonian, a privately owned airline with no ties to the ruling party in Macedonia, was forced to suspend operations for nonpayment of its debts for ground services at Macedonia's airports. Its rival, Makedonski Aviotransport (MAT), had its debts ignored, it is said, because of friendly relations between its directors and leaders of the ruling Social Democratic Union Party. Disputes about dividing the spoils among political factions in Albania, to cite another example, delayed performance for over two years of a contract Siemens had won to refurbish Tirana's airport. PSV, a Czech construction firm, was twice awarded a big contract to supply concrete railway ties to Czech Railways. Bidders against the firm protested the award, arguing that only PSV was aware of all required conditions and that the auction was rigged in the firm's favor. To no avail; and too bad for Czech Railways, which received substandard material likely to survive only one or two winters. (Unchastened, PSV says it will get things right once it is privatized!)

A mix of the private and public sectors in infrastructure is probably unavoidable—it would be unrealistic to expect that the state will get out altogether. But this creates its own problems as local businessmen are increasingly fed up with having to deal with, compete against, or operate alongside, bloated public-sector infrastructure enterprises. Andras Pakay, a former executive at Malev who now works for a Western investment bank in Budapest and deals with investment opportunities farther east, suggests that Russia's aviation, like other aspects of its infrastructure, will never reach its full potential so long as the state "maintains its heavy-handed control. Such power means that I have to deal with bureaucrats everyday. I'd rather pay more taxes than face that."

Slovenia's private-sector transport managers are particularly bitter. In Ljubljana, which has neither a tram nor metro, buses are the only system of mass transit. Nonetheless, LPP (a local bus company) has lost money for six straight years, mostly because the government sets the routes it must run and the prices it must charge. The local city council covers some of this loss with a subsidy, but managers would be happy to do without this handout if they could also rid themselves of government oversight.

The problems of infrastructure are thus not exclusively questions of ownership, but also of the anticompetitive effects of subsidies and state regulation. One of the basic rules of the transition is that efficient and effective economic enterprise requires that all entities act on an equal basis: that is, whenever possible, that they are all subject to market discipline. This means that governments can no longer run infrastructure industries primarily for social and political rather than economic ends. Therein lies the rub. What is the point of state control if the state must run its firms as if they were private ones?

There is some hope for change, however. A modicum of sense is often introduced by the budget constraints of governments themselves, and the flow of subsidies may be diminishing as consumers are increasingly charged prices closer to the real costs of the services they consume. Poland, Slovenia, Estonia, and Latvia have all squeezed infrastructure companies to varying degrees. Bulgaria was forced to do so by the IMF, which insisted that credits to Bulgarian State Railways be curtailed, fares be pegged to inflation, and secondary lines eliminated to rationalize usage. (The company's response? "The government has turned its back on its own social policy," said its chairman, Angel Dimitrov.) The new Romanian government installed in late 1996 under President Emil Constantinescu also says that it wants to end direct government management of all infrastructure and will begin by cutting (no calls yet for eliminating) subsidized loans.

Squeezing of this sort helps. Increasingly, governments now take pains to emphasize that infrastructure industries, like normal firms, must learn to stand on their economic feet. Five years ago, for example, all transition country airlines were in critical condition, with government-imposed performance regimens and strict price controls. Few in the region questioned the state's involvement in air transport through a subsidy here, a decree there, and a bias against foreign ownership or even minority investments. In the past few years, with energy prices rising and government budgets under the gun, things are beginning to take a turn.

Governments have learned from bitter experience. Over-capacity, foreign competition (on both regional and international routes), and an inability to invest in up-to-date technology and modern management techniques have meant fewer passengers and freight shipments. "Politicians have learned that the longer you try to win time, the worse it is," says Bazyli Samojlik, the vice president for finance at the Polish LOT airline, which began to be organized as a commercial entity in 1992. "You cannot stop the world."

10. 4 The Privatization Way

Even if the present environment for private capital continues, private investments in infrastructure in the region are likely to triple by the end of the century. Inconceivable a mere five years ago, private infrastructure projects—from privately owned bus companies that carry 36 % of all commuters in Odessa to a myriad of private trucking businesses in Poland— are sprouting in every transition country.

But a break with outmoded economics and an infusion of new thinking is required if infrastructure investment in the region (which, given local capital shortages, must in part be fueled by foreign finance) is to take off in earnest. Even if it may not be possible for different railroads to compete for business on the same routes, substitute forms of transport nearly always provide a sufficient competitive challenge. Trucking has been taking a large part of railroad business in the West, and the same holds true in the East. According to the EBRD, rail freight volume in the region declined 50 % between 1989 and 1994 (see figure 10.2), and although some of this decline can be attributed to falling output, much of the rest has been picked up by aggressive new private trucking companies. Instead of leading to more efficient and leaner railroads, this competitive failure often leads to a new clamor for subsidization.

In fact, it is often government itself, adhering to mistaken theories, that creates and sustains monopolies in infrastructure, even while notions about natural monopoly are crumbling in the face of evidence from a series of bold experiments in decentralization and privatization around the world. A comparison of

333

Figure 10.2

**Change in Volume of Rail Freight Traffic
(in Thousands of Tons)**

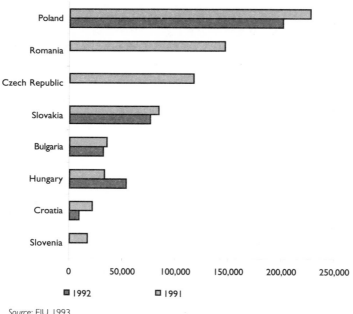

Source: EIU, 1993.

Western Europe with North America provides a good example. For years, the Europeans (except for the British) have been coddling their money-losing airlines and railroads, making sure they do not compete with each other. Prices of air tickets are kept ridiculously high, maintaining air travel as a luxury, while rail tickets are kept artificially low to stimulate demand for what is in reality a very expensive way to travel.

All the while, air travel has been radically deregulated in the United States, and fierce competition ensued. Upstart airlines grabbed a market share at the expense of such venerable names as Pan Am, TWA, and Eastern. Indeed, Pan Am (the world's pioneer in civil aviation) and a number of other big airlines were allowed to go bankrupt (something that would be unthinkable in the case of a habitually subsidized state airline, such as Air France), without any noticeable disruption in services. The result? America's private airlines have been slashing prices and making flying affordable for almost everyone. Small wonder then that the Europeans fight tooth and nail to keep U.S. airlines from flying between European cities, even though the American retaliation for this exclusion keeps them from expanding into the lucrative American market.

Trucking is another example. Never a "natural monopoly," road transport was often made to mimic one by governments, which regulated prices and restricted competition. Unions could be kept happy in this way (by reducing pressure on wages), and railroads, traditional beneficiaries of state largesse, could keep their share of the freight business because trucking costs were kept artificially high. Deregulation in the United States showed, again, the high cost of these practices. Prices in the trucking industry were decontrolled in 1980. By 1990, rates had fallen by a third and the industry's payroll by half. Labor productivity grew by 9% a year, and today there are 17% more full-time truckers than in 1980. Managers invested in information technology—computers, cellular phones, etc.—to track freight, redesigned rolling stock to carry more goods more safely, and concentrated on winning "intermodal" traffic that travels part of its journey by some other means of transport. After a bloody restructuring, freight volume and revenues are growing.

The lessons for the transition countries are clear: market-friendly infrastructure strategies work best, providing incentives for private property ownership; reliable enforcement of contracts; a liberal pricing regime; low taxes; and a hearty welcome for foreign investors. Economists argue about how much weight to attach to one of these factors or another, but most agree with this broad proposition: a key to growth is granting infrastructure firms the same freedom to respond to market incentives that is now increasingly available to ordinary private businesses.

When private enterprise is granted even a little bit of that liberty to operate, money begins to pour into infrastructure improvements. In 1995 alone, $1.82 billion in loans from international banks flowed to 19 private regional infrastructure companies in the transition countries. Private ownership is finding its way into infrastructure in a number of ways. In some cases, infrastructure enterprises have been privatized, in part or in total. In others, new projects are constructed on the build-operate-transfer (BOT) basis, which allows contractors to build a project and then to make money by keeping a fixed share of the revenues the project generates. Governments are pushed to consider privatization because it makes it easier to meet demands for new roads, air flights, or port services without straining public finances. Most importantly, as Hungary discovered, this is the form of privatization that can bring a serious cash infusion into state coffers.

10.5 No Buying Time

The thirst for infrastructure improvements goes hand in glove with the region's thirst for capital. Only the Czechs, otherwise the region's flag-waving privatizers, can afford to fund most infrastructure projects directly from state funds: of the CK420 billion in planned transport improvements for the next decade, the government intends to finance CK359 billion itself. (In a strange manifestation of this policy, a junior minister in the Klaus government publicly threatened suicide two years ago if a planned foreign investment in infrastructure was allowed to go ahead.) But other transition countries, with their budgets in the red, do not have this luxury and will have to look to the world capital markets for help. This means that countries that want to succeed must not only open their infrastructure industries to competition, but also increase transparency in order to be able to finance the construction projects they so vitally need.

This is because lenders need information. However, transition country infrastructure managers have little experience in opening their books to outsiders. Moreover, their accounting systems are usually far from reliable, both in assessing the value of the assets they control and in costing their activities. Investors are then asked to jump into the dark.

When, in 1992, Air France purchased a stake in CSA, the Czech flagship airline, it thought it was getting a good deal. In fact, the French also brought the EBRD (whose head, Jacques Attali, happened to be the brother of Air France's president) into the deal. Perhaps only a state airline (a lesson here to be sure) would enter into a deal worth $60 million without adequate information. But when CSA's assets were finally examined by international accountants Ernst and Young, it turned out that the existing books overvalued them by $25 million. The partnership fell apart in 1994 amid acrimonious disputes. (Loss of this particular Western investor may have been no bad thing, after all. CSA lost $40 million in the last year of its common venture with Air France and claimed to be making money in 1996. Air France is still a financial basket case.)

Most investors, however, are more demanding, and the very fact that infrastructure companies in transition countries now need to gain outside finance or private capital imposes greater commercial discipline. When Romania tried to partially privatize its state airline, Tarom, several Western investment banks refused to bid for the mandate because the company's books were in such a mess. Muddled finances always make investors wary. In response to such pressures, LOT, CSA, Hungary's Malev, and even Aeroflot have recently adopted the standard airline financial accounting recommended by the International Air Traffic Association (IATA) to its members.

There are four main places that managers and governments in search of nonstate finance for infrastructure can go: international institutions, the world's commercial banks, stock markets, and bond markets. By tradition, international institutions such as the World Bank and the EBRD are usually the first port of call because they have long global experience in making substantial loans for infrastructure projects and are willing to lend where commercial banks fear to tread. This, however, is a stopgap solution. Private capital markets dwarf international institutions in the financial resources at their command. But most commercial banks remain haunted by the debt crisis of the 1980s, which was linked to infrastructure development in the Third World (though heavy government borrowing in Poland and Hungary also played a part in causing this financial anxiety). One investment banker in Prague comments that it is "extraordinary how few Western banks seem to be serious lenders" for infrastructure purposes in the region.

Commercial banks may be cautious; equity markets appear to be more gung-ho. Between 1990 and 1995, report economists at the World Bank's Private Infrastructure Database, transition countries raised $2.8 billion through infrastructure privatizations (a sum that excludes telecommunications). Such privatizations are likely to gather pace. In 1996, investors have snapped up stakes in Lithuanian and Estonian ports, and Russia began to sell shares in everything from rails to shipyards.

Bond finance is another option. In several respects it looks like a good fit in the region. Bond markets command large amounts of capital and are comfortable with maturities of fifteen or twenty years, long periods of time that tend to bother bankers. The Czech Republic is considering turning to the Euromarket to raise $500 million over the next two years to help finance infrastructure. Yet issues from even the most fiscally prudent of transition governments, such as the Czechs, are more sellable if they are government-linked. Lending to projects that are not underwritten by a government is very tricky, even for bond investors. Governments may need to guarantee payment if privatized or commercialized infrastructure firms are to succeed in the bond market. The snag is that such sovereign guarantees may be bad incentives for nominally private businesses and are, in any case, likely to be in increasingly short supply as governments worry about their existing debts.

State guarantees are usually a necessity when a third source of funding—institutional investors such as pension funds—is sought. Funds that specialize in private infrastructure developments are attractive because they offer flexible deals, often mixing secured and subordinated debt, equity and bridge financing that can cover the stages of a project that pose the most risk, that is, the initial construction work, when unanticipated problems often come to the fore. The EBRD reckons that there are at least sixteen big funds that specialize in this activity, but only two of them (with a combined investment capacity of mere $150 million) are active in the transition region, and these are present only because they have received backing from the EBRD or the World Bank's commercial arm, the International Finance Corporation. More hope for this type of funding may come when transition countries develop their own institutional investors in the form of vital domestic pension fund and life insurance industries.

It may be possible to sell a deal without a government guarantee. Estonia's planned privatization of the Port of Tallinn is being propelled by Finnish, Swedish, and Danish maritime firms willing to finance port improvements without government guarantees, but only if they get a piece of the port's ownership. In Slovenia, a consortium of Austrian and Italian banks have come up with a scheme for lending to the country's international rail freight lines modeled on aircraft leasing. Yet the ingenuity and rarity of these projects is telling. The problem is that, given the so-called political risk in the postcommunist world, coming up with a reliable way of delivering long-term project finance for infrastructure in the transition countries, without the need for governments to underwrite it in some way, will be difficult for many years to come.

10.6 The Risk Business

The most obvious source of difficulties for infrastructure projects is politics. Many of those in search of finance make great play of their political connections. When Lithuanian construction firms were making a pitch to German investors interested in supporting reconstruction of the highway linking the three Baltic countries, the Lithuanians made great boasts about their closeness to the then ruling postcommunist government. Now that the postcommunists have lost power, that advantage has disappeared instantly. The same problem existed in Romania, where state infrastructure managers were often closely allied to the former president, Ion Iliescu.

Even if the risk of political upheaval is put aside, political risk can still exist. Investors in freight companies, for example, want a reasonable return on their investment. In many countries, however, the rates that shippers can charge are substantially controlled, and the state often exploits its licensing procedures and property ownership when it leases equipment to competitors. Ukraine provides many ripe examples here. In 1996, Kiev's cabinet of ministers tried to force nonstate shipping companies to pay licensing fees set at more than the value of their gross revenues.

Innovative companies have been hit particularly hard. Kiev Airlines got off the ground in the chaotic early days of the country's independence, when the former Moscow-centered system of air travel within and without the old Soviet Union broke down. Kiev Airlines, a private operation, began to lease unused state-owned aircraft. It set a fixed schedule (including flights to eleven countries that previously had no direct air links with Ukraine) and stuck to its promised prices, attracting customers who were unwilling to rely on the new state airline, Air Ukraine.

Efficient ticket distribution was established by the upstart airline, including free home delivery of tickets—high-quality consumer services unheard of in Ukraine. Kiev Airlines even invested $1.5 million in rehabilitating airports throughout the country. By 1993, the airline commanded 16% of total passenger flights originating with Ukrainian air enterprises. But in Ukraine, it seems, no business success can go unpunished. Bureaucrats began to bully and meddle, and by 1995, the company found itself with its back to the wall, its working capital impounded and its directors under arrest.

That tale would be more shocking if it were not so common and governments not so slow in learning the lessons of such debacles. These lessons are straightforward: investors will put in financial capital only if they can be sure that a government will, in return, commit its political capital to the tricky business of establishing transparent regulatory procedures enforced by law, phasing out price controls and ending the grotesque subsidies and rampant favoritism available to state-owned infrastructure companies.

There are also more direct financial consequences of political uncertainty. Foreigners will lend to infrastructure projects in dollars or D-marks, but an airline or port will earn money in rubles or krowns. If the krowns were suddenly to fall in value against the dollar or D-mark, how will the currency risk be balanced between borrowers and lenders? Questions like these are particularly problematic in the transition countries, where few currencies are both stable and convertible and the question exists as to whether or not access to foreign exchange can be guaranteed at all.

Looking further into the future, some investors are also beginning to worry about the environmental risks associated with infrastructure investments. What if "green" parties gain ground in the region and begin to insist that investors clean up the toxic environments—usually found around infrastructures such as ports and rail yards—that communism left behind? The amount of environmental damage in the region suggests that investors run a big risk of one day being saddled with big clean-up costs.

Balancing risks makes concluding infrastructure investments notoriously complicated. Haggling between governments, contractors, and bankers over big projects like airport development can take years, as it did in Ukraine. In this tug-of-war between investors and borrowers, investors have the upper hand in one powerful way: the longer governments delay in undertaking reform and reconstruction, the more urgent their infrastructure needs become. And international financiers have no shortage of projects clamoring for capital around the globe. This competition for capital will help to determine much of the future of the transition countries.

Because suppliers of capital are spoiled, with a wide range of places in which they can invest, borrowers are locked in a virtuous circle in which, aware of the fierce competition, they struggle to improve their attractiveness to investors. And investors, as they look around the region, need to know how easy it will be for them to get their money into or out of a country or to sell their stakes. They must look at market access, the competition their investment will receive from subsidized state activities, the legal and regulatory environment, the transparency of business procedures, and the reliability and financial health of local partners. They must weigh the allure of giant markets such as Russia and Ukraine, with their monumental infrastructure needs (and thus potential for big profits), against the relative certainty of doing business in the more developed markets of Slovenia, Poland, Hungary, the Czech Republic, Estonia, and even Slovakia (despite the mercurial Vladimir Meciar).

10.7 Flying Low

The Geneva-based IATA estimates that, combined, airlines in the region will need to spend at least $15 billion before the end of the century to replace aircraft that are becoming either technologically or legally obsolete. But fare wars (as competition increases) and excess capacity have made the profits needed to sustain such investment elusive. Latvia's state airline, indeed, went bankrupt last year. So, too, would others if governments, out of fear of political consequences, did not stubbornly subsidize these expensive ways to wave the flag. Instead of biting the bullet and sorting out their problems on their own, most airline managers—and the aircraft and engine makers who supply them—are placing their hopes on the notion that economic recovery will herald their salvation.

To be sure, infrastructure in the region is a big and growing business. Russia's eighty-seven regions, republics, autonomous areas, and territories, for example, are clamoring for the airline services that tradition-bound Aeroflot and other state lines cannot meet. Tartarstan's government is buying its own fleet of small jets. "Bush pilot" operations are mushrooming throughout the provinces of the "Wild East." So persistent is the demand for aircraft that, although most Russian defense companies have fallen on hard times, at least two hundred are surviving by meeting such pent-up demands for small, light aircraft estimated at 10,000 units per year.

But although economic growth spurs demand for certain kinds of air travel, overall supply in the transition countries over the past six years tended to exceed demand. In 1995, the region's scheduled airline services carried 3% fewer passengers than in 1990, the first year of transition, and according to IATA estimates, there was little or no change in 1996. Yet over the same period airlines increased the number of available seats by 5%, primarily due to the entrance of Western competitors such as Lufthansa, Delta, and Austrian Airlines. The irony, and part of the reason for excess supply, is that hidebound state airlines do not adapt to new conditions and tend to concentrate their flights, and thus their losses, on the same routes. Almost all of Eastern Europe's airlines fly passengers to Moscow and St. Petersburg, where landing and other fees are high. IATA pundits reckon the number of seats unfilled on these flights is equal to one jet load per day.

In the world of airlines in the countries of transition, the yield from each air passenger is thus now a function of competition. This means, inevitably, lower prices, best afforded not by giants like Aeroflot, with their aging equipment and inflated payrolls, but by lower-cost national entrants like Air Estonia and Adria (Slovenia), using second-hand airplanes bought for next to nothing. Still, shedding capacity—IATA estimates that one third of flights in the region are permanent loss makers—is easier said than achieved. An aircraft cannot recoup its maintenance cost by sitting on the ground. But putting it in the air adds extra seats to an already saturated market, and these will be sold only at a cut price determined by the market, not by the airline's need for profit. In that situation, nobody wins except—in the short term at least—the consumer.

The directors of Aeroflot (a state airline dismissed by one executive of Poland's increasingly competitive LOT as an "employment agency") argue that cutting prices and routes leads to self-destruction. At a meeting with Dutch bankers in 1996, the airline's executives pointed out that if a more efficient carrier cuts its prices to take market share from less efficient competitors, or to meet the challenge of new competitors, the less efficient one must match the cut to keep its passengers and stay in business. Unless the prices stimulate a significant increase in demand, both carriers will supposedly earn less than before, and the more efficient carrier will follow the less efficient on the flight path to collapse.

Aeroflot's analysis of regional airline economics enrages reformers. Why, they argue, should the more efficient carrier collapse since the less efficient would collapse first and thus remove excess capacity to the benefit of the surviving carrier? But the thesis cannot be ignored when some of the region's least efficient airlines remain in ministerial hands and are, all too obviously, political status symbols: like those wayward European airlines Alitalia and Air France, many transition country airlines remain immune to bankruptcy or normal commercial pressures.

Indeed, throughout the region, airline policy has primarily focused on the idea of creating flag-carrying champions. Free-market-oriented Estonia, for example, has balked at selling its state airline to foreign investors (SAS in particular) for fear that Tallinn will become merely a stopover and not a hub. Only Moldova has succeeded in completely privatizing its airline industry, at least on paper. Two distinct companies—Moldovan Airlines and Renan—have been forged from the local rump of Aeroflot that Moldova inherited on independence. The international airport at Chisinau has also been put into the hands of an independent authority. But without the big handouts all three companies get from the treasury, none would still be in business.

Nor is privatization making great strides in the area of airport construction and management. Some of its enemies are surprising, at least at first glance: international airlines are often among the biggest opponents, fearing that privately owned airports would levy higher charges than state-owned terminals. But it often simply suits international airlines to keep airports weak. To gain landing rights, airlines often promise to help to defray any deficit in an airport's operating budget; sometimes this promise is in exchange for giving the airlines a share in the airport's commercial revenues from restaurants and parking concessions. Such arrangements also usually convey the power to veto airport development and hence, perhaps, to keep out competitors' flights. A recent study by the World Bank found this type of deal most common at airports where one airline has a big hub.

There is also another barrier to the private sector's ability to provide the region with the modern airports it needs. Permission to build or expand an airport is always politically sensitive. (This holds true for most infrastructure projects. In the Czech Republic, for example, construction on a proposed highway link with Germany has been stalled for years by the objections of a few small towns.) Even when permission is granted, airport construction is expensive and risky, whoever is paying: remodeling Budapest's Ferihegy is reckoned to have skyrocketed to three times the price it was supposed to cost. Reconstruction of Kiev's Borispol Airport, supposedly a government priority, took two years longer than planned because of the government's inability to repay the first part of a DM 4.65 million loan advanced by Daimler Benz Aerospace.

10. 8 Flying High

Still, stirrings of aviation reform are becoming visible. After Latvia's state-owned airway Latavio went bankrupt (a casualty of the country's savage banking crisis, when a Riga court ordered Latavio's financial assets frozen because they were deposited in a bank under investigation), it was replaced by Air Baltic, a joint venture with Sweden's SAS that insists on workplace innovation. Despite local labor laws that demand detailed job descriptions, for example, Air Baltic's employees must be versatile, with accountants turning their hands to sales and managers asked, at times, to unload luggage. In Poland, Hungary, and the Czech Republic, the change at state airlines LOT, Malev, and CSA has been slow, but pervasive. Many loss-making flights within the region have been abandoned. Employees now receive extensive training in serving customers, who used to be taken for granted. Instead of lavishing funds on pricey headquarters for managers, LOT's bosses squat in a disused army barracks on the edge of Warsaw's airport.

LOT's mechanics department, moreover, has been transformed into an individual profit center and has so improved its performance that most Western airlines now use it to service flights stopping in Warsaw, instead of keeping their own personnel on the ground as they do, say, in Kiev. A buying spree early in the transition process that saddled the Ministry of Transport, not LOT, with debt, has given the airline one of the most modern air fleets in the world. Sales at both LOT and Malev have increased since 1995, and net income has improved to the point that both companies claim to be breaking even, at the very least. But the job is not finished, particularly as LOT continues to employ more than twice the number of people it needs to get the job done. One reason for this is a law that forbids LOT from sacking its employees, forcing the company to get around this restriction by transferring some unnecessary workers to the profitable casinos it operates jointly with Marriott Hotels.

Because its managers are more independent, LOT has been set free to borrow a winning strategy from the United States. This is the "hub" system, whereby one airport acts as a central point where passengers are delivered in order to transfer to second flights that will take them to their final destination. Hubs save money because they assure that more flights are filled, and they eliminate the need for a large, expensive ground support staff at each airport. LOT's scheme is deceptively simple: because it maintains a web of flights throughout Eastern Europe and the NIS, it is able to funnel passengers from such countries as Ukraine, Russia, Romania, and Moldova (these travelers often prefer LOT's gleaming new Boeing jets to the decaying Ilyushins and Tupolevs flown by their national airlines) through Warsaw on their way to the West, and Western passengers through Warsaw on their way to destinations in the east. One result of this is that LOT's passenger volume is up 16% in the years between 1994 and 1996, perhaps the best performance in the region.

The success of such transformations of infrastructure enterprises into commercially oriented firms has been made possible in part by an often belated realization by politicians that they make bad infrastructure managers. This depoliticization of management begins to expose firms to such normal market pressures as contract enforcement and bankruptcy. Moreover, the managers of Malev and LOT have had financial goals, if not yet profitability, added to the performance criteria written into management contracts.

These incentives are also reinforced by the desire of all these airlines to attract outside investors. Such investments have come in: Malev sold 30% of its shares to Alitalia, and another 5% to Italy's Simset at a price of $77 million in 1992. (It also succeeded in privatizing its maintenance operations through the formation of a joint venture with the American Lockheed.) Airline industry wags suggest, however, that sales to European state airlines will do little or nothing to help transition airlines to reform. "What are they going to teach us?" quipped one CSA executive who participated in forging the airline's stormy marriage to Air France. "How to pad the payroll and surrender to unions? At this, we are already expert."

The experience of CSA is probably an exception. Usually, outside influence means growing pressure on firms to improve their performance in order to raise shareholder value. Moreover, to attract outside investors the Polish, Hungarian, and Czech governments were forced to insulate the airlines from ministerial manipulation, both by enshrining the private property status of airline assets in law and by developing a transparent system of pricing and other aspects of commercial regulation. The EBRD argues that this latter reform is of fundamental importance. For when states are simultaneously owners and regulators, "they retain more scope for involvement in the activities of infrastructure enterprises."

10.9 Off the Tracks

Are such reforms good enough to restore crumbling infrastructure services? For all its newfound commercial veneer, LOT and other airlines in the region, like their rail and sea counterparts, still receive considerable indirect subsidies in the form of tax write-offs of debt and other invisible handouts. Subsidies are even more entrenched in such areas as small rural rail, air, and barge routes that will never be economically efficient, whoever owns them. Slovakia's Ministry of Transport reckons that such stretches of rail track account for about a third of the cost of the government's railroad subsidies. These areas might be better served by bus. However, until they have been placed in the private sector, no one will be able to tell.

Railway executives in the transition countries are usually as hostile as the region's airline managers to change and movements toward privatization, with ministers often staunchly supporting managerial obstructionism. A former Bulgarian deputy minister of transport, Latchezar Lalov, was not unusually hidebound by the region's standards: "While I am in this post," he declared, "I will not allow the state to be sold out." Zoltan Rigo, the longtime head of MAV, Hungary's state railway, declared in 1996 that "naive reforms" were the biggest threat to the transport sector, not the sclerotic policies and miserly investment that eat away at rail services in his country—last year, indeed, 90 % of freight trains in Hungary failed to complete runs within two hours of schedule. Small wonder, then, that Mr. Rigo's head rolled in November 1996, a sign perhaps that even entrenched infrastructure managers are beginning to feel ministerial wrath.

Such signs are still more of an exception, rather than the rule. Romanian rail passengers, for example, have patiently borne six national strikes and uncountable local wildcat walkouts in the past two years, and Romanian taxpayers are preparing to take on all railway debts (estimated at $2 billion) as part of a vague restructuring plan cooked up during the final days of the Iliescu regime. All the while, every year since 1989, the Romanian railway has received less in fares and freight charges than it does in government handouts.

Throughout the region railways are a surreal business, an activity where commercial criteria are, if ever applied, usually wrongly applied. According to the EU's transport commission, transition country railways have gulped down subsidies equal to 60% of their operating budgets since 1991 and yet have still managed to lose market share, both in commuter services and in freight carried. Between 1991 and 1996, the use of passenger rail declined by 40% (despite increased subsidies for passenger tickets, as governments force railways to bear some of the costs of falling incomes), while the use of cars and trucks has more than quadrupled. Although the overall freight market in the region has grown since 1994, rail's share of it has fallen. Altogether, from the dominant position it held in the socialist era, in 1996 rail held only 28% of the passenger market and 43% of the freight market.

The delay in reforming railways is not unique to the region. In Europe, only Britain has privatized its rail network. In France, subsidies to state intercity lines (SNCF) have been growing by three times the rate of inflation in the 1990s. Reform, however, is not impossible. The British have divided their rail services into distinct passenger, freight, and international companies, with commercial standards set for each. These changes have delivered substantial new private investments despite a corresponding decline in state subsidies.

Reform, however, must be comprehensive, including management changes and financial responsibility. Pruning bloated staff, for example, while useful, is unlikely to deliver enough savings to increase investment or efficiency. In Slovakia, the EU transport department figures that one in five rail jobs that existed in 1990 has disappeared. Yet Slovak railways are still riddled with inefficiencies, as freight continues to travel, on average, at a speed of only twenty kilometers per hour, one third of the speed of trucks. No surprise, then, that rail transport is losing more and more business to the country's myriad of usually low-cost private haulers. Trucks, indeed, have been increasing their share of freight hauled by 10% a year in each of the past five years.

One reason railways remain somewhat immune to change is that oversight responsibility for them is divided among a jumble of ministerial departments. In Slovenia, four different ministries need to sign off on any changes to rail subsidies, passenger services, or freight deliveries. (The same sort of bureaucratic web holds other infrastructure industries in thrall. In Russian aviation, for example, there were in 1994—the last time the government made an official count, already a worrying factor—111 distinct design bureaus for aircraft and 134 aviation plants. Responsibility for these was divided between the ministries of interior, economy, foreign trade, and defense.) Most countries, moreover, possess at least four different sorts of rail operations: long-distance and international passenger trains, intercity and commuter trains, urban metros and trams, and freight, each with both its managers and committees of managers supposedly charged with coordinating their activities. Such coordination, however, usually takes the form of stifling competition between the services. In no country in the region is oversight for any one of these vested in one ministry alone.

The companies that provide these services vary enormously. At one extreme, Estonia has sold shares in its metros and a few of its commuter lines to investors. Hungary, belatedly, has set commercial standards that MAV must meet and has opened transport service to penetration by private companies (mostly through leasing arrangements). At the other extreme, Ukrainian State Railways must be one of the few empires still run according to a five-year plan. In the middle are such countries as Latvia, Slovakia, and Slovenia, who are dithering over reforms and privatization schemes.

In almost every country, governments are admitting that change must come. The situation is, indeed, desperate. Rail freight volume has fallen by over 50% throughout the region, and 25% of all track is reckoned by the EBRD to be in unsatisfactory technical condition. Even in Romania, the state railway authority acknowledges that it has to alter its ways.

While Western Europe—where many countries in the region look for models—may not be the best example, experiences in other parts of the world show that railways need not always be a bottomless pit for state subsidies. In several Asian countries, even commuter railways can make money. The Kowloon-Canton Railway Corporation (KCRC) in Hong Kong receives no subsidies at all and yet made a profit of HK $901 million on sales of HK $3 billion last year; it is planning to invest HK $75 billion in a railway through the west of the territory that it claims will bring a 12% return on investment. KCRC and other Asian metros seize two advantages also available to transition country rail lines: low wages and particularly crowded cities. According to a recent study by the American management consultancy firm A. T. Kearney, the Paris metro carried the same number of passengers per kilometer as KCRC, but its labor-adjusted costs per passenger were four times higher.

More generally, according to the study, the reason for the success of Asian companies is that they have been given far greater freedom to set their own fares and fee schedules and to reinvest in equipment and rolling stock as they wish. Like other businesses in the region, they have had to plan for the future and prepare their own solutions to problems. Can similar things happen in the transition countries? Budapest's Mayor Gabor Demszky has said that his city's metro—its original line is the oldest on the European continent—must "be a business." Some of his advisors want to do the same with suburban lines by separating track from rolling stock and then opening rail track to and from the city to all comers. On other types of lines, some of the free-market-oriented advisors around Romania's president Constantinescu want to make it easier for railway companies of one country to run services across the tracks of another. They think that such competition will spur competitive juices among Bucharest's somnolent rail managers.

This is the right way to go. The easy solution—throwing money at the problem, as in France with its pricey high-speed trains—is unavailable to postcommunist ministers who can barely make ends meet now. Instead, transport ministers should use their poverty to force through the types of reforms that will make railways more competitive, setting ticket prices to cover both commuter and freight costs; charging managers with the job of meeting financial goals, not merely with providing ersatz social services; focusing companies on one particular activity, say, intercity travel or freight services, where managers can look for specific opportunities to make profits instead of floundering about trying to maintain all the old services they used to perform when budgets didn't matter. Restructuring of this sort will be painful, no doubt, but without it railways will continue to slip into economic irrelevance.

10.10 Roads to Riches?

There is another way to bring the discipline of the market to bear: concession and leasing arrangements. These forms of commercialization deliver managerial discipline and the incentive of profit, but politicians are often afraid of them, especially in those areas, such as roads, that have always been accessible without any charge.

Most politicians in the region are convinced that charging motorists for the use of roads is political poison. With so many people enjoying the pleasures of car ownership for the first time (the number of privately owned automobiles in the transition countries increased tenfold since 1990, reckoned the European Driver's Union), road pricing is the last thing that most ministers want to contemplate. (The Czechs, however, charge hefty fees for special licenses required to drive on the country's motorways.) And yet they have not been able to rule out the idea entirely, if only because their own officials tell them that tolls may be a good way to attract sorely needed investors to the area of road construction, and transport economists reckon that charging drivers may be the only way to prevent today's traffic jams from becoming tomorrow's gridlock.

Transition countries roads are starved for investment. Taxes earmarked for this purpose are often diverted. In Bulgaria, for example, only 30% of the funds collected for road maintenance through fuel, auto, and truck levies in 1995—a mere 8 million lev—was actually turned over to the ministry of transport to fund road improvement: the rest stayed in the general state coffers.

One way around the roadblock of uncertain finance is to offer concessions for private investors. Here Hungary has been a pioneer. The country's most advanced truck terminal, near the town of Zahony in northeast Hungary, for example, was built by a private company, Europark. Truckers are attracted not only because the terminal's facilities are a big improvement on other terminals, but because its operators help to speed the process of crossing into nearby Ukraine. A system has been established whereby trucks receive customs clearance one mile before the border customs post used by other road vehicles, often saving hours of waiting. The trucks are then formed into a convoy and taken across the border into Ukraine.

Toll roads are another Hungarian experiment. Like elsewhere in the region, responsibility for the state of roads is divided between central and local governments. Unlike other countries, however, Hungary has bitten the bullet to make investors in road building welcome. The First Hungarian Concession Motorway Co. (ELMKA), for example, was granted the right to build and operate a 42-kilometer toll portion of the country's M1 motorway between Gyor and Hegyeshalom, the toll concession is set to last for thirty-five years, and another fifteen years may be added if both parties agree. A second concession followed soon after for constructing and operating tolls on a portion of the M15 between Mosonmagyarovar and Rajka. A new bridge over the Danube at Szekszard is also being constructed on a concession basis.

ELMKA is able to make a go of this concession because the toll the firm charges is hefty: in Greece, for example, the average toll is equivalent to 2.3 forints per kilometer, and in France tolls average something like 12.80 forints per kilometer. Along ELMKA's stretch of the M1, tolls equal 30.10 forints per kilometer. Karoly Lederer, ELMKA's president, justifies the high costs because his company does not receive any state guarantees for the risk it took in building and agreeing to maintain the motorway. Motorists don't seem to be put off by these fees; traffic on the motorway was heavy during the first six months of its existence, despite there being a free alternative route running parallel to the north. The concession the state offered for the Mosonmagyarovar motorway was even more generous. Here tolls could be placed on a stretch of the road the government itself had already begun to build before turning over construction to the concessionaire.

Just how tricky the concession and road building business can be, however, was illustrated by a recent spat between the Bulgarian government and would-be Austrian investors. In 1993, an auction was held for foreign bidders to construct a new motorway linking Bulgaria with Serbia. Austria's Macolan Holdings won with the highest bid and was contracted to build-not only the highway, but also hotels and other amenities along the route. Macolan's concession to administer the road was to last thirty years.

Soon, however, the government began to balk at the toll levels agreed upon in the contract. Once it began to be picked over by bureaucrats hostile to privatization, the deal started to unravel. During one of the country's numerous changes of government, Macolan was ousted and an Italian firm was awarded the contract. Although many reform-minded Bulgarian municipalities have succeeded in contracting out road maintenance to private firms, the episode with Macolan set outside investors, and not only those in Bulgaria, to thinking. If tolls charged to affluent car users are so politically vulnerable, how is it possible that a subway or bus system can be made commercially viable? And if fares or freight charges are subsidized, can investors rely on governments to make up the revenue shortfall?

10.11 Against the Tide

While timid in taking such steps in road building and other infrastructure services, several countries have embraced maritime privatization, if not enthusiastically then at least solidly, and are trying to improve the efficiency of these industries by turning ports and shipping lines into globally competitive companies. Here Russia has gone fast and far. The Russian shipping industry has benefited enormously from decentralization and the competition that results. For the most part, the Kremlin has phased out direct operating subsidies, while docks and ship repair have been taken out of central administrative hands and given to local authorities, who are made responsible for their financial wellbeing as well as for operations.

Maritime restructuring began soon after the fall of communism. Shipping lines, which previously were linked to specific ports for their operations, were hived off to become independent entities. Central Moscow control of ports was abolished in favor of an independent "marine administration" headquartered at each port. These bodies are left to sort out the port's activities and prospects on their own, and they now compete fiercely for business with each other. Without oversight from Moscow, and mindful of the choices open to shippers to unload their goods elsewhere, marine administrators no longer have an excuse to avoid hard decisions, particularly as no local government has the wherewithal to subsidize big and continuing losses.

Tough decisions, however, remain. One concerns the unitary nature of port administration. No Russian port has yet seen fit to divide itself into distinct businesses such as harbor pilots for guiding ships to their berths, stevedore companies to load and unload ships, container operations, warehousing, and transport (by truck, rail, or both) of goods to and from port. By keeping all activities under one management, Russian ports invite inefficiency and overmanning. They need look no further than next-door Estonia to see that dividing port functions pays off. Market opening activities within port operations helped to spur continuing increases in use: the passenger flow through the Port of Tallinn alone, for example, grew from 2.3 million in 1994 to 3.9 million in 1995, as ferry services competed for passengers, to cite just one possible cause. Tonnage passing in and out of the port has been growing at more than 15% a year for five consecutive years, one reason being, perhaps, that a variety of firms compete to move goods out of the port more efficiently and at more competitive prices.

When it comes to shipping lines, change in Russia has been as pervasive as any in regional infrastructure industries. Today, nine big domestic shipping lines compete in the Russian market and vie for business in shipping natural resources and importing capital goods to and from Asia's booming markets. Although domestic industrial production has fallen monumentally over the past five years, Russia's shipping lines have managed to capture the bulk of the country's new imports (meaning that their budgets are met by contract, not subsidy) and are winning a growing share of world shipping between non-Russian ports. To spur even greater innovation, Murmansk Shipping has set up "profit centers" for each of its businesses, borrowed pricing structures from Finnish shipping lines, and encouraged staff with bonuses for exceeding promised delivery dates. Such steps, humdrum in most Western industries, have made Russian shippers able to compete head-to-head with the most efficient lines in the world, according to economists at London's Baltic Exchange, the world's premier maritime market.

In the future, Russian shipping companies will have to compete even in the local markets many now take for granted, where they possess monopoly control usually established with the connivance of politicians. The national maritime agency is asking for the power to vet and, if necessary, veto all deals that will bring a particular line into monopoly position at any port. As deregulation strips companies of the cozy rules that used to govern them, the danger is that they will try to secretly fix prices among themselves. Last year, the government raided the offices of two Baltic shippers in search of evidence of a suspected cartel. To further insure competition, a national mergers authority is empowered to prevent mergers among shipping companies for the next ten years.

Foreign investors are taking note: shares in shipping companies are among the most active on the Moscow exchange. Not only are the assets of ports and shipping lines relatively easy to evaluate, at least when compared to other Russian firms, but shippers carry little or no debt and thus have considerable leeway to borrow for fleet refurbishment. The EBRD, indeed, has already "pre-qualified" five of these shipping lines for loans. Shipping companies, moreover, hold another advantage for investors: ships can be seized in foreign ports if loans are not repaid and contracts are not honored.

10.12 Facing the Facts

Only by freeing infrastructure industries from the state's dead hand can the region's hopes for improved services and growing investment in infrastructure be fulfilled. Grudgingly, the process is underway. Poland, Estonia, the Czech Republic, Latvia, Slovenia, Hungary, and Russia have removed some of the complex ministerial oversight that paralyzed infrastructure managers and forced them to respond to a bureaucratic maze of masters. Companies such as CSA have introduced bonuses based on performance for managers in an attempt to align managerial interests with the interest of private shareholders.

Pressure for continued reform will come from all directions: investors, businessmen, consumers, government. Each will become more demanding, not less. Investors bring flocks of accountants and advisors in their wake. Stock market analysts—Hungary is a good example here—help to diagnose the problems facing infrastructure firms. Bankers will tell the firms they advise to take the often bitter pills they recommend in order to secure the credits they need and the rising share prices they desire. These advisors will be constant catalysts for change.

With commercialization, concessioning, and outright privatization another ghost will disappear: the monopoly that governments ostensibly feared but, in fact, established. For competition is the greatest force for change. Whether it is LOT and Aeroflot that are facing Western competitors like Delta and British Airways, or national railroads that are challenged eventually on intercity passenger and freight routes by Europe's high-tech systems, competition will incite greater efficiency, as firms will have to fight hard to keep the most lucrative parts of their business.

In the end, infrastructure reform demands investment, but that can come only with improvements in corporate control. Great strides have been taken, as we have seen. Yet progress remains erratic, and more needs to be done, particularly to improve transparency and allow domestic and international investors to throw their weight around in infrastructure industries' boardrooms.

Sometimes the rhetoric of reform is merely a foil for old-fashioned intrigue, as we saw in Ukraine's airline industry. Nonetheless, as in other areas of industry, real reform cannot be long in coming. Infrastructure managers may still try to ignore investors and consumers as long as they can. There was a time when all they had to do was obey their ministerial masters. That time is gone.

11
The Taxman Cometh
Taxation and the Postcommunist Transition

"The art of taxation," quipped Jean-Baptiste Colbert, treasurer to Louis XIV, "consists in so plucking the goose as to obtain the largest amount of feathers with the least possible amount of hissing." Colbert's Gallic wisdom seems nowadays to be the motto of the postcommunist governments, one seconded by the IMF and a bevy of international advisers.

Countries in the region, indeed, are revising their tax systems and seeking to improve collection so as to close the gap between what states spend and the revenues they manage to raise. Failure here, everyone seems to agree, will make them slide back into recession. The hissing that governments fear most comes from cuts in social spending, not increased taxation.

This survey is written with the view of the geese in mind. Whether the plucking process delivers an abundance of down comforters for those doing the plucking is not something about which the geese are much concerned. They don't mind surrendering some feathers, especially when they get something back in exchange. But they do not want the process to make them freeze or strip away their ability to fly. Before that happens, quite a few geese are likely to take off with their feathers, stashing them where they are of more use to themselves. So the transition governments must do their plucking with care, skill, and, given the high murder rate among tax collectors, a lot of luck. Above all, for governments to succeed, they must learn to live with less.

10.1 State Penury

Throughout the postcommunist world, government budgets are in disarray because, it is alleged, the state is too weak to raise the money it needs. Until recently, Russia was billions of dollars and months behind in paying state pensions. So dire do Kremlin finances remain, indeed, that a few soldiers starved to death last spring in Siberia for lack of army provisions. Elsewhere, the situation is equally chaotic: rural teachers go unpaid in Kyrgyzstan, state hospitals go without supplies in Moldova and Romania, Bulgarian bureaucrats strike (and take bribes) because, they say, the state does not pay them.

In the more successful countries of Central Europe, the state can generally pay its bills, but some of it is done by printing more money, which makes inflation a monster that has nowhere been fully slain. While the advanced economies of the West are running inflation below 5%, even the paragons of financial discipline in the transition countries, such as Poland or Hungary, are still well in double-digit figures. Farther east or farther south, inflation is constantly threatening to destroy even the semblance of stability that has recently been won.

Why are governments in this fiscal mess? The conventional wisdom is that tax collection is outdated and inefficient, and tax evasion ubiquitous. As is usual with conventional wisdom, there are grains of truth in what it says. In this particular case, however, there is even more that is misleading.

People everywhere hate taxes, so getting a system that works—one viewed as basically fair and legitimate, in which evasion is not rampant, and which manages to fill the state coffers sufficiently to run a government that functions—is not something that can be put together either quickly or easily. So the transition countries start with a huge handicap. They have a highly developed (many would say—and we shall argue—highly overdeveloped) state that craves a big chunk of the meager wealth they produce to keep going. But like just about everything else inherited from the previous regime, the mode of financing the state is woefully inadequate under today's new conditions.

Under communism, taxation was a trivial job. Although citizens seemingly paid no taxes, social burdens were nevertheless imposed on them via low and unpaid wages, distorted prices, and the near-universal use of the so-called turnover tax—a charge on an enterprise's gross production, not its profits. Because production was mostly in state-owned enterprises and tightly controlled by planning authorities, and since the quantities as well as prices of goods sold (to other state companies) were also determined by state bureaucrats, the state simply had to decide what portion of what was produced was needed to satisfy its own demands. Evasion was, for all practical purposes, impossible—and irrelevant as well,—because the state could always print the money it needed and fund itself by inflation and/or shortages to consumers.

When communism collapsed, it was probably too much to ask that socialist forms of taxation disappear overnight. Although some governments started to rewrite them systematically, most grafted new tax laws onto the trunk of the old tax system. As a result, their tax codes resemble Frankenstein's monster—part living, part dead. And as taxes multiply, the cost of collection goes up and compliance goes down.

A survey by Russian Economic Barometer, a Moscow think-tank, shows that two-thirds of Moscow's small businessmen think vague and contradictory tax laws, and their enforcement, are the greatest threats to their firms. Another survey, conducted in 1996 by the World Bank economists Daniel Kaufmann and Paul Siegelbaum, found that Ukrainian managers were wasting 36% of their time dealing with tax matters. All the while, Ukrainian small shop owners have had to grapple with 150 different changes in the rate of Value Added Tax (VAT) and open their books to the prying eyes of six different government departments. (Small wonder that, according to the UN Economic Commission for Europe, Ukraine has the slowest pace of business start-ups in the postcommunist world.) Similar polls in Romania, Bulgaria, and Croatia reveal similar conclusions.

Even in the most advanced Central European countries, the value of stability is not something governments understand. Hungary's "Personal Income Tax" (PIT) law, for example, was the first income tax regime in the region. But, instead of allowing people to become accustomed to it and plan their lives accordingly, the law has had at least 20 different major amendments since its introduction. On top of these legislative changes, interpretation of the rules also constantly changes: in 1993, new PIT interpretations were issued only in late December, while employers should have deducted taxes from their employees' salaries according to these rules for the entire year.

10.2 Shadowlands

No surprise, then, that tax avoidance is rampant everywhere. By definition, of course, the shadow or black economy, where people hide from the taxmen, cannot be measured precisely. Even in the most developed economies guessing at its size and scope requires detective work. But including both legal earned income that goes unreported and illicit activities like drug dealing and smuggling, the shadow economy may account for up to half of total output in countries like Belarus, Bulgaria, Russia, and Ukraine. Romania, in fact, is planning to adjust official statistics to take account of its shadow economy—the size of which is estimated at anywhere between 20% and 40% of GDP.

Shadow activity may be even greater in Latvia. Riga's port has a long heritage of acting as a (sometimes secret) backdoor into Russia—a tradition revived since 1991 because of heavy-handed import/export controls in Russia and strong-armed governance in Belarus. Contraband destined for Belarus alone may equal 12% of total Latvian imports by volume, reckons the Latvian Ministry of Trade, but little or no taxes are gained from such smuggling.

Backstreet labor exchanges—unregulated labor markets—have arisen throughout the region. Builders hire workers when needed, with no obligation other than to pay them for that day's work (sometimes, among unscrupulous bosses, not even that). Job-seekers, many illegal or unwanted immigrants (Georgians in Moscow, Ukrainians in Prague, Lithuanians in Warsaw, Romanians in Budapest, Belarusians in Riga) are keen to work this way because they are paid in cash.

What makes this ubiquitous evasion possible is the change in the way people earn their livelihoods. In the old days, the tax collector could just sit comfortably in his office and count the money that flowed in. Now the economies of the postcommunist countries allow people to make money in a great variety of ways, without the state being able to control the flow.

A new service sector has mushroomed everywhere, as did other small businesses, shops, and manufacturing firms. Self-employment and part-time work are also common. In Lithuania and Slovakia, for example, as late as 1991 over 70% of household income arrived in old-fashioned wage packets. By 1996 only

45% and 40% respectively was declared as coming from that source: much of the remainder derived from self-employment or small businesses, many operating off the books and tax rolls.

These trends make it easier to hide in the shadows: concealing a business consultancy run from home is far simpler than concealing a state manufacturing plant or a salary from employment in it. Cash transactions multiply, and governments have difficulty monitoring such unadvertised person-to-person exchanges. Indeed, many people employed in the gray economy not only avoid paying taxes, but supplement their incomes by claiming unemployment benefits, thus exacerbating even more the fiscal problems of the state. Jobless rates in places like Hungary, which claims an official total of 20%, probably grossly overstate the true level of unemployment.

Because tax avoidance is so rampant, and underreporting of income and profits is taken for granted by tax officials, companies that honestly report their true income are assumed by tax collectors to be hiding even more, and so additional charges are imposed. This old communist trick, which was used to crush the last vestiges of private economic activity, continues in such places as Russia, Croatia, Ukraine, Macedonia, Moldova, and Lithuania. In Ukraine, for example, low-level tax officials are empowered to calculate a company's tax bill according to their own estimates, and as a result taxpayers confront three bleak choices: pay a heavy and unjust tax bill, bribe the taxman, or fight the charge and face a stiff fine on top of the taxes already assessed.

More thuggish enforcement also abounds. In Russia, Bulgaria, Belarus, and Ukraine masked and heavily armed police are known to swoop down on unsuspecting businesses, carting off any currency they may find, as well as any paperwork that may hint at where other wealth may be hidden. Slovak, Croatian, Moldovan, and Latvian tax police are fond of lurking outside restaurants, shops, and barbers, ready to pounce on businesses that cannot produce a record of a completed sale. (Both shop owners and customers can be fined if no receipt is found.) When caught, Bulgarian tax dodgers can expect three years in jail. Latvia prefers to beat its tax cheats with fines that can go as high as 25% of the value of a firm's annual turnover.

Given the size of the gray economy and the stakes often involved, tax collection in the transition countries is not only erratic, but dangerous. Last year, 26 tax collectors were killed in Russia, 74 seriously injured, six kidnapped, and 41 others saw their homes burned to the ground. Hungary has responded, in part, to the threats to its taxmen by forming a special 300-man "flying squad" of elite, specially trained tax collectors who act under the authority of the national police, not the tax bureaucracies of the Ministry of Finance.

But the biggest tax evaders are not the small shopkeepers and backstreet traders. Many of the region's elites nowadays frame tax laws so as to skew taxation away from industries they, or their cronies, control, curtailing (when not eliminating altogether) the elite's contributions to state revenues. Gazprom is undoubtedly Russia's most notorious example. Tax-exempt "stabilization funds" helped Gazprom salt away every year untaxed profits equal to its declared ones—perhaps $3.5 billion in 1996 alone. Only recently, after a shove from the IMF, did the government crack down and insist on Gazprom paying higher taxes. And Gazprom is not alone, because energy industry bosses everywhere in the transition countries are adept at skirting taxes.

10.3 Rich or Poor?

With the focus on fighting inflation and modernizing the state that is everywhere seen as necessary to push through economic reforms and assure future growth, international organizations insist that transition governments put their tax systems in order and reform their collection mechanisms. Indeed, they make their aid conditional on progress here. Unless the state can run a noninflationary budget and at the same time pay for the safety net required to cushion the side effects of the transition, these advisers say, economic reforms will become politically unsustainable. What modernization usually means, in this view, is that the old turnover taxes must be abolished, an efficient income tax system instituted, and VAT and other indirect taxes introduced.

Modernization of the state in general, and of tax collection systems in particular, is an important objective. But this survey points to another, much deeper problem at the root of the difficulties the transition governments face in making ends meet. It is not that they collect too little, but that they spend too much. Not a little too much, either, but far more than what any country in their position can afford, without choking off growth and heading into deeper trouble.

Moreover, in many places tax collection cannot be genuinely improved unless taxes go down, for part of the problem is that when taxes are sky-high, avoidance is much too attractive for the region's bloated and bumbling states to fight, and the cost of doing it skyrockets as well.

When the first postcommunist countries started their reform process, they were told—mostly by the IMF, which lent them money to stabilize their economies—that they must reduce subsidies to state businesses and force them to face the music of the market. Many countries—though by no means all—listened in that they stopped or reduced the myriad of price subsidies and some outright transfers, at least to enterprises without special political clout. This does not mean that these kinds of transfers have vanished or even that they are small. Poland, for example, spends a great deal per year to keep its inefficient coal mines in operation (polluting entire regions in the process).

Hungary (and nearly all other transition countries) went through a series of bank "recapitalizations," which is another name for putting billions of dollars into banks that do not know how to lend money, and thus indirectly into companies that borrow and don't pay back. About 7 % of Russia's GDP continues to go to enterprise subsidies, which largely benefit managers of badly run state enterprises, and various "state guarantees" for credits (which tend to be actual gifts) constitute additional hidden subsidies for the rich. Energy prices are nearly nowhere what the market demands. Still, the ubiquitous redistribution of income among enterprises is certainly down from what it was in the old days of the communist regime.

What neither the IMF nor reformers in the transition countries insisted on was that, beyond the industrial cross-subsidization, postcommunist states were running a myriad of other expensive programs on a scale they could not possibly afford. Here the proximity of Western Europe is partly to blame. Czechs, Estonians, Hungarians, Poles, and Slovenes have always felt, not without reason, if it was not for the communist boot they would be little different from Austria, Spain, or Italy. Many postcommunist countries, indeed, see themselves as an integral part of Europe, and they view Western Europe not only as a model for their own development, but also as something that is within their reach. Because Western Europe has been running governments that devour around 50 % of GDP, the transition countries took this hypertrophy of the state as something normal.

Should their Western neighbors (and the advisers paid by them) have told the postcommunist countries that they were deluding themselves? They may not have been in a good position to do this, but they certainly should have. This survey is not the place to discuss whether the level of government spending in Western Europe is sustainable or will need to be seriously scaled down. What is certain, however, is that no country ever got from where the transition economies are today to where their Western neighbors are now, while at the same time running government programs—*nota bene* consisting mostly of income transfers, rather than productive infrastructure investments—costing more than half of what the country produced.

Western Europeans themselves did not really develop their cradle-to-grave welfare systems until the last twenty or thirty years, i.e., when they were already quite rich. In the years when the West was growing fast (and thus getting rich), tax rates were far below what they are now. One common denominator among the rapidly expanding economies of Southeast Asia is the small size of their social welfare systems.

Indeed, as figure 11.1 shows, even compared to Western Europe, many transition countries are big spenders. When the extent of their spending is juxtaposed with their wealth, the contrast is striking: with GDP per capita five or ten times smaller than Western Europe, the share of government spending in the GDP of the transition countries is of a similar magnitude. Hungary grabs a greater percent of national wealth (50.6%) than rich, high-tax Germany (49%); Poland (48%), Czech Republic (45%), Slovakia (48%), and Slovenia (46%) take more than Britain (41.9%) and Ireland (37.6%).

Even the down-and-nearly-out Russia (41%) and Ukraine (39.3%) grab as a percent of national income more than the wealthy United States (33.3%) and Japan (36.2%). And all of these countries are way above what the truly fast-growing economies pay for their states: Thailand (16%), Taiwan (18%), Korea (20%), Chile (21%), or even the very rich and very paternalistic Singapore (26%).

Strangely, in some places things may be getting worse, not better. In Slovakia, for example, the share of GDP taken by the state, according to the Slovak Association of Taxpayers, is growing much faster than the economy. Indeed, the Meciar government now takes in almost 10% more of GDP in taxes than just four years ago. The government's lust for tax revenues is begin-

Figure 11.1

Government Spending

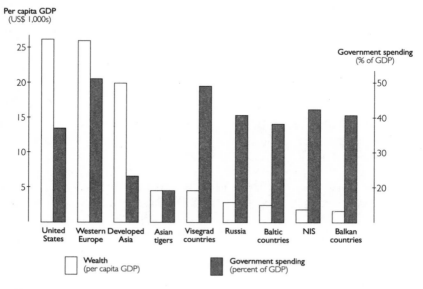

Per capita GDP
(US$ 1,000s)

Government spending
(% of GDP)

- Wealth (per capita GDP)
- Government spending (percent of GDP)

Note:
Western Europe: Germany, Austria, Netherlands
Developed Asia: Japan, Korea, Singapore, Taiwan
Asian tigers: Indonesia, Malaysia, Thailand
Visegrad countries: Czech Republic, Hungary, Poland, Slovakia
NIS: Belarus, Ukraine
Balkan countries: Bulgaria, Romania

Source: 1. GDP, spending and tax revenues: S&P (unless noted otherwise). 2. Tax and Social Security rates:1996 International Tax Summaries (Coopers & Lybrand). Wiley, 1996 (unless noted otherwise).

ning to bite. Ivan Miklos, architect of Slovakia's early privatization successes and a former minister, argues that tax arrears are
now growing at 10% annually.

10.4 Welfare for the Well-to-Do

Next to the belief that dizzying state expenditures of the transition countries are "normal," the greatest obstacle to curbing the
state's appetite is the widespread view that the state is spending
huge sums so as to provide a "safety net" for the poor, the old,
the unemployed, and the disadvantaged. How can we cut the

"social safety net," defenders of the state ask, at the very time when economic reforms create an ever-greater need to help those who have difficulties adjusting?

The fundamental flaw with this argument, says the Swedish economist Anders Aslund, who has studied state expenditures in several countries of the region, is that most of the money the state spends does not go to those who really need help. It is diverted, instead, from the general population to the better-off.

Russia, for example, which is, by far, not among the highest spenders in the region, spent 24% of its GDP for social expenditures in 1994. Of this amount, a mere 0.4% of GDP went to the "employment fund," and only half of that consisted of unemployment benefits, which went to truly poor people. "Social benefits" accounted for 2.4% of GDP, but about half of it was composed of subsidized holidays for the privileged. Family allowances, included in social benefits, amounted to about 1% of GDP, but working poor with several children did not receive this assistance. Actual social welfare for the poorest was only a fraction of 1% of GDP.

Much is heard about the misery of Russian pensioners. In fact, Russia's largest social transfers in 1994 were pensions—5.5–6% of GDP. But almost a third of this went to people under 60, who would not be retired in Western Europe. Many of these and other "pensioners" continue to work, while aged and ill people do not get needed additional support. Hardly any of these substantial social transfers are targeted to the truly poor. All the while nearly 5% of GDP went to housing subsidies, which are regressive: the larger your apartment, the more your housing is subsidized, and the poorest fifth of the population received no housing subsidies because they had no dwellings of their own. Aslund calculates that public expenditures could be cut by at least 15% of GDP in Russia and Ukraine from their 1996 levels, without any harm to the poor.

Interestingly, the most "reformed" countries of Central Europe are among the most profligate spenders on social programs that benefit the better-off. While government spending in the Central Asian post-Soviet republics has been brought down from its absurd heights (from 35% to 14.5% of GDP in Kyrgyzstan, for example, and to 19% in Kazakhstan) Hungary, the Czech Republic, Poland, and Slovakia devote no less than

30–35% of GDP to social expenditures, more than total public expenditure (including defense and infrastructure) in the United States, Switzerland, and Japan.

The reasons for this? Here is one small example: As far back as the 1950s, Polish peasants learned that being classified as "disabled" led to lower obligatory deliveries of foodstuffs and produce to the state, required by the communist authorities. Today, the rate at which Poland's citizens receive "disability" benefits would seem to make it a nation of cripples. In fact, the state simply lost control of the benefits it confers on people who often hold jobs and run businesses, while supplementing their income from the state coffers.

The ultimate explanation with regard to why the postcommunist states do not cut spending is the same as everywhere: politics. The truly poor and needy are not a large population bloc, and they tend to vote less often. The mostly rich and middle-class recipients of government largesse, by contrast, are politically active and tend to punish politicians who cut their benefits, no matter how inequitable. When spending gets cut, therefore, it is often where it is least justified: education (which builds human capital for the future) has taken huge cuts everywhere, as did infrastructure expenses (which increase the value of the existing capital stock and encourage more private investment). Welfare for the rich and the middle class, however, persists or is only minimally rationalized.

10.5 More is Less

Unless spending is cut, tax systems are unlikely to improve as states establish punishing rates of taxation to continue funding their extensive social welfare schemes. The most important comparative advantage of the transition countries is supposed to be their skilled labor available at low cost. Indeed, wages in the region are still quite low, as compared with the rest of Europe (though not with places like China, Indonesia, or Thailand, with which Eastern Europe does not like to be compared, but in which the GDP per capita is in fact much closer).

Cheap labor, however, begins to look much less cheap when social security contributions, falling mostly on employers, are added to the wages workers actually receive. The payroll tax in Thailand is 3%. Americans pay a 15% social security tax for their unemployment and state retirement benefits. Singaporeans get their pensions in exchange for a 20% tax on income up to a certain limit. Ultra socialist Sweden provides its proverbially generous benefits against the very large 45% payroll charge. None of these countries, however, can equal Hungary which imposes a whacking 54% payroll tax, or Poland, where the state takes 48 cents in social insurance for every dollar received by the worker (who must then pay an additional 21–45 % in income taxes), or the Czech Republic where the payroll tax is 47.5%. Bulgaria, Romania, Russia, and others are only a few percent behind (see figure 11.2).

Figure 11.2

Social Security Contributions

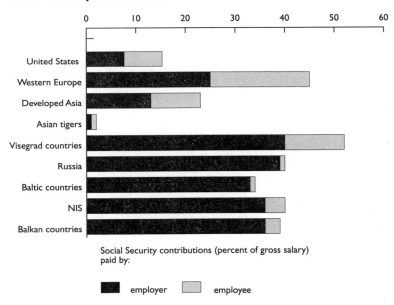

Social Security contributions (percent of gross salary) paid by:

■ employer   □ employee

Note:
Western Europe: Germany, Austria, Netherlands
Developed Asia: Japan, Korea, Singapore, Taiwan
Asian tigers: Indonesia, Malaysia, Thailand
Visegrad countries: Czech Republic, Hungary, Poland, Slovakia
NIS: Belarus, Ukraine
Balkan countries: Bulgaria, Romania

Source: 1. GDP, spending and tax revenues: S&P (unless noted otherwise). 2. Tax and Social Security rates: 1996 International Tax Summaries (Coopers & Lybrand). Wiley, 1996 (unless noted otherwise).

Payroll taxes are a fraction of the direct taxes the transition states impose on businesses and individuals. Corporate income taxes run around 40% throughout the region, and individual incomes are taxed at top marginal rates of between 40% and 50%. Moreover, unlike other countries, in which the highest rates of income tax are paid only by the highest earners, most transition countries allow inflation to push a much greater proportion of their taxpayers into the highest brackets.

In both 1993 and 1995, for example, Hungary failed to adjust its brackets even though inflation was well above 20%, meaning that people were paying higher taxes without earning any more money in real terms. This "bracket creep" meant that large and ever-increasing numbers of Hungarian taxpayers in 1995 were finding themselves in the highest tax bracket. Only when forecasts showed that it would not be long before an average income earner was taxed at the highest rate were brackets adjusted upward. That tax brackets are not indexed to inflation probably makes governments—not just in Hungary—quite a bit more tolerant of rising prices, as they in effect "raise" taxes by stealth so that politicians do not have to take the unpopular step of actually voting for a tax hike.

Results throughout the region are nothing short of ridiculous. In Ukraine, for example, after accounting for income, social security taxes, and VAT, the total cost of employing a worker averages three times the amount the worker takes home. When taxes rise to such levels, avoidance and evasion rise with them. This in turn makes the so-called tax base (the income subject to effective taxation) smaller, requiring still higher tax rates to maintain the same levels of revenues. At some point, which may have been reached in a number of countries, setting up a legitimate business is no longer a viable option.

Take the case of Nadezhda Derevyanko, a Muscovite who thought she had good a business idea. From a small boutique near Petrovsky Passage, she expanded into a full-scale clothing manufacturing firm called Linya, selling outfits popular with television personalities on Moscow's NTV. Then she ran afoul of taxes that haunt the small and successful in Moscow. Weeks after she filed her income statements to authorities in 1995, the city government quadrupled Linya's real estate taxes. Soon, two days a week had to be spent going to various ministries filling out tax forms. To make herself less visible, Derevyanko closed her shops and began selling directly to stores from an unlisted address.

High taxes in Russia and elsewhere also have other, unintended consequences. Many people complain, for example, that Russian companies do not disclose any information to their shareholders. Predictably, this depresses their value to outside investors, who refuse to put their money into companies that might produce the long-awaited recovery. But if Russian companies open their books to shareholders, they could not keep them closed to tax auditors. Unless they continue hiding their income from tax authorities, however, they will be broken by the excessive taxes they now avoid. This is also not what their shareholders want. What begins with taxes that are too high ends with large-scale corruption and stunted development of capital markets (see figure 11.3).

Given punishing rates of taxation, tax evasion, against which transition governments and their foreign advisers never cease to inveigh, may indeed be a saving grace without which things would be even worse. For businesses in the best position to evade—new and unburdened with the communist past, small, and often in the neglected service sector—are also the very ones that constitute the most dynamic sector of the transition economies, creating viable new jobs and wealth.

Many transition governments and international organizations, indeed, are trying hard to devise some means to assist new businesses through a myriad of preferential credits and other advantages. As every banker trying to lend to small businesses knows, however, these methods are quite costly, not the least because it is very difficult to identify those among new businesses (many of which will fail) that have a chance of success and deserve assistance. An effective tax exemption may just fit the bill: it is of value only to the successful (which have income to shield), and does not help the others.

Whatever the truth, life in the shadows imposes a high price. It is hard for underground businesses or individuals to advertise or otherwise reach potential customers. It is next to impossible for them to borrow money from legal sources, which increases their vulnerability to mafias and other criminal elements. They have no redress against corrupt or arbitrary officials, and the dead hand of the state must always be pushed aside. In the end, corruption may improve the life span and efficiency of individual businesses, but systemic tolerance for corruption will make the state's performance even more corrupt and its role in the economy even more invasive.

Figure 11.3

Corporate Taxes

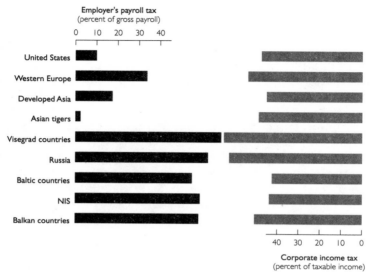

Note:
Western Europe: Germany, Austria, Netherlands
Developed Asia: Japan, Korea, Singapore, Taiwan
Asian tigers: Indonesia, Malaysia, Thailand
Visegrad countries: Czech Republic, Hungary, Poland, Slovakia
NIS: Belarus, Ukraine
Balkan countries: Bulgaria, Romania

Source: 1. GDP, spending and tax revenues: S&P (unless noted otherwise). 2. Tax and Social Security rates:1996 International Tax Summaries (Coopers & Lybrand). Wiley, 1996 (unless noted otherwise).

10.6 Less is More

Tax reform is important, and modernization of tax collection is a part of it. But the only way to go for the transition countries is to cut taxes, not increase them through a systemic reform and improved collection. In part, this will have to come through politically painful (but socially and economically salutary) cuts in the redistributive social programs to which the people in the region became accustomed during the decades of communist inefficiency. But in part, lower rates may produce only a temporary dip in state revenues and lead to higher intakes in the future.

Lower tax rates, indeed, may produce a "virtuous circle"—a mirror image of the vicious one associated with high rates. The idea was made popular in the 1980s by the economist Arthur Laffer. When taxes are low they do not distort economic activity: people simply don't mind paying and do what they would do without them.

As taxes are raised above a certain threshold, however, incentives to work may decrease (leading to less wealth production) and incentives to avoid may increase, so that a 1% tax hike brings less than an additional 1% of income. Now, suppose that taxes are raised to 100%. Since no one will work (at least not legally) if the state takes everything, the revenues such a levy will bring will be zero, the same as when no taxes are raised. But this means that at some point, well below tax rates of 100%, increasing taxes will not only bring less revenue on the margin, but also less revenue overall.

Economists are not sure where the point lies at which the marginal yield from increased taxes begins to shrink (tax rates around 20–30% are mentioned), and they know even less when increased taxes will lead to lower overall revenues. But it may be taken as given that the transition countries are well past the first point, and many may even be past the second. What this means is that if tax rates are significantly lowered, people may work more and avoid less, and after the initial dip, revenues may rise to levels higher than they are today. At the minimum, the social gain from lowering taxes will be an increase in what the countries produce (GDP).

So far the only transition countries that learned this lesson were those that had no other choice because their revenues simply collapsed and the governments had to make do with less. They are not the most advanced postcommunist countries, which persist in the illusion that they can imitate the generous social policies of Germany or France, but rather the usual laggards in economic and political reform.

Kazakhstan's state, for example, spends only 19.1% of GDP and collects even less (11.6%) in taxes, and other Central Asian republics are also more realistic about what they can afford. Not counting Albania, where the state collapsed, Moldova's government, alone among European transition countries, spends less than 30% of GDP and collects less than a mere 23% in taxes, and the size of Lithuania's state is at a still modest 31% of GDP (with 27.8% of GDP collected through the tax system).

Latvia and Estonia have not made similar strides in controlling state expenditures (at 44% and 42%, respectively), but they have made significant progress in simplifying their tax systems—which may be a prelude to spending reductions.

Latvia learned its lesson the hard way. Before 1995, Latvian companies faced a range of tax brackets, from 35% to 65%, depending on their classification. No surprise, then, that managers wasted an awful lot of time trying to get their firms reclassified in a lower tax category rather than on increasing the firm's competitiveness. Then, the government established a 25% tax as the common, and only, rate businesses must pay. According to economists at Den Danske Bank, a Danish bank with interests in the country, the number of companies filing tax returns doubled in 1996, the first year of the new system. That success was soon imitated in the field of personal income taxes, where a flat 25% rate now applies to all incomes between 4,000 and 60,000 lats, with an additional 10% applied to incomes above that bracket.

Estonia did even better. It has built a tax system that is so simple that the annual filing takes but a single page. Because personal and business income are taxed at the same 26% rate, there is no inefficient shifting of monies from one category to another. No army of accountants and tax lawyers prowls Tallinn; the costs of tax collection are less than 1% of the revenues collected (in America the Internal Revenue Service needs ten times that). "We inherited this ridiculous Soviet system, where everybody spent weeks filling in forms, so we changed it to something very convenient, easy to check, not so easy to cheat," says Karlev Jarvelill, Estonia's thirty-something tax chief. As a result fiddling scarcely exists, and people seem willing to pay their share. The system may also be a contributing factor in fostering strong private-sector growth. Indeed, 45% of all employment in Estonia is now in small firms, the sort that are most vulnerable to the pressure of high, and heavy-handed, taxation.

10.7 Taxation and Democracy

The side effects of heavy taxation are not confined to the economy. For taxation, growth, and democracy have always been linked. After all, revolts against taxes by the new middle class were catalysts in the rise of the first modern republics. Taxes can be used either to redistribute wealth or to concentrate it, to enhance centralized political control or to fracture it in favor of (usually weaker) local bodies.

Economic reform paving the way for markets is supposedly the idea that tops the agenda in the transition countries. The state should retreat from the omnipresent role it played in the communist system, we are told: liberalization and privatization are to lead to a system based on more freedom as well as efficiency. Countries like Poland were very proud to announce that more than 50% of their economies are now in private hands. But all the while 50% of the new wealth produced by this infant private sector has been systematically appropriated and spent by the state.

Because wealth is power, the states in the postcommunist countries are not only sapping the energies of the private sector—they remain far too powerful. National elections in a country in which government spends 50% of GDP are not about foreign policy or the interest of the national community. They are about a conflict among interest groups clamoring for the state to help them help themselves to what they could not gain through the market, with its voluntary transactions between willing buyers and willing sellers. In other words, they are about coercive redistribution of wealth from the more to the less efficient and, even sadder, from the have-nots to the haves.

Sometimes redistribution is just. There are people who do poorly in the market and need help to be able to lead the type of dignified existence that, in a civilized society, should be everyone's right. All to often, however, redistribution is simply a function of political power, devoid of any moral claim, wielded by state bureaucrats jealous of their jobs and privileges, farmers unwilling to modernize their production, manufacturers incapable of meeting the challenge posed by their competitors.

In a state that disposes of a lion's share of the national wealth, selfish and cabalistic concerns replace the idea of the common good, and politics becomes debased. Vested interests dominate and individual freedom suffers. So, in the end, heavy and incoherent taxation not only inhibits growth, it stunts democracy too.

Index

Capitalism with a Comrade's Face

was designed and composed by Judit Mihala
in Usherwood 11 pt
printed and bound by
Gyomai Kner Nyomda Rt.

in its 115th year of operation
on 100-gram Kossuth paper, bound in Holland linen
and published by
Central European Universiy Press